REFORMED READER:
A SOURCEBOOK IN CHRISTIAN THEOLOGY

REFORMED READER: A SOURCEBOOK IN CHRISTIAN THEOLOGY

VOLUME 1
Classical Beginnings, 1519–1799

Edited by

WILLIAM STACY JOHNSON
and
JOHN H. LEITH

WESTMINSTER/JOHN KNOX PRESS
Louisville, Kentucky

Book design by Publishers' WorkGroup

First edition

This book is printed on acid-free paper that meets the American National Standards Institute Z39.48 standard. ⊚

Published by Westminster/John Knox Press
Louisville, Kentucky

PRINTED IN THE UNITED STATES OF AMERICA

2 4 6 8 9 7 5 3 1

Library of Congress Cataloging-in-Publication Data

Reformed reader : a sourcebook in Christian theology / edited by William Stacy Johnson and John H. Leith.—1st ed.
    p.   cm.
Includes bibliographical references and index.
Contents: v. 1. Classical beginnings, 1519–1799.
ISBN 0-664-21957-8 (v. 1 : alk. paper)

    1. Theology, Doctrinal—History—Modern period, 1500– 2. Reformed Church—Doctrines. I. Johnson, William Stacy. II. Leith, John H.
BT27.R39   1993
230'.42—dc20
                                                  92-46620

For Liz

CONTENTS

CONTENTS

ACKNOWLEDGMENTS

Acknowledgment is made to the following publishers and authors for permission to reprint selections from copyrighted material:

Mrs. Marion Davis Battles. Excerpt from *The Piety of John Calvin: An Anthology Illustrative of the Spirituality of the Reformer,* edited by Ford Lewis Battles. Published, 1978.

Harvard University Press. Reprinted by permission of the publishers from *Bonifacius: An Essay Upon the Good,* by Cotton Mather: Cambridge, Mass.: The Belknap Press of Harvard University Press. Copyright © 1966 by the President and Fellows of Harvard College.

Labyrinth Press. Excerpts from *The Marrow of Theology,* by William Ames. Translated by John D. Eusden. Published, 1983 (reprint; Pilgrim Press edition published 1968). Also from *Ulrich Zwingli: Early Writings.* Edited by Samuel Macauley Jackson. Published, 1987. And from *Zwingli: On Providence and Other Essays.* Edited by William John Hincke for Samuel Macauley Jackson. Published, 1983. Also from *Commentary on True and False Religion: Zwingli.* Edited by Samuel Macauley Jackson and Clarence Nevin Heller. Published, 1981.

Librairie Droz, S.A. Excerpt from *The Political Thought of Peter Martyr Vermigli: Selected Texts and Commentary.* Edited by Robert M. Kingdon. Published, 1980.

Oliver and Boyd. Plate from *Architecture in Worship,* by André Biéler. Translated by Odette and Donald Elliott. Published, 1965.

ACKNOWLEDGMENTS

Oxford University Press. Excerpts from *Reformed Dogmatics: J. Wollebius, G. Voetius, F. Turretin.* Translated and edited by John W. Beardslee III. Copyright © 1965 by Oxford University Press, Inc. Reprinted by permission.

Pickwick Publications. Excerpts from *A Little Book of Christian Questions and Responses,* Theodore Beza. Translated by Kirk M. Summers. Published, 1981. And excerpts from *In Search of True Religion: Reformation, Pastoral and Eucharistic Writings,* by Huldrych Zwingli. Translated by H. Wayne Pipkin. Volume 2 of *Huldrych Zwingli Writings.* Edited by E. J. Furcha and H. W. Pipkin. Published, 1984.

University of Oregon Press. Excerpts from *The Philosophy of Jonathan Edwards From His Private Notebooks.* Edited by Harvey G. Townsend. Published, 1955.

Unwin Hyman. Excerpts from *Reformed Dogmatics: Set Out and Illustrated from the Sources* by Heinrich Heppe. Translated by G. T. Thompson. Edited and revised by Ernst Bizer. Published, 1950.

Van Gorcum. Excerpt from *Defensio fidei catholicae de Satisfactione Christi adversus Faustum Socinum Senensem* by Hugo Grotius. Translated by Edwin Rabbie. Edited and with an introduction and notes by Hotze Mulder. Published, 1990.

Western Publishing Company and **Macmillan Publishing Company.** Excerpt from *Constitutionalism and Resistance in the Sixteenth Century.* Translated and edited by John H. Franklin. Published, 1969.

Yale University Press. Excerpts from *The Works of Jonathan Edwards,* edited by John E. Smith. Published, 1957–.

ABBREVIATIONS AND SHORT TITLES

Ames, *Marrow*
William Ames, *The Marrow of Theology.* Translated and edited by John D. Eusden from the 3d Latin edition of 1629. Boston and Philadelphia: Pilgrim Press, 1968.

Arminius, *Works*
The Works of James Arminius. The London Edition. Translated by James Nichols and William Nichols. 3 volumes. London, 1825–75. Reprint, Grand Rapids: Baker Book House, 1986.

Barth, *Church Dogmatics*
Karl Barth, *Church Dogmatics.* Edinburgh: T. & T. Clark, 1936–77.

Beardslee, *Reformed Dogmatics*
Reformed Dogmatics: J. Wollebius, G. Voetius, F. Turretin. Translated and edited by John W. Beardslee III. New York: Oxford University Press, 1965.

Beza, *Questions and Responses*
Theodore Beza, *Questionum et responsionum Christianarum.* Geneva, 1570. Eng. trans.: *A Little Book of Christian Questions and Responses.* Translated by Kirk M. Summers. Princeton Theological Monograph Series 9. Allison Park, Penna.: Pickwick Press, 1981.

Bucer, *De Regno Christi*
Martin Bucer, *De Regno Christi.* Edited by Francois Wendel. Gutersloh: Bertelsmann, 1955 = Vol. 15 of *Martini Buceri Opera Latina.*

Calvin's New Testament Commentaries
John Calvin, *Calvin's New Testament Commentaries.* Edited by David W. Torrance and Thomas F. Torrance. 12 vols. Edinburgh and London: Oliver & Boyd; Grand Rapids: Wm. B. Eerdmans, 1963–74.

Calvin, *Romans*
John Calvin, *The Epistle of Paul to the Romans and Thessalonians.* Trans-

lated by R. Mackenzie. Edinburgh: Oliver & Boyd, 1960; Grand Rapids: Wm. B. Eerdmans, 1973 = *Calvin's New Testament Commentaries,* vol. 8.

Cochrane, *Confessions*

Arthur C. Cochrane, ed. *Reformed Confessions of the Sixteenth Century.* Philadelphia: Westminster Press, 1966.

CO

Joannis Calvini Opera Quae Supersunt Omnia. Edited by G. Baum, E. Cunitz, and E. Reuss. Brunsvigae, 1863–1900 = *CR* 29-87.

CR

Corpus Reformatorum. Halle and Berlin, 1934– . Leipzig, 1906– .

Decades

Heinrich Bullinger, *Sermonum decades quinque, de potissimis Christianae religionis capitibus, in tres tomos digestae, authore Heinrycho Bullingero, ecclesiae Tigurinae ministro.* Zurich, 1552. Published separately in Latin between 1549–51 in Zurich: The First and Second Decades, originally *Sermonum decades duae De potissimus verae religionis capitibus . . .* , 1549; the Third, *Sermonum decas tertia,* and the Fourth, *Sermonum decas quarta,* 1550; the Fifth, *Sermonum decas quinta,* 1551. Eng. trans.: *The Decades of Henry Bullinger.* Translated in 1587. 4 vols. Cambridge: Parker Translation Society, 1852. Reprint, New York: Johnson Reprint Corp., 1968.

Edwards, *Works* (1834)

The Works of Jonathan Edwards. And a Memoir by Sereno E. Dwight. Revised and corrected by Edward Hickman. 2 vols. London, 1834. We cite this edition rather than the Worcester or original Dwight editions because it is presently in print and thus is accessible to contemporary students of Edwards.

Edwards, *Works* (Yale)

The Works of Jonathan Edwards. Edited by John E. Smith. 10 vols. New Haven: Yale University Press, 1957– .

Jonathan Edwards, Jr., *Works*

The Works of Jonathan Edwards, D.D. 2 vols. Andover, 1842.

Heppe, *Reformed Dogmatics*

Heinrich Heppe, *Reformed Dogmatics: Set Out and Illustrated from the Sources.* Translated by G. T. Thompson. Edited and revised by Ernst Bizer. London: George Allen & Unwin, 1950; Grand Rapids: Baker Book House, 1978.

Institutes

John Calvin, *Institutes of the Christian Religion* (1559). Translated by Ford Lewis Battles. Edited by John T. McNeill. Library of Christian Classics. Philadelphia: Westminster Press, 1960. The page numbers refer to the

Westminster edition. The Latin text, *Institution Christianae Religionis,* may be found in *OS,* vols 3 and 4.

Leith, *Creeds*

John Leith, ed. *Creeds of the Churches: A Reader in Christian Doctrine from the Bible to the Present.* Atlanta: John Knox Press, 1982.

LCC

Library of Christian Classics.

Melanchthon and Bucer

Melanchthon and Bucer. Edited by Wilhelm Pauck. LCC. Philadelphia: Westminster Press, 1969.

OS

Ioannis Calvini Opera Selecta. Edited by P. Barth, G. Niesel, et al. Munich: Chr. Kaiser, 1926–52.

Owen, *Works*

John Owen, *The Works of John Owen.* 16 vols. London: Johnstone & Hunter, 1850–53.

Perkins, *A Golden Chain*

William Perkins, *A Golden Chain, or The Description of Theology.* 1590, 1592. In *The Work of William Perkins.* Edited by Ian Breward. Courtenay Library of Reformation Classics 3. Appleford, Eng.: Sutton Courtenay Press, 1970.

Schaff, *Creeds*

Philip Schaff, ed. *The Creeds of Christendom.* 3 vols. New York: Harper & Brothers, 1877. Reprint, Grand Rapids: Baker Book House, 1966.

SS

Huldreich Zwingli's Werks. Edited by M. Schuler and J. Schulthess. 8 vols. Zurich, 1828–42. (The first edition of Zwingli's works, now being supplanted by *CR*).

Treatises

Calvin: Theological Treatises. Translated by Geoffrey Bromiley. LCC. Philadelphia: Westminster Press, 1953.

Ursinus, *Commentary*

The Commentary of Dr. Zacharius Ursinus on the Heidelberg Catechism. Translated by G. W. Williard. 2d American ed. Columbus, Ohio, 1852.

WA

D. Martin Luthers Werke: Kritische Gesamtausgabe. Weimar: Böhlau, 1883– .

Zwingli and Bullinger

Zwingli and Bullinger. Translated by Geoffrey Bromiley. LCC. Philadelphia: Westminster Press, 1953.

Zwingli, *In Search of True Religion*
Huldrych Zwingli, *In Search of True Religion: Reformation, Pastoral and Eucharistic Writings.* Translated by H. Wayne Pipkin. Vol. 2 of Zwingli, *Writings.*

Zwingli, *Sämtliche Werke*
Huldrych Zwingli's Sämtliche Werke. Edited by E. Egli, et al. Berlin, Leipzig, Zurich, 1905– = *CR* 88–101.

Zwingli, *Works*
The Latin Works and the Correspondence of Huldrych Zwingli. 3 vols. Vol. 1: *Early Writings.* Edited by Samuel Macauley Jackson. New York: G. P. Putnam Sons, 1912. Reprint, Durham, N.C.: Labyrinth Press, 1986. Vol. 2: *On Providence and Other Essays.* Edited by Samuel Macauley Jackson and William John Hinke. Philadelphia: Heidelberg Press, 1922. Reprint, Durham, N.C.: Labyrinth Press, 1981. Vol. 3: *Commentary on True and False Religion.* Edited by Samuel Macauley Jackson and Clarence Nevin Heller. Philadelphia: Heidelberg Press, 1929. Reprint, Durham, N.C.: Labyrinth Press, 1983.

Zwingli, *Writings*
Huldrych Zwingli Writings. Edited by E. J. Furcha and H. W. Pipkin. Allison Park, Penna.: Pickwick Press, 1984.

PREFACE

Out of the religious ferment of sixteenth-century Europe the Reformed tradition emerged as a particular way of believing and practicing the Christian faith. Its message was simple: all glory goes to God alone, who is authoritatively revealed by scripture alone, which proclaims salvation by grace alone, achieved by God through Christ alone, and received by believers through faith alone. The aim of this message for all its simplicity was nothing less than revolutionary: Reformed Christians sought the reformation of the whole of life, not only at the level of individual faith and conduct but also at the level of the church and the wider community, its governing structures, institutions, and bases of power. Today there are Christians all over the world, both inside and outside of Reformed churches, whose faith has been nurtured, knowingly and unknowingly, by the ethos and theology of the Reformed tradition.

The purpose of this book is to exhibit the major themes and characteristic emphases of Reformed theology by making available in an accessible format short selections from representative primary sources. Some are offered here in English translation for the first time, and others come from translations obtainable only in the archives of major research libraries.

This volume draws upon texts dating from Reformed Christianity's birth in the 1519 Zurich reform of Huldrych Zwingli through its earliest encounters with the eighteenth-century Enlightenment. A companion volume, edited by George W. Stroup, continues the tradition into the modern era, beginning with Friedrich Schleiermacher's epoch-making 1799 *Speeches*.

The selections here come principally from the formal, systematic treatises and confessions of professional theologians but also include material from sermons, catechisms, hymns, prayers, and devotional guides, which, although also composed by preachers and theologians, provide an indirect insight into the spiritual lives of many ordinary men and women of faith.

The range of selections illustrates both the distinctiveness and the diversity of early Reformed theology. The most important comprehensive statement of this theology is of course John Calvin's *Institutes of the Christian Religion*. Yet the Reformed tradition flows from a broader stream than John Calvin alone; although Calvin is of inestimable significance for the tradition, and although his theology counts as one of the singular achievements of Western Christianity, the sixteenth-century origins of Reformed theology include equally important, although perhaps lesser-read figures such as Huldrych Zwingli, Heinrich Bullinger, Peter Martyr Vermigli, and Wolfgang Musculus. Similarly, the later tributaries of Reformed theology range further than the single current sometimes labeled "Calvinism." To illustrate the diverse branches that run from the early sixteenth-century origins, we include a range of figures from the post-Reformation period, including not only the orthodox continental Reformed—theologians such as Theodore Beza, Antoine de la Roche Chandieu, Zacharias Ursinus, Girolami Zanchi, Johannes Wollebius, Pierre du Moulin, and François Turretin—but also the English Puritans, for example, William Ames, Richard Baxter, Richard Sibbes, John Owen, and Philip Doddridge; the Dutch covenantal theologians Johannes Cocceius and Herman Witsius; and the early American theologians Thomas Shepard, John Cotton, Cotton Mather, Jonathan Edwards, Samuel Hopkins, and Jonathan Edwards, Jr. In order to illustrate the reach of Reformed theology into public life and culture, there are also selections from Reformed statesmen such as Phillipe de Plessis-Mornay and James Madison and from Reformed philosophers such as Pierre Bayle, Francis Hutcheson, and Thomas Reid.

In addition, the Reformed tradition cannot be understood apart from certain pivotal figures who, while standing within the tradition, were struggling at the same time to transform it, and who in some instances actually moved beyond it: Jacob Arminius and Hugo Grotius, for example, who drew their intellectual origins from Reformed thought but who also sought to liberalize the dominant interpretation of Calvinism; Moïse Amyraut, advocate of universal grace whom some branded a heretic but who believed himself to be an authentic heir of Calvin; and those pietistically inclined theologians of the late seventeenth century, Jean de Labadie, Jacodus van Lodensteyn, and Anna Maria van Schuurman, who were zealous to effect an ever-deeper practical reform of the religious life. Whether we interpret figures such as these as inside or outside the Reformed camp, they were clearly raising issues that were suggested to them by the Reformed theological framework itself.

Each chapter discusses a traditional doctrine—the doctrine of God, Creation, Christology, and so forth. This structure organizes both volumes 1 and 2, with only a few deviations. Although the order of doctrines does not match the approach of any single theologian, it allows the reader to trace every major doctrine as it develops through the years and thus to gain a composite picture of the Reformed tradition. Since all doctrinal spheres are interrelated, the outline is for organizational convenience alone and does not imply any sort of reified division among the doctrines.

Keeping in mind both the busy pastor and the student struggling to master a profusion of new material, we have chosen passages which for the most part are concise, pithy, and short of digressions. We have also sought not to duplicate sources already widely available in collections of creeds and in other anthologies. In many cases the selections have been edited to make their point in the briefest possible compass (in these instances the word "edited" appears in the Source), although in so doing we have endeavored to preserve the original flow of the author's argument. Limitations of space have prevented us in some cases from including rich and often quite lengthy sections of biblical exposition which provided the grist and the ultimate authority for the theological conclusions being expressed. Sometimes we have indicated the relevant biblical passages in brackets but in many cases this would have been too cumbersome. Bear in mind, then, that each reading is but a glimpse at the whole, and the reader is encouraged to return to the sources themselves (*ad fontes*), where there is always more to be found.

In presenting a diversity of passages, from many sources and spanning a significant stretch of time, we have no desire to encourage a method that dissevers texts from their original contexts. Even less do we desire to perpetuate the habits of the theological dilettante who samples widely but masters little. There is no substitute for firsthand mastery of classical texts combined with proper attention to the times in which they were written. On the other hand, traditions span diverse contexts, and it is helpful to have a map of the general features of a historic tradition that will enable further exploration for ever greater detail. To that end, each passage is prefaced by a brief introduction, and most are accompanied by a bibliography with suggestions for further study.

We offer this collection of readings not merely as a window to illumine some remote historical landscape but as a doorway by which to enter terrain still alive with possibilities for contemporary theological reflection and for growth in spiritual understanding. These texts are important to us today not so much for their own sakes as for the sake of the reality to which they bear witness. As in all human reflection, the theology contained in these pages is flawed and falls well short of its appointed task. By no means can it simply be repeated in our current situation, as though a mere dusting off, tightening up, and refinishing of old furniture would make for a suitable theological habitation. Instead, theology in every age and every generation must settle in and begin to build again from the beginning. Yet no theology makes these new beginnings out of nothing. In a time such as ours, characterized by widespread ignorance of the historic Christian faith and by the lack of a common spiritual language or shared interpretive paradigm, one of the most urgent tasks faced by the church in the West is the recovery of a common Christian memory, a memory live enough to sustain faith, focused enough to rekindle and fortify hope, and rich enough to give love a transformative direction and content.

In the end, however, theology is more than texts, and faith is more than appropriating a tradition. Faced with many new challenges in our day, faith and theology in the Reformed way of being Christian must live, as ever, by grace alone, awaiting the transfiguration of all of life to the praise and glory of God.

A number of persons and institutions have contributed to the making of this volume. The following persons made suggestions about texts to be included, for which we are indebted: Brian Armstrong of Georgia State University, Edward A. Dowey of Princeton Theological Seminary, Clarissa Atkinson and Mark U. Edwards of Harvard Divinity School, and Joseph McLelland, of McGill University, who also contributed a translation. A special word of gratitude is due to the late Mary Beaty of Davidson College, Charles Raynal, Minister of Davidson College Presbyterian Church, and Iain Maclean, Minister of the Presbyterian Church of Southern Africa and doctoral candidate at Harvard Divinity School, who prepared translations of several of the selections.

We have also been beneficiaries of the wealth of materials in the Andover-Harvard Library of Harvard Divinity School, the Speer Memorial Library of Princeton Theological Seminary, and the library of Union Theological Seminary in Virginia. We are especially appreciative of help we received at Harvard from Donna McGuire, Laura Whitney, and Charles Willard, and from William Harris at Princeton. A number of persons donated their time in helping to assemble these materials for publication, among them, Missy Daniel, Ann Colley, Jeanne French, Dan Griswold, Elizabeth Johnson, Virginia Samuels, and William E. Samuels, each of whom we gratefully acknowledge.

William Stacy Johnson
Assistant Professor of Systematic Theology
Austin Presbyterian Theological Seminary
Austin, Texas

John H. Leith
Center of Theological Inquiry
Princeton, New Jersey

INTRODUCTION

"Reformed" is the name that has been given to the Christian community and to the theology that was shaped by the Protestant Reformation under the leadership of, in Zurich, Huldrych Zwingli (1484–1531) and Heinrich Bullinger (1504–75); in Basel, Hussgen (John) Oecolampadius (1482–1531); in Bern, Berthold Haller (1492–1536); and in Geneva, Guïllaume (William) Farel (1489–1565) and John Calvin (1509–64).[1]

The Reformation in Switzerland and the upper Rhineland acquired a character of its own that distinguished it from Lutheranism and from the left wing of the Reformation. The Reformation spread in particular through France and the Low countries, to England and Scotland. Reformed communities grew up along the Rhine and in modern-day Hungary, the Czech regions, and Poland. In Strasbourg the Reformation initially developed with affinities for the pattern in Zurich, although Martin Bucer (1491–1551) had first been influenced to participate in the reform by Martin Luther and Lutheran influence predominated in Strasbourg after 1549.

The Reformation in Switzerland was closely related to Christian humanism. Basel was the center of a distinguished humanist society that included Erasmus, Beatus Rhenanus, Conrad Pellican, and Caspar Hedio. Luther lived and grew to maturity in the monastery wrestling with the profoundly religious question of guilt and forgiveness. Huldrych Zwingli, who was never a monk, had been mightily influenced by the humanists Erasmus (1466–1536) and Thomas Wyttenbach (1472–1526).

The Reformation in Switzerland was more concerned about the authority

---

1. See Richard A. Muller, *Post-Reformation Reformed Dogmatics* (Grand Rapids: Baker, 1987); Timothy George, *Theology of the Reformers* (Nashville: Broadman, 1987); Steven Ozment, *The Age of Reform 1250–1550* (New Haven: Yale University Press, 1980); Barth, *Church Dogmatics* 1.2; Emil Brunner, *The Christian Doctrine of God: Dogmatics*, vol. 1 (Philadelphia: Westminster, 1950), 89–107; Brian Armstrong, *Calvinism and the Amyraut Heresy* (Madison: University of Wisconsin Press, 1969); John H. Leith, *Introduction to the Reformed Tradition* (Atlanta: John Knox, 1977).

of scripture and the question Is there a word from God? than about the issue of forgiveness, although this contrast is not absolute. The Swiss Reformed under the influence of Christian humanism were much more willing to break radically with medieval Catholicism than Luther had been. Whereas Luther wished to eliminate from the life of the church everything the Bible condemned, the reformers in Switzerland wished to eliminate everything that did not have a positive warrant from scripture.

In addition, the Reformation in Switzerland became at times a war against idolatry.[2] The cleansing of the church of images and pictures was much more radically undertaken than in Lutheranism or Anglicanism. When the Lutherans and the Reformed considered church union in the nineteenth century, it was argued that Lutheranism was primarily concerned about forms of works righteousness, whereas the Reformed were primarily concerned with idolatry, that is, the attempt to fasten the infinite and indeterminate God to anything that was finite, determinate, and in the control of human beings.

"Reformed" became the common designation for this particular type of Reformation, in part because of its radical character. Originally the Swiss had been called Zwinglians, Calvinists, and Sacramentarians. The term "Reformed" can rightly be applied to all Protestants and to other reforming groups in the sixteenth century. Yet it has come to be applied to the Swiss Reformation, which Elizabeth I distinguished from the Lutheran as "more reformed."[3]

The definitions of Reformed theology and the Reformed community have never been clearcut, and there is no authority with the right to make a final decision as to who is Reformed and who is not. The reformers themselves rejected any one pattern of reform that would be normative, as well as any normative book of confessions.[4] Reformed confessions were always occasional, written by Christians in a particular time and place. Theological works such as Calvin's *Institutes of the Christian Religion,* and confessions such as the Second Helvetic Confession, the Heidelberg Catechism, and the Scots Confession of 1560 had widespread influence, not because of the decision of any church court but simply by their usage in the Christian community.

CHARACTERISTICS OF REFORMED THEOLOGY

Reformed theology intended to be a catholic theology, that is, a theology for the one, Christian church. All of the original reformers appealed not only to

2. Carlos Eire, *War Against the Idols: The Reformation of Worship from Erasmus to Calvin* (New York: Cambridge University Press, 1986).
3. Schaff, *Creeds* 1:358–59. Cf. M. Eugene Osterhaven, *The Spirit of the Reformed Tradition* (Grand Rapids: Wm. B. Eerdmans, 1971), appendix, 171–78.
4. Schaff, *Creeds* 1:389–90. Cf. Peter Hall, *The Harmony of Protestant Confessions* (London: John F. Shaw, 1842), introduction.

scripture but to the theologians of the ancient church and to the first four ecumenical councils. Reformed theology is catholic in its affirmation of the doctrine of the person of Christ, as formulated at Chalcedon, and the doctrine of the Triune God. It is also catholic in its acknowledgment of the authority of Augustine, as well as other ancient theologians.

Heinrich Bullinger, in publishing his *Decades,* fifty sermons containing a popular statement of Christian faith, included an opening chapter of eleven creeds of the ancient church and an imperial decree for the catholic faith. He affirmed the theological statements of the first four ecumenical councils and omitted the fifth and sixth only because, in his view, they did not add anything new to the first four. Bullinger affixed this opening chapter to the *Decades* because it was his intention to state the faith of the holy, catholic church.[5] He also wanted to demonstrate that the faith that was being proclaimed was not heretical but was in agreement with the ancient church. In the body of the *Decades,* Bullinger included a full exposition of the Apostles' Creed. John Calvin likewise affirmed the first four ecumenical councils and drew much of his theology from the work of Augustine, Chrysostom, Athanasius, and other early church theologians. He also intended that the polity and the worship of the church should be in significant congruity with early practices. He expounded the Apostles' Creed in his catechism and organized the *Institutes* upon the structure of the Apostles' Creed.

Reformed theology is not only catholic but also Protestant. Zwingli was always sensitive about his relationship to Luther and contended that he came to his decisions independently from Luther.[6] As it developed, however, the Swiss Reformation is understandable only in the light of Luther. All early Reformed theology emphasized the teachings of Luther's great writings of 1520. Calvin himself always spoke of Luther with the highest regard, and some have argued that he had accepted Lutheran principles as a young man.[7] In any case, the fundamental doctrines of Luther's writings of 1520 came to dominate the classical period of Reformed theology: the supreme authority of the Holy Spirit speaking through the words of scripture; justification by grace through faith alone; the priesthood of all believers; the sanctity of the common life; and the necessity of faith that expresses itself in a responsible, deliberate decision for the reception of the sacraments. Zwingli, Calvin, and Luther had different educational backgrounds and cultural experiences that shaped the distinctive features in their theologies. Calvin was never a priest, and neither Zwingli nor Calvin was ever a monk. Whereas the minds of Zwingli

---

5. Heinrich Bullinger, *The Decades of Henry Bullinger,* ed. Thomas Harding (Cambridge: Cambridge University Press), vol. 1.
6. See G. W. Locher, *Zwingli's Thought* (Leiden: E. J. Brill, 1981).
7. Brian Gerrish, "Calvin on Luther" in *Interpreters of Luther,* ed. Jaroslav Pelikan (Philadelphia: Fortress, 1968), 67–96.

and Calvin were shaped by the leading humanists of the sixteenth century, Luther's formation came more from the religious life of medieval Catholicism. Yet all the reformers recognized a common faith. Calvin and Bullinger alike were eager for an ecumenical conference that would have brought the Protestants together under the vision of one organized church. The early Reformed community had great variety, but all Reformed theologians intended to be not only catholic but also what we today call "Protestant."

Within Catholic and Protestant Christianity, Reformed theology gradually acquired a recognizable identity. What is this identity?

From the beginning Reformed theology has been identified by particular methodological commitments. The Ten Conclusions of Bern (1528) begin with the affirmation "The holy, Christian church, whose only Head is Christ, is born with the Word of God, and abides in the same, and listens not to the voice of a stranger." The remaining nine conclusions repeatedly emphasize that all theology stands under the authority of the Bible. The distinctive emphasis of the disputations, which helped to establish the Protestant community in Switzerland, all appeal to the supreme authority of the Bible. The Tetrapolitan Confession of 1530 entitled the first chapter "Of the Subject Matter of Sermons," and it enjoined "our preachers to teach from the pulpit nothing else than is either contained in Holy Scripture or hath sure ground therein."

Reformed theology is characterized by a great emphasis upon the authority of the scriptures as the written revelation of God. It is the coherent explication of scripture in the language of ordinary discourse.[8] The characteristic that dominates the theological work of the Reformed theologians is the subordination of all theology to the authority of the scriptures.

Reformed theology has also been characterized by an emphasis on Christian experience, especially the experience of regenerating grace, and the concreteness of the situation in which theology is written. Calvin himself subjected his theology to the criticism of common sense, human wisdom, and experience. In the Reformed perspective, revelation orients human experience and to that extent transcends it, but revelation at the same time is believed not to contradict human experience or common sense.

Reformed theology is also distinguished by an emphasis on the practical and spiritually edifying rather than the theoretical and speculative. All the early Reformed theologians objected to flights of speculation and showed little interest in or concern for abstract questions of theory. They believed that the purposes of theology are to glorify God, save human souls, and transform human life and society. Questions and issues that do not directly bear on these

8. *Institutes of the Christian Religion* 1.13.3.

practical concerns received scant attention in the sixteenth century. One significant test of the authenticity of any doctrine for these early reformers was its power to edify. While the emphasis on edification was not eliminated in the seventeenth century, as evidenced in the profound movement of Reformed piety known as "Puritanism," later Reformed orthodoxy was marked by increasing preoccupation with the more speculative questions of scholasticism.

Reformed theology for the most part adopted the language of ordinary discourse for theological work and rejected the specialized vocabulary developed in the schools. Theology is to be written without ornate, rhetorical flourishes, but with transparent clarity, in the language people spoke on the street and in the church. Even the more cumbersome style one encounters in some of the seventeenth-century literature comes alive when read aloud, since much of it originated as lectures or sermons.

Reformed theology also reflects particular themes and perspectives that unify it and give it its distinctive character. The theology of Zwingli and Calvin, for example, is marked by a profound sense of the majesty and awesomeness of God. Calvin's theology cannot be comprehended apart from an intense awareness of the holy, an awareness that encompassed everything he said and did. The Reformed theologians conceived of God as personal and inherently communicative, overflowing in energy, power, moral purpose, and intentionality. God calls into being that which is not, and God raises the dead (Rom. 4:17). Although predestination is certainly not the "central doctrine" from which other doctrines are deduced,[9] every doctrine in Calvin's theology presupposes the prevenient grace of God that received its classic statement in the doctrine of predestination.

Reformed theology emphasizes the all-encompassing character and "transcendence" of God. The greatness of God called for a radical distinction between who the Creator is and who the creature is, and it raised the perennial theological problem of relating God's transcendence to God's immanence. The Reformed could not abide a perspective which would mix or confuse the two. In this sense, Reformed Christology has greater affinity with the tradition of the ancient school of Antioch rather than that of Alexandria, although these distinctions cannot be drawn with absolute strokes. On the one hand, Reformed theologians insisted that God cannot be fastened or made available to human manipulation in any finite or determinate form; God must always remain God. On the other hand, they insisted equally upon the integrity of human history and of human beings as moral, responsible, historical crea-

---

9. Cf. Alexander Schweizer, *Die Protestantischen Centraldogmen: in ihrer Entwicklung innerhalb der Reformirten Kirche*, 2 vols. (Zurich: Orell, Füssli, 1854, 1856).

tures; the greatness of God does not imply the denigration of humanity. On the contrary, God's greatness is demonstrated precisely in choosing to elevate humanity, in enabling human beings to be transformed after the image of God. The net result was that Reformed theology desacralized created existence. It jealously guarded the integrity of the Creator and the creature alike, allowing for no confusion or mixture. This opened the door to a new appreciation of secular existence and a depreciation of the sacralized view of the church.

The Reformed thought of the transcendence and immanence of God in personal categories. God is personally and immediately active in the created order. None of the early Reformed theologians showed much interest in developing a doctrine of the structures and the processes of the created order, except when pressured to do so. Both Calvin and Zwingli recognized the integrity of secondary causes, but this is not where the center of their theology rested.

These particular emphases of Reformed theology receive practical focus in the Reformed protest against idolatry. The polemic against idolatry infused Reformed Christianity with an implicit impetus toward social and political criticism. In Zurich one demonstrated one's allegiance to Protestantism through acts which were as overtly political as religious in their implications: shattering the statues of medieval cathedrals or eating sausages during the Lenten season of fasting.[10]

Reformed theology also has a particular way in which it puts together justification by faith and sanctification, the forgiveness of sins and the renewal of life. In principle, as Reinhold Niebuhr has observed, neither God's grace as mercy nor God's grace as power is subordinated to the other. In fact, the Reformed have generally placed the greatest emphasis upon sanctification.[11] The Puritan movement in the British Isles built upon Reformed theology. The Reformed have sometimes become self-righteous and obscurantist in prematurely identifying the will of God with a particular pattern of life.

This particular way of combining justification and sanctification is also reflected in other doctrines. Calvin never set the law and the gospel against

10. E. G. Ullmann, *Zur Charakteristik der reformirten Kirche. Mit Beziehung auf neuere literarische Erscheinungen*, Theologische Studien und Kritiken, vol. 16 (Berlin, 1843), 749ff. Alexander Schweizer, *Die Glaubenslehre der evangelische—reformirten Kirche dargestellt und aus den Quellen belegt* (Zurich: Orell, Füssli, 1844), 1:45; F. C. Baur, "Über Princip und Charakter des Lehrbegriffs der reformirten Kirche in seinen Unterschied von dem lutherischen, mit Rücksicht auf A Schweizer's Darstellung der reformirten Glaubenslehre," *Theologische Jahrbücher* 6 (1847): 333; Matthias Schneckenburger, "Die neueren Verhandlungen, betreffend das Prinzip des reformirten Lehrbegriffs," *Theologische Jahrbücher* 7 (1848): 74.

11. Reinhold Niebuhr, *The Nature and Destiny of Man*, vol. 2 (New York: Charles Scribner's Sons, 1941, 1943), chap. 7.

each other; the law contains the gospel, and the gospel contains the law. Likewise, Reformed theology never simply opposes nature and grace. Redemption affirms creation, but redemption is more than creation, not simply its completion but, in the light of sin, its transformation. The practical priority in Reformed theology is always redemption. Calvin, for example, refused to discuss the possibility of whether the Word would have become flesh if human beings had not sinned.[12]

Reformed theology has always been unified by a vision of the human community under the authority of God. The Reformed communities worked out this vision in different ways. Calvin, for his part, insisted in the Genevan context on the relative distinction and independence of the church and the state, whereas Zwingli and Bullinger were content to allow a Christian state to carry out some aspects of the church's mission. Reformed theology and preaching characteristically sought "to draw the world to God and to build a kingdom of our Lord Jesus Christ that he may rule among us."[13] Reformed theology never defined the Christian life in terms of personal piety alone.

Simplicity is likewise a characteristic of Reformed theology and Reformed church life. Calvin did not use two words when one would do. He advocated moderation in food and drink and in one's general way of life. The insistence upon plainness is reflected in the rejection of clerical clothing for ministers. In general, the Reformed abhorred the pompous, the pretentious, the ostentatious, the baroque, the contrived, and the artificial. Simplicity for Calvin was very close to sincerity: the simple uncovers reality; the pretentious covers it up. It is interesting to note that Samuel Rutherford opposed bishops in the church in part because he did not believe it was possible to be a bishop and to live a simple life.

HISTORY OF
REFORMED THEOLOGY

The history of Reformed theology can be divided into six fairly distinct phases.

1517–1564: The Classical Reformation

We may date the formal beginning of the Protestant Reformation with Martin Luther's nailing of the ninety-five theses on the church door at Wittenberg in 1517. The Reformation in Zurich, which marked the beginning of "Reformed"

---

12. *Institutes* 2.12.4.
13. Sermon on II Timothy 2:16–19.

Christianity, had its dramatic inauguration when Huldrych Zwingli threw out the lectionary and began preaching straight through the Gospel of Matthew in January 1519. With the death of Calvin in 1564, the classical formation of Reformed theology and its time of the initial enthusiasm may be considered closed. From 1519 to 1564, Reformed theology received its influential statements in articles from disputations, as, for example, the Ten Conclusions of Berne in 1528, in a plethora of confessions, and in basic theological works such as Zwingli's *True and False Religion*, Bullinger's *Decades*, and Calvin's *Institutes*. All of the early Reformed theologians were preachers and pastors. The theology they proclaimed was worked out not in an academic setting but in the church. Its intentions were to edify the community and to shape the community as the communion of saints.

1564–1799: Orthodox and Puritan Theology

The preacher's theology of the classical Reformation was followed, especially on the continent of Europe, by theology that had more of the characteristics of the school. This was an inevitable development. The previous theology of the classical period, even Calvin's *Institutes*, was not a finished work. It had no specifically defined vocabulary, it contained inconsistencies, and it failed to take full advantage of the real theological achievements of medieval theology.

The scholastic tendencies of the seventeenth century have sometimes been set in opposition to the approach of the classical reformers. Although the theological style of the seventeenth century is unquestionably different, the theological substance flows out of the commitments of the sixteenth-century tradition; it is not the same, but neither does it contradict the theology of the earlier period.

Scholastic theologians defined words more precisely and wrote theology in logical, coherent, consistent statements. They made use of the theological achievement of medieval scholasticism. They also incorporated into the Reformed consensus covenant theology, which was, along with Arminianism and Saumur theology, a seventeenth-century attempt to modify late-sixteenth- and early-seventeenth-century Calvinism. The Westminster Confession of Faith and Catechisms (1643–47) became the dominant statement of Reformed theology in the English-speaking world. In contemporary theology, both Paul Tillich and Karl Barth have praised the theological quality of this scholastic theology.[14] It had remarkable powers to serve the church, not only in Europe but also in America. American Reformed theologians were indebted

---

14. Karl Barth, "Foreword," in Heppe, *Reformed Dogmatics*, v–vii; Paul Tillich, *A History of Christian Thought* (New York: Simon & Schuster, 1967), 276–83.

particularly to the theology of François Turretin in Geneva, the Westminster Confession and Catechisms, and the theology of the Synod of Dort.

Scholasticism was not the only trend of the post-Reformation period. The Protestant Reformation was preeminently a spiritual movement, and the Reformed emphasis on piety was continued in the later streams of the tradition. This accent on piety was most evident in English Puritanism, but it also manifested itself among such scholastic theologians as Gisburtus Voetius and figures who defy easy categorization, such as Jean de Labadie.

The seventeenth and eighteenth centuries also witnessed Reformed theology's first encounters with Enlightenment philosophy. Although there were intermittent attempts to come to grips with the Enlightenment—sometimes with brilliant results, as in the case of Jonathan Edwards—the problems of Enlightenment thought were for the most part deferred to the nineteenth century.

1738–1880: New England Theology

New England theology was the most persistent and fascinating effort to modify the dominant seventeenth-century Reformed theology without changing its basic presuppositions. Its preeminent theologian was Jonathan Edwards (1703–58). His theological work took into account three new developments. The first was the work of Isaac Newton (1642–1727), whose *Principia Mathematica* (1686) had described an orderly world that operated according to its own laws. God was increasingly unnecessary in a universe that seemed to be self-operating and intelligible in accordance with its own rules. Second was the British Enlightenment, and John Locke (1632–1704) in particular, which had crafted a philosophy that emphasized the empirical basis of knowledge and the "reasonableness" of Christianity. Third, the religious revivals in which Edwards himself participated raised the old question of human freedom and divine sovereignty with a new urgency. Edwards's modification of Reformed theology was continued by a remarkable succession of theologians, including Jonathan Edwards, Jr., Samuel Hopkins, Joseph Bellamy, Timothy Dwight, and Bennet Tyler, concluding in the work of Nathaniel William Taylor (1786–1858). With Edwards, they wrestled with the relationship between human freedom and grace and with the intelligibility of the Christian conception of God. They made accommodations in the doctrines of original sin and the atonement. They opened the way to bursts of Christian activity, missions, and social reform; and they prepared their people for the more difficult questions that the nineteenth century would raise. Yet for the most part, they remained within the boundaries of the traditional Reformed orthodoxy and the Westminster Confession. In the 1880s they were superseded by liberal theologians less bound by the tradition.

1799–1918: The Nineteenth-Century Response to the Enlightenment

This period begins with the publication of Friedrich Schleiermacher's 1799 *Speeches* and ends with the First World War. The eighteenth-century Enlightenment confronted the church in the nineteenth century with many challenges. Descartes, who had written his *Discourse on Method* in 1637, challenged the assumptions of traditional theology. How does one know the truth? Traditionally the church had said one knows the truth by consulting the authorities: the authoritative person, the authoritative book, the authoritative institution. Descartes, however, maintained that to know the truth one begins with the human subject, by doubting, in particular, by doubting the authorities. One can depend upon that which survives radical doubt and which is authenticated by its clarity and distinctiveness to human reason.

Immanuel Kant, writing in 1784 in answer to the question, What is Enlightenment? declared that Enlightenment is an exodus (*Ausgang*) from intellectual bondage; it is daring to accept responsibility for oneself. The immature sell themselves in tutelage to other people. The Enlightenment meant daring to think for oneself, decide for oneself, take responsibility for one's own life. This liberty was still a liberty bound by the authority of reason.

A new cultural attitude toward change began to become common. Change had previously been regarded as abnormal, and what remained the same as normal. Increasingly, these judgments were reversed, with change seen as normative, the unchanging as aberrant. Kant, for instance, exulted in the events of the French Revolution.

Modern science, from Copernicus (1473–1543) (*The Motion of Celestial Bodies* [1543]) to Darwin (*The Origin of Species* [1859]), to Einstein (1879–1955), created a new picture of the world. The older picture had been easy to accommodate to Christian theology. God was above the world; below the world were hell and the nether regions; and in between, the drama of human life was lived out. In the new world, where is God and what is there for God to do?

Karl Marx (1818–83) criticized the church's role in society and identified the ideological and illusory character of faith. He explained away religion as the consequence of the way people earn a living and their economic status. Sigmund Freud (1856–1939) likewise explained away religion as wish fulfillment and said it took away the dignity of human freedom. Freud was aware that Copernicus had taken away the dignity of creation and Darwin the dignity of human origins; now he would explain away human freedom. Another illusionist, Ludwig Feuerbach (1804–72), early in the nineteenth century contended in *The Essence of Christianity* (1841) that theology was a projection of the human spirit.

In the nineteenth century the Christian community also became increasingly aware of other religions. Ironically, the nineteenth-century missionary outreach made Christianity no longer a merely European but an increasingly global religion and also had the eventual impact of relativizing Christian uniqueness. On the social front, the industrial revolution raised important questions about how Christians should live in the modern world. Critical historical studies, moreover, examined the Bible as just another book and raised questions that required answers from theologians, especially questions concerning the reliability of scripture. Above all, the nineteenth century raised the question of historical relativity. This question, posed paradigmatically by Ernst Troeltsch, is still begging to be answered in our own day.

The Christian community responded to all of this in diverse ways. Liberals sought to assimilate the wisdom of the Enlightenment. They wanted to be modern people and Christians at the same time. Conservatives endeavored to preserve the traditional faith by ignoring, at least in some measure, the new developments. The fundamentalists declared by fiat that the typical nineteenth-century answers were not true and thus rejected them. The social gospel attempted to work out, at first in very simple terms (Charles Sheldon, *In His Steps* [1896]), then in the prophetic theology of Walter Rauschenbusch (*A Theology for the Social Gospel* [1918]), and finally in even more sophisticated ways of relating the Christian way of living to an industrialized, modern society (Reinhold Niebuhr, *Moral Man and Immoral Society* [1932]). Reformed theologians are to be found working in all these responses: in liberalism, in conservatism, in fundamentalism, and in the social gospel movement.

The lines of Reformed theology are difficult to trace in the nineteenth century. Accommodating the new situation and resisting the changes often became more important than interpreting the gospel faith. The question, therefore, must be raised as to whether these theologians are best classified by their responses to the Enlightenment and the nineteenth century or by their relationship to an earlier tradition. In this period it became difficult to speak of *the* tradition and more appropriate to speak of traditions in transformation.

Many liberals, preeminently Friedrich Schleiermacher (1768–1834), thought of themselves as Reformed theologians. Although there are striking continuities, they also minimized many classical Reformed doctrines such as the authority of the scriptures, especially the Old Testament, the personal activity of God in the created order, and the traditional Reformed understandings of the significance of the death and resurrection of Jesus Christ. The conservative reaction, which often turned into fundamentalism, also modified the older Reformed tradition by its great emphasis on such doctrines as the virgin birth as a test of orthodoxy and by its new, more rigid understanding of the infallibility of scripture. Fundamentalism was also characterized by a doctrinal authoritarianism that had not been true of the early tradition.

Many conservative theologians, such as Charles Hodge (1797–1878) at Princeton, continued to theologize quite capably within the presuppositions of seventeenth-century Reformed theology, but proceeded largely as if the Enlightenment had not happened. Hodge did incorporate the warm-hearted experience of the revivals into his theology, but he also boasted that nothing "new" had been taught at Princeton Theological Seminary during his tenure.

1918–1955: New Reformation Theology

A revival of Reformed theology came with the advent of new Reformation studies. In 1917 Karl Holl initiated the modern study of the Reformers with an essay on Luther's understanding of religion that insisted that ethics issues from religion, not the reverse, as progressive religious thought had assumed since Kant. The herald of the new era of Reformed theology was Karl Barth's commentary on Paul's Letter to the Romans (1918), especially the second edition, published in 1922. The nineteenth-century theologians had been impressed by the new knowledge, but Barth was impressed by the Word of God which stands in judgment over all human achievements and knowledge. God is in heaven. Humanity is on earth; therefore, let one's words be few. The liberal theologians had emphasized continuity—the continuity between God and the world, between Christian and non-Christian, between God's revelation in Jesus Christ and God's revelation everywhere else. Barth emphasized the discontinuity, the difference, arguing furthermore, that God is the Creator who is sovereignly free. God speaks when and where God chooses. God is not at people's beck and call. In short, Barth reaffirmed the classic Christian affirmations about God, about the human condition and human salvation. Yet he did so as a person of the twentieth century, accepting what had happened in the Enlightenment and the nineteenth century. He did not deny the reality of the scientific revolution, historical-critical study, or the industrial revolution. He was neither a fundamentalist nor a liberal, and both were unhappy with him. Barth was supported by many fellow theologians, in particular, Emil Brunner, John Baillie, Donald Baillie, and Reinhold Niebuhr. This revival of theology had a great influence on the life of the church and upon the proceedings of the World Council of Churches, particularly under the leadership of Willem Visser 't Hooft, a Reformed theologian.

The new era in theology began in America with the publication of Reinhold Niebuhr's *Moral Man and Immoral Society* in 1932. Niebuhr found the optimism of liberal theology to be unwarranted in light of the impulsive nature and the self-centeredness of human beings. The best that human beings can hope for is a society in which sin and the need for force will be continuing factors and in which centers of power will be sufficiently balanced against each other to make possible a tolerable degree of justice.

1955 to the Present: A Period of Experimentation

The adequacy of the new Reformation theology began to be challenged in the 1950s. Many believed that it had answered prematurely and too easily some of the questions of the nineteenth century about history, language about God, and responsibility for the created order. Yet no theology in the subsequent period has achieved commanding authority and none has proved to be persuasive to contemporary people, although this had been one of the primary intentions of the theologians of this period.

Theology since 1955 has been dominated by experimentation, emphasizing new themes and causes, especially the cause of the oppressed. These new emphases have done a great service to the church. Yet many theologians today identify themselves more by the particular themes of their own historical situation than by the effort to proclaim again the Christian faith and in particular the classical Protestant and Reformed faith in a new cultural situation.

Now as in the nineteenth century, there persist theologies that can be described as critically orthodox. These theologies are orthodox in that they accept the authority of the ancient catholic creeds and the guidance of theologians such as Augustine and also in that they accept the persuasive guidance of classical Protestant theology, in particular the historic statements of the Reformed tradition. These theologies are critical in their attempts to articulate the traditional faith with an awareness of the new knowledge that has come to us in our times and of the new warrants of credibility which society demands after the Enlightenment.

Christian theology is never a finished task. It builds on the past, but it must be thoroughly redone, rewritten, and respoken in every new time and place. The final human authority for the adequacy of any of these theologies, their integrity as statements of the faith, and their persuasiveness for contemporary people is the judgment made by common-sense wisdom guided by the testimony of the Holy Spirit, in the life of the worshiping, believing, Christian community over a period of time.

REFORMED READER:
A SOURCEBOOK IN CHRISTIAN THEOLOGY

1

CONCERNS AND
METHODS OF THEOLOGY

THE TASK OF THEOLOGY

Huldrych Zwingli: Short Account of
the 1519 Zurich Reform

Reformed theology began as the correction, edification, and improvement of
the established church's fundamental belief and practice.[1] Hence when in
January 1519 Huldrych Zwingli (1484–1531) ascended the pulpit of the Gröstminster church in Zurich as its newly appointed parish priest, he set upon
a radically new strategy of preaching. Laying aside the lectionary, Zwingli
resolved to proceed in order through the Gospel of Matthew, proclaiming
Jesus Christ in straight, expository style. Reformation commitment had preceded Zwingli to the city and indeed had led to Zwingli's being called there.
During the ensuing months, however, the reform intensified to the point that
in May of 1522 Zurich received a stern rebuke from its Roman Catholic
overseer, the Bishop of Constance. Although the bishop's letter did not mention Zwingli by name, he nonetheless assumed the task of drafting a response.
A portion of that response is our opening selection.

SOURCE

Huldrych Zwingli, *Apologeticus Archeteles* (August 22–23, 1522), in *Sämtliche Werke*
1:256–327; ET: In Zwingli, *Works* 1:238–41 (edited).

BIBLIOGRAPHY

Fritz Büsser, *Huldrych Zwingli: Reformation als prophetischer Auftrag*, Persönlichkeit
und Geschichte 74/75 (Göttingen: Musterschmidt, 1973). Idem, ed., *1484–1984: Zwingli*

---

1. See, e.g., John Calvin, *Necessity of Reforming the Church*, in *Treatises*, 187. In this treatise,
directed to the Roman Catholic Emperor Charles V on the eve of the Diet of Spires, Calvin argues
that the reformation of the church centers around three areas of contention: doctrine (especially
the doctrines of worship and salvation), sacraments, and polity.

und die Züricher Reformation (Zurich: Theologischer Verlag, 1984). Idem, *Wurzeln des Reformation im Zurich: zum 500. Geburtstag des Reformators Huldrych Zwingli* (Leiden: E. J. Brill, 1985). E. J. Furcha, ed., *Huldrych Zwingli, 1484–1531: A Legacy of Radical Reform* (Montreal: McGill University Faculty of Religious Studies, 1985). Ulrich Gäbler, *Huldrych Zwingli: His Life and Work*, trans. Ruth C. L. Gritsch (Philadelphia: Fortress, 1986). Christof Gestrich, *Zwingli als Theologe: Glaube und Geist beim Zürcher Reformator* (Zurich: Zwingli Verlag, 1967). Gottfried W. Locher, *Zwingli's Thought: New Perspectives*, Studies in the History of Christian Thought 25 (Leiden: E. J. Brill, 1981). G. R. Potter, *Zwingli* (Cambridge: Cambridge University Press, 1976). Jean Rilliet, *Zwingli: Third Man of the Reformation* (Philadelphia: Westminster, 1964).

Three years ago now . . . I preached the entire Gospel according to Matthew. . . . I added the Acts of the Apostles to the Gospel immediately, that the Church of Zurich might see in what way and with what sponsors the Gospel was carried forth and spread abroad. Presently came the First Epistle of Paul to Timothy, which seemed to be admirably adapted to my excellent flock. For there are contained in it certain canons, as it were, of the character worthy of a Christian. Here, inasmuch as certain smatterers showed perverted opinions of the faith, I postponed the Second Epistle to Timothy until I should have expounded that to the Galatians. Then I added the other. But the before-mentioned smatterers now went to such a pitch of mad impiety that they well-nigh made the name of Paul a disgrace. . . . So I also expounded both the Epistles of Peter, the standard-bearer of the Apostles, that they might see clearly whether both men [Paul and Peter] spoke under the inspiration of the same spirit, and when I had finished these I began the Epistle to the Hebrews, that they might recognize more plainly the goodness and glory of Christ. . . .

I call my flock absolutely away, as far as I can, from hope in any created being to the one true God and Jesus His only begotten Son, our Lord, he that trusteth in whom shall never die. I try with all my might to make them ask forgiveness of him who desires to be freely asked even though we are sinners. . . . I never boasted that I had the spirit of God, but I confidently hope meanwhile that He will not be absent from His own work, He whom I have so often found prospering the things He was accomplishing through me.

John Calvin: Theology as the Knowledge of God and of Humanity

The object and principal theme of Reformed theology is God. Reformed theology is God-centered theology. But God is not known in naked abstraction from God's relationship to humanity in Christ. This is apparent from these initial paragraphs of Calvin's *Institutes* in which knowledge of God and humanity are held in intimate correlation. All of Calvin's theology oscillates between these two poles.

SOURCE

Institutes I.1.1–2, pp. 35–38 (edited). The Latin may be found in *OS* 3 and 4.

BIBLIOGRAPHY

William A. Bouwsma, *John Calvin: A Sixteenth-Century Portrait* (New York: Oxford University Press, 1988). Edward A. Dowey, *The Knowledge of God in Calvin's Theology* (New York: Columbia University Press, 1952). Idem, "The Structure of Calvin's Theological Thought as Influenced by the Two-Fold Knowledge of God," in *Calvinus Ecclesiae Genevensis Custos*, ed. W. Neuser (Frankfurt am Main: Peter Lang, 1984), 137–46. Alexandre Ganoczy, *The Young Calvin*, trans. David Foxgrover and Wade Provo (Philadelphia: Westminster, 1987), chaps. 18–21. John H. Leith, "Calvin's Theological Method and the Ambiguities in His Theology," in *Reformation Studies: Essays in Honor of R. H. Bainton*, ed. F. H. Littell (Richmond, Va.: John Knox, 1962), 106–14. Idem, "Calvin's Awareness of the Holy, and the Enigma of His Theology," in *In Honor of John Calvin 1509–1564: Papers from the 1986 International Calvin Symposium, McGill University*, ed. E. J. Furcha (Montreal: Faculty of Religious Studies, McGill University, 1987). Wilhelm Niesel, *The Theology of Calvin*, trans. H. Knight (Philadelphia: Westminster, 1956). T.H.L. Parker, *Calvin's Doctrine of the Knowledge of God*, 2d ed. (Edinburgh: Oliver & Boyd, 1969). G. R. Potter and M. Greengrass, *John Calvin*, Documents of Modern History (New York: St. Martins, 1983). Suzanne Sellinger, *Calvin Against Himself: An Inquiry in Intellectual History* (Hamden, Conn.: Archon Books, 1984). François Wendel, *Calvin: Origins and Development of His Religious Thought*, trans. Philip Maret (New York: Harper & Row, 1963; reprint: Durham, N.C.: Labyrinth, 1987).

Nearly all the wisdom we possess, that is to say, true and sound wisdom, consists of two parts: the knowledge of God and of ourselves. But, while joined by many bonds, which one precedes and brings forth the other is not easy to discern. In the first place, no one can look upon himself without immediately turning his thoughts to the contemplation of God, in whom he "lives and moves" [Acts 17:28]. . . . Then, by these benefits shed like dew from heaven upon us, we are led as by rivulets to the spring itself. . . . Accordingly, the knowledge of ourselves not only arouses us to seek God, but also, as it were, leads us by the hand to find him.

Again, it is certain that man never achieves a clear knowledge of himself unless he has first looked upon God's face, and then descends from contemplating him to scrutinize himself. For we always seem to ourselves righteous and upright and wise and holy—this pride is innate in all of us—unless by clear proofs we stand convinced of our own unrighteousness, foulness, folly, and impurity. Moreover, we are not thus convinced if we look merely to ourselves and not also to the Lord, who is the sole standard by which this judgment must be measured. For, because all of us are inclined by nature to hypocrisy, a kind of empty image of righteousness in place of righteousness itself abundantly satisfies us. . . .

As long as we do not look beyond the earth, being quite content with our own righteousness, wisdom, and virtue, we flatter ourselves most sweetly, and fancy ourselves all but demigods. Suppose we but once begin to raise our thoughts to God, and to ponder his nature, and how completely perfect are his righteousness, wisdom, and power—the straightedge to which we must be shaped. Then, what masquerading earlier as righteousness was pleasing in us will soon grow filthy in its consummate wickedness. What wonderfully impressed us under the name of wisdom will stink in its very foolishness. What wore the face of power will prove itself the most miserable weakness. That is, what in us seems perfection itself corresponds ill to the purity of God.

Zacharius Ursinus:
Early Reformed Prolegomena

The early reformers carried on a polemic against what they saw as the unnecessary complexity of medieval scholasticism.[2] Once the Reformed churches became established, however, they felt the need for greater precision in defining theological terms and in stating the presuppositions and principles of their positions. This was necessary both for the internal integrity of the nascent tradition as well as for external definition over against various theological opponents. One witnesses after the middle of the sixteenth century, therefore, the development of dogmatic "prolegomena" (i.e., declaration of theological first principles) of which our selection from Zacharius Ursinus (Bär or Beer, meaning "Bear"; hence the Latin, Ursinus) (1534–83) is one of the earliest Reformed examples.[3] In 1561, at the request of the Reformed Prince Frederick III, Ursinus, a man of classical learning and a student of the Lutheran theologian Philipp Melanchthon (1497–1560), was called from Breslau to a chair in

---

2. Calvin's complaint is typical: "Do you remember what kind of time it was when the Reformers appeared, and what kind of doctrine candidates for the ministry learned in the schools? . . . [I]t was mere sophistry, and so twisted, involved, tortuous and puzzling, that scholastic theology might well be described as a species of secret magic. . . . And when those who had been formed in that workshop wished to carry the fruit of their learning to the people with what skill, I ask, did they edify the Church?" (John Calvin, *Reply to Sadolet* [1539], in *Treatises*, 233).

3. See Richard A. Muller, *Post-Reformation Reformed Dogmatics*, Vol. 1: *Prolegomena to Dogmatics*, 73–82.

theology at Heidelberg, where he performed admirably until the death of Frederick in 1576 and the subsequent imposition of a Lutheran creed. These are Ursinus's lectures given in Heidelberg on the *Heidelberg Catechism,* of which he was principal author.[4]

SOURCE

Explicationum catecheticarum D. Zachariae Ursini Silesii absolutum opus totiusque theologiae purioris quasi novum corpus; Davidis Parei opera extrema recognitum (Neustadt, 1594, 1598); ET: General Prolegomena, in Ursinus, *Commentary,* 1–3, 9–10 (edited). This edition of the lectures was edited posthumously by David Paraeus, a student of Ursinus. The original version, *Doctrinae christianae compendium,* appeared in 1584, the year following Ursinus's death.

BIBLIOGRAPHY

G. H. Hinkle, "The Theology of the Ursinus Movement" (Ph.D. diss., Yale University, 1964). Erdmann K. Sturm, *Der junge Zacharias Ursin: Sein Weg vom Philippismus zum Calvinismus (1534–1562),* Beiträge zur Geschichte und Lehre der Reformierten Kirche 33 (Neukirchen: Neukirchener Verlag, 1972). Derk Visser, *Zacharius Ursinus: The Reluctant Reformer, His Life and Times* (New York: United Church Press, 1983).

On the development of Reformed prolegomena, see Richard A. Muller, *Post-Reformation Reformed Dogmatics,* Vol. 1, *Prolegomena to Theology* (Grand Rapids: Baker, 1987).

What Is the Doctrine of the Church?

The doctrine of the church is the entire and uncorrupted doctrine of the law and gospel concerning the true God, together with his will, works, and worship; divinely revealed, and comprehended in the writings of the prophets and aspostles, and confirmed by many miracles and divine testimonies; through which the Holy Spirit works effectually in the hearts of the elect, and gathers from the whole human race an everlasting church, in which God is glorified, both in this, and in the life to come. . . .

What Are the Parts of the Doctrine of the Church, and in What Do They Differ from Each Other?

The doctrine of the church consists of two parts: the Law, and the Gospel; in which we have comprehended the sum and substance of the sacred Scriptures. The law is called the Decalogue, and the gospel is the doctrine concerning Christ the mediator, and the free remission of sins, through faith. . . .

---

4. On the Heidelberg Catechism, see pp. 59–60, below.

5

What Are the Various Methods of Teaching and Learning the Doctrine of the Church?

The method of teaching and studying Theology is three-fold. The *first* is the system of catechetical instruction, or that method which comprises a brief summary and simple exposition of the principal doctrines of the christian religion, which is called catechising. This method is of the greatest importance to all, because it is equally necessary for all, the learned as well as the unlearned, to know what constitutes the foundation of true religion.

The *second method* is the consideration and discussion of subjects of a general and more difficult character, or the Common Places, as they are called, which contain a more lengthy explanation of every single point, and of difficult questions, with their definitions, divisions, and arguments. This method belongs more appropriately to theological schools. . . .

The *third method* of the study of theology is the careful and diligent reading of the Scriptures or sacred text. This is the highest method in the study of the doctrine of the church. To attain this, the two former methods are to be studied, that we may be well prepared for the reading, understanding, and exposition of the holy Scriptures. For as the doctrine of the catechism and Common Places are taken out of the Scriptures, and are directed by them as their rule, so they again lead us, as it were, by the hand to the Scriptures. The catechism of which we shall speak in these lectures, belongs to the first method of the study of theology.

Johannes Wollebius and William Ames: Orthodox and Puritan Theology

As previously mentioned, Reformed theology is God-centered theology. Its object is God in relation to the human subject. But the theocentric character of Reformed theology differs depending upon whether one places relative emphasis upon the divine object in relation to the human subject or upon the human subject in relation to the divine object. The first type pursues theology as a science, a rational and demonstrative discipline describing an external object. For the other type, theology is more affective and experiential, emphasizing the subjective apprehension of inward benefits over objective perception of externals. Note that this is a matter of relative emphasis and not an absolute distinction.

Representing the first type is the Basel theologian Johannes Wollebius (Wolleb) (1586–1629). Wollebius was ordained in 1607 at the age of twenty and in 1618 became cathedral preacher at Basel and assumed the chair of Old Testament theology. His theology exhibits classic seventeenth-century continental orthodoxy in a form derived largely from his teacher Amandus Polanus von Polansdorf (1561–1610). This theology is relatively objectivist, emphasizing doctrine as a deposit of conceptualized truth. According to Wollebius, it is a "body of teachings" oriented toward God alone, the "principle of the being of theology."

The English Puritan theologian William Ames (Gulielmus Amesius) (1576–1633) exemplifies the second type of theology. In keeping with the experiential focus of his Cambridge teacher William Perkins,[5] Ames defines theology as θεοζωία, or "living to God." Ames was for most of his life an emigré in the Netherlands, where he participated in the Arminian controversies and was professor at Franecker. His theology was a fountainhead both for Puritanism and Pietism. However far we may want to press the difference in nuance between Ames and Wollebius, both presupposed the committed, engaged stance of the believer and the theologian in dynamic relationship to their object: namely, God as revealed in Jesus Christ.

SOURCES

(A) Johannes Wollebius, "Prolegomena to Christian Theology" 1. I-III, XX-XXII; 2. I, *Compendium Theologiae Christianae* (Basel, 1626); ET: In Beardslee, *Reformed Dogmatics*, 29–30, 35. (B) William Ames, *Medulla SS. Theologiae* (Amsterdam, 1623, 1629), Book I, chaps. 1 and 2; ET: "The Definition or Nature of Theology," and "The Divisions or Parts of Theology," in Ames, *Marrow*, 77–80 (edited).

BIBLIOGRAPHY

Karl Reuter, *Wilhelm Amesius, der führende Theologe des erwachsenden reformierten Pietismus*, Beiträge zur Geschichte und Leben der Reformierten Kirche 4 (Neukirchen: Neukirchener Verlag, 1940); ET: *William Ames, The Leading Theologian in the Awakening of Reformed Pietism*, trans. Douglas Horton (Cambridge: Andover Harvard Divinity School Library, 1965). Hugo Visscher, *Guilielmus Amesius: Zijn Leven en Werken* (Haarlem: J. M. Stap, 1894); ET: *William Ames, His Life and Works*, trans. Tjaard Georg Hommes (Cambridge: Andover Harvard Divinity School Library, 1965). William Perkins, *A Golden Chain, or The Description of Theology*.

A. JOHANNES WOLLEBIUS

(1)

Christian theology is the doctrine concerning God, as he is known and worshiped for his glory and for our salvation.

Propositions

I. The word "theology," which has many meanings, will be used in this

---

5. For Perkins, "Theology is the science of living blessedly forever" (*A Golden Chain, or The Description of Theology*, 177).

work to describe that knowledge of God which a Christian may attain in this life from God's own word. . . .

True theology is rightly distinguished as original and derived. The original is the knowledge by which God knows himself. In reality this does not differ from the essence of God. Derived theology is a kind of copy of the original, first in Christ the God-man, and secondarily in Christ's members. Some of Christ's members are triumphant in heaven, and others militant on earth; the theology of the triumphant may be called the theology of the blessed, and that of the militant, the theology of the wayfarers.

II. Theology is not regarded in this work as a faculty of the intellect, but as a system of teachings, and therefore is described as doctrine. . . . Theology consists of both contemplation and action. It is both wisdom and prudence; wisdom in that it apprehends principles through divinely illumined intelligence and reaches conclusions from them through knowledge; and prudence, in that it guides the human soul in its actions.

III. The principle of the being of theology is God; the principle by which it is known is the word of God. . . .

XX. As God is the peculiar [*proprius*] and primary object of theology, so is he also its primary and final end.

XXI. Since, therefore, its final end and the highest good [*summum bonum*] are the same, it is obvious that only Christian theology can rightly teach us concerning the highest good.

XXII. A subordinate end of sacred theology is our salvation, which consists of communion with God, and enjoyment of him.

(2)

There are two divisions of theology: the first concerns the knowledge of God, the second the service of God. The first consists of faith or things to be believed [τὰ πιστά]; the second, of works or things to be done [τὰ πρακτά].

B. WILLIAM AMES

I.

1. Theology is the doctrine or teaching [*doctrina*] of living to God. . . .
2. It is called doctrine, not to separate it from understanding, knowledge, wisdom, art, or prudence—for these go with every exact discipline, and most of all with theology—but to mark it as a discipline which derives not from nature and human inquiry like others, but from divine revelation and appointment. . . .

3. The principles of other arts, since they are inborn in us, can be developed through sense perception, observation, experience, and induction, and so brought to perfection. But the basic principles of theology, though they may be advanced by study and industry, are not in us by nature. Matt. 16:17, *Flesh and blood has not revealed this to you.*

4. Every art has its rules to which the work of the person practicing it corresponds. Since living is the noblest work of all, there cannot be any more proper study than the art of living.

5. Since the highest kind of life for a human being is that which approaches most closely the living and life-giving God, the nature of theological life is living to God.

6. Men live to God when they live in accord with the will of God, to the glory of God, and with God working in them. . . .

7. This life in essence remains one and the same from its beginning to eternity. . . .

8. Although it is within the compass of this life to live both happily and well, εὐζωία, living well, is more excellent than εὐδαιμονία, living happily. What chiefly and finally ought to be striven for is not happiness which has to do with our own pleasure, but goodness which looks to God's glory. For this reason, theology is better defined as that good life whereby we live to God than as that happy life whereby we live to ourselves. . . .

9. Furthermore, since this life is the spiritual work of the whole man, in which he is brought to enjoy God and to act according to his will, and since it certainly has to do with man's will, it follows that the first and proper subject of theology is the will. . . .

10. Now since this life so willed is truly and properly our most important practice, it is self-evident that theology is not a speculative discipline but a practical one. . . .

13. Theology . . . may therefore not incorrectly be called θεοζωία, a living to God, or θεουργία, a working towards God, as well as theology.

II.

1. The two parts of theology are faith and observance.

Johannes Cocceius: Biblical Method in Covenant Theology

Covenant theology has exercised a pervasive influence in the Reformed tradition, being reflected in such important theological works as the Westminster Confession of Faith as well as in the civil polity of the government in the United States. While the theme of covenant was present from the beginning in

9

Zwingli, Bullinger, and Calvin, Johannes Cocceius (Coccejus) (1603–69) carried it to new levels of systematic sophistication. A skilled Hebraist—he was professor of biblical philology at Bremen from 1630 and professor of Hebrew at Franecker from 1636—Cocceius crafted his theology according to a conscientious exegetical method, developing the covenant theme from its Old Testament roots into a comprehensive theological paradigm.

SOURCE

Johannes Cocceius, "De Theologia, & ejus tradendae Methodo," Caput I, *Summa Theologiae* (1662), 133–36; ET: "Biblical Method of Covenant Theology," trans. Mary Beaty.

BIBLIOGRAPHY

Heiner Faulenbach, *Weg und Ziel der Erkenntnis Christi: Eine Untersuchung zur Theologie des Johannes Coccejus*, Beiträge zur Geschichte und Lehre der Reformierten Kirche 26. (Neukirchen: Neukirchener Verlag, 1973). Charles S. McCoy, "The Covenant Theology of Johannes Cocceius" (Ph.D. diss., Yale University, 1957). Idem, "Johannes Cocceius: Federal Theologian," *Scottish Journal of Theology* 16 (1963): 352–70. Gottlob Schrenk, *Gottesreich und Bund im ältern Protestantismus vornehmlich bei Johannes Coccejus: Ein Beitrag zur Geschichte des Pietismus und der heilsgeschichtlichen Theologie* (Gütersloh, 1923; reprint: Giessen: Brunnen Verlag, 1985).

Theology is the knowledge and speech of a theologian. A theologian (to omit those things which do not serve our purpose) is "one who speaks God from God in the presence of God for his glory." So Paul says that he "persuades God, not men" (Gal. 1:10); that is, he persuades obedience to God, not to men. Likewise the entirety which is set before faith is called the "name of God" (John 17:26). "I have declared to them your name," that is, what should be felt and said about you, and what your power is that must be celebrated and glorified. Therefore "to name the name of God" is used for the whole of religion [Joel 2:32; Rom. 10:13; 2 Tim. 2:19]. To give glory to God and to think and speak fittingly about him and to call him one's own God in truth—this is the whole of religion.

Therefore it is particularly the part of a theologian "to speak God" (Ps. 139:20), but "from God," for wisdom is from him (Prov. 2:6), and "in the presence of God," and "in God" (2 Cor. 2:17). "We speak the word of God in Christ as if from God in the sight of God." For God presides as a judge in the conscience and no one can speak Christ the Lord except in the Spirit of God (1 Cor. 12:3). Moreover it is very clear that a person must speak God and the things of God "on account of God," on account of whom and for whom all things exist. The person who speaks God and divine matters [but does so] not from love of God and for God's glory is not able to speak God truly, for he does not really know him and does not speak from God and in God. He speaks his own desire and does not speak in good conscience. That it is especially fitting for man to engage in theology, and that there is no work which befits him better, is clear from this: man is from God and it is evident that he cannot exist except from God, and it is certain that no truth (and to understand truth distinguishes man from beast) can be known apart from God and that there is no wisdom and no conception of right and wrong, good and evil, which is not founded in the knowledge of God. And finally [it is clear] that man, as all of God's works, was made for him and on account of him, and that man, uniquely endowed with the faculty of understanding and will, cannot exist for God and his glory unless he exists in accordance with God in whose image he was made, and unless he so loves God, whom alone he can love and seek well, and seeks him as his true good. It follows from all this that it is man's greatest power not only to know and love God but also, from that love, to name the name of God in truth for his glory.

The knowledge of the theologian which he has in this life concerning God is not the knowledge which God has about himself and in himself and by which the Father knows the Son and the Son (in whom is the name of God, Exod. 23:21) knows the Father, or [by which] the Holy Spirit searches out the depths of God (1 Cor. 2:10), nor [is it] that by which we know God in our native land [i.e., heaven] when we shall know even as we are known; but [it is only knowledge] in part, as in an enigma (1 Cor. 13:8, 9, 10, 13); it is [merely] an archetype which God has determined to make known about himself in this life at distinct times and to allow to be known.

Meanwhile the knowledge is true, even if not made equal. Things known about God are known partly in a negative way, by separating those things which are weak and imperfect, partly in the imagination, and partly through attribution of their inaccessible loftiness (we recognize that he dwells in inaccessible light). These are without falsehood, though there is more in the subject matter itself than we can understand.

Not only is the theology "of the way" imperfect when compared to the theology "of the native land," but in all respects it is more imperfect than it was possible to know in the way. Which of the apostles or prophets understood all the mysteries in the Word of God? To say nothing of the others who were not prophets and apostles and who came to the point that they could learn nothing further from the Word of God and nothing further could be revealed through it. In that imperfection, therefore, which is joined with constant progress, are [those] who have "the spirit of faith" by which they affix themselves to God as he is making revelations, and they rest in the salvation of God, prepared to learn true wisdom and prudence through the instruction of the Holy Spirit. There are those, likewise, who have received "the word of wisdom" by which is revealed to the conscience the connection to divine truths and their conformity and plenitude and certainty, and [by which] all falsehoods are refuted—there are those who have received "the word of circumspection" or prudence, for avoiding the evil way, for approving the better things, for discerning the Spirit—there are those who have received a word of prophecy, namely, that ordinary [type] by which the Word of God is set forth. The apostle speaks of them in 1 Cor. 12:8, 9, and 10.

Although the theology of the way is imperfect, it is nonetheless useful in that those who are saved receive true knowledge of God through its ministry, so that they can be said "to know the truth," even "to know all things" [1 John 2:20, 21]. . . .

We have said that the glory of God is set before theology, so that a man may be toward God, which cannot happen unless God once becomes glorious and admirable in man (2 Thess. 1:10) and satiates and fills him as his good, and in him is everything (1 Cor. 15:28). As a result also, those who boast in the hope of eternal life and the enjoyment of God are said "to boast in the hope of the glory of God" (Rom. 5:2) because the glory of God (that is, for God to become glorious in us) is our good, and the object of our hope. Next, since theology is totally provided for glorifying God, loving him, seeking him, believing in him, rejoicing in him, and worshiping him, it cannot be doubted that it is practiced. Certainly it teaches this praxis, and teaches it in such a way that there is no truth in the theology which does not teach praxis through itself. Take this [as an example]: "God exists." Immediately comes the thought: Therefore it is for us to know God, not to deny him but rather with mind, tongue, and work to confess that he exists and is our Lord. . . .

The person who has known God to such a point that he desires to have a good conscience and to obey the word he has heard already finds it easy to know the doctrine of Christ from which it comes. Those who put away from themselves a zeal for a good conscience (1 Tim. 1:19) cannot hear the Word of Christ, and those who cannot hear him cannot know him; (John 8:43): "Why do you not understand my speech? Because you cannot hear my Word." That is, your mind shrinks away from my word so that you do not withstand hearing it for a wise inquiry. In this respect what [Gregory] Nazianzus says in *Oratio* 29, "Concerning the Dogma and the Constitution of the Bishops," is correct.

What we have said, then, that theology is from God and that men do not know what should be said about God unless he is [their] preceptor— this leads us to think about the beginnings of theology, or about the medium through which God teaches man the things he wants known about himself, and the things which man needs to know about him in order to be able to be his image.

Gisburtus Voetius: Between Pietism and High Scholasticism

High Scholasticism marks a period of more intense systematizing of the creative works of previous Reformed theology. It was not, however, devoid of concern for the practical life of the church, as evidenced in this selection on practical theology by Gisburtus Voetius (Gysbert Voët) (1589–1676). A Dutchman, Voetius attended the University of Leyden (modern Leiden), studying under both the strict Calvinist, Francis Gomarus (1563–1641), and the more liberal Jacob Arminius (1560–1609). He later sided with Gomarus and the other Calvinists against the followers of Arminius as a representative to the Synod of Dort (Dordrecht) in 1618–19 (pp. 94–96). In 1634 he was appointed to the faculty at Utrecht. During his tenure there he opposed both the new Cocceian system of theology[6] and the new philosophical method of René Descartes (1596–1650).[7] Notwithstanding Voetius's strict orthodoxy, he was a pietist who supported the spiritual reform of Jean de Labadie[8] and who stood as a forerunner of the seventeenth-century Lutheran pietists, Johann Arndt (1555–1621), Philip Jacob Spener (1635–1705), and August Hermann Francke (1663–1727).

SOURCE

Gisburtus Voetius, *Selectae disputationes theologicae*, 5 vols. (Utrecht, 1648–69); ET: "Concerning Practical Theology," in Beardslee, *Reformed Dogmatics*, 265–68, 289–95 (edited).

6. One of the chief differences between Voetius and Cocceius was over Sabbath observance. Voetius followed the observant position of Francis Gomarus (1563–1641), while Cocceius held that the gospel had overturned observance as a religious duty, a position which tracked that of Gomarus's opponent on this issue, Antonius Walaeus (1573–1639).

7. Descartes forged a philosophy grounded in methodological doubt, accepting only such "clear and distinct" truths as could be supported by reason and the data of human consciousness (René Descartes, *Discours de la méthode* [1637]; ET: *Discourse on Method and the Meditations*, trans. F. E. Suttcliffe [New York: Penguin, 1968]).

8. Voetius did, however, repudiate Labadie's separatism, thus reflecting another Reformed dispute in this period: that between Presbyterians and Independents. On Labadie, see pp. 265–66.

BIBLIOGRAPHY

The standard Dutch biography is A. C. Duker, *Gisburtus Voetius*, 3 vols. and index vol. (Leiden: E. J. Brill, 1897–1915). See also the recent symposium, *De Onbekende Voetius: Voordrachten Wetenschappelijk Symposium*, ed. Johannes van Oort (Kampen: J. H. Kek, 1989). See Ernst Bizer, "Reformed Orthodoxy and Cartesianism," *Journal for Theology and Church* 2 (1965): 20–82.

I. "Practical theology" may mean, in the broad sense, all theology that follows Scripture or is based upon it, whether expressed in commentaries, *loci communi* ("common places"), or catechisms, because all theology among pilgrims on earth is in its nature practical, and no portion of it can be correctly and completely discussed unless it is developed practically; that is, applied to the practice of repentance, faith, hope, and love, or to consolation or exhortation. . . .

In a more narrow sense the expression may mean:

(1) A practical and specific exposition or application of the content of the polemic or didactic exposition of theological topics. This is designated practical or casuistic theology, or the practice of faith, hope, love, repentance, or amendment of life. . . .

(2) [Another restricted use of the expression "practical theology" is] to indicate the exact and full presentation of that part of theology which is distinct from the first part, concerning faith or the dogmas of the faith. This is sometimes called moral theology, and sometimes, by synecdoche, casuistry. This in turn may be understood either broadly or narrowly. In the first sense it includes all theological topics except those which refer to the faith and to the articles that must be believed; that is, those concerning Scripture, God, the works of God, redemption by Christ, the person and offices of Christ, the winning and applying of salvation, which we have discussed earlier, in the section dealing with theological difficulties. In the narrower sense [practical theology] means simply the exposition of the decalogue, or moral theology and cases of conscience involving particular precepts of the decalogue, with the needed introductions. Thus it is to be distinguished from special treatments of the practice of religion, which are called ascetic theology and ecclesiastic polity, although these two branches, by many writers on the *loci*, are combined with interpretations of the decalogue or moral problems and casuistical theology.

Anna Maria van Schuurman: Theology of the Heart

Theology is a life and not just an academic discipline. The remarkably gifted lay theologian Anna Maria van Schuurman (1607–78) illustrates this in her

Eukleria, one of the major theological works of the Labidist movement. Van Schuurman had mastered a wide range of classical medieval theology but found new life in her conversion to Reformed Christianity and in her later association with Jean de Labadie (1610–74). Although women were not admitted to the university, Voetius allowed her to attend his lectures on theology hidden behind a curtain. The highly personal nature of van Schuurman's writing is typical of pietism. Her work has so far received little attention in the English-speaking world.

SOURCE

Anna Maria van Schuurman, *Eukleria, seu melioris partis electio; tractatus brevem vitae eius Deliniationem exhibens* (Altona: C. van der Meulen, 1673) = *Eucleria, of uitkiezing van het beste deel* (Amsterdam: J. van de Velde, 1684). The text is from the opening paragraphs of chap. 4. The translation is by Iain S. Maclean and W. S. Johnson, based on both the Dutch and Latin.

BIBLIOGRAPHY

Heinrich Heppe, *Geschichte des Pietismus und der Mystik in der reformierten Kirche, namentlich der Niederlande* (Leiden, 1879). Albrecht Ritschl, *Geschichte des Pietismus in der reformierten Kirche* (Bonn, 1880). T. J. Saxby, *The Quest for the New Jerusalem: Jean de Labadie and the Labidists, 1610–1744* (Dordrecht: Martin Nijhoff Publishers, 1987). G.D.J. Schotel, *Anna Maria van Schuurman* (Leyden, 1853). F. Ernest Stoeffler, *The Rise of Evangelical Pietism* (Leiden, 1965).

[I]t appears sufficiently demonstrated [from what I have related about my life] that I have labored much in superfluous things. For I knew no limit in the pursuit of the academic sciences. Thus I [found that I] had to hasten to the truths of Reformed theology and to the exercises of holiness to which I [now] subject all other things.

These academic sciences, in which I seemed to have made such [intellectual] progress, while they are blessings, they are judged in the light of the Reformed faith. And so it seemed that [in my studies] I no longer progressed directly and significantly forward but moved only in a circle, finding that, in general and in regarding particular matters, I needed continually to go back to the beginning. Not only did I exercise myself in contemplation of reality, but I also desired in my own way, and within my own limits, the grace to exert myself in positive theology. Just as in most things the comprehension and the thing itself differ completely, so I now learned every day the great distinction between truths grasped in the understanding, which are depicted in the conscience, and the love by which something is appropriated in the heart, between a conversion of the conscience and the [deeper] conversion of the heart, and between conversion itself and progress.

I acknowledge that to a certain extent I understood all of theology and loved it, so that in contemplating it I would well have died. And therefore in order that nothing should slip my mind, and because I did not always know what might happen to me, I devised orderly tables both of theoretical [dogmatic] and of practical theology (that which antiquity called the exercise of asceticism), complete with all their distinctions, subdistinctions, and descriptions. In these tables I could dutifully contemplate all these princes of the sciences as in the blinking of an eye. But what indeed had I more than a mere cultivated form and image of science?

Who can say why I did not rest content in this but along with this knowledge deeply sought to exercise godly fruits of piety? And so I invested a great deal of pious energy in fasting and praying, both in public and in private, in ordinary and extraordinary exercises, and I could gladly be found pursuing these without ceasing. . . . I led others through praying morning and evening at home, and covenanted myself each day so far as was possible to pray alone three times at set hours after the example of the prophet Daniel; and I reckon that this was no unpleasant offering for God because I so singularly sought to do my best, although often in these prayers the heavenly oil and rejoicing were lacking. . . . So that I eventually through experience learned that man in place of [heartfelt prayer] labors in vain with chosen words, that one ought more to use humble sighings and above these must become contemplative. And this agrees with the holy scriptures which command us to pray without ceasing, in spirit and in truth. . . . I think that Lactantius has also noticed this when he said that to have a great heart is the best religion. But the apostle has defined it with true evangelical words when he had to address the children of God, saying, "The Spirit comes to help us in our weaknesses. I know not what I should pray but the Spirit comes with irrepeatable sighs." Therefore it is necessary that the Spirit of Christ be in us for he prays that our heart and strength might be joined with God so that he might sink us into the unending ocean of the divine.

THE AUTHORITY AND INTERPRETATION OF SCRIPTURE

The confession "scripture alone" (*sola scriptura*) has formed the bedrock of Reformed teaching and practice. Before it is anything else, Reformed theology, historically, has been the faithful attempt to interpret the Word of God in scripture. The Reformed affirmation of scripture as the necessary and sufficient source for saving knowledge of God and thus for true doctrine was in accord with medieval Augustinian conviction. The Roman Catholic formulation of authority, however, linked scripture and its interpretation to an authoritative and infallible ecclesiastical institution. It was this that Protestant theology, and the Reformed in particular, rejected. The so-called scripture principle was there from the earliest days of Reformed theology; the formalized theory of scriptural authority came only later. After the First Helvetic Confession (1536), a large number, but not all, of the Reformed confessions opened with a statement of the authority of scripture.

BIBLIOGRAPHY

Barth, *Church Dogmatics* II/2, pp. 457–740. Karl Barth, "Das Schriftprinzip der reformierten Kirche," *Zwischen den Zeiten* 3 (1925): 215–45. G. C. Berkouwer, *Holy Scripture* (Grand Rapids: Wm. B. Eerdmans, 1975).

Huldrych Zwingli: The Clarity and Certainty of the Word of God

As part of his ongoing effort to convert the Roman Catholic monasteries to the reform movement, Zwingli preached this sermon in the early part of 1522 to the nuns at the Dominican convent in Oetenbach. It was published that same year in September. The sermon is a straightforward exposition, delivered in the vernacular and replete with scriptural references, in which Zwingli announced the efficacy and perspicacity of God's Word made effectual in believers through the power of the Holy Spirit. God's Word is *certain* in its ability to accomplish that which it seeks, namely, the salvation of the sinner. Its *clarity*, located in the "true and natural sense" of the text, eliminates the need for official ecclesiastical interpretation. Instead, the Spirit speaks this Word directly to the mind or soul of the recipient without any intermediary. This is possible, says Zwingli, because, even after the fall into sin, human beings retain the image of God as reflected in a universal thirst after God and salvation. To the end that believers should persevere in seeking and receiving the Word of grace, Zwingli concludes the sermon by imparting practical advice for coming to a true experiential understanding to the scriptural Word. It is this bit of concluding advice which comprises our text.

SOURCE

Huldrych Zwingli, *Von Klarheit und Gewissheit des Wortes Gottes* (1522), *Sämtliche Werke* 1:338–84; ET: "The Clarity and Certainty of the Word of God," in *Zwingli and Bullinger*, 93–95.

BIBLIOGRAPHY

W. P. Stephens, *The Theology of Huldrych Zwingli* (Oxford: Clarendon, 1986), chap. 2.

[O]ur view of the matter is this: that we should hold the Word of God in the highest possible esteem—meaning by the Word of God only that which comes from the Spirit of God—and we should give to it a trust which we cannot give to any other word. For the Word of God is certain and can never fail. It is clear, and will never leave us in darkness. It teaches its own truth. It arises and irradiates the soul of man with full salvation and grace. It gives the soul sure comfort in God. It humbles it, so that it loses and indeed condemns itself and lays hold of God. . . .

Blessedness begins indeed in this present time, not essentially, but in the certainty of consoling hope. May God increase it in us more and more, and never suffer us to fall from it. Amen.

I thought it might be good at this point to give some instruction in the way to come to a true understanding of the Word of God and to a personal experience of the fact that you are taught of God. For if we are not versed in Scripture, how are we to tell whether the priest who teaches us is expounding the pure truth unadulterated by his own sinful desires?

First, we must pray inwardly to God, that he will kill off the old man who sets such great store by his own wisdom and ability.

Second, when the old man is killed off and removed, that God will graciously infill us, and in such measure that we believe and trust only in him.

Third, when that is done we shall certainly be greatly refreshed and comforted, and we must constantly repeat the words of the prophet: Lord, God, strengthen that which thou hast wrought in us. For "let him that thinketh he standeth take heed lest he fall," as Paul says.

Fourth, the Word of God does not overlook anyone, and least of all the greatest. For when God called Paul, he said to Ananias: "He is a chosen vessel unto me, to bear my name before the princes and kings of the earth." Again, he says to the disciples (Matt. 10): "And ye shall be brought before governors and kings, that ye may testify unto them concerning me."

Fifth, it is the nature and property of the Word to humble the high and mighty and to exalt the lowly. That was the song of the Virgin Mary: "He hath put down the mighty from their seats, and exalted them of low degree." And again, John proclaimed concerning Christ (Luke 3): "By him shall all the hills be brought low, and the valleys filled, etc."

18

Sixth, the Word of God always attracts and helps the poor, comforting the comfortless and despairing, but opposing those who trust in themselves, as Christ testifies.

Seventh, it does not seek its own advantage: for that reason Christ commanded his disciples to take neither scrip nor purse.

Eighth, it seeks only that God may be revealed to men, that the obstinate may fear him and the lowly find comfort in God. Those who preach in that manner are undoubtedly right. Those who cautiously beat about the bush for their own advantage, defending the teaching of man instead of holding and expounding the doctrine of God, are false prophets. Know them by their words. They make a fine outcry: The holy Fathers! Is it nothing that man can do? and the like. But for all their complaining they do not complain that the Gospel of Christ is slackly proclaimed.

Ninth, when you find that the Word of God renews you, and begins to be more precious to you than formerly when you heard the doctrines of men, then you may be sure that this is the work of God within you.

Tenth, when you find that it gives you assurance of the grace of God and eternal salvation, it is of God.

Eleventh, when you find that it crushes and destroys you, but magnifies God himself within you, it is a work of God.

Twelfth, when you find that the fear of God begins to give you joy rather than sorrow, it is a sure working of the Word and Spirit of God.

May God grant us that Spirit. Amen.

John Calvin: Inspiration and Authority

Through his sermons, commentaries, and the *Institutes*, John Calvin set the standard for Protestant biblical interpretation. Unlike pre-Vatican II Roman Catholicism which, at the Council of Trent (1545–63), held tradition and scripture in equal authority, Calvin sought to base his theology on scripture alone. Scripture, for Calvin, must be interpreted by the "analogy of faith," according to which believers have been nurtured through the ages by the "plain meaning" of a single inspired book under the competent guidance of the Holy Spirit. The need for the Spirit to illumine the believer in interpreting the Word means that scriptural authority does not lie naked on the printed page. The Word, while committed to humanity for its edification, is not simply given to human disposal but always works subject to the dynamic movement of God. The Spirit is continually at work in the Word; but unlike some among the radical wing of the reform, Calvin denies that revelation new and different from that already given in scripture will be forthcoming. Claims to possess the Spirit separate from the Word are unreliable; efforts to read the Word apart from the Spirit are void.

SOURCES

(A) *Institutes* I.6.1–4, pp. 69–74. (B) John Calvin, Commentary: Galatians 4:22 (1548); *CO* 50; ET: In *The Epistles of Paul the Apostle to the Galatians, Ephesians, Philippians and Colossians*, trans. T.H.L. Parker = *Calvin's New Testament Commentaries* 11:84–85. (C) *Institutes* I.7.1–5, pp. 74–81 (edited). (D) *Institutes* IV.8.8–9, pp. 1155–58 (edited).

BIBLIOGRAPHY

Jack Forstman, *Word and Spirit: Calvin's Doctrine of Biblical Authority* (Stanford: Stanford University Press, 1962). John T. McNeill, "The Significance of the Word of God for Calvin," *Church History* 28 (1959): 131–46. Thomas F. Torrance, *The Hermeneutics of John Calvin*, Monograph Supplements to the Scottish Journal of Theology (Edinburgh: Scottish Academic Press, 1988).

A. THE AUTHORITY OF SCRIPTURE

[I]t is worth-while to say something about the authority of Scripture, not only to prepare our hearts to reverence it, but to banish all doubt. . . . The Scriptures obtain full authority among believers only when men regard them as having sprung from heaven, as if there the living words of God were heard. . . .

But a most pernicious error widely prevails that Scripture has only so much weight as is conceded to it by the consent of the church. As if the eternal and inviolable truth of God depended upon the decision of men!

[W]hile the church receives and gives its seal of approval to the Scriptures, it does not thereby render authentic what is otherwise doubtful or controversial. But because the church recognizes Scripture to be the truth of its own God, as a pious duty it unhesitatingly venerates Scripture. As to their question—How can we be assured that this has sprung from God unless we have recourse to the decree of the church?— it is as if someone asked: Whence will we learn to distinguish light from darkness, white from black, sweet from bitter? Indeed, Scripture exhibits fully as clear evidence of its own truth as white and black things do of their color, or sweet and bitter things do of their taste. . . .

[C]redibility of doctrine is not established until we are persuaded beyond doubt that God is its Author. Thus, the highest proof of Scripture derives in general from the fact that God in person speaks in it.

B. THE PLAIN MEANING OF SCRIPTURE

Scripture, they say, is fertile and thus bears multiple meanings. I acknowledge that Scripture is the most rich and inexhaustible fount of all wisdom. But I deny that its fertility consists in the various meanings which anyone may fasten to it at his pleasure. Let us know, then, that the true meaning of Scripture is the natural and simple one (*verum sensum scripturae, qui germanus est et simplex*), and let us embrace and hold it resolutely. Let us not merely neglect as doubtful, but boldly set aside as deadly corruptions, those pretended expositions which lead us away from the literal sense (*a literali sensu*).

C. WORD AND SPIRIT

[T]he testimony of the Spirit is more excellent than all reason. For as God alone is a fit witness of himself in his Word, so also the Word will not find acceptance in men's hearts before it is sealed by the inward testimony of the Spirit. The same Spirit, therefore, who has spoken through the mouths of the prophets must penetrate into our hearts to persuade us that they faithfully proclaimed what had been divinely commanded. Isaiah very aptly expresses this connection in these words: "My spirit which is in you, and the words that I have put in your mouth, and the mouths of your offspring, shall never fail" [Isa. 59:21]. Some good folk are annoyed that a clear proof is not ready at hand when the impious, unpunished, murmur against God's Word. As if the Spirit were not called both "seal" and "guarantee" [II Cor. 1:22] for confirming the faith of the godly; because until he illumines their minds, they ever waver among many doubts! . . .

Let this point therefore stand: that those whom the Holy Spirit has inwardly taught truly rest upon Scripture, and that Scripture indeed is self-authenticated.

D. THE MANNER OF INSPIRATION

Let this be a firm principle: No other word is to be held as the Word of God, and given place as such in the church, than what is contained first in the Law and the Prophets, then in the writings of the apostles; and the only authorized way of teaching in the church is by the prescription and standard of his Word.

From this also we infer that the only thing granted to the apostles was that which the prophets had had of old. They were to expound the ancient Scripture and to show that what is taught there has been fulfilled in Christ. Yet they were not to do this except from the Lord, that is, with Christ's Spirit as precursor in a certain measure dictating the words. . . .

Yet this, as I have said, is the difference between the apostles and their successors: the former were sure and genuine scribes of the Holy Spirit, and their writings are therefore to be considered oracles of God; but the sole office of others is to teach what is provided and sealed in the Holy Scriptures. We therefore teach that faithful ministers are now not permitted to coin any new doctrine, but that they are simply to cleave to that doctrine to which God has subjected all men without exception.

Heinrich Bullinger:
Reformed Hermeneutics

One of the problems posed by the scripture principle is how to determine who has arrived at the authoritative interpretation of the text. The abundance of interpretations may seem to undercut the claim that scripture provides the unique and clarifying mediation of divine revelation. For the Roman Catholics, the presence of many conflicting interpretations argued for hierarchical intervention to establish the true meaning based on the weight of tradition. Here the Swiss reformer Heinrich Bullinger (1504–75) offers hermeneutical rules to mitigate this problem. Scripture exposition, in order to be valid, must be catholic, charitable, sensitive both to the immediate context and to the whole content of scripture (i.e., allowing scripture to interpret scripture), and guided by the Holy Spirit.

SOURCE

Heinrich Bullinger, "Of the Sense and Right Exposition of the Word of God, and by What Manner of Means It May Be Expounded," in *Decades*, 75–80. The *Decades* were required reading for many English pastors, and hence they had a profound impact upon English Reformed theology.

BIBLIOGRAPHY

Works on Bullinger in English are few. See J. Wayne Baker, *Heinrich Bullinger and the Covenant: The Other Reformed Tradition* (Athens, Ohio, 1980). Edward Dowey, "Heinrich Bullinger as Theologian: Thematic, Comprehensive, Schematic," in *Calvin Studies V*, ed. John H. Leith (colloquium on Calvin studies, Davidson College, Davidson, N.C., 1989), 41–60. David C. Steinmetz, *Reformers in the Wings* (Philadelphia: Fortress, 1971; reprint: Grand Rapids: Baker, 1981).

Standard works include André Bouvier, *Henri Bullinger réformateur et conseiller oecuménique, le successeur de Zwingli, d'après sa correspondance avec les réformés et les humanistes de langue française* (Neuchatel: Delachaux & Niestlé, 1940). Joachim

Staedtke, *Die Theologie des jungen Bullinger,* Studien zur Dogmengeschichte und systematischen Theologie 16 (Zurich: Zwingli Verlag, 1962).

On Bullinger as an interpreter of scripture, see Susi Hausammann, *Römerbriefauslegung zwischen Humanismus und Reformation: Eine Studie zu Heinrich Bullingers Römerbriefvorlesung von 1525,* Studien zur Dogmengeschichte und Systematischen Theologie 27 (Zurich: Zwingli Verlag, 1970).

I will teach you the manner, and some ready ways, how to interpret the scriptures. The handling of these points shall take away the impediments which drive men from the reading of the word of God, and shall cause the reading and hearing of the word of God to be both wholesome and fruitful.

And first of all, that God's will is to have his word understood of mankind, we may thereby gather especially, because that in speaking to his servants he used a most common kind of speech, wherewithal even the very idiots were acquainted. Neither do we read that the prophets and apostles, the servants of God and interpreters of his high and everlasting wisdom, did use any strange kind of speech: so that in the whole pack of writers none can be found to excel them in a more plain and easy phrase of writing. Their writings are full of common proverbs, similitudes, parables, comparisons, devised narrations, examples, and such other like manner of speeches, than which there is nothing that doth more move and plainly teach the common sorts of wits among mortal men. There ariseth, I confess, some darkness in the scriptures, by reason of the natural property, figurative ornaments, and the unacquainted use of the tongues. But that difficulty may easily be helped by study, diligence, faith, and the means of skilful interpreters. . . .

[T]hough the scripture be manifest and the word of God be evident, yet, notwithstanding, it refuseth not a godly or holy exposition; but rather an holy exposition doth give a setting out to the word of God, and bringeth forth much fruit in the godly hearer. . . .

In the mean season, all the ministers of the church must beware, that they follow not herein their own affections any whit at all, or else corrupt the scriptures by their wrong interpretations; and so by that means set forth to the church their own inventions, and not the word of God. . . .

And now, dearly beloved, the place and time require us to say somewhat unto you touching the interpretation of the holy scriptures, or the exposition of the word of God. Wherein I will not speak any thing particularly of the skilful knowledge of tongues, or the liberal sciences, which are things requisite in a good interpreter; but will briefly touch the generalities alone. And first of all ye must understand, that some things in the scriptures, or word of God, are so plainly set forth, that they have need of no interpretation, neither will admit any exposition: which if any man go about with his own expositions to make more manifest, he may seem to do as wittily as he, which with fagot-light and torches would help the sun at his rising to give more light unto the world. As for those things which are so set down, that they seem to require our help to expound them, they must not be interpreted after our own fantasies, but according to the mind and meaning of him, by whom the scriptures were revealed. . . .

And therewithal ye must mark a few certain rules, which I mean briefly to touch and to shew unto you, in those few words which I have yet to speak.

First, since the apostle Paul would have the exposition of the scriptures to agree fitly, and in every point proportionally with our faith; as it is to be seen in the twelfth to the Romans: and because again in the latter epistle to the Corinthians he saith, "Seeing then that we have the same spirit of faith (according as it is written, I believed, and therefore have I spoken), we also believe, and therefore do we speak:" let it therefore be taken for a point of catholic religion, not to bring in or admit any thing in our expositions which others have alleged against the received articles of our faith, contained in the Apostles' Creed and other confessions of the ancient fathers. . . .

Furthermore, we read in the gospel, that the Lord doth gather a sum of the law and the prophets, saying: "Thou shalt love the Lord thy God with all thy heart, with all thy soul, and with all thy mind: this is the chief and great commandment. And the second is like unto it: Thou shalt love thy neighbour as thyself. In these two commandments hangeth the whole law and the prophets." Matt. xxii. . . .

We must therefore, by all means possible, take heed that our interpretations do not tend to the overthrow of charity, but to the furtherance and commendation of it to all men. . . .

Moreover, it is requisite in expounding the scriptures, and searching out the true sense of God's word, that we mark upon what occasion every thing is spoken, what goeth before, what followeth after, at what season, in what order, and of what person any thing is spoken. By the occasion, and the sentences going before and coming after, are examples and parables for the most part expounded. Also, unless a man do always mark the manner of speaking throughout the whole scriptures, and that very diligently too, he cannot choose in his expositions but err very much out of the right way. . . .

There is also, beside these, another manner of interpreting the word of God; that is, by conferring together the places which are like or unlike, and by expounding the darker by the more evident, and the fewer by the more in number. Whereas therefore the Lord saith, "The Father is greater than I"; we must consider, that the same Lord in another place saith, "My Father and I are all one." And whereas James the apostle saith, that Abraham and we are justified by works, there are many places in St. Paul to be set against that one. And this manner of interpreting did Peter the apostle allow, where he saith: "We have a right sure word of prophecy, whereunto if ye attend, as unto a light that shineth in a dark place, ye do well, until the day dawn, and the day-star arise in your hearts." . . .

And finally, the most effectual rule of all, whereby to expound the word of God, is an heart that loveth God and his glory, not puffed up with pride, not desirous of vainglory, not corrupted with heresies and evil affections; but which doth continually pray to God for his holy Spirit, that, as by it the scripture was revealed and inspired, so also by the same Spirit it may be expounded to the glory of God and safeguard of the faithful. . . .

Thus much hitherto have I said touching the sense and exposition of God's word: which, as God revealed it to men, so also he would have them in any case to understand it. Wherefore there is no cause for any man, by reason of a few difficulties, to despair to attain to the true understanding of the scriptures. The scripture doth admit a godly and religious interpretation.

Antoine de la Roche Chandieu: Theology and the Word of God

Chandieu (Sadeel or Sandeel) (1534–91) was pastor of the Reformed church in Paris prior to the St. Bartholomew's Day massacre (August 23–24, 1572), after which he fled to Switzerland. This passage from *De verbo Dei scripto* is a straightforward statement of the scriptural foundation of Reformed theology.

SOURCE

Antoine de la Roche Chandieu, *De verbo Dei scripto adversus humanas traditiones* (1580), in *Opera Theologica* (1592), trans. Mary Beaty.

Certain outstanding philosophers teach that the singular nature of the sciences is that they rest upon fixed principles beyond which it is not permitted to rise. If it were permitted, investigation would be infinite and there would therefore be no science, since the philosophers regard this almost as an oracle: there is no science of the infinite.

If, therefore, you should command a theologian to test his own principles, how could he do this except through some principle higher than those principles [to be tested]? And if this should happen, he would have moved into the infinite, which philosophers shudder at as if at some disgraceful act in science.

At this point a distinction of principles must be observed. One is the principle or cause of each conclusion (of these principles some are mediate, others are truly immediate); the other is a principle or axiom of science to which that syllogism should be referred. Outstanding philosophers [teach] many things about these matters.

The theological principle seems to me to be an axiom about sacred matters, undemonstrated and self-authenticated, and once it is set, an evident and necessary conclusion follows about matters which pertain to religion. This axiom is of that sort: "Sacred scripture is altogether inspired by God" [lit., θεόπνευστος, God-breathed]. No Christians are in doubt about this. Therefore every time sacred matters are discussed and someone has pointed out that "it has been so written by the prophets and apostles," the person on whom that primeval light has shined will agree: "It is absolutely true and certain, that scripture is inspired of God [θεόπνευστος], and scripture is true because God is truthful, and that is true because God said it"; and it will not be allowed to go any further, an untrodden way for the wise and the unwise.

Theologians, therefore, ought to be different in this respect, that they should never have to demonstrate their principles. There can be no science without undemonstrable principles about the truth of which those who profess the sciences feel no doubt. Has any mathematician ever doubted that the whole is greater than its parts? What philosopher has called into doubt this demonstrative principle . . . that . . . on whatever subject, a true affirmation or denial is immediately opposed to it. If anyone doubts this, the philosophers are of the opinion that he should be tortured until he acknowledges that it is one thing to be tortured and another not to be tortured. If anyone therefore does not admit the principles of some science, the philosophers command either that he not be disputed or that the error be conclusively proven by reducing the arguments to absurdity.

Human reason cannot be a principle of theology, for it would acquire the authority of sacred scripture and thus human reason would be superior to or more true than sacred scripture, and this would be not to be reasonable but to be insane, to blaspheme. . . .

Likewise, proof of sacred doctrine is not adduced to prove its own principles but is adduced from its own principles for conclusions. "Nothing can be a principle of theology which is inconsistent with sacred scripture or is condemned by it." Antithesis rather often occurs between human reason and sacred doctrine, since there is so little continuity. Hence it comes about that not all those endowed with human reason recognize and approve the true Christian religion, but more often they oppose it. Human reason therefore is not a theological principle.

Finally we must return to this point, that all reasons applied to believing are sought either from sacred scripture or from another source. If from sacred scripture, this accords with our wishes; if from elsewhere, then higher objections will always militate against them. I am not unaware that a person has certain shared ideas, but if those ideas are inconsistent with the Word of God, they must be rejected as altogether false. But if they accord with the Word of God, as do those preconceived ideas such as "God is one," "God must be obeyed," and similar ideas, then the truth of them is fundamental and certainty ought to be sought from God's Word. . . .

Christians today should prove articles of faith only by the authority of holy scripture. Nor does divine scripture need human wisdom, as Chrysostom correctly said. He also says it is very dangerous to commit matters of faith to human reason. Just as, therefore, holy scripture is inspired of God, so those who believe holy scripture are taught by God.

The Westminster Confession of Faith

One can hardly find a more eloquent expression of Reformed theology's high view of scripture than the opening chapter of the Westminster Confession. Scripture forms the bedrock upon which the confession's whole theological framework rests. Although God is manifest in "the light of nature" and in "the works of creation and providence," only from scripture comes the knowledge of God that leads to salvation. Scripture is "the word of God written," the "infallible truth and divine authority," and the "rule of faith and life." The confession sets forth no particular theory of how inspiration occurs or of the precise meaning of the term "infallibility," although it does speak of scripture's "entire perfection" and its being "immediately inspired by God." By leaving the specifics of inspiration somewhat open, Westminster invites the allegiance of all those who hold a high view of scriptural authority, however much they may differ as to the particulars of the theology of inspiration.

A product of the Westminster Assembly (1643–69), the confession is a preeminent statement of seventeenth-century Reformed faith and practice. It has been used and adapted by many church bodies, including Presbyterians, Congregationalists, and Baptists.

SOURCE

"Of the Holy Scripture," Westminster Confession of Faith (1647), in Schaff, *Creeds*, 3:600–606. For a critical edition, see S. W. Carruthers, ed., *The Westminster Confession of Faith* (Manchester, Eng.: R. Aikman & Son, 1937).

BIBLIOGRAPHY

A. F. Mitchell, *The Westminster Assembly* (Philadelphia: Presbyterian Board of Publication, 1884). Jack Bartlett Rogers, *Scripture in the Westminster Confession* (Grand Rapids: Wm. B. Eerdmans, 1967). John H. Leith, *Assembly at Westminster: Reformed Theology in the Making* (Richmond, Va.: John Knox, 1972). B. B. Warfield, *The Westminster Assembly and Its Work* (New York: Oxford University Press, 1931).

OF THE HOLY SCRIPTURE

I. Although the light of nature, and the works of creation and providence, do so far manifest the goodness, wisdom, and power of God, as to leave men inexcusable; yet are they not sufficient to give that knowledge of God, and of his will, which is necessary unto salvation. . . .

VI. The whole counsel of God, concerning all things necessary for his own glory, man's salvation, faith, and life, is either expressly set down in Scripture, or by good and necessary consequence may be deduced from Scripture: unto which nothing at any time is to be added, whether by new revelations of the Spirit, or traditions of men. Nevertheless we acknowledge the inward illumination of the Spirit of God to be necessary for the saving understanding of such things as are revealed in the Word; and that there are some circumstances concerning the worship of God, and government of the Church, common to human actions and societies, which are to be ordered by the light of nature and Christian prudence, according to the general rules of the Word, which are always to be observed.

VII. All things in Scripture are not alike plain in themselves, nor alike clear unto all; yet those things which are necessary to be known, believed, and observed, for salvation, are so clearly propounded and opened in some place of Scripture or other, that not only the learned, but the unlearned, in a due use of the ordinary means, may attain unto a sufficient understanding of them. . . .

IX. The infallible rule of interpretation of Scripture is the Scripture itself; and therefore, when there is a question about the true and full sense of any Scripture (which is not manifold, but one), it must be searched and known by other places that speak more clearly.

X. The Supreme Judge, by which all controversies of religion are to be determined, and all decrees of councils, opinions of ancient writers, doctrines of men, and private spirits, are to be examined, and in whose sentence we are to rest, can be no other but the Holy Spirit speaking in the Scripture.

Helvetic Formula of Consensus:
Scholastic Theology Codified

A product of high orthodoxy, the Helvetic Formula of Consensus was composed for the Swiss Reformed Church in 1675 by Johann Heinrich Heidegger (1633–98), with some assistance from the Geneva theologian François Turretin (1623–87)[9] and from Lucas Gernler of Basel (d. 1675). The occasion of the confession, which was meant only to supplement the standing Swiss confessions and not to constitute a new and complete work, was to reject the supposed "heresy" promulgated by the Reformed school at Saumur in France (pp. 39, 99–100). There the Hebrew scholar Louis Cappel (1585–1658) had argued that the vowel points of the Masoretic text of the Old Testament had not originated with Moses but came sometime after the compilation of the Babylonian Talmud.[10] This position was rejected by many Calvinists at the time, and some of the Swiss sought to codify this rejection in the Formula. Unlike the Westminster Confession, which set forth no theory of inspiration and took no position on the authorship of particular books, the Helvetic Formula teaches the literal verbal inspiration of the original text, down to the Masoretic vowel points, and implicitly embraces Mosaic authorship of the Pentateuch. This belief was not just a reaction to the Saumur school but had predecessors in Amandus Polanus von Polansdorf (1561–1602) and in

---

9. For Turretin's doctrine of scripture, see his *Institutio theologiae elencticae* (Geneva, 1679–85), Locus II; see also pp. 31–32.

10. Louis Cappel, *Critica sacra* (1650). The Babylonian Talmud was completed sometime around the fifth century C.E. The Masoretic vowel-pointing system may have been completed around the ninth or tenth century C.E.

Voetius.[11] The Formula was binding only in Switzerland and only for a limited time, but the theological position it represents endured and has adherents to this day.

SOURCE

Formula Consensus Ecclesiarum Helveticarum Reformatarum (composed, 1675; printed, Zurich, 1714); ET: Helvetic Formula of Consensus (1675), Canons 1–3, in Leith, *Creeds*, 309–11; Latin ed., *Collectio Confessionum*, ed. H. A. Niemeyer (Leipzig: Iulii Klinkhardti, 1840), pp. 729–39.

BIBLIOGRAPHY

James L. Good, *History of the Swiss Reformed Church Since the Reformation* (Philadelphia: Reformed Church, 1913). Schaff, *Creeds* 1:477–89.

I. God, the Supreme Judge, not only took care to have His word, which is the "power of God unto salvation to every one that believeth" (Rom. i. 16), committed to writing by Moses, the Prophets, and the Apostles, but has also watched and cherished it with paternal care ever since it was written up to the present time, so that it could not be corrupted by craft of Satan or fraud of man. Therefore the Church justly ascribes it to His singular grace and goodness that she has, and will have to the end of the world, a "sure word of prophecy" and "Holy Scriptures" (2 Tim. iii. 15), from which, though heaven and earth perish, "one jot or one tittle shall in no wise pass" (Matt. v. 18).

II. But, in particular, the Hebrew Original of the Old Testament, which we have received and to this day do retain as handed down by the Jewish Church, unto whom formerly "were committed the oracles of God" (Rom. iii. 2), is, not only in its consonants, but in its vowels— either the vowel points themselves, or at least the power of the points—not only in its matter, but in its words, inspired of God, thus forming, together with the Original of the New Testament, the sole and complete rule of our faith and life; and to its standard, as to a Lydian stone, all extant versions, oriental and occidental, ought to be applied, and wherever they differ, be conformed.

III. Therefore we can by no means approve the opinion of those who declare that the *text* which the Hebrew Original exhibits was determined by man's will alone, and do not scruple at all to remodel a Hebrew

---

11. Polanus, *Syntagma theologiae christianae* (Hanover, 1609), 479–80, 486. Voetius, *Selectae disputationes theologicae* (Utrecht, 1648), 1:29, 44. The source for this information is Barth, *Church Dogmatics* I/2, p. 524.

reading which they consider unsuitable, and amend it from the Greek Versions of the LXX and others, the Samaritan Pentateuch, the Chaldee Targums, or even from other sources, yea, sometimes from their own reason alone; and furthermore, they do not acknowledge any other reading to be genuine except that which can be educed by the critical power of the human judgment from the collation of editions with each other and with the various readings of the Hebrew Original itself—which, they maintain, has been corrupted in various ways; and finally, they affirm that besides the Hebrew edition of the present time, there are in the Versions of the ancient interpreters which differ from our Hebrew context other Hebrew Originals, since these Versions are also indicative of ancient Hebrew Originals differing from each other. Thus they bring the foundation of our faith and its inviolable authority into perilous hazard.

François Turretin: The Meaning of Verbal Inspiration

The Genevan François Turretin [Francisco Turretini][12] (1623–87) wrote one of the most capable and widely read systematic theologies of the seventeenth century. A theologian and pastor, Turretin presents a reasonable and lucid account, sensitive to theological nuance, of the verbal plenary inspiration of scripture.

SOURCE

François Turretin, *Institutio theologiae elencticae* (Geneva, 1679–85), Locus II, q. 4, sec. 3–6. An English translation of this entire work, by George Musgrave Giger, is housed at Speer Memorial Library, Princeton Theological Seminary. A complete translation of Locus II is available: *The Doctrine of Scripture: Locus 2 of Institutio theologiae elencticae*, ed. and trans. John W. Beardslee III (Grand Rapids: Baker, 1981). The translation below is by W. S. Johnson, based on the copy in the rare book room of Andover Harvard Library.

The authority of scripture . . . is simply the stature and ability with which the holy writings compel faith and obedience as to the articles of belief and practice contained therein. This authority rests on the divine and infallible truth contained in these books, whose author is God, who alone has the authority to bind humanity in faith and obedience. . . .

12. This is an Italian variation. Turretin was for a time the pastor to the Italian congregation in Geneva.

Moreover, [scriptural] authenticity pertains either to history and narrative, or to truth and norms. Regarding [history and narrative] whatever scripture chronicles is true in the telling, whether it is [an account of] good or evil or truth or falsity. Regarding things which are true in and of themselves, these are things spoken as the norm of faith and practice. Nor does everything in scripture possess this normative authority, since it contains utterances of blasphemers and the devil, but as to historical authenticity, everything is true.

Now the issue is not whether the sacred writers, in their capacity as human beings and in private [opinions] might commit error. This we are quick to acknowledge. Even less is the issue whether they could have committed error in their capacity as holy men led by the Holy Spirit as to the overall substantive message. To this I believe not one of our opponents would subscribe. . . . The issue, rather, is whether in the act of writing, they were guided and inspired by the Holy Spirit such that their writings, both in substance and in the words themselves, are authentic and of God. . . .

The scripture manifests itself to derive authoritatively from God, according to straightforward testimony, when it speaks of itself as [θεόπνευστος] "God-breathed" . . . and [according to] reason, from the evidences of being from God which God has so incontrovertibly impressed upon them.

The Psalter: Psalm 19:7–8

One of the chief ways in which Reformed piety and conviction were mediated to lay people was through the singing of the psalter. This text, which is but a portion of Psalm 19, was interpreted as a statement of the reliability of the truth of scripture in living the Christian life.

How perfect is the Law of God,
    how is his covenant sure,
Converting Souls, and making wise
    the simple and obscure.
Just are the Lord's Commandments,
    and glad both heart and mind:
His precepts pure, and giveth light
    to eyes that be full blind.

REVELATION

John Calvin and General Revelation: The Universal Sense of Divinity and the Wonders of Creation

Here Calvin asserts the existence of a sense of divinity (*sensus divinitatis*) in all persons, whether Christian or not. The sense of divinity constitutes a basic element in being human. It is a divinely planted seed (*semen divinitatis*) which naturally would have taken root and grown into piety, or true religion, had not sin intervened. It is not just a vague feeling but is truly a matter of knowledge (*notitia*) which is vividly present, so much so that it constitutes a taste (*gustus divinitatis*) and an experience (*experientiae* and *sentire*) which leaves humanity without excuse for turning away from God. Similarly, in the second selection, Calvin speaks of a general revelation in the cosmos, a mirror of the invisible God. Yet because of sin, neither the sense of divinity nor the cosmic revelation now avails for salvation; and thus this general revelation is made efficacious only through the clarifying and refining lens of scripture.[13]

SOURCES

(A) *Institutes* I.3.1, 3, pp. 43–44, 45–47. **(B)** *Institutes* I.5.1, I.6.6, pp. 51–52, 69–70, 72.

BIBLIOGRAPHY

For the twentieth-century neo-orthodox debate over the proper interpretation of Calvin on this score, see *Natural Theology: Comprising "Nature and Grace" by Professor Dr. Emil Brunner and the Reply "No!" by Dr. Karl Barth*, trans. Peter Fraenkel (London: Geoffrey Bles, 1956). See also G. C. Berkouwer, *General Revelation* (Grand Rapids: Wm. B. Eerdmans, 1955).

A. THE SENSE OF DIVINITY

There is within the human mind, and indeed by natural instinct, an awareness of divinity. This we take to be beyond controversy. To prevent anyone from taking refuge in the pretense of ignorance, God himself has implanted in all men a certain understanding of his divine majesty. Ever

---

13. In addition to the *sensus divinitatis* and the wonders of creation, Calvin sees evidence of God's general revelation in the human conscience (*conscientia*), in the sciences and liberal arts, and in the providential guidance of human history (*Institutes* I.1–10). Cf. Egil Grislis, "Calvin's Use of Cicero in the *Institutes* I:1–5—A Case Study in Theological Method," *Archiv für Reformationsgeschichte* 62 (1971): 5–37.

renewing its memory, he repeatedly sheds fresh drops. Since, therefore, men one and all perceive that there is a God and that he is their Maker, they are condemned by their own testimony because they have failed to honor him and to consecrate their lives to his will. If ignorance of God is to be looked for anywhere, surely one is most likely to find an example of it among the more backward folk and those more remote from civilization. Yet there is, as the eminent pagan says, no nation so barbarous, no people so savage, that they have not a deep-seated conviction that there is a God. And they who in other aspects of life seem least to differ from brutes still continue to retain some seed of religion. So deeply does the common conception occupy the minds of all, so tenaciously does it inhere in the hearts of all! Therefore, since from the beginning of the world there has been no region, no city, in short, no household, that could do without religion, there lies in this a tacit confession of a sense of deity inscribed in the hearts of all.

B. THE WONDERS OF CREATION

You cannot in one glance survey this most vast and beautiful system of the universe, in its wide expanse, without being completely overwhelmed by the boundless force of its brightness. The reason why the author of The Letter to the Hebrews elegantly calls the universe the appearance of things invisible [Heb. 11:3] is that this skillful ordering of the universe is for us a sort of mirror in which we can contemplate God, who is otherwise invisible. The reason why the prophet attributes to the heavenly creatures a language known to every nation [Ps. 19:2 ff.] is that therein lies an attestation of divinity so apparent that it ought not to escape the gaze of even the most stupid tribe. The apostle declares this more clearly: "What men need to know concerning God has been disclosed to them, . . . for one and all gaze upon his invisible nature, known from the creation of the world, even unto his eternal power and divinity" [Rom. 1:19–20].

That brightness which is borne in upon the eyes of all men both in heaven and on earth is more than enough to withdraw all support from men's ingratitude—just as God, to involve the human race in the same guilt, sets forth to all without exception his presence portrayed in his creatures. Despite this, it is needful that another and better help be added to direct us aright to the very Creator of the universe. It was not in vain, then, that he added the light of his Word by which to become known unto salvation.

Jonathan Edwards: Special Revelation in the Divine and Supernatural Light

The theology of Jonathan Edwards (1703–58) stands on the dividing line between the premodern and modern milieu.[14] On the level of basic doctrinal commitment, Edwards was a highly orthodox theologian steeped in the theology of Protestant scholasticism. On the level of explaining and justifying his theology, however, Edwards forged his reflections against the cutting edge of eighteenth-century philosophy and science. This combination, together with the unmatched skill with which he thought and wrote, makes him the most important theologian America has produced and one of its most insightful philosophers.

Whereas the previous passage from Calvin spoke of a revelatory "sense" which is present in all, this sermon from Edwards describes another kind of sense located solely in the hearts of believers. This saving "sense of the heart" is wrought by the Holy Spirit through a "divine and supernatural light" which, in communicating to the believer's heart, does not act in contravention of natural human capacities but works *through* them to create a new indwelling "principle"[15] which thereafter inspires and guides true belief and holy action. Like Calvin, Edwards divides human psychology into the understanding and the will. A merely "notional" knowledge of God residing solely in the "understanding" is insufficient. Instead, the kind of revelatory knowledge Edwards has in mind is a perception of who God is which attracts the full devotion of the self. Edwards preached this sermon to his congregation at Northampton (now in Massachusetts) in August of 1733. It was published early in 1734.

SOURCE

Jonathan Edwards, Sermon: "A Divine and Supernatural Light, Immediately Imparted to the Soul by the Spirit of God, Shown to be both Scriptural and Rational Doctrine," (Northampton, Conn., 1734), in Edwards, *Works* (1834) 2:14.

BIBLIOGRAPHY

An important source for Edwards's understanding of the "sense of the heart" is his *Miscellany* 782, "Ideas. Sense of the Heart" (ca. 1745). It is available in *The Philosophy*

14. Twentieth-century Edwards scholarship has split over whether Edwards was primarily a forward-looking innovator or one who merely synthesized the reigning concepts of his day. The truth is that he was both. For the classical work emphasizing Edwards as innovator, see the still-informative but now significantly modified thesis of Perry Miller, *Jonathan Edwards*; and more recently, Sang Hyun Lee, *The Philosophical Theology of Jonathan Edwards* (Princeton: Princeton University Press, 1988). For a summary of views emphasizing Edwards's intellectual conformity, see Nathan O. Hatch and Harry S. Stout, eds., *Jonathan Edwards and the American Experience* (New York: Oxford University Press, 1988).

15. Here the term "principle" connotes an innate disposition or inner spring of action rather than an external rule or law.

of Jonathan Edwards from His Private Notebooks, transcribed and edited by Harvey G. Townsend (Eugene: University of Oregon Press, 1955), 119–21; and in Perry Miller, "Jonathan Edwards on the Sense of the Heart," *Harvard Theological Review* 41 (1948): 123–45. The classic introduction to Edwards is Perry Miller, *Jonathan Edwards* (New York: W. Sloane, 1949). The best contemporary introduction is Robert Jenson, *America's Theologian: A Recommendation of Jonathan Edwards* (New York: Oxford University Press, 1988). On the eighteenth-century background of his thought, see Norman Fiering, *Jonathan Edwards' Moral Thought and Its British Context* (Chapel Hill: University of North Carolina Press, 1981). See also the bibliographies in other Edwards selections herein.

[The divine and supernatural light is:] A true sense of the divine excellency of the things revealed in the word of God, and a conviction of the truth and reality of them thence arising. This spiritual light primarily consists in the former of these, *viz.* A real sense and apprehension of the divine excellency of things revealed in the word of God. A spiritual and saving conviction of the truth and reality of these things, arises from such a sight of their divine excellency and glory; so that this conviction of their truth is an effect and natural consequence of this sight of their divine glory. There is therefore in this spiritual light,

1. A true sense of the divine and superlative excellency of the things of religion; a real sense of the excellency of God and Jesus Christ, and of the work of redemption, and the ways and works of God revealed in the gospel. There is a divine and superlative glory in these things; an excellency that is of a vastly higher kind, and more sublime nature, than in other things; a glory greatly distinguishing them from all that is earthly and temporal. He that is spiritually enlightened truly apprehends and sees it, or has a sense of it. He does not merely rationally believe that God is glorious, but he has a sense of the gloriousness of God in his heart. There is not only a rational belief that God is holy, and that holiness is a good thing, but there is a sense of the loveliness of God's holiness. There is not only a speculatively judging that God is gracious, but a sense how amiable God is on account of the beauty of this divine attribute.

There is a twofold knowledge of good of which God has made the mind of man capable. The first, that which is merely notional; as when a person only speculatively judges that any thing is, which, by the agreement of mankind, is called good or excellent, *viz.,* that which is most to general advantage, and between which and a reward there is a suitableness,—and the like. And the other is, that which consists in the sense of the heart; as when the heart is sensible of pleasure and delight in the presence of the idea of it. In the former is exercised merely the speculative faculty, or the understanding, in distinction from the will or disposition of the soul. In the latter, the will, or inclination, or heart are mainly concerned.

Thus there is a difference between having an *opinion*, that God is holy and gracious, and having a *sense* of the loveliness and beauty of that holiness and grace. There is a difference between having a rational judgment that honey is sweet, and having a sense of its sweetness. A man may have the former that knows not how honey tastes; but a man cannot have the latter unless he has an idea of the taste of honey in his mind. So there is a difference between believing that a person is beautiful, and having a sense of his beauty. The former may be obtained by hearsay, but the latter only by seeing the countenance. When the heart is sensible of the beauty and amiableness of a thing, it necessarily feels pleasure in the apprehension. It is implied in a person's being heartily sensible of the loveliness of a thing, that the idea of it is pleasant to his soul; which is a far different thing from having a rational opinion that it is excellent.

2. There arises from this sense of the divine excellency of things contained in the word of God, a conviction of the truth and reality of them.

FAITH AND OTHER
SOURCES OF KNOWLEDGE[16]

Zacharius Ursinus: The Difference
Between Reformed Theology,
Other Faiths, and Philosophy

The broad rubric "faith and other sources of knowledge" was treated by classical theology under the heading "faith and reason." Here Ursinus articulates the epistemological privilege of the church's theology, but he does not reject knowledge from sources originating outside the church. "Philosophy" here means human reason unguided by special revelation. The term serves a certain monolithic, all-encompassing function in comparison to contemporary rationality which is less inclined to reify "reason" or "philosophy" and which distinguishes a variety of academic disciplines. This passage is a con-

16. For a general survey of Western philosophy in the period covered here, see the following volumes in the series Readings in the History of Philosophy, Paul Edwards and Richard H. Popkin, gen. eds.: Richard H. Popkin, ed., *The Philosophy of the Sixteenth and Seventeenth Centuries* (New York: The Free Press, 1966); Lewis White Beck, ed., *Eighteenth Century Philosophy* (New York: Free Press, 1966).

tinuation of Ursinus's prolegomena, the early part of which has already been treated (pp. 4–6).

SOURCE

Zacharius Ursinus, *Explicationum catecheticarum* (1594), General Prolegomena; ET: "In what does the Doctrine of the Church differ from that of other Religions and from Philosophy," in Ursinus, *Commentary*, 3–4.

BIBLIOGRAPHY

See p. 5, above.

The doctrine of the church differs from that of all other religions, in four respects. *First:* the doctrine of the church has God for its author, by whom it was delivered, through the prophets and apostles, whilst the various religious systems of sectarists have been invented by men, through the suggestion of the devil. *Secondly:* the doctrine of the church alone, has such divine testimony in confirmation of its truth, as is sure and infallible, and which is calculated to quiet the conscience, and convict all the various sects of error. *Thirdly:* in the church the law of God is retained entire and uncorrupted, whilst in other systems of religion it is narrowed down and basely corrupted; for the advocates of these false religions entirely reject the doctrine of the first table, concerning the knowledge and worship of the true God, either setting forth some other God besides him who has revealed himself to the church by his word and works, and seeking a knowledge of God, not in his Son, but out of him, or worshipping him otherwise than he has commanded in his word. And not only so, but they are also equally ignorant of the inward and spiritual obedience of the second table; and whatever truth and excellence there is in these systems of religion, it is nothing more than a part of the precepts of the second table, in relation to the external deportment of the life, and the civil duties which men owe to each other. *Fourthly:* it is only in the church that the gospel of Christ is fully taught, and rightly understood. . . .

It is, however, different with *Philosophy*. True philosophy, although it also differs very much from the doctrine of the church, yet, it does not array itself against it, nor is it a wicked fabrication, and device of Satan, as is true of the false doctrines of the Sects; but it contains truth, and is, as it were, a certain ray of the wisdom of God, impressed upon the mind of man in his creation. It is a doctrine that has respect to God and his creatures, and many other things that are good and profitable to man-

kind, and has been drawn out from the light of nature, and from principles in themselves clear and evident, and reduced to a system by wise
and earnest men.

Moïse Amyraut: A Treatise Concerning Religion

Moïse Amyraut (Moses Amyrauldus) (1596–1664) was one of the leading
theologians of the Saumur Academy in France. His thoughts on religion
reflect his conviction that God's grace extends beyond the limits of the church
visible, a belief which he shared with Huldrych Zwingli (pp. 385–87, below).
Thus God's providential activity works upon non-Christians to produce an
inchoate apprehension of God. Still, Amyraut stood within the mainstream of
Reformed theology to the extent that he believed any who may be saved were
saved solely by God's sovereign election (pp. 99–100, below). In this passage
Amyraut defends the concept that non-Christian religions reflect a brand of
general revelation.

SOURCE

Moïse Amyraut, *Traitté des religions contre ceux qui les estiment toutes indifferentes*
(Saumur, 1631); ET: *A Treatise Concerning Religions, In Refutation of the Opinion which
accounts all Indifferent* (London: M. Simmons, 1660), chap. 1, pp. 137–38, 145, 148,
150–51 (edited, with orthography and punctuation revised).

BIBLIOGRAPHY

Brian G. Armstrong, *Calvinism and the Amyraut Heresy: Protestant Scholasticism and
Humanism in Seventeenth-Century France* (Madison: University of Wisconsin Press,
1969). Roger Nicole, "Amyraut, Amyraldus, Amyraldianism, etc." in *Encyclopedia of
Christianity*, ed. Edwin Palmer (Wilmington, Del.: Michael Glazier, 1964), 1:184–93.
Idem, *Moyse Amyraut: A Bibliography* (New York and London: Garland, 1981). Idem,
"Moyse Amyraut (1596–1664) and the Controversy on Universal Grace" (Ph.D. diss.,
Harvard University, 1966).

As all the World contents in this fundamental Truth, That there is
a God (which the Epicureans themselves dare not deny) and likewise
that God governs all the transactions upon Earth; (since the number of
those that deny is inconsiderable in comparison of its assertors; and
they which profess to [doubt] the same, are constrained, as we have
formerly shown, to confess that they have no other knowledge of God
but by the traces and instance of his Providence); so we may observe an
universal Instinct of Nature in this that all nations have accounted it
necessary to the rendering to God the honor belonging to him, that there

be one certain determinate form of constitution called Religion, containing the rules according to which men ought to guide and comport themselves therein. For never was there any nation that thought it enough to serve God in thought only, without making demonstration of their devotion by gestures and external actions, and observation of certain ceremonies; unless, perhaps, some one among those where barbarism rules all, and which in that respect we usually term savages. . . .

Socrates [for instance] being condemned to die, professed that it was God that raised him up to teach Philosophy and to reform the manners of his fellow citizens by his precepts; and pronounces resolutely that though they should open the prison doors to him with injunction never to philosophize more, he would not go forth, but would rather obey God than men. And Pythagoras when he had found out an excellent demonstration in geometry went and sacrificed a hundred oxen: for what reason, saving that he acknowledged that God had favored him with his assistance therein? And truly they had reason on their side. I would not so much derogate from the dignity of the humane mind as to take from it all power of inventing excellent things and of profound disquisition. But there appeared such a Providence of God in what I have alleged that he that bears not a great measure of obstinacy in his breast will suffer himself to be persuaded that God presided therein.

Herman Witsius: Proof for the Existence of God

The invocation of various "proofs" for the existence of God was typical although not universal in seventeenth- and eighteenth-century Reformed theology. Variations on the cosmological and teleological arguments were employed, but the ontological argument has exercised a persistent fascination for Reformed theologians. This proof, which originated with Anselm of Canterbury (ca. 1033–1109) was brought to the fore once again in the seventeenth century by René Descartes (1596–1650).[17] This proof finds the existence of God contained in the very concept of God as "that than which a greater

---

17. René Descartes, *Meditationes de prima philosophia* (1641), esp. the third meditation; ET: *Meditations on First Philosophy,* in *Philosophical Works of Descartes,* vol. 1, trans. E. S. Haldane and G.R.T. Ross (Cambridge: Cambridge University Press, 1934); and *Discourse on Method and Meditations,* trans. F. E. Sutcliffe (Baltimore, Md.: Penguin, 1971), 95–169, esp. 113–31. For a good example of Cartesian influence on seventeenth-century religious thought, see Abbé de Choisy and Abbé de Dangeau, *Quatre Dialogues* [1684], *suivis de l'Apologie de Pierre Jurieu* [1685], ed. Richard Parish, Editions Universitaires Fribourg Suisse (Fribourg: Editions Universitaires, 1981). The Reformed theologian Pierre Jurieu (1637–1713), who authored the negative tract appended to this edition, was a prominent Huguenot apologist and advocate of orthodoxy.

cannot be conceived." All the traditional proofs were subjected in 1781 to searching criticism by the philosopher Immanuel Kant (1724–1804).[18] In the passage below, the covenant theologian Herman Witsius (1636–1708), who was influenced by Descartes, reproduced the ontological argument in the routine discourse of an exposition of the Apostles' Creed.

SOURCE

Herman Witsius, *Exercitationes sacrae in symbolum, quod Apostolorum dicitur* (1681); ET: "On the Faith of the Existence of God," in *Sacred Dissertations on What Is Commonly Called the Apostles' Creed*, trans. and ed. Donald Fraser, 2 vols. (Edinburgh, 1823), 1:71–72.

BIBLIOGRAPHY

Michael Peterson, William Hasker, Bruce Reichenbach, and David Basinger, eds., *Reason and Religious Belief: An Introduction to the Philosophy of Religion* (New York and Oxford: Oxford University Press, 1991), chap. 5. Alvin Plantinga, ed., *The Ontological Argument: From St. Anselm to Contemporary Philosophers* (Garden City, N.Y.: Doubleday & Co., 1965).

The existence of God is so necessary and so evident a truth, that to one rightly attending to the subject, scarcely any thing can appear more certain, more obvious, more manifest. It is clear even from that notion of a Deity which is common to all nations. Whoever speaks of God, speaks of a Being infinitely perfect. Such a Being, however, cannot even be conceived of in thought, without including in our conception the necessity of his existence. For, since it is a greater perfection to exist than not to exist; to exist necessarily than to exist contingently and according to the pleasure of another; to exist from eternity and to eternity, than to exist at one time and not to exist at another time;—it follows that existence, even a necessary and eternal existence, is implied in the essence of a most perfect Being without necessary existence, as an idea of a mountain without a valley.

Besides, the man who denies that there is a God, denies, at the same time, that it is possible for an absolutely perfect and eternal Being to exist. For if he at any time begin to exist, he will not be eternal, and therefore not absolutely perfect, and consequently not God.

18. Immanuel Kant, *Der Kritik der reinen Vernunft* (1791); ET: *Critique of Pure Reason*, trans. Norman Kemp Smith (London: Macmillan; New York: St. Martins, 1929). Although the literature on Kant is voluminous, the best introductory work is Stephan Körner, *Kant* (London and Baltimore, 1955; reprint: New Haven: Yale University Press, 1989).

Pierre Bayle: Faith and Reason in Conflict

Pierre Bayle was born the son of a French Huguenot pastor in a small town south of Toulouse in 1647 and died an expatriate in Holland in 1704. He is most famous for his *Dictionnaire historique et critique* (Historical and critical dictionary) (1695–97) which employed skeptical arguments to bring into question the whole range of intellectual endeavor of his age. Although later thinkers such as Voltaire (1694–1778) and David Hume (1711–76) would read Bayle as an ally in irreligious skepticism, he was actually a sincere believer in the Christian faith. Except for a one-and-a-half-year lapse into Roman Catholicism, Bayle remained loyal to the Reformed faith throughout his life. Bayle's critique of the powers of philosophy, far from leading him to abandon religion, led him instead to embrace faith alone as the foundation of religious knowledge.

SOURCES

(A) Pierre Bayle, *Critique générale de l'histoire du Calvinisme du P. Maimbourg* (1684); ET: *New Critical Letters on the "History of Calvinism."* **(B)** Pierre Bayle, *Commentaire philosophique sur ces paroles de Jesus-Christ, Contrain-les d'entrer* (1686); ET: *A Philosophical Commentary upon These Words of Jesus: "Compel Them to Come In,"* in *The Great Contest of Faith and Reason: Selections from the Writings of Pierre Bayle*, Milestones of Thought, trans. and ed. Karl C. Sandberg (New York: Frederick Unger, 1963), 37, 39, 49, 52, 55–56 (edited).

BIBLIOGRAPHY

Pierre Bayle, *Historical and Critical Dictionary: Selections*, trans. Richard H. Popkin (Indianapolis, Ind.: Hackett Publishing Co., 1991). Ludwig Feuerbach, *Pierre Bayle. Ein Beitrag zur Geschichte der Philosophie und Menschheit* (Leipzig, 1848). Paul Hazard, *The European Mind: The Critical Years, 1680–1715*, trans. Lewis May (New Haven: Yale University Press, 1953). John Kilcullen, *Sincerity and Truth: Essays on Arnauld, Bayle, and Toleration* (Oxford: Clarendon Press, 1988). Elizabeth Labrousse, *Pierre Bayle*, 2 vols. (The Hague: Nijhoff, 1963–65). H. T. Mason, *Pierre Bayle and Voltaire* (London: Oxford University Press, 1963).

A. REASON AND NATURAL CONSCIENCE

[I]n questions of religion one must not wait until he has acquired all of the evidence asked for in the philosophy of Mr. Descartes before making a decision and consenting to believe.

In order to establish this principle we must pose a second, something like this, that *in questions of religion the standard of judgment is not in the understanding but in the conscience,* that is, we must receive objects not according to the clear and distinct ideas acquired by a severe examination, but according to the dictates of our conscience by which we feel that in accepting them we will do what is pleasing before God. We must necessarily come to this point. The faith which the Holy Spirit instills in us fills us with a full persuasion without the aid of a long examination. On the other hand, if we wished to depend only upon the light of understanding, we could not accept the dogmas of a religion without having observed all of the precepts of Mr. Descartes. Now this undertaking surpasses the capabilities of almost all Christians, and if it were necessary, there would not be two Christians out of ten thousand who could maintain their belief except by a "criminal temerity."

Some people will perhaps tell me that the question appears very difficult to me because of the smallness of my mind. They will be right. I would therefore be very happy for some accomplished person to cast more light upon this fine subject and to show, if he can, that in matters of religion we are, through the providence of God, led by reason and not by instinct, as we are often led in other matters. It has been said that the principal concern of a rich man is not to know how he became rich, but to be rich. Cannot we say the same of faith? Whether faith enters into our mind by our education, or by our prejudices, or by chance, or by reasonings, the most important thing is to possess it. . . . (Postscript to Chapter XI of *Critical Letters*).

B. REASON AND TOLERANCE

[N]ow I come to the particular subject and the specific matter of my commentary on these words of the passage "Compel them to come in," and this is how I reason: the literal meaning of these words is contrary to the most distinct ideas which reason teaches us; therefore, it is false. . . .

To try to convert people by force to a religion they do not profess is consequently in evident contradiction with common sense and natural light, the general principles of reason, and, in a word, with the original and basic rule of discerning the true from the false, the good from the bad. The clear and distinct ideas which we have of the essence of certain things persuade us invincibly that God cannot reveal to us anything which contradicts them. (For example, we are entirely certain that God cannot reveal that the whole is smaller than its parts; that it is proper to prefer vice to virtue; that we should esteem our dog above our friend and our country; that to go from one place to another by sea we should start out at a gallop on a horse; that in order to prepare a field for an abundant harvest we must not cultivate it.) It is then evident that God has not commanded us in His word to force acceptance of the Gospel upon people by means of beatings or other such violences. Thus, if we find in the Gospel a passage which commands us to do the contrary, we may be assured that the meaning is figurative and not literal. . . .

If you ask a man to do any more [than to follow his conscience], it is clear that you are asking him to fix his love and zeal only upon the absolute truth, infallibly recognized as such. Now in our present human condition it is impossible for us to know with certainty that that which appears to us to be truth is in fact the absolute truth. (I am speaking here of the particular truths of religion, and not of the properties of numbers, nor of the first principles of metaphysics, nor of the maxims of geometry.) Indeed, all we can do is to be fully persuaded that we possess the absolute truth, that we are not mistaken, and that our opponents are mistaken. But this persuasion is an equivocal mark of the truth since it is found in the most hopelessly lost heretics. It is therefore certain that it is impossible for us to find any sure sign by which we might discern our true ideas, which we believe to be true, from our false ideas, which we also believe to be true.

Thomas Reid: The Scottish "Common Sense" Philosophy

Thomas Reid (1710–96), born in Strachan, Scotland, is well-known in philosophical circles as the originator of the so-called common sense philosophy. This philosophy proceeds according to certain innate, self-evident first principles (e.g., the existence of other minds, of objects outside our perception) the authority of which is grounded in the constitution of our common human nature. What is perhaps less well-known is that, before becoming regent of King's College (1751–64) and later the successor of Adam Smith to the Chair of Moral Philosophy at Glasgow (1764–96), Reid was for fourteen years (1737–51) pastor of a Presbyterian congregation in New Machar. The central problem posed by Reid's work was to provide a way out of the skeptical impasse which philosophy had reached as a result of the work of Descartes, John Locke (1632–1704), and Reid's fellow Scot, David Hume. Moving from this impasse took Reid deep into the intricacies of empirical psychology, as evidenced in the titles of his major works: *An Inquiry into the Human Mind on the Principles of Common Sense* (1764), *Essays on the Intellectual Powers of Man* (1785), and *Essays on the Active Powers of Man* (1788). The problems of theology always lay in the background of Reid's philosophy, and his work exercised significant sway over Reformed theology in Scotland and America in the nineteenth century. Reid continues to influence twentieth-century thought through such diverse figures as G. E. Moore, Ludwig Wittgenstein, Roderick M. Chisholm, and Alvin Plantinga.

In his *Lectures on Natural Theology*, from which the first selection is taken, Reid argues that belief in God is not one of the first principles of common sense but may be deduced from those principles, thereby providing the basis of a "natural religion." Revelation supplements and completes natural religion, but by itself revelation constitutes an insufficient ground of theological knowledge and requires reason in order to determine which is the true revelation and to avoid superstition. The second selection, a commonly cited section from the *Essays on the Intellectual Powers of Man*, identifies belief as the "mainspring of the life of man" and is inspired in human beings by the work of God.

SOURCES

(A) Thomas Reid, "Natural Theology," Lecture 73 (February 11, 1780), in *Lectures on Natural Theology*, transcribed and edited by Elmer H. Duncan (Washington, D.C.: University Press of America, 1981), 1–2. (B) Thomas Reid, "Of the Evidence of Sense, and of Belief in General," *Essay on the Intellectual Powers of Man* (1785), in *The Works of Thomas Reid, D.D.*, 2 vols., ed. William Hamilton (Edinburgh, 1846), essay 2, chap. 20, pp. 327–30 (edited).

BIBLIOGRAPHY

Selwyn Grave, *The Scottish Philosophy of Common Sense* (Oxford: Clarendon, 1960). Keith Lehrer, *Thomas Reid*, The Arguments of the Philosophers, ed. Ted Honderich (London and New York: Routledge, 1989). James McCosh, *The Scottish Philosophy: From Hutcheson to Hamilton* (New York: Robert Carter, 1875).

A. NATURAL THEOLOGY

Of all the animals which God has made it is the prerogative of Man alone to know his Maker. There is no kind of knowledge that tends so much to elevate the Mind as the knowledge of God. Duty to God forms an important part of our duty and it is the support of every virtue; it gives us magnanimity, fortitude and tranquility; it inspires with hope in the most adverse circumstances, and there can be no rational piety without just notions of the perfections and providence of God. It is no doubt true that Revelation exhibits all the truths of Natural Religion, but it is no less true that reason must be employed to judge of that revelation; whether it comes from God. Both are great lights and we ought not to put out the one in order to use the other. Revelation is of use to enlighten us with regard to the use of Natural Religion, as one Man may enlighten another in things that it was impossible could be discovered by him, it is easy then to conceive that God could enlighten Man. And that he has done so is evident from a comparison of the doctrines of Scripture with the systems of the most refined heathens. We acknowledge then that men are indebted to revelation in the matter of Natural Religion but this is no reason why we should not also use our reason here. Revelation was given us not to hinder the exercise of our reasoning powers but to aid and assist them. 'Tis by reason that we must judge whether that Revelation be really so; 'Tis by reason that we must judge of the meaning of what is revealed; and it is by Reason that we must guard against any impious, inconsistent or absurd interpretation of that revelation. As the best things may be abused so when we lay aside the exercise of reason Revelation becomes the tool of low Superstition or of wild fanaticism and that man is best prepared for the study and practice of the revealed Religion who has previously acquired just Sentiments of the Natural. The best notions of the divine Maker which we can form are imperfect and inadequate and are all drawn from what we know of our own Mind. We cannot form an idea of any attribute intellectual or moral as belonging to the deity, of which there is not some faint resemblance or image in ourselves. As we cannot form the least conception of Material objects but must somehow or other resemble those we perceive by our senses so our knowledge of Deity is grounded on our knowledge of the human Mind.

B. BELIEF

Belief must have an object. For he that believes must believe something; and that which he believes, is called the object of his belief. Of this object of his belief, he must have some conception, clear or obscure; for, although there may be the most clear and distinct conception of an object without any belief of its existence, there can be no belief without conception. . . .

Not only in most of our intellectual operations, but in many of the active principles of the human mind, belief enters as an ingredient. Joy and sorrow, hope and fear, imply a belief of good or ill, either present or in expectation. Esteem, gratitude, pity, and resentment, imply a belief of certain qualities in their objects. In every action that is done for an end, there must be a belief of its tendency to that end. So large a share has belief in our intellectual operations, in our active principles, and in our actions themselves, that, as faith in things divine is represented as the main spring in the life of a Christian, so belief in general is the main spring in the life of a man.

That men often believe what there is no just ground to believe, and thereby are led into hurtful errors, is too evident to be denied. And, on the other hand, that there are just grounds of belief can as little be doubted by any man who is not a perfect sceptic.

We give the name of evidence to whatever is a ground of belief. To believe without evidence is a weakness which every man is concerned to avoid, and which every man wishes to avoid. Nor is it in a man's power to believe anything longer than he thinks he has evidence.

What this evidence is, is more easily felt than described. Those who never reflected upon its nature, feel its influence in governing their belief. . . .

First, It seems to be quite different from the evidence of reasoning. All good evidence is commonly called reasonable evidence, and very justly, because it ought to govern our belief as reasonable creatures. And, according to this meaning, I think the evidence of sense no less reasonable than that of demonstration. If Nature give us information of things that concern us, by other means than by reasoning, reason itself will direct us to receive that information with thankfulness, and to make the best use of it. . . .

Many eminent philosophers, thinking it unreasonable to believe when they could not shew a reason, have laboured to furnish us with reasons for believing our senses; but their reasons are very insufficient, and will not bear examination. Other philosophers have shewn very clearly the fallacy of these reasons, and have, as they imagine, discovered invincible reasons against this belief; but they have never been able either to shake it in themselves, or to convince others. The statesman continues to plod, the soldier to fight, and the merchant to export and import, without being in the least moved by the demonstrations that have been offered of the non-existence of those things about which they are so seriously employed. And a man may as soon, by reasoning, pull the moon out of her orbit, as destroy the belief of the objects of sense. . . .

There is, no doubt, an analogy between the evidence of sense and the evidence of testimony. Hence, we find, in all languages the analogical expressions of the *testimony of sense,* of giving *credit* to our senses, and the like. But there is a real difference between the two, as well as a similitude. In believing upon testimony, we rely upon the authority of a person who testifies; but we have no such authority for believing our senses.

Shall we say, then, that this belief is the inspiration of the Almighty? I think this may be said in a good sense; for I take it to be the immediate effect of our constitution, which is the work of the Almighty. But, if inspiration be understood to imply a persuasion of its coming from God, our belief of the objects of sense is not inspiration; for a man would believe his senses though he had no notion of a Deity. He who is persuaded that he is the workmanship of God, and that it is a part of his constitution to believe his senses, may think that a good reason to confirm his belief. But he had the belief before he could give this or any other reason for it.

The Psalter: Psalm 14, "The Fool Says in His Heart, 'There Is No God' "

There is no God, as foolish men,
    affirm in their mad mood:
Their drifts are all corrupt and vain,
    not one of them does good.
The Lord beheld from Heaven high,
    the whole race of mankind:
And saw not one that sought indeed
    the living God to find.

2

THE DOCTRINE
OF GOD

THE REALITY, MAJESTY,
AND GLORY OF GOD

Reformed Christianity seeks to live for the praise of God. This doxological emphasis in Reformed theology rests in the conviction that all of life exists for the praise and glory of God. God is the fundamental reality, and God is to be worshiped for God's own sake and not primarily for the sake of benefits received, whether in this life or the next. To give allegiance to anything that is not God or to worship any God other than the one who is revealed in Jesus Christ is idolatry.

Doxology

Huldrych Zwingli: Regarding God
and His Worship

Zwingli penned his *Exposition of the Christian Faith* in 1531, the year of his death, but it did not appear in print until 1536, with a preface by Bullinger. It is one of the most concise and well-constructed pieces Zwingli produced and the last full-length work to come from his hand. The following selection exhibits two of the chief motifs in Zwingli's theology: his strong convictions that God is transcendent and sovereign over creation, and that one must always properly distinguish the Creator and the creature. Invoking the classical Augustinian distinction between employment (use) and enjoyment,[1]

---

1. For Augustine's use/enjoyment distinction, see *De doctrina Christiana* (397) (ET: *On Christian Doctrine*), in *Patrologiae Cursus Completus, Series Latina*, ed. J. P. Migne (Paris, 1857–66), 34.15–127. A number of English translations are available. See also Oliver O' Donavan, *The Problem of Self-Love in St. Augustine* (New Haven and London: Yale University Press, 1980).

Zwingli exhorts his readers to trust in God alone. Far from embodying an abstraction, this perspective gives a concrete shape to the Christian life in which one is a pilgrim loving and serving God for God's own sake and handling all things in a manner appropriate to their relation to God.

SOURCE

Huldrych Zwingli, *Fidei expositio* (1536) (originally titled *Professio Fidei*), in *SS* 4:44–78; ET: "Regarding God and His Worship," *Exposition of the Christian Faith*, in *Zwingli and Bullinger*, 249–51.

BIBLIOGRAPHY

W. P. Stephens, *The Theology of Huldrych Zwingli* (Oxford: Clarendon, 1986), chap. 3.

All being is either created or uncreated. God alone is uncreated, for only one thing can be uncreated. For if there were many uncreated things there would be many eternal: for uncreated and eternal are closely interrelated, so that the one is also the other. And if there were many eternal things there would be many infinite, for these too are very similar, and interrelated, so that if a thing is eternal it is also infinite, and if it is infinite it is also eternal. But only one thing can be infinite, for once we allow that there are two infinite substances, the one is immediately limited by the other. Hence it is certain that God alone is uncreated. And this is the origin and source and basis of the first article of the Creed: when we say, "I believe in God the Father Almighty, Maker of heaven and earth," we state emphatically that ours is an infallible faith because it rests upon the one and only God. Pagans and unbelievers and all those who trust in what is created have to admit that they may be deceived in their belief or opinion because they trust in what is created. But those who build upon the Creator and beginning of all things, who never began to be but caused all other things to exist, can never fall into error. Certainly no creature can be the object and basis of the inflexible and never-wavering power which is faith. For that which has a beginning at one time did not exist. And when it did not exist, how could anyone trust in what was not? That which has a beginning cannot therefore be the natural object or basis of faith. Only the eternal and infinite and uncreated God is the basis of faith. . . .

For if we are to enjoy only God, we must trust only in God: we must trust in what we are to enjoy and not in what we are to employ.

John Calvin: Piety as Having to Do
with the Living God

God's transcendence does not mean that God is disconnected from the world, still less from the Christian life. Quite the opposite: God's transcendence enables God to be in relationship to every event and every person. Thus in every aspect and event in life, according to Calvin, human beings are transacting business with God (*negotium cum Deo*); it is God with whom they have to deal. This does not mean that human beings encounter God *a se*, i.e., God in God's own being. They have no access, through speculative thought or otherwise, to "what God is" but must remain content to know "of what sort" God is, as made available in God's self-witness of revelation in Jesus Christ. And the particular character of this revelation means, in turn, that God will be known by Christians primarily as a God of benevolent grace. Hence Calvin defines piety as "that reverence joined with love of God which the knowledge of his benefits induces."

SOURCE

Institutes I.2.1–2, pp. 41–43 (edited).

What is God? [*quid sit Deus?*] Men who pose this question are merely toying with idle speculations. It is more important for us to know of what sort he is and what is consistent with his nature [*qualis sit Deus*]. What good is it to profess with Epicurus some sort of God who has cast aside the care of the world only to amuse himself in idleness? What help is it, in short, to know a God with whom we have nothing to do [*negotii*]. Rather, our knowledge should serve first to teach us fear and reverence; secondly, with it as our guide and teacher, we should learn to seek every good from him, and, having received it, to credit it to his account. For how can the thought of God penetrate your mind without your realizing immediately that, since you are his handiwork, you have been made over and bound to his command by right of creation, that you owe your life to him?

For, to begin with, the pious mind does not dream up for itself any god it pleases, but contemplates the one and only true God. And it does not attach to him whatever it pleases, but is content to hold him to be as he manifests himself; furthermore, the mind always exercises the utmost diligence and care not to wander astray, or rashly and boldly to go beyond his will.

Here indeed is pure and real religion: faith so joined with an earnest fear of God that this fear also embraces willing reverence, and carries with it such legitimate worship as is prescribed in the law. And we ought to note this fact even more diligently: all men have a vague general veneration for God, but very few really reverence him; and wherever there is great ostentation in ceremonies, sincerity of heart is rare indeed.

Jonathan Edwards: The Interplay of Doxology and Happiness

If the doxological focus of Reformed theology means seeking God for God's own sake, then where does human happiness fit in? The traditional way of reconciling the divine glory and human happiness was to affirm that seeking God's glory would in some way redound to one's own ultimate benefit: one who seeks to secure one's life will lose it, while one who loses one's life for God's sake will save it (Mark 8:34; Matt. 10:38; Luke 17:33; John 12:25).

In the eighteenth century the idea of the subordination and connection of human happiness to the divine glory underwent a shift. Instead of the good for humanity being defined in reference to God (or, in the vocabulary of the eighteenth century, God's "benevolence"), now the goodness of God was defined in reference to God's desire to bring about the wants, wishes, and desires of human beings.[2] Into this situation stepped Jonathan Edwards. He tried to reformulate the eighteenth-century outlook to make it conform to the traditional Reformed conviction of the priority and deity of God. In this selection from Edwards's notebooks,[3] divine and human happiness are seen to coalesce in a common pursuit of the divine glory.

SOURCE

Jonathan Edwards, *Miscellanies* 92, 208, 243, 247, in *The Philosophy of Jonathan Edwards from His Private Notebooks*, transcribed and edited by Harvey G. Townsend (Eugene: University of Oregon Press, 1955), 129.

92. How then can it be said that God has made all things for Himself, if it is certain that the highest end of the creation was the communication of happiness? I answer, that which is done for the gratifying of a

---

2. For an accessible account of this shift by a leading contemporary philosopher, see Charles Taylor, *Sources of the Self: The Making of the Modern Identity* (Cambridge: Harvard University Press, 1989), esp. chap. 16.

3. Throughout his life Edwards diligently kept a set of notebooks, the most important of which is the *Miscellanies*, which comprises nine manuscript volumes. Quotations here from the *Miscellanies* are taken from the redacted editions, which are already publicly available. A definitive, critical edition will eventually be published in the Yale edition of Edwards's works based on Thomas Schafer's transcription which is housed in the Beinecke Rare Book Room and Manuscript Library of Yale University.

natural inclination of God may very properly be said to be done for God. God takes complacence in communicating felicity and He made all things for this complacence. His complacence in this making happy was the end of the creation. Revelations 4:11, "For thy pleasure they are and were created."

208. Glory of [God]. God loves His creatures so, that He really loves the being honored by them, as all try to be well thought of by those they love. Therefore, we are to seek the glory of God as that which is a thing really pleasing to Him.

243. Glory of God. The first part of the 14th chapter of John, and the 28th verse of the 12th chapter and Isai. 48:11, and Isai. 42:8, and many other such passages of Scripture make me think that God's glory is a good independent of the happiness of the creature; that it is a good absolutely, and in itself, and not as subordinate to the creature's happiness, but [a] good—not only because 'tis the creature's highest good—a good that God seeks (if I may so speak) not only as He seeks the creature's happiness, but for itself, seeks absolutely as an independent ultimate good. And though [there are] many passages in the Old Testament that seem to speak as if the end of His doing this or that was His honor's sake or His name's sake, it still appears to me exceeding plain that to communicate goodness is likewise an absolute good and what God seeks for itself, and that the very being of God's goodness necessarily supposes it. For to make happy is not goodness if it be done purely for another, superior end.

247. Glory of God. For God to glorify Himself is to discover Himself in His works or to communicate Himself in His works, which is all one. For we are to remember that the world exists only mentally, so that the very being of the world implies its being perceived or discovered. For God to glorify Himself is in His acts *ad extra* to act worthy of Himself, or to act excellently. Therefore, God don't seek His own glory because it makes Him the happier to be honored and highly thought of, but because He loves to see Himself, His own excellencies and glories, appearing in His works.

Samuel Hopkins: Willingness to Be "Damned for the Glory of God"

This selection from Samuel Hopkins (1721–1803) shows that the legendary question, Are you willing to be damned for the glory of God? was a serious subject of debate for some within the Reformed tradition, even if other Reformed theologians considered the question at best fruitless or at worst grotesque. The question was intended as a "test" or "tool" to plumb the motives of one's allegiance to God; however, it too easily became a source of metaphysical reflection as an end in itself.

Hopkins, a representative of the New Divinity, or New England, theology and a devotee of Jonathan Edwards, considered the foundation of the Christian life to be "disinterested benevolence." Practicing disinterested benevolence as an antidote to selfishness meant subordinating one's private happiness when it conflicted with the good of all. According to Hopkins's logic, embracing the good of the whole required one even to assent to one's own destruction if one were to discover that God deemed it good for the sake of the whole. We should note that Hopkins's mentor, Edwards, had specifically rejected this question as a violation of the way God has constructed the human psychology of self-love.

When Hopkins drafted the dialogue excerpted below, it is likely that he had in mind such moderate Calvinists as his ministerial colleague in Newport, Rhode Island, Ezra Stiles (later president of Yale). Stiles had debated this and other such questions with Hopkins and concluded that the New Divinity theology was overly speculative and lacking in social utility. The more severe aspects of the New Divinity helped turn many in the next generation of New Englanders to Unitarianism.

SOURCE

Samuel Hopkins, "A Dialogue Between a Calvinist and a Semi-Calvinist" (ca. 1799), in *The Works of Samuel Hopkins*, ed. Edwards Amasa Park, 3 vols. (Boston, 1852), 1:143–44, 156–57 (edited).

BIBLIOGRAPHY

Richard Birdsall, "Ezra Stiles and the New Divinity Men," *American Quarterly* 17 (1965): 248–58. William Breitenbach, "New Divinity Theology and the Idea of Moral Accountability" (Ph.D. diss., Yale University, 1978). Idem, "The Consistent Calvinism of the New Divinity Movement," *William and Mary Quarterly* 41 (1984): 241–64. Joseph A. Conforti, *Samuel Hopkins and the New Divinity Movement* (Grand Rapids: Christian University Press, 1981). Joseph Haroutunian, *From Piety to Moralism* (New York: Henry Holt, 1932). Bruce Kucklick, *Churchmen and Philosophers: From Jonathan Edwards to John Dewey* (New Haven and London: Yale University Press, 1985), chap. 4.

Some of the major works of the New Divinity theologians include Joseph Bellamy, *True Religion Delineated* (1750); Nathaniel Emmons, *The Gospel Scheme of Grace* (1789); Samuel Hopkins, *System of Doctrines*, 2 vols. (1793). See also the works of Timothy Dwight, Jonathan Edwards, Jr., and Leonard Woods.

SEMI-CALVINIST. Sir, I have wanted, for some time, to talk with you about the notion which some lately advance, viz., that Christians may, yea, that they ought, and must, be willing to perish forever, in order to be

Christians. This is a shocking doctrine to me; for I believe it absolutely impossible for any one to be willing to be eternally wretched; and if it were possible, it would be very wicked; for we are commanded to do that which is directly contrary to this, viz., to desire and seek to escape damnation, and to be saved; as all our most considerable and best divines have taught, which I could easily prove, were it necessary.

CALVINIST. I can decide nothing upon this matter until I know what is meant by being *willing to be miserable forever* by those who assert this, or you who oppose it. Let me then ask you, Do you suppose that by being willing to be miserable is meant a being pleased with damnation, or choosing to be miserable forever, for its own sake, or in itself considered, and preferring misery, eternal misery, and being just as the damned will be, to eternal happiness and being just as the blessed will be forever, considering the former as being in itself better than the latter? This is, doubtless, impossible, and, if it were not, would be very unreasonable and wicked. And I question whether any one ever believed this, or meant to assert it, by saying that Christians ought to be willing to perish forever. But if by being willing to be cast off by God forever be meant, that however great and dreadful this evil is, yet a Christian may and ought to be willing to suffer it, if it be necessary in order to avoid a greater evil, or to obtain an overbalancing good, if such a case can be supposed; this, I think, is true, and ought to be maintained, as essential to the character of a Christian, and that the contrary doctrine is dangerous and hurtful. For it is essential to true benevolence to prefer a greater good to a less, and a less evil to a greater, and that whether it be private or public good or evil, or his own personal good or evil, or that of others. . . .

A belief of this doctrine, and exercises answerable, will bring and keep in view true, unreserved resignation to the will of God, and prevent his deceiving himself with an imagined resignation which is not true resignation, but the exercise of wicked selfishness and impiety, and with which many are deceiving themselves. For instance, when a parent loses a dear and only child he is resigned and willing his child should be taken from him by death, if God will make it happy forever. This condition spoils the resignation, and it expresses no true regard to God, but only a regard to his child; which the most selfish parent has, as well as the most benevolent. So one who thinks himself a Christian is willing to be poor and despised, to be sick and suffer great pain, if it may work for his good, and God will make him eternally happy at last, and thinks this true resignation, and that in a high and uncommon degree; whereas this is not real resignation to the will of God, and expresses nothing but selfishness, in making God a tool to answer our own selfish ends. He will consent that God should make him happy, and answer his ends, and is willing to be in his hands on no other condition. This expresses no true regard to God, or the general good. To conclude, the Christian who believes this truth, and has feelings and exercises answerable to it, with pleasure gives himself into the hands of God, and rejoices that he and all things are in his hands, and that he will glorify himself by all men, either in their salvation or damnation, and says to God, "If it be most for thy glory that I should be cast off, thy will be done. 'Father, glorify thy name.' I have no condition to make; let God be glorified, and his kingdom be most happy and glorious, whatever becomes of me." And the stronger and more clear these exercises are, the greater evidence he will have, when he reflects upon them, that he is a true friend to God, and that it is most for his glory, and for the greatest general good, that he should be perfectly holy and happy in his kingdom forever.

Isaac Watts: *All Praise to God*

Isaac Watts (1674–1748) was a nonconformist pastor and hymn-writer of the Independent wing in England. His hymns are among some of the most noteworthy in the English language, and they were pivotal in prompting the transition away from the Psalter as the sole form of congregational singing and toward the singing of freely composed popular hymns.

SOURCE

Isaac Watts, Hymn: "From All That Dwell Below the Skies," in *The Psalms of David* (1719).

BIBLIOGRAPHY

Harry Escott, *Isaac Watts Hymnographer: A Study of the Beginning, Development and Philosophy of the English Hymn* (London: Independent Press, 1962).

From all that dwell below the skies
    Let the Creator's praise arise:
  Alleluia! Alleluia!
Let the Redeemer's name be sung
    Through every land, in every tongue.
  Alleluia! Alleluia! . . .

Eternal are Thy mercies Lord;
    Eternal Truth attends Thy Word:
  Alleluia! Alleluia!

Thy praise shall sound from shore to shore,
   'Til suns shall rise and set no more.
Alleluia! Alleluia!

Idolatry

John Calvin: "God Is the Only Proper Witness to Himself"

Having made it clear that humanity needs revelation in order to apprehend God in a spiritual and saving way (pp. 19–22, 33–34, above), Calvin now capsulizes this conviction in a formulaic principle: "God himself is the sole and proper witness to himself." As we have seen, God performs this self-witness first in nature generally and then with persuasive clarity in the Word made operative through the Holy Spirit. In contrast to this definitive revelation of God in the Word, human nature is prone to fashion God according to its own devices and thus makes of itself a veritable "factory of idols."

SOURCES

(A) *Institutes* I.11.1–4, pp. 99–105 (edited). **(B)** *Institutes* I.11.8–9, pp. 107–10. **(C)** *Institutes* I.11.12, p. 112.

BIBLIOGRAPHY

Carlos Eire, *War Against the Idols: The Reformation of Worship from Erasmus to Calvin* (New York: Cambridge University Press, 1986).

A. GOD THE ONLY PROPER WITNESS TO HIMSELF

But as Scripture, having regard for men's rude and stupid wit, customarily speaks in the manner of the common folk, where it would distinguish the true God from the false it particularly contrasts him with idols. It does this, not to approve what is more subtly and elegantly taught by the philosophers, but the better to expose the world's folly, nay, madness, in searching for God when all the while each one clings to his own speculations. Therefore, that exclusive definition, encountered everywhere, annihilates all the divinity that men fashion for themselves out of their own opinion: for God himself is the sole and proper witness of himself. . . .

God, indeed, from time to time showed the presence of his divine majesty by definite signs, so that he might be said to be looked upon face to face. But all the signs that he ever gave forth aptly conformed to his plan of teaching and at the same time clearly told men of his incomprehensible essence. For clouds and smoke and flame [Deut. 4:11], although they were symbols of heavenly glory, restrained the minds of all, like a bridle placed on them, from attempting to penetrate too deeply. . . .

B. HUMANITY A FACTORY OF IDOLS

For whence came the beginning of idols but from the opinion of men?. . . [A]ll we conceive concerning God in our own minds is an insipid fiction. . . . For surely there is nothing less fitting than to wish to reduce God, who is immeasurable and incomprehensible, to a five-foot measure! And yet custom shows this monstrous thing, which is openly hostile to the order of nature, to be natural to men.

Now we ought to bear in mind that Scripture repeatedly describes superstitions in this language: they are the "works of men's hands," which lack God's authority. . . .

[W]hat is held in the book of Wisdom concerning the origin of idols is received virtually by public consent: that the originators of idols were those who conferred this honor on the dead, and thus superstitiously worshiped their memory. Of course, I admit that this perverse custom was very ancient, nor do I deny that it was a torch with which to fire men's mad dash into idolatry all the more; yet I do not concede that this was the original source of the evil. For it appears from Moses that idols were in use before this eagerness to consecrate images of the dead prevailed, which is frequently mentioned by secular writers. When he relates that Rachel stole her father's idols [Gen. 31:19], he is speaking of a vice that was common. From this we may gather that man's nature, so to speak, is a perpetual factory of idols. . . .

So it goes. Man's mind, full as it is of pride and boldness, dares to imagine a god according to its own capacity: as it sluggishly plods, indeed is overwhelmed with the crassest ignorance, it conceives an unreality and an empty appearance as God.

To these evils a new wickedness joins itself, that man tries to express in his work the sort of God he has inwardly conceived. Therefore the mind begets an idol; the hand gives it birth. The example of the Israelites shows the origin of idolatry to be that men do not believe God is with them unless he shows himself physically present. . . .

Daily experience teaches that flesh is always uneasy until it has obtained some figment like itself in which it may fondly find solace as in an image of God. In almost every age since the beginning of the world, men, in order that they might obey this blind desire, have set up symbols in which they believed God appeared before their bodily eyes.

C. OF THE RIGHT USE OF ART

And yet I am not gripped by the superstition of thinking absolutely no images permissible. But because sculpture and painting are gifts of God, I seek a pure and legitimate use of each, lest those things which the Lord has conferred upon us for his glory and our good be not only polluted by perverse misuse but also turned to our destruction. We believe it wrong that God should be represented by a visible appearance, because he himself has forbidden it [Ex. 20:4] and it cannot be done without some defacing of his glory. And lest they think us alone in this opinion, those who concern themselves with their writings will find that all well-balanced writers have always disapproved of it. If it is not right to represent God by a physical likeness, much less will we be allowed to worship it as God, or God in it. Therefore it remains that only those things are to be sculptured or painted which the eyes are capable of seeing: let not God's majesty, which is far above the perception of the eyes, be debased through unseemly representations.

The Westminster and Heidelberg Catechisms: What Is the "Chief End of Man"? and What Is Idolatry?

The Westminster Shorter Catechism (1647) is one of the most widely read and influential of the Reformed catechisms, especially among Presbyterians. The opening lines are a classic expression of Reformed piety:

QUESTION: What is the chief end of man?
ANSWER: To glorify God and enjoy him forever.[4]

The Heidelberg Catechism was drafted at the direction of the Palatinate Prince, Frederick III, by Zacharius Ursinus in 1562, with some aid from Caspar Olevianus (Olewig), and approved by a general synod and distributed in 1563. It is divided into three parts which parallel Paul's Epistle to the Romans: sin (qs. 3–11; Rom. 1:18—3:20), redemption in Christ (qs. 12–18; Rom. 3:21—11:36), and the Christian life (qs. 86–129; Romans 12–16).[5]

---

4. Schaff, *Creeds* 3:676.
5. Schaff, *Creeds* 1:540.

The Heidelberg Catechism is highly personal and focuses upon the work of Christ on the believer's behalf:

QUESTION: What is your only comfort, in life and in death?
ANSWER: That I belong—body and soul, in life and in death—not to myself but to my faithful Savior, Jesus Christ, who at the cost of his own blood has fully paid for all my sins and has completely freed me from the dominion of the devil; that he protects me so well that without the will of my Father in heaven not a hair can fall from my head; indeed, that everything must fit his purpose for my salvation. Therefore, by his Holy Spirit, he also assures me of eternal life, and makes me wholeheartedly willing and ready from now on to live for him.

In their different ways, both Heidelberg and Westminster are aiming at complete devotion to God. Because of its pastoral tone and experiential approach to doctrine, Heidelberg is the most widely used Reformed catechism in Europe and rivals Westminster in popularity worldwide.

In the selection from Heidelberg below, the Reformed opposition to idolatry is brought to bear practically in the Christian life.

SOURCE

Catechismus oder Kurtzer Unterricht Christlicher Lehre (Germantown, Mass.: Christoph Saur, 1755). Latin: H. A. Niemeyer, *Collectio Confessionum* (Leipzig, 1840), 390–461. A. Wolters, *Heidelberger Katechismus in seiner ursprünglichen Gestalt, herausgegeben nebst der Geschichte seines Textes im Jahre 1563*, 1864; ET: *Heidelberg Catechism* (1563), q. 95, in Cochrane, *Confessions*, 325.

BIBLIOGRAPHY

Karl Barth, *Learning Jesus Christ Through the Heidelberg Catechism*, trans. Shirlie C. Guthrie, Jr. (Grand Rapids: Wm. B. Eerdmans); previously published as *The Heidelberg Catechism for Today* (Richmond, Va.: John Knox, 1964). Lyle D. Bierma, "The Covenant Theology of Caspar Olevian" (Ph.D. diss., Duke University, 1980). James J. Good, *The Heidelberg Catechism* (Philadelphia: Reformed Church, 1914). Walter Hollweg, *Neue Untersuchungen zur Geschichte des Heidelberger Katechismus* (Neukirchen: Neukirchener Verlag, 1961). Schaff, *Creeds* 1:529–54.
    On Ursinus, see pp. 4–5, above. On the Westminster Assembly, see pp. 27–28, above.

Q. 95. *What is idolatry?*
A. It is to imagine or possess something in which to put one's trust in place of or beside the one true God who has revealed himself in his Word.

Lord's Day 35

Q. 96. *What does God require in the second commandment?*

A. That we should not represent him or worship him in any other manner than he has commanded in his Word.

Q. 97. *Should we, then, not make any images at all?*

A. God cannot and should not be pictured in any way. As for creatures, although they may indeed be portrayed, God forbids making or having any likeness of them in order to worship them, or to use them to serve him.

Q. 98. *But may not pictures be tolerated in churches in place of books for unlearned people?*

A. No, for we must not try to be wiser than God who does not want his people to be taught by means of lifeless idols, but through the living preaching of his Word.

Lord's Day 36

Q. 99. *What is required in the third commandment?*

A. That we must not profane or abuse the name of God by cursing, by perjury, or by unnecessary oaths. Nor are we to participate in such horrible sins by keeping quiet and thus giving silent consent. In a word, we must not use the holy name of God except with fear and reverence so that he may be rightly confessed and addressed by us, and be glorified in all our words and works.

Peter van Mastricht: Whether God Should Be Objectified in Thought as an "Old Man"?

The logical extension of the Reformed polemic against idolatry is that not only should the physical attempt to embody Deity be eliminated but so should mental concepts which attribute a corporeal form to God. Thus the question asked by Peter (Petrus) van Mastricht (1630–1706) whether God should be conceived as an old man is not a facetious one. Notwithstanding the negative theology (*via negativa*) implied by the Reformed anti-idolatry polemic, it does not leave one to resort to mystical silence. Instead God's self-witness in scripture reveals those positive statements about God that are permissible.

Peter van Mastricht was a Dutch pastor who held several academic posts, succeeding Gisburtus Voetius as professor of theology at Utrecht in 1677.

SOURCE

Peter van Mastricht, *Theoretica-practica Theologia* II.iv.12 (1714), cited in Heppe, *Reformed Dogmatics*, 64.

[Is it right] in divine worship when praying to objectify God to oneself as an "old man"? . . . Because the Lutherans have long since lost the use of images in public worship, which cannot but generate such stupid conceptions in onlookers, they cannot with any sort of ἐπιείκεια ["graciousness" or "forbearance"] find fault. They declare that such conceptions of God in the guise of an elderly man do not import any sin, provided they do not insist that God's essence has such a figure. In order to get at them with both nails the *Reformed* say that it is lawful to have a concept of God, in fact it is highly necessary, unless we would be atheist; yet they hold that a concept of God under the guise of a man or anything else corporeal is quite out of order. [The reasons are as follows:] (1) The Saviour Jn. 4:24 bids us hold such a conception of God, as agrees with God's nature, describes God as Spirit and of course He wishes to be worshipped and adored in spirit, i.e., spiritually, without any sort of figures; and in truth, or with true thoughts agreeable to the concept. (2) Such conceptions of God are false, according as they do not agree with the God conceived; in fact they are illicit. (3) Such concepts are vain Rom. 1:21. (4) They obscure the glory of the incorruptible God and as it were change it ἐν ὁμοιώματι εἰκόνος φθαρτοῦ ἐιθρώπου ["for images resembling a mortal human being" (Rom. 1:23)]. (5) By these concepts the heart is clouded and the mind rendered foolish.

HEINRICH BULLINGER AND JOHANNES COCCEIUS: THE NAMING OF GOD

We have seen that Reformed theology's high view of divine transcendence does not mean that God resides in sublime detachment from the world. Neither does it mean that God remains some vague and unintelligible force, a mere personification of the myriad powers that impinge upon human life. Instead, God is personal, a being whom we may address by name. In Bullinger and Cocceius we have two of the early Reformed treatments of the naming of God. For these theologians, the divine name is a matter not of human invention but of God's self-revelation. In these passages, rich in biblical exegesis, Bullinger and Cocceius focus on the Old Testament names, and particularly the name Yahweh.[6] The passages reflect the seriousness with which classical Reformed theology took the Bible and its study in the original languages.

SOURCES

(A) Heinrich Bullinger, "Of God," in *Decades* 3:123–37 (edited). (B) Johannes Cocceius, "De Nominibus Dei," chap. IX, *Summa Theologiae* (1662), 166; ET: "The Divine Names," trans. Mary Beaty. (This chapter runs from pp. 166–70 and includes detailed exegesis of all the Old Testament names.)

A. HEINRICH BULLINGER

Very eloquently, truly, and godly doth Tertullian in his book *De Trinitate* say: "The proper name of God cannot be uttered, because it cannot be conceived. For that is called by a name, that is conceived by the condition of its own nature: for a name is the significant notifying of that thing which may be conceived by the name. But when the thing, which is handled, is of such sort that it cannot be rightly conceived by our very senses and understanding, how shall it be rightly named by an apt term and fit nomination? which, while it is beyond understanding, must needs also be above the significancy of the term whereby it is named: so that when God upon certain causes or occasions doth annex or declare to us his name in words, we may think and know that the very property of the name is not expressed so much in words, as a certain significancy is set down, to which while men in prayers do run, they may seem to be able by it to call upon and obtain the mercy of God." . . .

But whatsoever may be thought of him shall still be less than he: and whatsoever in speech is shewed of him, being compared with him, shall be much less than he. For in silence to ourselves we may partly perceive him: but as he is, in words to express him, it is altogether impossible. For if you call him Light, then do you rather name a creature of his than him, but him you express not: or if you call him Virtue, then do you rather name his power than him, but him you declare not: or if you call him Majesty, then do you rather name his honour than him, but him you describe not. And why should I, in running through every several title, prolong the time? I will at once declare it all. Say all of him whatsoever thou canst, and yet thou shalt still rather name something of his than himself. . . .

---

6. For a contemporary treatment of the divine names in the Old Testament, see Tryggve N. D. Mettinger, *In Search of God: The Meaning and Message of the Everlasting Names*, trans. Frederick H. Cryer (Philadelphia: Fortress, 1988); on the meaning of the name "Yahweh," see esp. 28–49.

The first and chiefest way to know God is derived out of the very names of God attributed unto him in the holy scripture. Those names are many and of sundry sorts, because his virtue, his wisdom, I mean, his goodness, justice, and power are altogether infinite. I will reckon up and expound unto you, according to my skill the most excellent and usual among the rest.

Among all the names of God that is the most excellent which they call *Tetragrammaton*, that is (if we may so say), the four-lettered name: for it is compounded of the four spiritual letters, and is called JEHOVAH. . . .

Like to this also are these names of God, *Jah*, and *Hu*. Whereof the first is oftener found in the Psalms than once: for David saith, *Hallelu-Jah*," that is, "Praise ye the Lord." . . .

But the Hebrews do not read or express the four-lettered name of God by calling it Jehovah, but instead of it they use the word *Adonai*. For they say that Jehovah must not be uttered. Now all interpreters in their translations, where they turn it into Latin, do call it *Dominus*, that is, Lord: for God is the Lord of all things, both visible and invisible. Neither is there in all the world any other Lord but this one, and he alone, to whom all things in the world are subject and do obey: for he hath a most mere dominion and absolute monarchy over all his creatures. And therefore for plainness sake sometime the word *Sabbaoth* is annexed to the name of God; which some translate "the Lord of powers," and some "the Lord of hosts." For God, being almighty, doth by his power or strength shew forth and in his host declare, what mighty things he is able to do, and of how great power and might he is. . . .

Sometimes there is ascribed to the Lord the word *Æleon*, and the Lord is called *Æleon*, that is to say, high. For in the one hundred and thirteenth psalm we read: "The Lord is higher than all nations, and his glory is above the heavens. Who is like the Lord our God, which setteth himself so high in his habitation?" And in the ninety-seventh psalm he saith: "Thou, Lord, art higher than all that are in the earth; thou art exalted far above all gods."

Again, God is called *El*, because of his strength. For what he will, that can he do, and therefore is he called a strong God, or a giant. . . .

But now the scripture doth attribute the plural number, *Elohim*, not to God alone, but also to angels, to judges, and to men in authority: because God is always present with them, while they labour in that office which he hath appointed them unto; and doth by the ministry of them work the things which he himself will, and which are expedient for the welfare of mortal men. And although the word *Elohim* be of the plural number, yet is it set before verbs in the singular number. . . .

Moreover, in the league which God maketh with our father Abraham God giveth himself another name. For he saith: "I God am *Schaddai*," that is, sufficient, or sufficiency. Therefore God is called *Schaddai*. . . .

Last of all we read in the third of Exodus that God said to Moses: "Thus shalt thou say to the children of Israel, The Lord God of our fathers, the God of Abraham, the God of Isaac, and the God of Jacob, hath sent me unto you. This is my name for ever, and this is my memorial from one generation unto another." So then here now we have another name of God; for he will be called the God of Abraham, of Isaac, and of Jacob. . . .

And now by the way, it is not without a mystery that, when he is the God also of other patriarchs, as of Adam, Seth, Enos, and especially of Enoch and Noah, yet out of all the number of them he picked those three, Abraham, Isaac, and Jacob, and to every one of their names prefixed severally his own name, saying: "I am the God of Abraham, the God of Isaac, and the God of Jacob." For so he did evidently teach the mystery of the Trinity in the unity of the divine substance, and that every one of the persons is of the same divinity, majesty and glory; that is, that the Father is very God, the Son very God, and the Holy Ghost very God; and that these three are one God; for he saith, "I am God, &c." Of which I will speak in place convenient.

Thus much hitherto concerning the names of God, out of which an indifferent knowledge of God may easily be gathered. I know that one Dionysius hath made a busy commentary upon the names of God: but I know too, that the godly sort, and those that are studious of the apostles' doctrine do understand, that the disciples of the apostles did far more simply handle matters belonging unto religion.

B. JOHANNES COCCEIUS

We know God not through his essence but through his acts and through his name by which he has been willing to reveal to us his "virtues" (1 Pet. 2:9), which is "his divinity" (Rom. 1:20).

"The name of God" in scripture signifies all that which can be known about God and which God has been willing for us to know about him for his greatest praise. It therefore comprehends all things that are known or can be known about God by nature, and those that have been revealed to us about God beyond the natural knowledge of God, not only things that are natural to God but also the actions which, through his good pleasure, are made known by God for the purpose of showing his worthiness and riches.

"The name of God" is said "to be adored" because God is adored and glorified in this name. All things that God has been willing to have known and believed about himself are glorious. "We invoke the name of God" because we distinguish God from false gods when we invoke him by his name, that is, by those things which he has said about himself, and in believing them we invoke God, seeking and hoping for that which is in accordance with his name. "We trust the name of God," that is, we trust him who has become known to us and whom we trust to be such as he said himself to be, and by our trust in him we give the glory to his name. "The name of God" was revealed to Moses (Exod. 34:5, 6, 7), that is, all the "goodness" of God, and "his ways and acts" (Exod. 33:19; Ps. 103:7). The truth of his name is known in Christ (John 17:26).

The names that are given to God in scripture are partly of his person and partly of his essence. And these, again, are partly substantive (and they are either incomprehensible and incommunicable to created beings in any way or they are God's own in appearance but nonetheless communicated to created beings in a certain way) and partly adjectival, denominating God by his attributes.

Although all are incommunicable to created beings, so that they cannot exist in them as they exist in God, nevertheless they are partly enunciated by the names that are attributed also to created beings on account of a certain harmony they have with God or even on account of his image that is in them. Others are of such a sort that their names cannot in any way agree with created beings and be granted to them. There are also names that come from acts. In the schools [i.e., scholastic theology], it is held that some of the divine terms are called "names"; others are called "attributes." . . .

THE TRIUNE GOD

Classical Reformed theology embraced the Nicene trinitarian faith in one God subsisting in three persons, Father, Son, and Holy Spirit, united and equal in "essence" but differentiated in "subsistence" according to the distinct relations among the persons (*ad intra*) and in their mode of operation upon the world (*ad extra*).[7] Thus its approach to trinitarian doctrine was not especially innovative. Yet there were certain distinct emphases in the Reformed approach to the Trinity, as exemplified in the following material.

---

7. See G. L. Prestige, *God in Patristic Thought*, 2d ed. (London: SPCK, 1952); J.N.D. Kelly, *Early Christian Doctrines*, rev. ed. (New York: Harper & Row, 1978).

John Calvin: The Use
of Traditional Terminology

Calvin in his coverage of the Trinity is typically circumspect concerning the use of abstract, metaphysical terminology to speak about the divine essence. Nevertheless, for the sake of preserving a true confession of who God is, Calvin endorses the classical patristic terms for speaking of the Trinity by which, in contrast to idolatrous speculation, God "offer[s] himself to be contemplated clearly."

SOURCE

Institutes I.13.1–2, 5, 6, 16, 18–19, pp. 121–23, 125–26, 128 (edited).

BIBLIOGRAPHY

For general information, see François Wendel, *Calvin: Origins and Development of His Religious Thought*, trans. Philip Maret (New York, 1963; reprint: Durham, N.C.: Labyrinth, 1987), 165–69.

On the accusation against Calvin of "Arianism" by the crypto-Protestant Pierre Caroli, see Edward Bähler, "Petrus Caroli und Johannes Calvin: Ein Betrag zur Geschichte und Kultur der Reformationszeit," *Jahrbuch für schweizerische Geschichte* 29 (1904): 62–82. William Nijenhuis, "Calvin's Attitude Towards the Symbols of the Early Church During the Conflict with Caroli," *Ecclesia Reformata: Studies on the Reformation* (Leiden: E. J. Brill, 1972). Philip Schaff, *History of the Christian Church*, 8 vols. (New York: Charles Scribner's Sons, 1910), Vol. 8: *Modern Christianity: The Swiss Reformation*, 251, 351–52, 376.

On Calvin's conflict with Servetus and the anti-trinitarians, see Roland F. Bainton, *Hunted Heretic: The Life and Death of Michael Servetus, 1511–1553* (Boston: Beacon, 1960). Antonio Rotondò, *Calvin and the Italian Anti-Trinitarians*, trans. J. and A. Tedeschi (St. Louis, Mo.: Foundation for Reformation Research, 1968). Philip Schaff, *Modern Christianity: The Swiss Reformation*, 628–37, 652–58. George H. Williams, *The Radical Reformation* (Philadelphia: Westminster, 1962), esp. 319–37, 580–669.

One of the ancients seems aptly to have remarked, "Whatever we see, and whatever we do not see, is God." According to this, he fancied that divinity was poured out into the various parts of the world. But even if God to keep us sober speaks sparingly of his essence, yet by those two titles that I have used he both banishes stupid imaginings and restrains the boldness of the human mind. Surely, his infinity ought to make us afraid to try to measure him by our own senses. Indeed, his spiritual nature forbids our imagining anything earthly or carnal of him. For the same reason, he quite often assigns to himself a dwelling place in heaven. And yet as he is incomprehensible he also fills the earth itself. . . .

For who even of slight intelligence does not understand that, as nurses commonly do with infants, God is wont in a measure to "lisp" in speaking to us? Thus such forms of speaking do not so much express clearly what God is like as accommodate the knowledge of him to our slight capacity. To do this he must descend far beneath his loftiness. . . .

But God also designates himself by another special mark to distinguish himself more precisely from idols. For he so proclaims himself the sole God as to offer himself to be contemplated clearly in three persons. Unless we grasp these, only the bare and empty name of God flits about in our brains, to the exclusion of the true God. Again, lest anyone imagine that God is threefold, or think God's simple essence to be torn into three persons, we must here seek a short and easy definition to free us from all error.

But because some hatefully inveigh against the word "person," as if humanly devised, we ought first to see with what justice they do this. The apostle, calling the Son of God "the stamp of the Father's hypostasis" [Heb. 1:3], doubtless assigns some subsistence to the Father wherein he differs from the Son. For to consider hypostasis equivalent to *essence* (as certain interpreters have done, as if Christ, like wax imprinted with a seal, represented in himself the substance of the Father) would be not only uncouth but also absurd. For since the essence of God is simple and undivided, and he contains all in himself, without portion or derivation, but in integral perfection, the Son will be improperly, even foolishly, called his "stamp." But because the Father, although distinct in his proper nature, expresses himself wholly in the Son, for a very good reason is it said that he has made his hypostasis visible in the latter. In close agreement with this are the words immediately following, that the Son is "the splendor of his glory" [Heb. 1:3; cf. Vg.]. Surely we infer from the apostle's words that the very hypostasis that shines forth in the Son is in the Father. From this we also easily ascertain the Son's hypostasis, which distinguishes him from the Father.

The same reasoning applies to the Holy Spirit: for we shall presently prove that he is God, and yet it is necessary for him to be thought of as other than the Father. Indeed, this is not a distinction of essence, which it is unlawful to make manifest. Therefore, if the testimony of the apostle obtains any credence, it follows that there are in God three hypostases. . . .

If, therefore, these terms were not rashly invented, we ought to beware lest by repudiating them we be accused of overweening rashness. Indeed, I could wish they were buried, if only among all men this faith were agreed on: that Father and Son and Spirit are one God, yet the Son is not the Father, nor the Spirit the Son, but that they are differentiated by a peculiar quality [*sed proprietat quadam esse distinctos*].

Really, I am not, indeed, such a stickler as to battle doggedly over mere words. For I note that the ancients, who otherwise speak very reverently concerning these matters, agree neither among themselves nor even at all times individually with themselves. . . .

But laying aside disputation over terms, I shall proceed to speak of the thing itself: "Person," therefore, I call a "subsistence" in God's essence, which, while related to the others, is distinguished by an incommunicable quality [*proprietate*]. By the term "subsistence" we would understand something different from "essence." For if the Word were simply God, and yet possessed no other characteristic mark, John would wrongly have said that the Word was always with God [John 1:1]. When immediately after he adds that the Word was also God himself, he recalls us to the essence as a unity. But because he could not be with God without residing in the Father, hence emerges the idea of a subsistence, which, even though it has been joined with the essence by a common bond and cannot be separated from it, yet has a special mark whereby it is distinguished from it. Now, of the three subsistences I say that each one, while related to the others, is distinguished by a special quality. This "relation" is here distinctly expressed: because where simple and indefinite mention is made of God, this name pertains no less to the Son and the Spirit than to the Father. But as soon as the Father is compared with the Son, the character of each distinguishes the one from the other. Thirdly, whatever is proper to each individually, I maintain to be incommunicable because whatever is attributed to the Father as a distinguishing mark cannot agree with, or be transferred to, the Son. Nor am I displeased with Tertullian's definition, provided it be taken in the right sense, that there is a kind of distribution or economy in God which has no effect on the unity of essence.

Jonathan Edwards: God's Inward Trinitarian Self-Communication

Jonathan Edwards's trinitarian theology centers upon God's inherent relationality and propensity to self-communication. In so doing, it attempts to solve the ancient problem of how God can be completely self-sufficient and yet genuinely related to the temporal order. God's self-existence (aseity), according to Edwards, is located in God the Father; but the prior actuality of God contains at the same time an essential predisposition to communication. This propensity to communicate occurs internally (*ad intra*) in the trinitarian life

69

and externally (*ad extra*) in the creation and sustenance of the world. Within the Trinity, the relations unfold like this: through God's self-reflective knowledge, the second person of the Trinity is a perfect repetition of the Father's actuality; and through God's reflexive loving of what God knows, the third person is the most perfect display of mutual trinitarian love. God the Father's "priority" in subsistence implies a certain "dependence" or "subordination" of the Son and Spirit but does not entail the latter's inferiority in essence. This is so because the Father's aseity is still the aseity of the entire Godhead. These relationships among the three persons are not formed arbitrarily but are "fitting" expressions of the divine character.[8]

SOURCE

Jonathan Edwards, *Observations Concerning the Scripture Oeconomy of the Trinity and the Covenant of Redemption* (New York: Charles Scribner's Sons, 1880), 21–36.

BIBLIOGRAPHY

Jonathan Edwards, *Treatise on Grace and Other Posthumous Writings Including Observations on the Trinity*, ed. Paul Helm (Greenwood, S.C.: Attic, 1971). Sang Hyun Lee, *The Philosophical Theology of Jonathan Edwards* (Princeton: Princeton University Press, 1988). Herbert W. Richardson, "The Glory of God in the Theology of Jonathan Edwards: A Study in the Doctrine of the Trinity" (Ph.D. diss., Harvard University, 1962).

We should be careful that we do not go upon uncertain grounds, and fix uncertain determinations in things of so high a nature. The following things seem to be what we have pretty plain reason to determine with respect to those things.

1. That there is a subordination of the Persons of the Trinity, in their actings with respect to the creature; that one acts from another, and under another, and with a dependance [*sic*] on another, in their actings, and particularly in what they act in the affairs of man's redemption. So that the Father in that affair acts as Head of the Trinity, and the Son under Him, and the Holy Spirit under them both.

2. It is very manifest, that the Persons of the Trinity are not inferiour one to another in glory and excellency of nature. The Son, for instance, is not inferiour to the Father in glory; for He is the brightness of His glory, the very image of the Father, the express and perfect image of His person. And therefore the Father's infinite happiness is in Him, and the

---

8. This interpretation of Edwards is significantly influenced by Lee, *The Philosophical Theology of Jonathan Edwards*, esp. chap. 7.

way that the Father enjoys the glory of the deity is in enjoying Him. And though there be a priority of subsistence, and a kind of dependance of the Son, in His subsistence, on the Father; because with respect to His subsistence, He is wholly from the Father and is begotten by Him; yet this is more properly called priority than superiority, as we ordinarily use such terms. There is dependance without inferiority of deity; because in the Son the deity, the whole deity and glory of the Father, is as it were repeated or duplicated. Every thing in the Father is repeated, or expressed again, and that fully: so that there is properly no inferiority.

3. From hence it seems manifest, that the other Persons' acting under the Father does not arise from any natural subjection, as we should understand such an expression according to the common idiom of speech; for thus a natural subjection would be understood to imply either an obligation to compliance and conformity to another as a superiour and one more excellent, and so most worthy to be a rule for another to conform to; or an obligation to conformity to another's will, arising from a dependence on another's will for being or well-being. But neither of these can be the case with respect to the Persons of the Trinity, for one is not superiour to another in excellency: neither is one in any respect dependant on another's will for being or well-being. For though one proceeds from another, and so may be said to be in some respects dependant on another, yet it is no dependance of one on the will of another. For it is no voluntary, but a necessary proceeding; and therefore infers no proper subjection of one to the will of another.

4. Though a subordination of the Persons of the Trinity in their actings, be not from any proper natural subjection one to another, and so must be conceived of as in some respect established by mutual free agreement, whereby the Persons of the Trinity, of their own will, have as it were formed themselves into a society, for carrying on the great design of glorifying the deity and communicating its fulness, in which is established a certain oeconomy and order of acting; yet this agreement establishing this Oeconomy is not to be looked upon as meerly [sic] arbitrary, founded on nothing but the meer pleasure of the members of this society; nor meerly a determination and constitution of wisdom come into from a view to certain ends which it is very convenient for the obtaining. But there is a natural decency or fitness in that order and oeconomy that is established. It is fit that the order of the acting of the Persons of the Trinity should be agreeable to the order of their subsisting. That as the Father is first in the order of subsisting, so He should be first in the order of acting. That as the other two Persons are from the Father in their subsistence, and as to their subsistence naturally origi-

nated from Him and are dependant on Him; so that in all that they act they should originate from Him, act from Him and in a dependance on Him. That as the Father with respect to the subsistences is the Fountain of the deity, wholly and entirely so; so He should be the fountain in all the acts of the deity. This is fit and decent in itself. Though it is not proper to say, decency *obliges* the Persons of the Trinity to come into this order and oeconomy; yet it may be said that decency requires it, and that therefore the Persons of the Trinity all consent to this order, and establish it by agreement, as they all naturally delight in what is in itself fit, suitable and beautiful. Therefore, of the Trinity with respect to their actions *ad extra,* is to be conceived of as prior to the covenant of redemption: as we must conceive of God's determination to glorify and communicate Himself as prior to the method that His wisdom pitches upon as tending best to effect this. For God's determining to glorify and communicate Himself must be conceived of as flowing from God's nature; or we must look upon God from the infinite fullness and goodness of His nature, as naturally disposed to cause the beams of His glory to shine forth, and His goodness to flow forth, yet we must look on the particular method that shall be chosen by divine wisdom to do this as not so directly and immediately owing to the natural disposition of the divine nature, as the determination of wisdom intervening, choosing the means of glorifying that disposition of nature. We must conceive of God's natural inclination as being exercised before wisdom is set to work to find out a particular excellent method to gratify that natural inclination. Therefore this particular invention of wisdom, of God's glorifying and communicating Himself by the redemption of a certain number of fallen inhabitants of this globe of earth, is a thing diverse from God's natural inclination to glorify and communicate Himself in general, and superadded to it or subservient to it. And therefore, that particular constitution or covenant among the Persons of the Trinity about this particular affair, must be looked upon as in the order of nature after that disposition of the Godhead to glorify and communicate itself, and so after the will of the Persons of the Trinity to act, in so doing, in that order that is in itself fit and decent, and what the order of their subsisting requires. We must distinguish between the covenant of redemption, that is an establishment of wisdom wonderfully contriving a particular method for the most conveniently obtaining a great end, and that establishment that is founded in fitness and decency and the natural order of the eternal and necessary subsistence of the Persons of the Trinity. And this must be conceived of as prior to the other.

It is evident by the Scripture, that there is an eternal covenant between some of the Persons of the Trinity, about that particular affair of men's redemption; and therefore that some things that appertain to the particular office of some of the Persons and their particular order and manner of acting in this affair, do result from a particular new agreement; and not meerly from the order already fixed in a preceding establishment founded in the nature of things, together with the new determination of redeeming mankind. There is something else new besides a new particular determination of a work to be done for God's glorying and communicating Himself. There is a particular covenant entered into about that very affair, settling something new concerning the part that some at least of the Persons are to act in that affair.

GOD'S NATURE AND ATTRIBUTES

Reformed Christianity worships the living God. For classical Reformed theology, God is the personal and spiritual being par excellence, a being who may be addressed by name; who possesses real, substantive existence; who is neither a composite of elements contained in the world nor a vague and undifferentiated force or power set loose within the world. For Reformed theology, God's scripturally revealed attributes are a genuine expression of God's reality, while at the same time they do not exhaust God's reality. Reformed theologians have adopted various ways of organizing the attributes of God: communicable and incommunicable, absolute and relative, moral and natural, and so forth. Although we can neither provide examples here of each way of organizing the attributes nor treat each attribute in all its fullness, the following selections provide an introduction to the classical beginnings of the distinctive Reformed approach to the nature and attributes of God.[9]

Huldrych Zwingli: God Is Known
Only Through God

Reformed reasoning about God begins in revelation, as noted in the first statement from Zwingli below: God is known only through God. But as Zwingli's second statement illustrates, the powers of human reason play a part

9. For a straightforward, accessible treatment of the classical Reformed approach to God's nature and attributes, see Charles Hodge, *Systematic Theology*, 3 vols. (New York, 1874; reprint: Grand Rapids: Wm. B. Eerdmans, 1989), 1:366–441. The twentieth-century classic that reworks the Reformed doctrine and provides copious historical excursuses is Barth, *Church Dogmatics* II/1, esp. pp. 322–677.

in explicating what the fundamental commitments derived from revelation mean. Thus Zwingli deduces the coinherence of divine attributes rationally from the more fundamental conviction of God's transcendent character as the One Creator God.

SOURCES

(A) Huldrych Zwingli, *Commentarius de vera et falsa religione* (1525); ET: *Commentary on True and False Religion*, in Zwingli, *Works* 3:58–67 (edited). **(B)** Huldrych Zwingli, *Fidei expositio* (1536), in *SS* 4:44–78; ET: *An Exposition of the Faith*, in *Zwingli and Bullinger*, 249.

A. GOD IS KNOWN ONLY
THROUGH GOD

What God is is perhaps above human understanding, but not *that* God is. For many of the wise have got so far as to have no doubt of the existence of God, though there have been some who attributed divinity to many beings—through their limited understanding, no doubt, which did not venture to attribute to one and only one being the great power and majesty that they saw must belong to divinity. . . .

Furthermore, *what* God is, we have just as little knowledge of from ourselves as a beetle has of what man is. Nay, this infinite and eternal divine is much farther separated from man than man is from the beetle, because a comparison between any kinds of created things can more properly be made than between any created thing and the Creator, and all perishable things are nearer and more closely related to each other than to the eternal and unbounded divine, however much you may find in them a likeness and footprints, as they say, of that divine. Since, then, we can in no way attain of our own effort to a knowledge of what God is . . . , it must be admitted that only by God Himself can we be taught what He is.

All, therefore, is sham and false religion that the theologians have adduced from philosophy as to what God is. If certain men have uttered certain truths on this subject, it has been from the mouth of God, who has scattered even among the heathen some seeds of the knowledge of Himself, though sparingly and darkly; otherwise they would not be true. But we, to whom God Himself has spoken through His Son and through the Holy Spirit, are to seek these things not from those who were puffed up with human wisdom, and consequently corrupted what they received pure, but from the divine oracles. . . .

B. REASONING ABOUT DIVINE
ATTRIBUTES

To sum up: the source of our religion is to confess that God is the uncreated Creator of all things, and that he alone has power over all things and freely bestows all things. . . .

Moreover, we think of God as follows: Since we know that God is the source and Creator of all things, we cannot conceive of anything before or beside him which is not also of him. For if anything could exist which was not of God, God would not be infinite: he would not extend to where that other is, seeing that it exists apart from him. In the Scriptures, as we see, Father, Son, and Holy Ghost are all described as God, but they are not creatures or different gods, but the three are all one, one essence, one *ousia* or existence, one power and might, one knowledge and providence, one goodness and loving-kindness. There are three names or persons, but each and all are one and the self-same God.

We know that this God is good by nature, for whatever he is he is by nature. But goodness is both mercy and justice. Deprive mercy of justice, and it is no longer mercy, but indifference or timidity. But fail to temper justice by kindness and forbearance and at once it becomes the greatest injustice and violence. Therefore when we confess that God is good by nature, we confess that he is both loving, kind and gracious, and also holy, just and impassible. But if he is just and righteous, necessarily he must abhor all contact with evil. Hence it follows that we mortals cannot have any hope of fellowship or friendship with him, since we are not only guilty of sin, but actually participate in it. On the other hand, if he is good, he must necessarily temper every resolve and act with equity and grace.

John Calvin: Divine Attributes
in Scripture

In keeping with his high view of the majesty and glory of God and his concomitant reticence to speculate concerning God's essence, Calvin never provides any highly refined reflections upon the attributes of God. Instead he links his understanding of God squarely to the witness of scripture as apprehended in human experience.

SOURCE

Institutes I.10.1–3, pp. 96–99 (edited).

God, the Maker of heaven and earth, governs the universe founded by him. Indeed, both his fatherly goodness and his beneficently inclined will are repeatedly extolled; and examples of his severity are given, which show him to be the righteous avenger of evil deeds, especially where his forbearance toward the obstinate is of no effect.

Indeed, in certain passages clearer descriptions are set forth for us, wherein his true appearance is exhibited, to be seen as in an image. For when Moses described the image, he obviously meant to tell briefly whatever was right for men to know about him. "Jehovah," he says, "Jehovah, a merciful and gracious God, patient and of much compassion, and true, who keepest mercy for thousands, who takest away iniquity and transgression, . . . in whose presence the innocent will not be innocent, who visitest the iniquity of the fathers upon the children and the children's children." [Ex. 34:6–7; cf. Vg.] Here let us observe that his eternity and his self-existence are announced by that wonderful name twice repeated. Thereupon his powers are mentioned, by which he is shown to us not as he is in himself, but as he is toward us: so that this recognition of him consists more in living experience than in vain and high-flown speculation. Now we hear the same powers enumerated there that we have noted as shining in heaven and earth: kindness, goodness, mercy, justice, judgment, and truth. For power and might are contained under the title *Elohim.*

By the same epithets also the prophets designate him when they wish to display his holy name to the full. That we may not be compelled to assemble many instances, at present let one psalm [Ps. 145] suffice for us, in which the sum of all his powers is so precisely reckoned up that nothing would seem to have been omitted [esp. Ps. 145:5]. And yet nothing is set down there that cannot be beheld in his creatures. Indeed, with experience as our teacher we find God just as he declares himself in his Word. In Jeremiah, where God declares in what character he would have us know him, he puts forward a less full description but one plainly amounting to the same thing. "Let him who glories, glory in this," he says, "that he knows that I am the Lord who exercise mercy, judgment, and justice in the earth" [Jer. 9:24; I Cor. 1:31]. Certainly these three things are especially necessary for us to know: mercy, on which alone the salvation of us all rests; judgment, which is daily exercised against wrongdoers, and in even greater severity awaits them to their everlasting ruin; justice, whereby believers are preserved, and are most tenderly nourished. When these are understood, the prophecy witnesses that you have abundant reason to glory in God. Yet neither his truth, nor power, nor holiness, nor goodness is thus overlooked. For how could we have the requisite knowledge of his justice, mercy, and judgment unless that knowledge rested upon his unbending truth? And without understanding his power, how could we believe that he rules the earth in judgment and justice? But whence comes his mercy save from his goodness? If, finally, "all his paths are mercy" [Ps. 25:10], judgment, justice [cf. Ps. 25:8–9], in these also is his holiness visible.

Theodore Beza: Reconciling the Justice and Mercy of God

One of the chief problems in presenting the attributes of God is how to reconcile qualities which often seem to conflict in human experience. In this passage we have a christological resolution of justice and mercy from the hand of Theodore Beza (Théodore de Bèze) (1519–1605]. Beza, a noted linguist and theologian, became Calvin's successor at Geneva in 1564. He is often credited with causing "Calvinism" to take the turn toward scholasticism, a thesis which is still subject to debate.[10] This selection comes from a short pamphlet framed in a question-and-answer format and designed to explain the essentials of the faith in a straightforward and intelligible manner.

SOURCE

Beza, *Questions and Responses*, qs. 16 and 17, p. 7.

BIBLIOGRAPHY

John S. Bray, *Theodore Beza's Doctrine of Predestination*, Bibliotheca Humanistica & Reformatorica 12 (Nieuwkoop: De Graaf, 1975). Walter Kickel, *Vernunft und Offenbarung bei Theodor Beza: zum Problem des Verhältnisses von Theologie, Philosophie und Statt* (Neukirchen: Neukirchener Verlag, 1967). Jill Raitt, *The Eucharistic Theology of Theodore Beza: Development of the Reformed Doctrine*, AAR Studies in Religion 4 (Chambersburg, Penna., 1972).

10. See Ernst Bizer, *Früorthodoxie und Rationalismus* (Zurich: EVZ-Verlag, 1963), 6–15; Basil Hall, "Calvin Against the Calvinists," in *John Calvin: A Collection of Essays*, ed. G. E. Duffield (Grand Rapids: Wm. B. Eerdmans, 1966), 22–28. Hans Emil Weber, *Reformation, Orthodoxie und Rationalismus* (Gütersloh: Gutersloher Verlag, 1967). But cf. John S. Bray, *Theodore Beza's Doctrine of Predestination*; John Patrick Donnelly, "Italian Influences on the Development of Calvinist Scholasticism"; Richard A. Muller, *Christ and the Decree: Christology and Predestination in Reformed Theology from Calvin to Perkins*, Studies in Reformed Theology 2 (Durham, N.C.: Labyrinth, 1986); Jill Raitt, *The Eucharistic Theology of Theodore Beza*.

Q15 So that you may know this, what in God should you chiefly consider?

A15 His perfect justice, and perfect mercy.

Q16 What do you mean by "justice" and "mercy"?

A16 They are not in God, as qualities, but through the justice of God, we know to so great an extent is the nature of God perfect, that He especially hates and most severely will punish all injustice. By the term "perfect mercy" we mean that whatever is bestowed upon us comes entirely from His free grace, especially the gift of eternal life.

Q17 Yet, these things seem to contradict. For how can He be the most severe punisher of them whom He condones by His free grace?

A17 The Father has revealed to us that these things agree perfectly in His Son, who paid the penalty for our sins completely, and was freely given to us by the Father.

Girolami Zanchi: Divine Attribute of Omnipotence in Explanation of the Divine Decrees

Girolami (Jerome) Zanchi (1516–90) was an Italian theologian who began studying at the University of Padua as an Augustinian friar. Under the influence of fellow Italian Peter Martyr Vermigli (Pietro Martire Vermigli) (1499–1562), Zanchi moved toward conversion to the Protestant faith, but his complete commitment came only after a protracted struggle of conscience that culminated in his flight from Italy in 1552 and ten months of study in Geneva under Calvin. Zanchi's work exemplifies the unambiguous entry into Reformed theology of the scholastic method, with its emphasis on deductive logic and metaphysical speculation. Zanchi's handling of the divine attributes focuses on the simplicity of God whose essence and attributes are one. When compared to Calvin's modest treatment of divine attributes, Zanchi's theology discloses a subtle shift toward inquiry into God *a se* (as God is in God's own being). This shift is not absolute, however, for Zanchi's approach to the attributes is noteworthy for using them as a way of securing the believer's certitude of predestination. For example, God's omnipotence (the attribute singled out below) is not considered in and of itself but is thought to reinforce confidence in the reliability of one's predestined salvation.

SOURCE

Girolami Zanchi, *De Predestinatione* (Strasbourg, 1562); ET: "Observations on the Divine Attributes," in Zanchi, *Absolute Predestination*, trans. Augustus M. Toplady (London, 1769; reprint: Evansville, Ind.: Sovereign Grace Book Club, 1960), 24, 42–51 (edited). Zanchi's work is collected in *H. Zanchii Operum Omnium Theologicorum*, 8 vols. (Geneva, 1617–19).

BIBLIOGRAPHY

Christopher Burchill, "Girolami Zanchi: Portrait of a Reformed Theologian and His Work," *Sixteenth Century Journal* 15/2 (1984): 185–207. John Patrick Donnelly, *Calvinism and Scholasticism in Vermigli's Doctrine of Grace*, Studies in Medieval and Reformation Thought 18 (Leiden: E. J. Brill, 1976). Idem, "Italian Influences on the Development of Calvinist Scholasticism," *Sixteenth Century Journal* 7/1 (1976): 80–101. Otto Gründler, *Die Gotteslehre Girolami Zanchis und ihre Bedeutung für seine Lehre von der Prädestination* (Neukirchen: Neukirchener Verlag, 1965; originally, "Thomism and Calvinism in the Theology of Girolami Zanchi" (Ph.D. diss., Princeton Theological Seminary, 1963). Idem, "The Influence of Thomas Aquinas upon the Theology of G. Zanchi," *Studies in Medieval Culture* (1964): 102–17. Norman Shepherd, "Zanchius on Saving Faith," *Westminster Theological Journal* 36 (1973): 25–44. Joseph Tylenda, "Girolomi Zanchi and John Calvin," *Calvin Theological Journal* 10 (1975): 101–41.

Although the great and ever-blessed God is a being absolutely simple and infinitely remote from all shadow of composition, He is, nevertheless, in condescension to our weak and contracted faculties, represented in Scripture as possessed of divers Properties, or Attributes, which, though seemingly different from His Essence, are in reality essential to Him, and constitutive of His very Nature.

Of these attributes, those on which we shall now particularly descant (as being more immediately concerned in the ensuing subject) are the following ones: I., His eternal wisdom and foreknowledge; II., The absolute freedom and liberty of His will; III., The perpetuity and unchangeableness both of Himself and His decrees; IV., His omnipotence; V., His justice; VI., His mercy.

Without an explication of these, the doctrine of Predestination cannot be so well understood, and we shall, therefore, briefly consider them by way of preliminary to the main subject. . . .

IV.—We now come to consider THE OMNIPOTENCE OF GOD.

Position 1.—God is, in the most unlimited and absolute sense of the word, Almighty. "Behold Thou hast made the heaven and the earth by Thy great power and stretched-out arm, and there is nothing too hard to Thee" (Jer. xxxii. 17). "With God all things are possible" (Matt. xix. 26).

The schoolmen, very properly, distinguish the omnipotence of God into absolute and actual: by the former, God might do many things which He does not; by the latter, He actually does whatever He will. For instance, God might, by virtue of His absolute power, have made more worlds than He has. He might have eternally saved every individual of mankind, without reprobating any; on the other hand, He might, and that with the strictest justice, have condemned all men and saved none. He could, had it been His pleasure, have prevented the fall of angels and men, and thereby have hindered sin from having footing in and among His creatures. By virtue of His actual power He made the universe; executes the whole counsel of His will, both in heaven and earth; governs and influences both men and things, according to His own pleasure; fixes the bounds which they shall not pass, and, in a word, worketh all in all (Isa. xlv. 7; Amos iii. 6; John v. 17; Acts xvii. 26; 1 Cor. xii. 6).

Position 2.—Hence it follows that, since all things are subject to the Divine control, God not only works efficaciously on His elect, in order that they may will and do that which is pleasing in His sight, but does, likewise, frequently and powerfully suffer the wicked to fill up the measure of their iniquities by committing fresh sins. Nay, He sometimes, but for wise and gracious ends, permits His own people to transgress, for He has the hearts and wills of all men in His own hand, and inclines them to good or delivers them up to evil, as He sees fit, yet without being the author of sin, as Luther, Bucer, Augustine, and others have piously and Scripturally taught.

(1) I would infer that, if we would maintain the doctrine of God's omnipotence, we must insist upon that of His universal agency; the latter cannot be denied without giving up the former.

(2) This doctrine of God's omnipotence has a native tendency to awaken in our hearts that reverence for and fear of the Divine Majesty, which none can either receive or retain, but those who believe Him to be infinitely powerful, and to work all things after the counsel of His own will.

(3) This doctrine is also useful, as it tends to inspire us with true humility of soul, and to lay us, as impotent dust and ashes, at the feet of sovereign Omnipotence.

(4) We are hereby taught not only humility before God, but likewise dependence on Him and resignation to Him.

(5) The comfortable belief of this doctrine has a tendency to excite and keep alive within us that fortitude which is so ornamental to, and necessary for us while we abide in this wilderness.

(6) This should stir us up to fervent and incessant prayer. For, does

God work powerfully and benignly in the hearts of His elect? and is He the sole cause of every action they do, which is truly and spiritually good? Then it should be our prayer that He would work in us likewise both to will and to do of His good pleasure, and if, on self-examination, we find reason to trust that some good thing is wrought in us, it should put us upon thankfulness unfeigned, and cause us to glory, not in ourselves, but in Him. On the other hand, does God manifest His displeasure against the wicked by blinding, hardening and giving them up to perpetrate iniquity with greediness? which judicial acts of God are both a punishment for their sin and also eventual additions to it, we should be the more incited to deprecate these tremendous evils, and to beseech the King of heaven that He would not thus "lead us into temptation." So much concerning the omnipotence of God.

John Milton: "Praise the Lord for He Is Kind"

John Milton (1608–74), one of the great English poets, stood in the Puritan tradition but always maintained a certain theological independence of mind. This verse from a popular hymn, composed when Milton was a young man, focuses on the divine qualities of mercy and kindness.

SOURCE

John Milton, Hymn: "Let Us With a Gladsome Mind" (1623) (altered).

Let us with a gladsome mind
   Praise the Lord for He is kind:
For His mercies shall endure,
   Ever faithful, ever sure.

Let us sound His name abroad,
   For of gods He is the God:
For His mercies shall endure,
   Ever faithful, ever sure.

He, with all-commanding might,
   Filled the new-made world with light:
For His mercies shall endure,
   Ever faithful, ever sure.

Westminster Shorter Catechism:
Definition of God

This statement, frequently quoted and often memorized by Reformed laity, capsulizes God's nature and attributes in a single sentence.

SOURCE

Westminster Shorter Catechism (1647), q. 4, in Schaff, *Creeds*, 3:676.

QUESTION: What is GOD?
ANSWER: God is a Spirit, infinite, eternal, and unchangeable, in his being, wisdom, power, holiness, justice, goodness, and truth.

Jonathan Edwards: God's Outward
Self-Communication

We noted God's propensity for self-communication inwardly (*ad intra*) in the selection from Edwards on the Trinity, above. In the passage below, Edwards explains how God desires to communicate outwardly (*ad extra*) to rational creatures. God's dynamic and essentially communicative nature means that God is not undifferentiated "pure act" (*actus purus*) as was the case for Thomas Aquinas and for some of the Reformed orthodox. Rather, God's being (through God's own choice) is inexhaustively productive of other beings. For Edwards, therefore, creation is an expression of God's nature: creation is allowed to echo, however inadequately, the dynamic life of God. And through the unceasing process of God's communication, in which everything flows from God and returns to God, there is realized the happiness and ennobling both of creatures and of God. Above all, in this process God's own being is glorified. By virtue of his trinitarian theology, Edwards is able to speak of this dynamic relationality of God toward the world in a way that still preserves God's prior actuality and sovereign control over everything that occurs.[11]

SOURCE

Jonathan Edwards, *Dissertation I: Concerning the End for which God Created the World*, (1753–54; posthumously published, 1788), in Edwards, *Works* (Yale) 8:432–33, 441–44.

BIBLIOGRAPHY

Jonathan Edwards, Sermon: "The Sole Consideration, That God is God, Sufficient to still all Objections to His Sovereignty" (June, 1735), in Edwards, *Works* (1834) 2:107–

11. See Lee, *The Philosophical Theology of Jonathan Edwards*, 196–210.

10. See also "The insufficiency of reason as a substitute for revelation" (= *Miscellany* 1274), *Miscellaneous Observations*, in Edwards, *Works* (1834) 2:483. The definitive work is Lee, *The Philosophical Theology of Jonathan Edwards*, esp. chaps. 7 and 8.

As there is an infinite fullness of all possible good in God, a fullness of every perfection, of all excellency and beauty, and of infinite happiness. And as this fullness is capable of communication or emanation *ad extra;* so it seems a thing amiable and valuable in itself that it should be communicated or flow forth, that this infinite fountain of good should send forth abundant streams, that this infinite fountain of light should, diffusing its excellent fullness, pour forth light all around. And as this is in itself excellent, so a disposition to this in the Divine Being must be looked upon as a perfection or an excellent disposition; such an emanation of good is, in some sense, a multiplication of it; so far as the communication or external stream may be looked upon as anything besides the fountain, so far it may be looked on as an increase of good. And if the fullness of good that is in the fountain is in itself excellent and worthy to exist, then the emanation, or that which is as it were an increase, repetition or multiplication of it, is excellent and worthy to exist. Thus it is fit, since there is an infinite fountain of light and knowledge, that this light should shine forth in beams of communicated knowledge and understanding: and as there is an infinite fountain of holiness, moral excellence and beauty, so it should flow out in communicated holiness. And that as there is an infinite fullness of joy and happiness, so these should have an emanation, and become a fountain flowing out in abundant streams, as beams from the sun. . . .

One part of that divine fullness which is communicated, is the divine knowledge. That communicated knowledge which must be supposed to pertain to God's last end in creating the world, is the creatures' knowledge of him. For this is the end of all other knowledge: and even the faculty of understanding would be vain without this. And this knowledge is most properly a communication of God's infinite knowledge which primarily consists in the knowledge of himself. God in making this his end makes himself his end. This knowledge in the creature is but a conformity to God. 'Tis the image of God's own knowledge of himself. 'Tis a participation of the same: 'tis as much the same as 'tis possible for that to be, which is infinitely less in degree: as particular beams of the sun communicated, are the light and glory of the sun in part.

Besides God's perfections, or his glory, is the object of this knowledge, or the thing known; so that God is glorified in it, as hereby his excellency is seen. As therefore God values himself, as he delights in his own knowledge; he must delight in everything of that nature: as he delights in his own light, he must delight in every beam of that light: and as he highly values his own excellency, he must be well pleased in having it manifested, and so glorified.

Another thing wherein the emanation of divine fullness, that is and will be made in consequence of the creation of the world, is the communication of virtue and holiness to the creature. This is a communication of God's holiness; so that hereby the creature partakes of God's own moral excellency, which is properly the beauty of the divine nature. And as God delights in his own beauty, he must necessarily delight in the creature's holiness; which is a conformity to, and participation of it, as truly as the brightness of a jewel, held in the sun's beams, is a participation, or derivation of the sun's brightness, though immensely less in degree. And then it must be considered wherein this holiness in the creature consists; viz. in love, which is the comprehension of all true virtue; and primarily in love to God, which is exercised in an high esteem of God, admiration of his perfections, complacency in them, and praise of them. All which things are nothing else but the heart's exalting, magnifying, or glorifying God; which as I showed before, God necessarily approves of, and is pleased with, as he loves himself and values the glory of his own nature.

Another part of God's fullness which he communicates is his happiness. This happiness consists in enjoying and rejoicing in himself, and so does also the creature's happiness. 'Tis, as has been observed of the other, a participation of what is in God; and God and his glory are the objective ground of it. The happiness of the creature consists in rejoicing in God; by which also God is magnified and exalted: joy, or the exulting of the heart in God's glory, is one thing that belongs to praise. So that God is all in all, with respect to each part of that communication of the divine fullness which is made to the creature.

Samuel Hopkins: God's Attributes the Ground of the Moral "Government" of the World

In the theology of Jonathan Edwards which we have just studied, God's ways with the world are not arbitrary; instead, God's actions are always "fitting" and in conformity with God's character. Building upon this framework, Samuel Hopkins and the New Divinity theologians spoke of the "government" of God, which is an external expression of God's character by which the world is ordered. The goodness of God's attributes guarantees the goodness of this "government"; therefore, this government conforms to the best and wisest of plans.[12]

SOURCE

Samuel Hopkins, "The Decrees of God," *System of Doctrines* (1792), in *The Works of Samuel Hopkins* 1:90–91.

BIBLIOGRAPHY

See p. 54.

II. It is abundantly evident and demonstrably certain from reason, assisted by divine revelation, that all the sin and sufferings which have taken place, or ever will, are necessary for the greatest good of the universe, and to answer the wisest and best ends, and therefore must be included in the best, most wise, and perfect plan.

1. This appears evident and certain from the being and perfections of God. God is omnipotent, his understanding is infinite, and he is equally wise and good. He is infinitely above all dependence and control, and hath done, and can and will do, whatsoever pleaseth him. It hence is certain that he will do nothing, nor suffer any thing to be done or take place, which is not, on the whole, good, wisest, and best that it should take place, and is not most agreeable to infinite wisdom and goodness. It is impossible it should be otherwise. Therefore, when we find that sin and misery have taken place in God's world, and under his government, we may be as certain that it is, on the whole, best it should be so, and that all this evil is necessary in order to answer the best ends, the greatest good of the universe, as we can be that there is a God omnipotent, and possessed of infinite wisdom, rectitude, and goodness; and he who denies or doubts of the former, equally questions and opposes the latter. If it be once admitted that any evil, or the least event, may or can take place, which is not, on the whole, best, and therefore not desirable that it should be, it must with equal reason be granted, that nothing but evil, and what is on the whole undesirable, may take place; and that the universe may become wholly evil, or infinitely worse than nothing. And all would be left without any ground or reason to trust in God, or any thing else, for the least good for himself, or any other being. The divine

---

12. Students of the eighteenth century will wish to compare Gottfried Wilhelm Leibniz, *Essais de Théodicée sur la bonté de Dieu, la liberté de l'homme et l'origine du mal* (1710); ET: *Theodicy*, ed. Austin Farrar (LaSalle, Ill.: Open Court, 1985).

perfections and character are the only security against this, and are the ground of an equal certainty that nothing has taken place, or ever will, which is not on the whole best, or necessary for the greatest good of the whole. And this is a sure and ample foundation for the trust, confidence, comfort, and joy of him who is a true friend to God, and desires the greatest good of the whole, and consequently is irreconcilably opposed to every event which is not on the whole wisest and best. If this foundation were taken away and destroyed, what could the righteous, the truly pious and benevolent, do? They must be left without any possible support, and sink into darkness and woe!

PREDESTINATION

In General

In its most general form, the doctrine of predestination asserts, first, that anyone who is saved is saved by the prior determination of the grace of God in Jesus Christ and, second, that anyone who is lost is lost by receiving—likewise at the determination of God—the just consequences of his or her sin. Recognizing the impenetrable mystery at the heart of predestination, Reformed theologians have labored to conceive these two assertions in a variety of ways, each theologian seeking to reconcile the divine attributes of love and holiness, and each, in conceptualizing God's ways with humanity, attempting neither to make God the author of sin nor to eviscerate the integrity of the believer's own acceptance of salvation.

For Reformed orthodoxy, the essential affirmation is that the elect are chosen by God to be holy; and this choosing is done on the basis of the mercy and justice of God's free will, and not on the basis of a holiness or merit which God has previously foreseen. Instead, by an eternal, pretemporal, unchangeable, and unconditional decision, the destinies of each individual person have been set definitively in the mind of God, with a fixed number being elected to salvation and the rest being passed over for damnation. Most divided this decision of God into two decrees: a decree for "election" of the saved and another for "reprobation" of the damned. While this rigorous interpretation of predestination has been a stumbling block for many in accepting Reformed theology, it should be noted that the doctrine finds its origins in the scriptures themselves[13] and has a historical pedigree which dates as far back as Augustine. In addition to its warrant in scripture and tradition, predestination was

---

13. Some important passages on predestination and the "decrees" of God in general are Gen. 18:19; Exod. 4:21; Isa. 6:10; Amos 3:2; Hos. 13:5; Acts 1:16; 2:23; 4:28; John 3:36; Rom. 8; 9; 11:2; Eph. 1:5; 2:3; 1 Pet. 1:2; 2:8; and Rev. 17:8.

especially persuasive to Reformed theology as a logical correlate of the doctrine of justification by grace alone.

One will notice in the examples that follow a continual tension between the universal reach of the gospel and the particularity of God's election. Classical Reformed theology moved toward an ever-greater focus upon particularity, although some, such as Bullinger early on and Amyraut in the seventeenth century, would attempt to hold the universal and the particular in a more or less even balance.

Heinrich Bullinger: A Summary of Moderate, Single Predestination

Bullinger gives us here, in a sermon on God the Creator, an admirably straightforward summary of predestination as a "comfort [for] godly worshippers of God." Bullinger's position is perhaps best characterized as a moderate, single predestination.[14] According to this view, the gospel is the free grace of God offered to all in the preaching of the church. The effectiveness of the gospel in the hearts of those who hear it is subject to the eternal decree of God. But this decree is a positive decree concerning the elect only; it is not accompanied by a specific decree to bring about the damnation of the reprobate.[15]

SOURCES

(A) Heinrich Bullinger, "Of the Gospel of the Grace of God," in *Decades* 3:32–34.
(B) Heinrich Bullinger, *Decades* 3:185–92.

BIBLIOGRAPHY

PRIMARY SOURCES: Heinrich Bullinger, "The Sum of the Christian Religion," in *Decades* 4:194–258. The Second Helvetic Confession in Cochrane, *Confessions*.

SECONDARY SOURCES: Gottfried Adam, *Der Streit um die Prädestination im ausgehenden 16. Jahrhundert*, Beiträge zur Geschichte und Lehre der Reformierten Kirche (Neukirchen: Neukirchener Verlag, 1970). J. Wayne Baker, *Heinrich Bullinger and the Covenant: The Other Reformed Tradition* (Athens: Ohio University Press, 1980). Richard Muller, *Christ and the Decree*, chap. 3. Joachim Staedtke, "Der Züricher Prädestina-

---

14. This is not meant to draw a sharp divide between Bullinger and Calvin. There are identifiable differences but within a common framework. See Muller, *Christ and the Decree*, 39–47. For an argument accenting the differences, see Baker, *Heinrich Bullinger and the Covenant*, chap. 2. Others, however, argue that the *Decades* come later than some of Bullinger's earlier disavowals of double predestination, and so they posit a shift in Bullinger's view toward that of Calvin (e.g., Staedtke, "Der Züricher Prädestinationsstreit von 1560").

15. While Bullinger's statement "God by his eternal and unchangeable counsel hath foreappointed who are to be saved, and who are to be condemned" may seem to imply a double decree, one for the elect and another for the reprobate, it must be interpreted in light of the next three sentences and in the context of the whole of Bullinger's other writings. The three sentences after the one just quoted indicate that the "fore-appointment" Bullinger has in mind is a general plan of salvation and not a double predestination. In addition, Bullinger avoids speaking of a double decree in all of his earlier works.

tionsstreit von 1560," *Zwingliana* 9 (1953): 536–46. Cornelis P. Venema, "Heinrich Bullinger's Correspondence on Calvin's Doctrine of Predestination, 1551–1553," *Sixteenth Century Journal* 17/4 (1986): 435–50. Hans Emil Weber, *Reformation, Orthodoxie und Rationalismus, Erster Teil, Von Der Reformation Zur Orthodoxie*, Zweiter Halbband. Beiträge zur Förderung christlicher Theologie 14 (Darmstadt: Wissenschaftliche Buchgesellschaft, 1966). See also the older material cited by these sources.

For an example of single predestination in a confession, see *The Thirty-Nine Articles of Religion of the Church of England* (Eng. ed., 1571; Amer. rev. ed., 1801), Article 17, in Schaff, *Creeds* 3:497–99.

A. OF THE GOSPEL OF THE GRACE
OF GOD

Thus hitherto we have heard that God, the Father of mercies, according to his free mercy taking pity upon mankind when it stuck fast and was drowned in the mire of hell, did, as he promised by the prophets, send his only-begotten Son into the world, that he might draw us out of the mud, and fully give us all things requisite to life and salvation. For God the Father was in Christ reconciled unto us, who for us and our salvation was incarnate, dead, raised from death to life, and taken up into heaven again.

And although it may by all this be indifferently well gathered, to whom that salvation doth belong, and to whom that grace is rightly preached; yet the matter itself doth seem to require in flat words expressly to shew, that Christ and the preaching of Christ his grace declared[1] in the gospel doth belong unto all. For we must not imagine that in heaven there are laid two books, in the one whereof the names of them are written that are to be saved, and so to be saved, as it were of necessity, that, do what they will against the word of Christ and commit they never so heinous offenses, they cannot possibly choose but be saved; and that in the other are contained the names of them which, do what they can and live they never so holily, yet cannot avoid everlasting damnation. Let us rather hold, that the holy gospel of Christ doth generally preach to the whole world the grace of God, the remission of sins, and life everlasting.

B. OF DIVINE PREDESTINATION

The doctrine of the foreknowledge and predestination of God, which hath a certain likeness[2] with his providence, doth no less comfort the godly worshippers of God. They call foreknowledge that knowledge in God, whereby he knoweth all things before they come to pass, and seeth even present all things that are, have been, and shall be. For to the knowledge of God all things are present; nothing is past, nothing is to come. And the predestination of God is the eternal decree of God, whereby he hath ordained either to save or destroy men; a most certain end of life and death being appointed unto them. Whereupon also it is elsewhere called a fore-appointment.[3] Touching these points some have diversely disputed; and many verily, curiously and contentiously[4] enough; and in such sort surely, that not only the salvation of souls, but the glory of God also, with the simple sort is endangered. The religious searchers or interpreters of the scriptures confess, that here nothing is to be permitted to man's wit; but that we must simply and wholly hang upon whatsoever the scripture hath pronounced.[5] And therefore these words of St. Paul are continually before their eyes and in their minds: "O the depth of the riches of the wisdom and knowledge of God! how unsearchable (or incomprehensible) are his judgments, and his ways past finding out! For who hath known the mind of the Lord? or who was his counsellor? or who hath given unto him first, and he shall be recompensed?" (Rom. 11). They never forget the admonition of the most wise man, Jesus Syrach, saying: "Seek not out the things that are too hard for thee; neither search after things which are too mighty for thee: but what God hath commanded thee, think thou always thereupon, and be not too curious in many of his works; for it is not needful for thee to see with thine eyes the things that be secret" (Ecclus. 3). In the mean time truly, they do not contemn neither yet neglect those things which it hath pleased God by the open scriptures to reveal to his servants touching this matter.

Of God's foreknowledge there are many testimonies, especially in the prophecy of [Isaiah] chap. 41 and in the chapters following; whereby also the Lord doth declare that he is the true God. Furthermore, God by his eternal and unchangeable counsel hath fore-appointed who are to be saved, and who are to be condemned. Now the end or the decree of life and death is short and manifest to all the godly. The end of predestination, or fore-appointment, is Christ, the Son of God the Father. For God hath ordained and decreed to save all, how many soever have communion and fellowship with Christ, his only-begotten Son; and to destroy or condemn all, how many soever have no part in the communion or fellowship of Christ, his only Son. Now the faithful verily have fellowship with Christ, and the unfaithful are strangers from Christ. . . .

Therefore, if thou ask me whether thou art elected to life, or predestined to death; that is, whether thou art of the number of them that are to be damned, or that are to be saved; I answer simply out of the scripture, both of the evangelists and the apostles: If thou hast communion or fellowship with Christ, thou art predestined to life, and thou art of the number of the elect and chosen: but if thou be a stranger from Christ, howsoever otherwise thou seem to flourish in virtues, thou art predestined to death, and foreknowledged, as they say, to damnation. Higher and deeper I will not creep into the seat of God's counsel. And here I rehearse again the former testimonies of scripture: "God hath predestined us, to adopt us into his sons through Jesus Christ. This is the will of God, that whoso believeth in the Son should live; and whoso believeth not should die." Faith therefore is a most assured sign that thou art elected; and whiles thou art called to the communion of Christ, and art taught faith, the most loving God declareth towards thee his election and good-will.

1. *Allatam vel annunciatam,* Lat.
2. *Cognationem,* Lat.
3. *Praefinitio,* Lat.
4. *Spinosa,* Lat.
5. *Agnoscunt modum, ut in rebus omnibus, ita in his imprimis, servandum;* Lat. omitted; they acknowledge that, as in all things, so in these matters especially, moderation is to be kept.

John Calvin: Double Predestination as a Part of the Christian Life

The selections below, drawn from Calvin's *Commentaries* and from his lengthy argument on predestination in the *Institutes*, point to the problem, which we have already encountered, of how to square the biblical passages, such as Ezek. 18:23, 1 Tim. 2:3–4, and 2 Pet. 3:9, which proclaim God's universal will to save, with the empirical observation that many reject the offer of salvation. For Calvin the answer to this question is twofold: there is, first, a universal but conditional will of God to save; then, second, there is a particular and unconditional will of God to save some but not others. This last affirmation is known as "double-predestination," according to which, before the foundation of the world, God chose to elect some to salvation and eternal life and to condemn others to death and eternal damnation. The radical particularity of God's choice in election and reprobation is a mystery the believer apprehends only in Christ. Those who are among the elect have no cause to boast, however, for election does not entitle the believer to a special *status* but only to the special *task* of serving God and humanity.

While Bullinger and Calvin agree that providence and predestination both proceed from the eternal purposes of God, Calvin locates predestination neither within the doctrine of God nor within the doctrine of Creation but makes it the penultimate theological subject of the Christian life, placing it just prior to the resurrection in the *Institutes*, Book III. Predestination, then, is not primarily meant to fuel abstract speculation about the fate of others but is offered as a consolation to the church and to the individual believer, the ripened fruit of God's work of sanctifying grace.

SOURCES

(A) John Calvin, Commentary: Ezekiel 18:23 (1565); *CO* 40; ET: In *Commentaries on the First Twenty Chapters of the Book of the Prophet Ezekiel*, trans. Thomas Myers, 2 vols. (Edinburgh: Calvin Translation Society, 1853) 2:247–48 = Vol. 12 of Calvin, *Commentaries*, 47 vols. (Edinburgh, 1843–59). **(B)** *Institutes* III.21.1, pp. 920–22. **(C)** *Institutes* III.21.1, pp. 922–23. **(D)** *Institutes* III.21.5, p. 926. **(E)** *Institutes* III.22.11, p. 947. **(F)** *Institutes* III.23.9, p. 957. **(G)** *Institutes* III.24.5, p. 970. **(H)** John Calvin, *Sermons on the Epistle to the Ephesians* (Latin: Geneva, 1559; French: Geneva, 1562); *CO* 51, trans. from the French by Arthur Golding (Oxford, 1577; rev. trans. Carlisle, Penna.: Banner of Truth, 1973), pp. 36–37.

BIBLIOGRAPHY

John Calvin, *Congrégation sur l'élection éternelle* (1551, pub. 1562), *CO* 8:85–138. Idem, *De aeterna Dei praedestinatione*; ET: *On the Eternal Predestination of God* (Geneva, 1552), trans. J.K.S. Reid (London: James Clarke, 1961); *CO* 8:249–56. Paul Jacobs, *Prädestination und Verantwortlichkeit bei Calvin* (Neukirchen: Buchhandlung des Erziehungsvereins, 1937). Richard Muller, *Christ and the Decree*, chap. 2. Alexander Schweizer, *Die Glaubenslehre der evangelisch-reformierten Kirche*, 2 vols. (Zurich, 1844–45). Idem, *Die Protestantischen Centraldogmen in ihrer Entwicklung innerhalb der Reformirten Kirchen*, 2 vols. (Zurich: Orell, Füssli, 1854–56). Schweizer argues the now-discredited thesis that predestination forms the "central doctrine" of Calvinism. François Wendel, *Calvin: Origins and Development of His Religious Thought*, 263–84.

A. IN WHAT SENSE GOD DESIRES ALL TO BE SAVED?

Have I any pleasure at all that the wicked should die? saith the Lord God; and not that he should return from his ways, and live? [Ezek. 18:23]

[T]he manner must be noticed in which God wishes all to be saved, namely, *when they turn themselves from their ways*. God thus does not so wish all men to be saved [if it means having] to renounce the difference between good and evil; [rather,] repentance, as we have said, must precede pardon. How, then, does God wish all men to be saved? By the Spirit's condemning the world of sin, [through] righteousness, and [through] judgment, at this day, by the Gospel, as he did formerly by the law and the prophets. God makes manifest to mankind their great misery, that they may [turn] themselves [around] to him: he wounds that he may cure, and slays that he may give life. We hold, then that God does not will the death of a sinner, since he calls all equally to repentance, and promises himself prepared to receive them if they only seriously repent. If anyone should object [that this interpretation eliminates election, here is the answer:] the prophet [Ezekiel] does not here speak of God's secret counsel, but only recalls miserable men from despair, that they may apprehend the hope of pardon, and repent and embrace the offered salvation. . . .

God is said not to wish the death of a sinner. How so? [it is because] he wishes all to be converted. Now we must see how God wishes all to be converted; for repentance is surely his peculiar gift: as it is his office to create men, so it is his province to renew them, and restore his image within them. . . . Since, therefore, repentance is a kind of second creation, it follows that it is not in man's power; and if it is equally in God's power to convert men as well as to create them, it follows that the reprobate are not converted, because God does not wish their conversion; for if he wished it he could do it: and hence it appears that he does not wish it.

B. THE EVIDENCE OF MANY WHO
REJECT SALVATION

In actual fact, the covenant of life is not preached equally among all men, and among those to whom it is preached, it does not gain the same acceptance either constantly or in equal degree. In this diversity the wonderful depth of God's judgment is made known. For there is no doubt that this variety also serves the decision of God's eternal election. If it is plain that it comes to pass by God's bidding that salvation is freely offered to some while others are barred from access to it, at once great and difficult questions spring up, explicable only when reverent minds regard as settled what they may suitably hold concerning election and predestination. A baffling question this seems to many. For they think nothing more inconsistent than that out of the common multitude of men some should be predestined to salvation, others to destruction.

C. AVOIDING SPECULATION

Human curiosity renders the discussion of predestination, already somewhat difficult of itself, very confusing and even dangerous.

First, then, let them remember that when they inquire into predestination they are penetrating the sacred precincts of divine wisdom. If anyone with carefree assurance breaks into this place, he will not succeed in satisfying his curiosity and he will enter a labyrinth from which he can find no exit. For it is not right for man unrestrainedly to search out things that the Lord has willed to be hid in himself, and to unfold from eternity itself the sublimest wisdom, which he would have us revere but not understand that through this also he should fill us with wonder. He has set forth by his Word the secrets of his will that he has decided to reveal to us. These he decided to reveal in so far as he foresaw that they would concern us and benefit us.

D. DISTINGUISHING "FOREKNOWLEDGE" AND "PREDESTINATION"

No one who wishes to be thought religious dares simply deny predestination, by which God adopts some to hope of life, and sentences others to eternal death. But our opponents, especially those who make foreknowledge its cause, envelop it in numerous petty objections. We, indeed, place both doctrines in God, but we say that subjecting one to the other is absurd.

When we attribute foreknowledge to God, we mean that all things always were, and perpetually remain, under his eyes, so that to his knowledge there is nothing future or past, but all things are present. And they are present in such a way that he not only conceives them through ideas, as we have before us those things which our minds remember, but he truly looks upon them and discerns them as things placed before him. And this foreknowledge is extended throughout the universe to every creature. We call predestination God's eternal decree, by which he compacted with himself what he willed to become of each man. For all are not created in equal condition; rather, eternal life is foreordained for some, eternal damnation for others. Therefore, as any man has been created to one or the other of these ends, we speak of him as predestined to life or to death.

E. REJECTION OF THE REPROBATE

"God has mercy upon whomever he wills, and he hardens whomever he wills" (Rom. 9:18). Do you see how Paul attributes both to God's decision alone? If, then, we cannot determine a reason why [God] vouchsafes mercy to his own, except that it so pleases him, neither shall we have any reason for rejecting others, other than his will. For when it is said that God hardens or shows mercy to whom he wills, men are warned by this to seek no cause outside his will.

F. HUMAN RESPONSIBILITY REMAINS

The reprobate wish to be considered excusable in sinning, on the ground that they cannot avoid the necessity of sinning, especially since this sort of necessity is cast upon them by God's ordaining. But we deny that they are duly excused, because the ordinance of God, by which they complain that they are destined to destruction, has its own equity—unknown, indeed, to us but very sure. From this we conclude that the ills they bear are all inflicted upon them by God's most righteous judgment.

G. ELECTION IS IN CHRIST

[T]hose whom God has adopted as his sons are said to have been chosen not in themselves but in his Christ [Eph. 1:4]; for unless he [God] could love them in him [Christ], he could not honor them [the elect] with the inheritance of his Kingdom if they had not previously become partakers of him. But if we have been chosen in him [Christ], we shall not find assurance of our election in ourselves; and not even in God the Father, if we conceive him as severed from his Son. Christ, then, is the mirror wherein we must, and without self-deception may, contemplate our own election.

H. ELECTION IS TO SERVICE

[W]e must always bear in mind that God's electing of us was in order to call us to holiness of life. For if he should let us alone still as wretched castaways, surely we could do nothing but all manner of wickedness according to the corruption that is in us. . . . For we are not elected to give ourselves over to permissiveness, but to show by our deeds that God has adopted us to be his children and taken us into his keeping in order to dwell in us by his Holy Spirit and to unite us to himself in all perfection of righteousness.

The Dutch Remonstrance versus the Synod of Dort

The Dutch theologian Jacob Arminius (Jakob van Harmenszoon; also Hermanns, Harmens, Harmannus) (1560–1609) formulated a view of predestination that significantly modified the standard sixteenth-century Reformed doctrine. In 1610, one year after Arminius's death, the views of his followers, the Arminians, were set forth in the Five Articles of the Remonstrance and addressed to the States-General of Holland and West Friesland. Written by

Arminius's associate Johannes Uitenbogaert and signed by forty-six ministers, the articles received political support from a peace-minded merchant class headed by Jan van Oldenbarneveldt and Hugo Grotius. This group favored a truce in the protracted war against Catholic Spain and supported the right of religious self-determination for each Dutch province.[16]

To resolve the Arminian controversy, the States-General convened a national synod at Dort (Dordrecht) from November 13, 1618 to May 9, 1619, in which Reformed theologians from not only the Netherlands and West Friesland but also East Friesland, Switzerland, the Palatinate, Nassau, Hesse, England, and Scotland participated. With the support of the nationalist and anti-Catholic Prince Maurice of Orange, the Remonstrants were soundly voted down; about two hundred Remonstrant clergy were divested and eighty banished; a few, including Grotius, were imprisoned; and Oldenbarneveldt was beheaded. The synod reaffirmed the Belgic Confession and the Heidelberg Catechism and adopted five articles confuting the Remonstrance. Commonly known by the acronym TULIP, the articles asserted (1) total depravity of humanity, (2) unconditional election, (3) limited atonement, (4) irresistible grace, and (5) perseverance of the saints.

Regarding predestination, the Remonstrants acknowledged the characteristic Reformed supremacy of God's will in the operation of grace, but they held that God's sovereignty is bound by God's justice. God's foreknowledge of a person's acceptance of Christ and perseverance in the faith precedes God's decree of election.[17] Faith and repentence still depend on God's prevenient grace as assistance but not on grace as unconditional and invincible. For the Calvinists at Dort, this position made God's will, and thus salvation, contingent upon human decision, thereby violating the principle of grace alone.

This defining episode in Reformed history identified theological issues that still divide Calvinists and Arminians; but we should also note that the debate had become inextricably caught up in the explosiveness of seventeenth-century European politics, thereby polarizing the parties and precluding constructive resolution of their differences.[18] The Remonstrant church, long a disenfranchised group, still exists in the Netherlands today, having been recognized in 1795 when church and state were finally separated.

---

16. Carl Bangs has summed up the politics of the Dutch fight for independence against Spain helpfully, if somewhat one-sidedly: "There would be a war party, militaristic, staunchly Calvinistic and anti-Catholic, predestinarian, centralist, politically even royalist, and ecclesiastically presbyterian. There would be a peace party, trade-minded, theologically tolerant, republican and Erastian. The first would support the war and fight Arminianism; the second would support a truce and fight Calvinism" (*Arminius*, 275).

17. For Arminius's statement of this, see the section on the *ordo salutis*, p. 114.

18. Cf. the proposals for ecumenical settlement discussed on pp. 302–6.

SOURCES

(A) *Articuli Arminiani sive Remonstrantia* (1610) [Dutch: *De Remonstrantie en het Remonstrantisme*], Article I; ET: *The Five Arminian Articles*, in Schaff, *Creeds* 3:544–46. **(B)** Jacob Arminius, *Verklarung van Jacob Arminius* (1608), Articles III and IV; a Latin translation appears in Arminius, *Opera theologica* (Leiden, 1629); ET: *Declaration of Sentiments*, in Arminius, *Works* 1:659–64 (edited). **(C)** *Canones Synodi Dordrechtanae* (1618–19), First Head of Doctrine, Articles VI–VIII; ET: "Of Divine Predestination," *Canons of the Synod of Dort*, in Schaff, *Creeds* 3:582–84 (Schaff reproduces the Latin of both the Remonstrance and Dort).

BIBLIOGRAPHY

Carl Bangs, *Arminius: A Study in the Dutch Reformation* (Nashville: Abingdon, 1971; reprint: 2d ed., Grand Rapids: F. Asbury, 1985). A. W. Harrison, *Arminianism* (London: Duckworth, 1932). Idem, *The Beginnings of Arminianism to the Synod of Dort* (London: University of London Press, 1926). G. C. Berkouwer, *Divine Election* (Grand Rapids: Wm. B. Eerdmans, 1960). Schaff, *Creeds* 1:512–15, 3:550–80. Alan P. F. Sell, *The Great Debate: Calvinism, Arminianism and Salvation* (Grand Rapids: Baker, 1983). Howard A. Slaatte, *The Arminian Arm of Theology* (Washington, D.C.: University Press of America, 1977). N. Tyacke, *Anti-Calvinists: The Rise of English Arminianism, c. 1590–1640* (Oxford: Oxford University Press, 1987). In addition, compare John Calvin, Commentary: Romans 9 (1540), in Calvin's *New Testament Commentaries* 8:190–219, with Jacob Arminius, *Analysis of the Ninth Chapter of St. Paul's Epistle to the Romans* (appended to the 1602 examination of William Perkins's predestination pamphlet but drafted years earlier during Arminius's tenure as pastor), in Arminius, *Works* 2:496–519 (edited). See also pp. 114, 153–56, 222–24, 262–65, 288–91, 302–6.

A. THE REMONSTRANCE

Art. I. That God, by an eternal, unchangeable purpose in Jesus Christ his Son, before the foundation of the world, hath determined, out of the fallen, sinful race of men, to save in Christ, for Christ's sake, and through Christ, those who, through the grace of the Holy Ghost, shall believe on this his Son Jesus, and shall persevere in this faith and obedience of faith, through this grace, even to the end; and, on the other hand, to leave the incorrigible and unbelieving in sin and under wrath, and to condemn them as alienate from Christ, according to the word of the gospel in John iii. 36: "He that believeth on the Son hath everlasting life: and he that believeth not the Son shall not see life; but the wrath of God abideth on him" and according to other passages of Scripture also.

B. JACOB ARMINIUS

In his primitive condition as he came out of the hands of his Creator, man was endowed with such a portion of knowledge, holiness, and power, as enabled him to perform THE TRUE GOOD, according to the commandment delivered to him: Yet none of these acts could he do, *except through the assistance of Divine Grace.*—But in his *lapsed and sinful state*, man is not capable, of and by himself, either to think, to will, or to do that which is really good; but it is necessary for him to be regenerated and renewed in his intellect, affections or will, and in all his powers, by God in Christ through the Holy Spirit, that he may be qualified rightly to understand, esteem, consider, will, and perform whatever is truly good. When he is made a partaker of this regeneration or renovation, I consider that, since he is delivered from sin, he is capable of thinking, willing, and doing that which is good, but yet *not without the continued aids of Divine Grace.* . . .

Divine Grace . . . (1) is a *gratuitous affection* by which God . . . in the first place, gives his Son, "that whosoever believeth in him might have eternal life,"—and, afterwards, he justifies him in Christ Jesus and for his sake, and adopts him into the right of sons, unto salvation.—(2) It is *an infusion* (both into the human understanding and into the will and affections,) of all those gifts of the Holy Spirit which appertain to the regeneration and renewing of man,—such as *faith, hope, charity*, etc.; for, without these gracious gifts, man is not sufficient to think, will, or do anything that is good.—(3) It is that *perpetual assistance* and continued aid of the Holy Spirit, according to which He acts upon and excites to good the man who has been already renewed, by in him salutary cogitations and by inspiring him with good desires, that he may thus actually will whatever is good; and according to which God may then will and work together with man, that man may perform whatever he wills.

In this manner, I ascribe to grace THE COMMENCEMENT, THE CONTINUANCE AND THE CONSUMMATION OF ALL GOOD,—and to such an extent do I carry its influence, that a man, though already regenerate, can neither conceive, will nor do any good at all, nor resist any evil temptation, *without this [prevenient] and exciting, this following and co-operating grace.*

C. THE SYNOD OF DORT

ART. VI. That some receive the gift of faith from God, and others do not receive it, proceeds from God's eternal decree. "For known unto God are all his works from the beginning of the world" (Acts xv. 18; Eph. i. 11). According to which decree he graciously softens the hearts of the elect, however obstinate, and inclines them to believe; while he leaves the non-elect in his just judgment to their own wickedness and obduracy. And herein is especially displayed the profound, the merciful, and at the same time the righteous discrimination between men, equally involved in ruin; or that decree of *election* and *reprobation*, revealed in the Word of God, which, though men of perverse, impure, and unstable minds wrest it to their own destruction, yet to holy and pious souls affords unspeakable consolation.

ART. VII. Election is the unchangeable purpose of God, whereby, before the foundation of the world, he hath, out of mere grace, according to the sovereign good pleasure of his own will, chosen, from the whole human race, which had fallen through their own fault, from their primitive state of rectitude, into sin and destruction, a certain number of persons to redemption in Christ, whom he from eternity appointed the Mediator and head of the elect, and the foundation of salvation.

This elect number, though by nature neither better nor more deserving than others, but with them involved in one common misery, God hath decreed to give to Christ to be saved by him, and effectually to call and draw them to his communion by his Word and Spirit; to bestow upon them true faith, justification, and sanctification; and having powerfully preserved them in the fellowship of his Son, finally to glorify them for the demonstration of his mercy, and for the praise of the riches of his glorious grace: as it is written, "According as he hath chosen us in him before the foundation of the world, that we should be holy and without blame before him in love; having predestinated us unto the adoption of children by Jesus Christ to himself, according to the good pleasure of his will, to the praise of the glory of his grace wherein he hath made us accepted in the Beloved" (Eph. i. 4–6). And elsewhere, "Whom he did predestinate, them he also called; and whom he called, them he also justified; and whom he justified, them he also glorified" (Rom. viii. 30).

ART. VIII. There are not various decrees of election, but one and the same decree respecting all those who shall be saved both under the Old and New Testament; since the Scripture declares the good pleasure, purpose, and counsel of the divine will to be one, according to which he hath chosen us from eternity, both to grace and to glory, to salvation and the way of salvation, which he hath ordained that we should walk therein.

ART. IX. This election was not founded upon foreseen faith, and the obedience of faith, holiness, or any other good quality or disposition in man, as the prerequisite, cause, or condition on which it depended; but men are chosen to faith and to the obedience of faith, holiness, etc. Therefore election is the fountain of every saving good; from which proceed faith, holiness, and the other gifts of salvation, and finally eternal life itself, as its fruits and effects, according to that of the Apostle. "He hath chosen us [not because we were, but] that we should be holy and without blame before him in love" (Eph. i. 4).

ART. X. The good pleasure of God is the sole cause of this gracious election; which doth not consist herein that God, foreseeing all possible qualities of human actions, elected certain of these as a condition of salvation, but that he was pleased out of the common mass of sinners to adopt some certain persons as a peculiar people to himself, as it is written, "For the children being not yet born, neither having done any good or evil," etc., "it was said [namely, to Rebecca] the elder shall serve the younger; as it is written, Jacob have I loved, but Esau have I hated" (Rom. ix. 11–13); and, "As many as were ordained to eternal life believed" (Acts xiii. 48).

ART. XI. And as God himself is most wise, unchangeable, omniscient, and omnipotent, so the election made by him can neither be interrupted nor changed, recalled nor annulled; neither can the elect be cast away, nor their number diminished.

Moïse Amyraut: Predestination at the Saumur Academy

Moïse Amyraut was from 1633 until his death in 1664 the celebrated professor of theology at the Saumur Academy in France. Amyraut, whose lectures were always well attended, belonged to the French humanist tradition and sought to revise the dominant Reformed orthodoxy of his day by putting forward his own more moderate position on predestination, a position which he considered a faithful interpretation of John Calvin. Notwithstanding God's will that all be saved, Amyraut found himself, like Calvin, having to account theologically for the empirical fact that indeed all are not saved. His *Brief traitté de la prédestination* (Brief treatise on predestination) of 1634 argued that salvation is universal in its provision but particular in its application to individual persons. God, motivated by benevolent love, desires the salvation of all persons in Jesus Christ, provided only that they repent, believe, and live unto righteousness. Because of the inability of human beings to repent by themselves, however, God must awaken some to conversion through a special and particular action of the Holy Spirit. God's "antecedent" will to save all persons on the condition that they believe, therefore, is effectuated only in the operation of God's "consequent" will to kindle faith. This position has been called "hypothetical universalism." It should not be confused, however, with the more modern brand of universalism which holds that all persons will in fact be saved.

To the orthodox Reformed, Amyraut seemed in no better position to account for human freedom than they, and, what is more, Amyraut seemed to skate dangerously close to Arminianism. As a result of all this, he faced heresy charges at the National Synod of Alençon in 1637. Nevertheless, he was not condemned but was only warned to avoid using what the orthodox perceived as ambiguous and inflammatory theological phrases. Amyraut never changed his theological position, however, and his various writings after the synod continued to provoke controversy.

SOURCE

Moïse Amyraut, *Brief traitté de la prédestination* (1634; corrected ed. 1658) (Saumur: Chés Isaac Desbordes, 1658), chap. 9, pp. 87–100 (edited), trans. Charles Raynal.

BIBLIOGRAPHY

In addition to the sources on pp. 29–30 (especially Armstrong, *Calvinism and the Amyraut Heresy*), see Hodge, *Systematic Theology* 2:265–67, 321–24. Jürgen Moltmann, "Gnadenbund und Gnadenwahl: Die Prädestinationlehre des Moyse Amyraut, dargestellt im Zusammenhang der heilsgeschichtlich-foederaltheologichen Tradition der Akademie von Saumur" (Ph.D. diss., Göttingen, 1951). Idem, "Prädestination und Heilsgeschichte bei Moyse Amyraut," *Zeitschrift für Kirchengeschichte* 65 (1954): 270–303. Leonard Proctor, "The Theology of Moise Amyraut Considered as a Reaction Against Seventeenth-Century Calvinism" (Ph.D. diss., University of Leeds, 1952). Schaff, *Creeds* 1:477–85. See also pp. 224–25, below.

CHAPTER IX
THE NATURE AND CAUSE OF THE ELECTION AND PREDESTINATION OF GOD
BY WHICH HE HAS ORDAINED TO ACCOMPLISH IN SOME PEOPLE THIS STATE AND TO LEAVE OTHERS ASIDE

Human nature is such that if God had not taken other counsel in ordaining to send his Son into the world to offer him to everyone as the universal Redeemer, no matter how great the charity from which this counsel proceeds, it would have been ineffective for the human race, and the sending and the suffering of his Son would have been entirely frustrated. It was thus incompatible with his wisdom to send his Son into the world, where he sustained an ignominious death, to produce nothing effective for human salvation and, with his clemency and his unfailing charity, to let the whole human race perish in its condemnation. No other means was left than for him to enter the world to display an effective manifestation of his power among humanity to overcome all the corruption in human understanding and will, so as to make them believe and embrace which is offered to them. The purpose, notwith-standing all the resistance maintained by the darkness of the intellect and the perversity of the will, was that humankind nevertheless yield to the evidence of the truth and acknowledge the necessity and excellence of the Redeemer and seek deliverance in him. So it is this counsel that we call *election* or *predestination*, in which God shows in the desire and abundantly excellent riches of his mercy toward those whom he has elected and predestined to give them faith, and the severity toward those whom he has abandoned to themselves, and his sovereign freedom in the dispensation of this worthy mystery.

And as far as mercy in concerned, it appears outside its own limits. For in that he saw the human race lying in such a miserable condition and indeed was touched by it, there is a good proof of a nature inclined to pity. But, on the other hand, inasmuch as justice required vengeance, he restricted his pity and prevented its being able to bear fruit in us. In that he was not content to remain touched with such pity, but rather sought in his wisdom the means of satisfying his justice, and in truth resolved to send his Son into the world and abandon him to the death on the cross for the universal salvation of the world, he showed a vehement compassion which was reinforced and, in a manner of speaking, was filled with wrath against the obstacles to his justice, and in reality overcame them. But nevertheless his compassion still presupposed that there was a condition in humanity that could be left behind and that makes it a matter of urgency, namely, by faith in the Redeemer proved by repentance. Apart from that repentance it does not appear that his mercy would be of any use to us. And just as a natural corre-spondence exists between the integrity of the creature and the bounty of the Creator, and some necessary relation between the human corruption and the justice of the judge of the world, it also seems that some appro-priate relation obtain between the faith and repentance of the sinner and the divine mercy. Accordingly, one can offer this foundation: God loves his creature when it is whole; God punishes man because he is sinful; thus one can propose this with some assurance: God pardons the sinner because with faith he relies on his mercy. But it is equally necessary that the love of God presuppose this condition to be in humankind and that it not be, even that it cannot be, unless he himself creates it by his power. Thus in this matter mercy exceeds all measure and all understand-ing. . . . [Here Amyraut cites Eph. 2:4-5, Rom. 8:29; 11:2; Ps. 1:6; Gal. 4:8-9; 1 Pet. 1:20; and elaborates the meaning of God's knowledge.]

The severity of God also appears in this counsel, in that he did not make this grace universal like the other, but restricted it to some and left others to themselves. For instead of the preceding grace envisioning the whole human race, as we have concluded above, this latter grace envisions only a portion and leaves the rest destitute. Moreover, those whom he elects and separates from the others in this way are much fewer in number; of them Christ said that many were called but few chosen [Matt. 20:16; 12:14]. It is indeed true, in that he proposed one same Redeemer universally for all, foreseeing that they would receive him, that he bore witness to a great charity as much to the ones as to the others. And those whom he has passed over do not have less than those whom he elected to recognize his mercy toward them. If they do not receive the Redeemer, they must attribute that to their own hardness and obstinacy; and if as a result of their incredulity they remain eternally lost, they cannot blame it upon anyone but themselves. For, as we will see later, if God is in respect to some the cause of faith and salvation, he is not the cause of the unbelief and of the damnation of others. If his election is efficacious in some, accomplishing really and in fact that upon which salvation depends, the incredulity of others does not come from their reprobation, as from the effective cause, but from their own blindness and perversity belonging to themselves. But in any case, that he employs such a mercy for some whose blindness and perversity he wishes to surmount, and does not employ it toward the others, and even that those he abandons to the hardness of their hearts are in greater numbers than the others, there is a just severity. . . . [Here Amyraut cites and comments on Rom. 9:18–21.]

And this freedom of which I have spoken is demonstrated again in this point. For thus one (and I have already said something about this earlier) might give some reason for the benevolence which God would manifest to his creatures if they had maintained their original integrity, and for the justice which he exercises when they degrade their original integrity, and also for the mercy which he grants them if they have recourse to it with assurance, and repentance, and that scripture itself is not silent about the reasons for the dispensation of these things. Neither does scripture teach us another reason for this choice of God to share with some the salutary gift of faith and leave other men behind in their condition than the free will of God. Otherwise it would seem strange that if misery is an object of compassion they be likewise miserable, and if the corruption of vice is an object of vengeance, they be likewise guilty. Neither, if you would look elsewhere than in the Word of God, would it be possible that you would discover anything other than this same free will. For where would you find it? Will it be in our works that God had foreseen from all eternity what we must do? Not at all! For all good works only follow faith and do not precede it. . . . [Here Amyraut cites and comments on Rom. 14:23; Heb. 11:6; Acts 15:9; Eph. 2:6–7; 2 Timothy 1:9; Rom. 10:17.]

For since faith does not come from us but is a gift of God, before foreseeing any faith in us, it was necessary that God ordain to put it there. And thus we seek the reason why he ordained it. And it appears that God has not ordained to give it to everyone . . . , otherwise everyone would believe, which is more than refuted by experience. For this reason, moreover [the apostle Paul] calls faith "the faith of the elect of God" to show that God has particularly elected some to give them this grace of believing. But it cannot be faith itself, as a thing foreseen and antecedent, which has moved some to believe rather than others. Would it then finally be because he had foreseen that they would use better than others the saving grace which is offered them? In no way! For the good use of saving grace consists in that one embrace it by faith, or in that after he has embraced it, one makes it bear fruit in good works. Therefore, since we have shown that this eternal decree to give faith cannot be founded on seeing faith beforehand nor on good works, it follows necessarily that it has not in a small way been founded on what God has foreseen to be the good use of grace. . . . [Here Amyraut repudiates attempting to distinguish degrees of efficacy in conversion and comments on Rom. 9:14.]

It is not that God, who is a wise being above everything that we can comprehend, has made this choice of men at random and has thrown upon them the arbitrary destiny as to who would perish and who would not. It might be that we have such thoughts. Although we might attribute it to the liberty of his good pleasure, let us not believe it proceeds with his ordinary wisdom. And St. Paul gives us to believe that after having proposed so beautiful an example of this liberty of God in the calling of the Jews rather than all the other nations of the world, then in the rejection of the Jews and in the calling of the nations to knowledge of him, and finally in the reunion of both these people in the same Christ by the mercy that God must one day offer to the posterity of Abraham, that he cries, "Oh the depth of the riches and the wisdom and the knowledge of God!" [Rom. 11:13]. This shows that it was not done without God having used his wisdom. But we want to say that in humankind there is no cause of this diversity of the favor of God and that he reveals to us nothing other than his will alone. So we who believe depend entirely on his mercy for our salvation; those who do not believe must attribute it to the hardness of their hearts; and those who seek the causes for which some have believed rather than others, some have been rejected rather than others, should adore the secrets of God

which cannot be fathomed and acknowledge that he is sovereignly free
in the dispensation of his graces.

Pierre du Moulin: On the Antecedent
and Consequent Will of God

Lutherans, Arminians, and Amyrauldians distinguished between God's antecedent and consequent wills. For them, God's antecedent will is the general
will of God which desires that all through Christ may be saved (cf. 1 Tim. 2:4).
But this expression of God's will is antecedent to the conduct of human
beings. Once confronted by grace, human beings may choose whether or not
to embrace the grace being offered them. It is this concrete choice of particular individuals that becomes the object of God's consequent will. By this
consequent will, God decrees to save those who through faith accept divine
grace.[19] The orthodox Reformed rejected this and similar distinctions. They
reasoned that since God is one, and thus not subject to human manipulation,
so too must we affirm the unity of God's will and its free operation in election,
irrespective of human merit.

Pierre du Moulin (Petrus Molinaeus) (1568–1658) was one of the most
capable theologians of his day, holding numerous positions including professor of philosophy and Greek at Leiden (1592–99), parish preacher at
Charenton (France) (1599–1620), and professor of theology at Sedan (France)
(1620–58). His *Anatome Arminianismi* was written in 1619 for the Synod of
Dort.

SOURCE

Pierre du Moulin, *Anatome Arminianismi, seu enucleatio controversiarum quae in Bel-
gio agitantur, super doctrinae de providentiae, de praedestinatione, de morte Christi, de
naturae et gratiae, et de conversione* (Leyden, 1619), chaps. 4 and 5; ET: "Of the Will of
God" and "Of the Antecedent and Consequent Will of God," *Anatomy of Arminianism*
(London, 1620), 20–41 (edited selections, with modified orthography, punctuation, and
grammar).

BIBLIOGRAPHY

Du Moulin's work covers a wide range of subjects. His classic study is *De cognitione dei
tractatus* (1624); ET: *A Treatise of the Knowledge of God, as excellently and compen-
diously handled by the famous and learned divine, Peter du Moulin*, trans. Robert
Codrington (London, 1634). See also Lucien Rimbault, *Pierre du Moulin, 1568–1658:
Un Pasteur classique à l'age classique* (Paris: Librairie Philosophique J. Vrin, 1966).

19. For a summary of the Lutheran view, see Heinrich Schmid, *The Doctrinal Theology of the
Evangelical Lutheran Church*, 3d ed., rev., trans. Charles A. Hay and Henry E. Jacobs (Philadelphia,
1889; reprint: Minneapolis: Augsburg, 1961), 278–84.

[The distinction in the will of God may in one sense be admitted], because there is a certain order among the purposes of God. Thus his will of creating man was in order prior to his will of feeding and clothing him. But with . . . Arminius it is called the "Antecedent" will of God, because it goes before the act of the human will; and they call the "Consequent" will of God that which is after the human will and which is thereby dependent on it. . . .

Between these two wills of God he puts this difference: that the antecedent will of God may be resisted, the consequent cannot. He would have it (a) that God should be disappointed in his antecedent will and fail of his propounded end; but (b) the consequent will of God cannot be frustrated but must necessarily be fulfilled. For he thinks that God does not always attain to that which he intends. . . .

Between these two wills of God (if any credit may be given to Arminius) the human will comes in which causes God to revoke his antecedent will . . . forces him to abandon his propounded end, leading him to turn toward another goal than that which he first intended. . . .

It is certainly plain that this "antecedent" will of God is not a will at all but only a desire . . . . And by this God is spoken of . . . as one wishing and desiring . . . [and thus] in an anthropopathic manner. . . .

It is also absurd, indeed impious, to affirm that God, to whom all things from eternity are not only foreseen but also provided for should intend anything that from eternity he knew would not come to pass. . . .

What a thing it is that hereby there is [posited] as resistance between these two wills of God, the latter of which corrects the former! For by this antecedent will God desires to do that which from eternity he is certain he shall not do. . . .

Herman Witsius: Predestination in Covenant Theology

This passage from the covenant theologian Witsius bases predestination in biblical sources, and, once again, displays the Reformed attentiveness to the original biblical languages. Covenant theology has been thought to temper the severity of orthodox predestinarian teaching by holding that God's decrees always operate in the context of a gracious covenantal relationship with humanity. The stress in the opening paragraph on the election of Christ himself has been renewed in the twentieth-century Reformed theology of Karl Barth.

SOURCE

Herman Witsius, *De oeconomia foederium Dei cum hominibur libri quattuor* (1677), Book 3, Chapter 4; ET: "Of Election," *The Oeconomy of the Covenants between God and Man, Comprehending a Complete Body of Divinity,* 3 vols. (New York: George Forman, 1798), 2:1–30.

BIBLIOGRAPHY

J. van Genderen, *Herman Witsius* ('s Gravenhage: Güido de Bres, 1953).

The beginning and first source of [the covenant of grace] is Election, both of Christ the Savior and of those to be saved by Christ. For even Christ was chosen of God, and, by an eternal and immutable decree, given to be our Savior; and therefore he is said to be foreordained before the foundation of the world (1 Pet. 1:20). And they whom Christ was to save were given to him by the same decree. They are therefore said to be chosen in Christ (John 17:6). That is, not only by Christ as God and consequently the elector of them, but also in Christ as Mediator . . . to be saved by his merit and power and to enjoy communion with him. . . .

We thus describe it: Election is the eternal, free, and immutable counsel of God about revealing the glory of his grace in the eternal salvation of some certain persons [cites Eph. 1:4–6].

We call election the counsel of God, by which term we mean that which is commonly called decree. Paul on this subject calls it πρόθεσις [*prothesis*], the "purpose" or "fore-appointment" of God. This term appears very choice to the apostle . . . and denotes a sure, firm, and fixed decree of God which he can never repent of and which depends on nothing out[side] of himself [i.e., not on human merit] but is founded only in [God's] good-pleasure [cites 2 Tim. 1:9; Eph. 1:11; Rom. 8:28; 9:11.]. . . .

This election to glory is not some "general" decree of God about saving the faithful and the godly who persevere in their faith and piety to the end of their life; but a particular designation of certain individual persons, whom God has enrolled as heirs of salvation. . . .

The very term προορίζειν [*proorizein*], "to predestinate," which the apostle more frequently uses on this subject, does not obscurely discover this truth. For as ὁρίζειν [*horizein*] signifies "to point out" or "ordain" a certain person [cites Acts 17:31; 10:42; Rom. 1:4] . . . so προορίζειν [*proorizein*], as applied to the heirs of eternal life, must signify "to enroll," "to write down" some certain persons as heirs in the eternal testament.

The Progress or Order of Salvation (Ordo Salutis)

As debate about predestination proceeded, differences arose over whether God's purpose to elect creatures to salvation logically preceded or succeeded God's purpose to create and allow the creature to fall. Since God's decisions, both to elect and to create, are eternal, what is at stake here is the *logical* and not the *temporal* procession of the order of salvation (*ordo salutis*), even though practically this is a subtle distinction to maintain. While the disputants agreed that God's decrees to permit humanity to fall and to rescue humanity from sin are eternally singular in the mind of God, the debate centered over whether to emphasize (a) the way in which creation and fall served the prior purpose of redemption, or (b) the way in which redemption follows creation and fall as a gracious remedy.

The first position, called "supralapsarianism," accents God's sovereign wisdom from before the foundation of the world. It envisions the *ordo salutis* thus: Election (motivated by the divine glory itself) → Creation → Fall → Justification → Sanctification → Glorification. Any other order, on this view, would posit a cause outside of God's will compelling the decree to elect. This scheme is *supra*lapsarian, since the decree to elect is logically *prior to* creation and fall (lapse). It emphasizes the unity of God's eternal purpose and depicts God as not being "surprised" by the fall nor as subsequently having to improvise salvation as a response. In supralapsarianism, the elect are chosen from among creatable (and thus not yet created) beings prior to their falling.

The second position, termed "infralapsarianism," believes the supralapsarian scheme implicitly makes the fall necessary in order for God to implement the prior decree to elect. This in turn implies, so they argued, that God is the author of evil. To avoid this result, the infralapsarians held that God's election is logically dependent upon and responds to humanity's lapse into sin. Thus for the infralapsarians the *ordo salutis* proceeds this way: Creation → Fall → Election → Justification → Sanctification → Glorification. This is called *infra*lapsarianism, since election occurs *within* the situation of fallen humanity. It emphasizes the diversity of the decrees, and it attempts to do greater justice to the fairness of God in that God does not determine the fate of individuals without noticing their sin. In infralapsarianism, the elect are chosen, in a manner of speaking, "after" the fall from among the mass of sinful humanity.

Supralapsarianism, represented below by Johannes Braun (1628–1708), professor at Gronigen, has claimed for its camp many of the most prominent theologians, including Zwingli and Calvin, although reference to these two is misleading since neither discussed any particular order in the decrees.[20] Infralapsarianism occupies the majority position in the Reformed confessions,[21] and it too claims many notable theologians, not the least being François Turretin, represented below.

Although overly abstruse reflection on the *ordo salutis* seems to violate the venerable Reformed insistence on avoiding speculative inquiry into the mystery of God's ways, the charts of Beza and Perkins show how the *ordo salutis* could provide pastors and other believers with an easily memorized theological framework for grasping the stages in the Christian life (see Rom 8:30).

Arminius, as one would expect, framed a different understanding of the order of the decrees reproduced below, to which Pierre du Moulin wrote a trenchant response.

Johannes Braun: Supralapsarianism

SOURCE

Johannes Braun, *Doctrina Foederum sive Systema Theologiae didacticae et elencticae* I. ii.9.24 (Amsterdam, 1688), in Heppe, *Reformed Dogmatics*, 160–61.

Some institute parts or acts of predestination from creation itself or from the fall of man; they are called sublapsarians because they so arranged things as if creation and the fall preceded every act of predestination. Others start its actions at the actual end which God has set before Himself in the creation of man, namely at the manifestation of His glory through the exercise of His justice and mercy. For creation itself and the lapse of man were predestinated by God; therefore predestination precedes creation and the fall. Therefore the parts or acts of predestination should be ordered in this way. (1) God decreed to manifest His glory by manifesting His mercy and righteousness. (2) He decreed to create a creature endowed with reason and after His own image, to whom He could manifest His glory. (3) He decreed to create that creature liable to lapse. (4) He decreed to permit his lapse. Who does not see so far that the object of predestination is man creatable and liable to lapse? There follow the remaining acts of predestination, which look

20. For examples of passages which may be interpreted as supralapsarian but which in fact make no mention of the order of the decrees, see Huldrych Zwingli, Sermon: "On the Providence of God" (1530), in Zwingli, *Works* 2:174–76; and John Calvin, *Institutes* III.22.7–8, pp. 955–57. For an account of high orthodox supralapsarianism, see Abraham Kuyper, Jr., *Johannes Maccovius* (Leiden: D. Donner, 1899).

21. See, e.g., *Confessio Fidei Gallicana* (Gallican Confession) (1559), Article 12 and *Confessio Belgica* (Belgic Confession) (1561, rev. 1619), Article 16, in Schaff, *Creeds* 3:366–67, 401 (for both the original French and ET).

to the means and execution or actual exercise of justice and mercy; therefore (5) He decreed to free certain men already lapsed from lapse and misery, to leave others in that state. In this sense the object of predestination is *homo lapsus,* not *labilis;* for he who is freed from wretchedness or left in it must of course have already lapsed into wretchedness. Those who say that lapsed man is the object of predestination, in arranging the act of predestination begin with this fifth and last act, that God wishes to free some from wretchedness, to leave others in wretchedness; but this is bad, since the end precedes the execution in every intention. Since then the end is the manifestation of God's glory, by the manifestation of His righteousness and mercy, at that point we must undoubtedly begin, since it is the first act in God's intention and so the first act in predestination. Thus strictly speaking the object of predestination as regards the end *homo creabilis et labilis.*

François Turretin: Infralapsarianism

SOURCE

François Turretin, *Institutio theologiae elencticae* (Geneva, 1688), q. 18; ET: "The Order of God's Decrees in Predestination: Whether any order is to be admitted in the Divine Decrees, and what it is?" The translation is modified from that of George Musgrave Giger, housed in Speer Memorial Library, Princeton Theological Seminary. Another translation is in Beardslee, *Reformed Dogmatics*, 443–44, 556–59.

Although Christian piety might readily spare this question, if people were content with things revealed, they would be content with knowing soberly, and would never strive to break into the secrets of God, for the purpose of rashly searching into his inscrutable counsels, and minutely dividing God's decrees, as if God was to be measured by the human rule. . . .

[Nevertheless] we embrace . . . the common one among the Reformed. . . .

XXII. According to this order, the *First* Decree with us is concerning the creation of man. The *Second,* concerning the permission of his fall, by which he drew with him into ruin and destruction all his posterity. The *Third,* concerning the election to salvation of some certain ones from the fallen human race, and the leaving of others in their native corruption and misery. The *Fourth,* concerning the sending of Christ into the world, as the Mediator and Surety of the Elect, who having appeased God's justice by his own most perfect obedience, might obtain for them alone full salvation. The *Fifth,* concerning effectually calling them by the preaching of Gospel, and the grace of the Holy Spirit, giving them faith, justifying, sanctifying and at length glorifying them.

XXIII. Three things principally prove that this order is indeed the most suitable. **1.** *The Scripture*: which subordinates the Mission of Christ, and Redemption to Election, Eph. i. 3, 4, 7; Rom. 29, 30; John iii. 16, and xvii. 2, 6; 1 Thess. v. 9; 1 Pet. i. 2; And derives from the merit of Christ all the saving gifts of the Spirit, to wit, faith and repentance, John xvi. 7; Rom. viii. 32; Eph. i. 3, 4, 5; Philip. i. 29; Heb. ix. 14, 15. **2.** *The nature of the thing*, because in the legitimate order of things the intention of the end ought to precede the intention of the means, so that in the execution the means should first be used, before the end is arrived at. Now here the end intended by God in the covenant of grace, is the salvation of the Elect, but the means to procure it are Christ, and the call to him by the Word and the Spirit: For neither would Christ ever have been sent into the world, unless the Elect were to be redeemed; Nor would the Gospel have been preached, unless the same were to be collected into the mystical Body of Christ; Whence Paul says *it pleased God* by the preaching of the Gospel, *to save them that believe by the foolishness of preaching*, 1 Cor. i. 21; and Eph. iv. 12, he teaches that the end of the ministry and of the gifts bestowed by Christ, is no other than *the perfecting of the saints and the edifying of the body of Christ*. For that reason it is necessary, that the Elect who alone are to be saved and edified in the Body of Christ, should be considered antecedently to the mission of Christ, and the preaching of the Gospel, which was instituted for their sake; and so the object of vocation are the elect, not of election the called. **3.** The *economical operation of the Persons of the Holy Trinity* in the work of salvation; For as each of them concurs to it according to the mode of working peculiar and proper to himself, the Father by electing the Son by redeeming, and the Holy Spirit by regenerating; so they ought to agree in the object about which they are occupied so that there may be the same periphery of the Election of the Father, of the Redemption of the Son, and the Regeneration of the Holy Spirit, so that as many as are elected by the Father, should be redeemed by the Son, regenerated by the Spirit, and no one be given to the Son to be redeemed, who was not elected by the Father, and who is not to be sanctified by the spirit.

XXIV. Although in truth we think the Decrees of God should be thus arranged, yet we must always bear in mind that this is said only with respect to our manner of conception, who are compelled to divide into various inadequate conceptions what we cannot compass in one single conception; but not on the part of God himself who decreed with himself all these things by a single and most simple act, as much those

110

things which look to the end, as those which look to the means; in which sense it is rightly said that there is in God only one single Decree, embracing at once the end and the means, by which he determined to have mercy unto salvation upon some above others, and to save them by and on account of Christ. In this we think we ought to acquiesce with simplicity and soberness; that we may be solicitous rather concerning the reducing to practice this saving doctrine by the desire of piety and sanctification, and concerning the confirmation of our Election and call by good works, than concerning the investigation of vain and interminable questions, which the profane temerity of men is accustomed to agitate here, feeding an idle curiosity, but not building up faith.

XXV. And here is the profitable and saving use of the doctrine of Predestination, that it may not afford any occasion either to *the desperation* of men, or to their profane *license*, the two terrible rocks, upon which the wicked, falsely abusing it, are accustomed to strike.

Theodore Beza and William Perkins: The "Table" or "Chain" of Salvation

SOURCES

(A) Theodore Beza, Diagram *ordo rerum decretarum*, or *Tabula praedestinationis*, in *Summa totius Christianismi* (1555), *Opera* I.170s; reproduced in Heppe, *Reformed Dogmatics*, 147–48. (B) William Perkins, "The Table Declaring the Order," from *A Golden Chain, or The Description of Theology*.

BIBLIOGRAPHY

Richard A. Muller, "Perkins' *A Golden Chaine*: Predestinarian System or Schematized *Ordo Salutis*?" *Sixteenth Century Journal* 9 (1978): 69–81. Muller argues that Perkins's table places Christ at the center of salvation thus avoiding a common criticism of Reformed theology, namely, that the decree of predestination subordinates and renders Christ superfluous. See also Perkins, "Of God's Work and His Decree," "Of Predestination," chap. 6 and chap. 7, par. 1 in *A Golden Chain, or The Description of Theology* (1590, 1592); ET: 183–86.

A. THEODORE BEZA: TABLE OF PREDESTINATION

See page 112.

B. WILLIAM PERKINS: A GOLDEN CHAIN

See page 113.

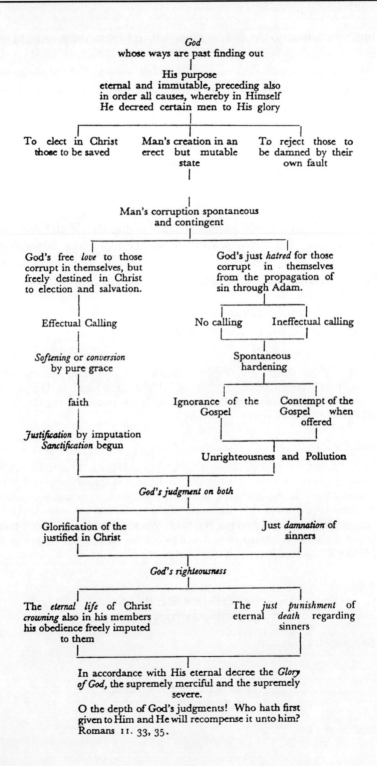

God
whose ways are past finding out

His purpose
eternal and immutable, preceding also
in order all causes, whereby in Himself
He decreed certain men to His glory

| To elect in Christ those to be saved | Man's creation in an erect but mutable state | To reject those to be damned by their own fault |

Man's corruption spontaneous
and contingent

God's free *love* to those corrupt in themselves, but freely destined in Christ to election and salvation.

God's just *hatred* for those corrupt in themselves from the propagation of sin through Adam.

Effectual Calling

No calling   Ineffectual calling

Softening or *conversion*
by pure grace

Spontaneous
hardening

faith

Ignorance of the Gospel   Contempt of the Gospel when offered

Justification by imputation
Sanctification begun

Unrighteousness and Pollution

God's judgment on both

Glorification of the
justified in Christ

Just *damnation* of
sinners

God's righteousness

The *eternal life* of Christ *crowning* also in his members his obedience freely imputed to them

The *just punishment* of eternal *death* regarding sinners

In accordance with His eternal decree the *Glory of God*, the supremely merciful and the supremely severe.

O the depth of God's judgments! Who hath first given to Him and He will recompense it unto him? Romans 11. 33, 35.

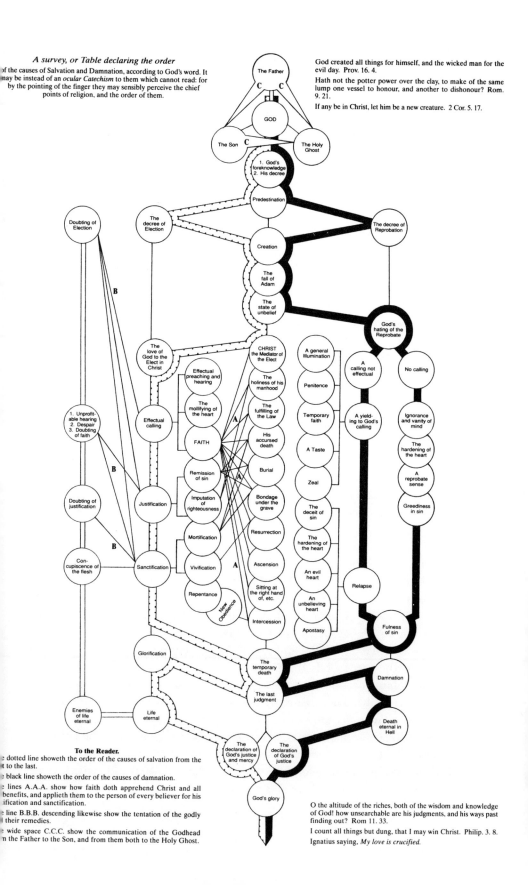

A survey, or Table declaring the order

of the causes of Salvation and Damnation, according to God's word. It may be instead of an *ocular Catechism* to them which cannot read: for by the pointing of the finger they may sensibly perceive the chief points of religion, and the order of them.

God created all things for himself, and the wicked man for the evil day. Prov. 16. 4.

Hath not the potter power over the clay, to make of the same lump one vessel to honour, and another to dishonour? Rom. 9. 21.

If any be in Christ, let him be a new creature. 2 Cor. 5. 17.

The Father

C   C

GOD

The Son   C

The Holy Ghost

1. God's foreknowledge
2. His decree

Predestination

Doubting of Election

The decree of Election

The decree of Reprobation

Creation

The fall of Adam

The state of unbelief

God's hating of the Reprobate

The love of God to the Elect in Christ

CHRIST the Mediator of the Elect

A general Illumination

A calling not effectual

No calling

Effectual preaching and hearing

The holiness of his manhood

Penitence

1. Unprofit-able hearing
2. Despair
3. Doubting of faith

Effectual calling

The mollifying of the heart

The fulfilling of the Law

Temporary faith

A yield-ing to God's calling

Ignorance and vanity of mind

FAITH

His accursed death

A Taste

The hardening of the heart

Remission of sin

Burial

Zeal

A reprobate sense

Doubting of justification

Justification

Imputation of righteousness

Bondage under the grave

The deceit of sin

Greediness in sin

Mortification

Resurrection

The hardening of the heart

Con-cupiscence of the flesh

Sanctification

Vivification

Ascension

An evil heart

Relapse

Repentance

New Obedience

Sitting at the right hand of, etc.

An unbelieving heart

Intercession

Apostasy

Fulness of sin

Glorification

The temporary death

Damnation

The last judgment

Enemies of life eternal

Life eternal

Death eternal in Hell

To the Reader.

e dotted line showeth the order of the causes of salvation from the t to the last.

e black line showeth the order of the causes of damnation.

e lines A.A.A. show how faith doth apprehend Christ and all benefits, and applieth them to the person of every believer for his ification and sanctification.

e line B.B.B. descending likewise show the tentation of the godly l their remedies.

e wide space C.C.C. show the communication of the Godhead m the Father to the Son, and from them both to the Holy Ghost.

The declaration of God's justice and mercy

The declaration of God's justice

God's glory

O the altitude of the riches, both of the wisdom and knowledge of God! how unsearchable are his judgments, and his ways past finding out? Rom 11. 33.

I count all things but dung, that I may win Christ. Philip. 3. 8.

Ignatius saying, *My love is crucified.*

Jacob Arminius: Predestinarian Decree
Subject to Human Belief

SOURCE

Jacob Arminius, *Verklarung van Jacobus Arminius* (1608), Article I, part 5; ET: *Declaration of Sentiments*, in Arminius, *Works* 1:653–54.

I have hitherto been stating those opinions concerning the article of Predestination which are inculcated in our churches and in the University of Leyden, and of which I disapprove. I have at the same time produced my own reasons, why I form such an unfavourable judgment concerning them; and I will now declare my own opinions on this subject, which are of such a description as, according to my views, appear most conformable to the word of God.

I. The FIRST absolute decree of God concerning the salvation of sinful man, is that by which he decreed to appoint his Son Jesus Christ for a Mediator, Redeemer, Saviour, Priest and King, who might destroy sin by his own death, might by his obedience obtain the salvation which had been lost, and might communicate it by his own virtue.

II. The SECOND precise and absolute decree of God, is that in which he decreed to receive into favour *those who repent and believe* and, in Christ, for HIS sake and through HIM, to effect the salvation of such penitents and believers as persevered to the end; but to leave in sin and under wrath *all impenitent persons and unbelievers,* and to damn them as aliens from Christ.

III. The THIRD DIVINE decree is that by which God decreed to administer *in a sufficient and efficacious manner* the MEANS which were necessary for repentance and faith; and to have such administration instituted (1) according to the *Divine Wisdom,* by which God knows what is proper and becoming both to his mercy and his severity, and (2) according to *Divine Justice,* by which He is prepared to adopt whatever his wisdom may prescribe and to put it in execution.

IV. To these succeeds the FOURTH decree, by which God decreed to save and damn certain particular persons. This decree has its foundation in the foreknowledge of God, by which he knew from all eternity those individuals who *would,* through his preventing grace, *believe,* and, through his subsequent grace *would persevere,*—according to the before-described administration of those means which are suitable and proper for conversion and faith; and, by which foreknowledge, he likewise knew those who *would not believe and persevere.*

Pierre du Moulin: Critique of Arminius

SOURCE

Pierre du Moulin, *Anatome Arminianismi* (1619), chap. 12; ET: "What Predestination Is," *Anatomy of Arminianism*, 85–86.

By [his account of the decrees of predestination] it is plain that Arminius did not understand what the decree of predestination was. For the decree of predestination is that whereby God appointed what he will do with us, and not that which he would have us do. It is unfitting therefore that Arminius places among the decrees of God that [supposed] will of God whereby God [is thought to have] appointed those to be saved who shall believe, because it incorrectly confuses the commandment of God with the will of God. . . . [T]he rules of the Gospel no more belong to the providence of God (and therefore not to predestination) than do the rules of the Law.

Therefore of [Arminius's] four decrees (see p. 114), the second [supposing that God decrees eternal life on the basis of belief foreseen] is to be wiped out and a place appointed for it instead under the doctrine of the Gospel and not in the eternal decree and secret predestination.

THE COVENANTS

From the formal declaration of God's gracious initiative toward humanity in election, we turn now to the substantive workings of that initiative in human history. One of the chief ways in which Reformed theology has understood this "history of salvation" is through the biblical concept of covenant. Based on the pronouncement "I will be your God, and you will be my people" (e.g., Jer. 7:23; 11:4; 30:22; 31:33; 32:38; Ezek. 36:28; Heb. 8:10), the Reformed theology of covenant participated in tensions, some of which we have already encountered and others which we shall encounter below: tensions between God's universal will to save and the particularization of that will in the life of some individuals but not others; between the consistency of God's gracious character and the diversity of God's acts in history; between God as transcendent object of theological thought and God as dynamic subject of theologically informed action; between the primacy of God's grace in salvation and the integrity of the human response to the conditions of righteous living.

Reformed covenantal reflection began in Zwingli's defense of infant baptism against the Anabaptists. This early Zurich theology proclaimed a single covenant of grace, a conviction no doubt emanating in significant part from the powerful Reformed belief in the unity of God. Over time, perception of the duality within the one covenant grew stronger, in part through an exegetical response to the biblical material, in part for the purpose of explaining the character of God's grace in election,[22] and perhaps in part under the impact of the dichotomizing logic of the influential French humanist, Peter Ramus (Pierre à la Ramée) (1515–72).[23] Thus the covenant was delineated into a general and special covenant, or a conditional covenant of works and an unconditional covenant of grace. The covenant of works provided a basis for explaining the moral and social responsibility of all persons.

BIBLIOGRAPHY

Barth, *Church Dogmatics* IV/1, pp. 22–34, 54–66. Louis Berkhof, *Systematic Theology*, 4th rev. ed. (Grand Rapids: Wm. B. Eerdmans, 1949; reprint, 1979), 211–18, 262–301. Jack W. Cottrell, "Covenant and Baptism in the Theology of Huldreich Zwingli" (Ph.D. diss., Princeton Theological Seminary, 1971). Heinrich Heppe, *Dogmatik des deutschen Protestantismus im sechzehnten Jahrhundert* (1857). Peter Y. De Jong, *The Covenant Idea in New England Theology: 1620–1847* (Grand Rapids: Wm. B. Eerdmans, 1945). Delbert R. Hillers, *Covenant: The History of a Biblical Idea* (Baltimore and London: Johns Hopkins University Press, 1969). D. J. McCarthy, *Treaty and Covenant* (Rome: Biblical Institute, 1978). Perry Miller, *The New England Mind: The Seventeenth Century* (Cambridge and London: Belknap, Harvard University Press), esp. Appendix B, "The Federal School of Theology." Holmes Rolston III, *John Calvin versus the Westminster Confession* (Richmond, Va.: John Knox, 1972). Gottlob Schrenk, *Gottesreich und Bund im älteren Protestantismus, vornehmlich Johannes Coccejus* (Gütersloh: Bertelsmann, 1923, 1987). Emanuel Graf von Korff, *Die Anfänge der Foederaltheologie und ihre Ausgestaltung in Zürich und Holland* (Bonn: Emil Eisele, 1908). David A. Weir, *The Origins of the Federal Theology in Sixteenth-Century Reformation Thought* (Oxford: Clarendon, 1990).
See also the material cited in the selections below.

Heinrich Bullinger: A Universal Covenant of Grace

The early Zurich theology preached a universal "postlapsarian"[24] covenant of grace which is bilateral, contemplating a mutual pact between God and

22. This is the thesis of the important work by David A. Weir, *The Origins of the Federal Theology in Sixteenth-Century Reformation Thought* (Oxford: Clarendon, 1990). Weir especially thinks the covenant theology sought to explain the tension between God's sovereignty and the advent of sin.
23. A Calvinist killed in the St. Bartholomew's Day Massacre, Ramus rejected the dominant Aristotelian logic and replaced it with a system which stressed rhetoric, humanistic studies, and the practical life. See Walter J. Ong, *Ramus, Method, and the Decay of Dialogue* (New York: Octagon Books, 1974); and Wilbur Samuel Howell, *Logic and Rhetoric in England, 1500–1700* (Princeton: Princeton University Press, 1956).
24. That is, the covenant was established after humanity's lapse into sin, or fall.

humanity, with the conditions that God makes certain promises and humanity undertakes certain duties of obedience. It is a single covenant, binding together all of God's covenantal transactions (or "leagues") with Adam, Noah, Abraham, and Moses in the Old Testament, which are seen as anticipations of the covenant in Jesus Christ. The unity of the covenant flows from the unity of God's ways with humanity. In the passage below, Heinrich Bullinger explains the covenant idea in a sermon on the law.

SOURCE

Heinrich Bullinger, "Of the Ceremonial Laws of God," in *Decades* 2:169–75.

BIBLIOGRAPHY

Heinrich Bullinger, *De testamento seu foedere Dei unico & aeterno* (Zurich: Froschauer, 1534); ET: *A Brief Exposition of the One and Eternal Testament or Covenant of God*, in *Fountainhead of Federalism: Heinrich Bullinger and the Covenantal Tradition*, trans. Charles S. McCoy and J. Wayne Baker (Louisville, Ky.: Westminster/John Knox, 1991). J. Wayne Baker, *Heinrich Bullinger and the Covenant: The Other Reformed Tradition*. Peter Walser, *Die Prädestination bei Heinrich Bullinger im Zusammenhang mit seiner Gotteslehre*, Studien zur Dogmengeschichte und systematischen Theologie 12 (Zurich: Zwingli Verlag, 1957).

[W]hen God's mind was to declare the favour and good-will that he bare to mankind, and to make us men partakers wholly of himself and his goodness, by pouring himself out upon us, to our great good and profit; it pleased him to make a league or covenant with mankind. Now he did not first begin the league with Abraham, but did renew to him the covenant that he had made a great while before. For he did first of all make it with Adam, the first father of us all, immediately upon his transgression, when he received him, silly wretch,[1] into his favour again, and promised his only-begotten Son, in whom he would be reconciled to the world, and through whom he would wholly bestow himself upon us, by making us partakers of all his good and heavenly blessings, and by binding us unto himself in faith and due obedience. This ancient league, made first with Adam, he did afterward renew to Noah, and after that again with the blessed patriarch Abraham. And again, after the space of four hundred years, it was renewed under Moses at the mount Sinai, where the conditions of the league were at large written in the two tables, and many ceremonies added thereunto. But most excellently of all, most clearly and evidently, did our Lord and Saviour Jesus Christ himself[2] shew forth that league; who, wiping away all the ceremonies, types, figures, and shadows, brought in instead of them the very truth, and did most absolutely fulfil and finish the old league. . . .

But now I return to the league which was renewed with Abraham.

We are expressly taught in Genesis, who they were that made the league; that is, the living, eternal, and omnipotent God, who is the chief maker, preserver, and governor of all things; and Abraham with all his seed, that is, with all the faithful, of what nation or country soever they be. For so doth the Apostle expound the seed of Abraham, especially in his epistle to the Galatians, where he saith, "If ye be Christ's, then are ye the seed of Abraham, and heirs by promise" [Gal. iii. 29.].

The time, how long this league should endure, is eternal, and without end or term of time. For although, in the renewings or declarations of the league, many things were added which afterward did vanish away, especially when Christ was come in the flesh; yet notwithstanding, in the substantial and chiefest points, ye can find nothing altered or changed. For God is always the God of his people: he doth always demand and require of them faithful obedience; as may most evidently be perceived in the new Testament.

For there are two points, or especial conditions, contained in this league: the first whereof declareth what God doth promise, and what he will do for his confederates; I mean, what we may look for at his hands: the second comprehendeth the duty of man, which he doth owe to God, his confederate and sovereign prince.

1. *jam profugum*, Lat.; now become an outcast.
2. *tandem*, Lat.; at length.

John Calvin: One Covenant Under the Old and New Testaments

Continuing the theme of a single covenant established after the fall, Calvin maintains the essential unity and consistency of the Old and New Testaments, which are both mediated through Jesus Christ and operate on the basis of grace.[25] Rather than Bullinger's bilateral covenant, Calvin thinks of a unilateral promise resting on God's saving action in Jesus Christ.

SOURCE

Institutes II.10.1–5, pp. 428–32.

BIBLIOGRAPHY

Institutes II.9–11. J. Wayne Baker, *Heinrich Bullinger and the Covenant*, 193–98. Everett H. Emerson, "Calvin and Covenant Theology," *Church History* 25 (1956): 136–44. Paul

25. To summarize, the Old Testament is handed down physically, the New Testament spiritually; the Old is but a shadow, the New the substance of truth; the Old follows the law's letter, the New its spirit; the Old operates through fear, the New leads to freedom; and the Old is limited to one nation, the New spreads to many nations.

Helm, "Calvin and the Covenant," *Evangelical Quarterly* (1983): 65–81. Anthony A. Hoekema, "The Covenant of Grace in Calvin's Teaching," *Calvin Theological Journal* 2 (1967): 133–61. M. E. Oesterhaven, "Calvin on the Covenant," *Reformed Review* 33 (1980): 136–49.

[A]ll men adopted by God into the company of his people since the beginning of the world were covenanted to him by the same law and by the bond of the same doctrine as obtains among us. It is very important to make this point. . . . Accordingly I shall add, by way of appendix, how far the condition of the patriarchs in this fellowship differed from ours, even though they participated in the same inheritance and hoped for a common salvation with us by the grace of the same Mediator. The testimonies that we have gathered from the Law and the Prophets to prove this make plain that God's people have never had any other rule of reverence and piety. Nevertheless, because writers often argue at length about the difference between the Old and the New Testament, thus arousing some misgiving in the simple reader's mind . . . , let us look in passing at the similarities and differences between the covenant that the Lord made of old with the Israelites before Christ's advent, and that which God has now made with us after his manifestation.

Both can be explained in one word. The covenant made with all the patriarchs is so much like ours in substance and reality that the two are actually one and the same. Yet they differ in the mode of dispensation. . . .

Here we must take our stand on three main points. First, we hold that carnal prosperity and happiness did not constitute the goal set before the Jews to which they were to aspire. Rather, they were adopted into the hope of immortality; and assurance of this adoption was certified to them by oracles, by the law, and by the prophets. Secondly, the covenant by which they were bound to the Lord was supported, not by their own merits, but solely by the mercy of the God who called them. Thirdly, they had and knew Christ as Mediator, through whom they were joined to God and were to share in his promises.

Zacharias Ursinus: Covenant Theology at Heidelberg

The University of Heidelberg, where Zacharias Ursinus was a prominent professor, seems to have been instrumental in the development of a dual concept of covenant. While it is true that Ursinus sees a duality of circumstances between the old and new covenants, this duality is still subordinate in substance to the one covenant in Jesus Christ.

SOURCE

Zacharius Ursinus, *Explicationum catecheticarum* (1594), commentary on q. 18; ET: "Of the Covenant of God," in Ursinus, *Commentary*, 96–100.

BIBLIOGRAPHY

In addition to works cited elsewhere, see the following, in which Ursinus is viewed as instrumental in the development of the double covenant: Robert Letham, "The *Foedus Operum*: Some Factors Accounting for Its Development," *Sixteenth Century Journal* 14/4 (1983): 457–67. David A. Weir, *The Origins of the Federal Theology in Sixteenth-Century Reformation Thought*.

For the argument that Ursinus was not an originator of a double covenant, see Derk Visser, "The Covenant in Zacharias Ursinus," *Sixteenth Century Journal* 18/4 (1987): 531–44.

A covenant in general is a mutual contract, or agreement between two parties, in which the one party binds itself to the other to accomplish something upon certain conditions, giving or receiving something, which is accompanied with certain outward signs and symbols, for the purpose of ratifying in the most solemn manner the contract entered into, and for the sake of confirming it, that the engagement may be kept inviolate. From this general definition of a covenant, it is easy to perceive what we are to understand by the Covenant here spoken of, which we may define as a mutual promise and agreement, between God and men, in which God gives assurance to men that he will be merciful to them, remit their sins, grant unto them a new righteousness, the Holy Spirit, and eternal life by and for the sake of his Son, our Mediator. And, on the other side, men bind themselves to God in this covenant that they will exercise repentance and faith, or that they will receive with a true faith this great benefit which God offers, and render such obedience as will be acceptable to him. This mutual engagement between God and man is confirmed by those outward signs which we call sacraments, which are holy signs, declaring and sealing unto us God's good will, and our thankfulness and obedience.

A testament is the last will of a testator, in which he at his death declares what disposition he wishes to be made of his goods, or possessions.

In the Scriptures, the terms Covenant and Testament are used in the same sense, for the purpose of explaining more fully and clearly the idea of this Covenant of God; for both of them refer to and express our reconciliation with God, or the mutual agreement between God and men. . . .

This covenant could only be made by a Mediator, as may be inferred from the fact that we, as one of the parties, were not able to satisfy God for our sins, so as to be restored to his favor. Yea, such was our miserable condition, that we would not have accepted of the benefit of redemption had it been purchased by another. Then God as the other party, could not, on account of his justice, admit us into his favor without a sufficient satisfaction. We were the enemies of God, and hence there could be no way of access to him, unless by the intercession of Christ, the Mediator, as has been fully shown in the remarks which we have made upon the question—Why was a Mediator necessary? We may conclude, therefore, that this reconciliation was possible only by the satisfaction and death of Christ, the Mediator. . . .

This covenant is one in substance, but two-fold in circumstances; or it is one as it respects the general conditions upon which God enters into an engagement with us, and we with him; and it is two as it respects the conditions which are less general, or as some say, as it respects the mode of its administration.

The Covenant is one in substance. 1. Because there is but one God, one Mediator between God and man, Jesus Christ, one way of reconciliation, one faith, and one way of salvation for all who are and have been saved from the beginning. . . .

2. There is but one covenant, because the principal conditions, which are called the substance of the covenant, are the same before and since the incarnation of Christ; for in each testament God promises to those that repent and believe, the remission of sin; whilst men bind themselves, on the other hand, to exercise faith in God, and to repent of their sins.

But there are said to be two covenants, the old and the new, as it respects the circumstances and conditions which are less general, which constitute the form, or the mode of administration, contributing to the principal conditions, in order that the faithful, by their help, may obtain those which are general.

Johannes Wollebius: Covenant of Works, Covenant of Grace

Here in the Basel theology of Johannes Wollebius (1586–1629), a student of Polanus (1561–1610), a clear duality has evolved between a covenant of works, in which humanity is expected to obey God's commands prior to the fall under threat of punishment, and a covenant of grace, in which God's gracious promise of salvation is revealed in Jesus Christ. Note that this contrast does not correspond to the traditional distinction between the Old and New Testaments, for, typical of Reformed theology, the dispensations of Israel and the church are both thought to be a part of the covenant of grace (pp. 118–19, above). In opposition to the theology of Zwingli, Bullinger, and Calvin, however, the covenant of grace is now no longer a universal covenant but a covenant made specifically with the elect after the fall. Note that Wollebius sees the entire Trinity at work in the covenant as its efficient cause.

SOURCE

Johannes Wollebius, *Compendium Theologiae Christianae* (Basel, 1626), Book I, chaps. 8, 21; ET: "God's Rule over Men in the State of Innocence," and "The Covenant of Grace," in Beardslee, *Reformed Dogmatics*, 64–65, 117–19.

Chapter VIII: God's Rule over Men in the State of Innocence

(I)

1. . . . . God's rule over human beings is apparent in the states of innocence and of misery, and finally in the state of glory and grace.

2. His rule over men in a state of innocence consisted of giving a covenant of works to him, by which, under the condition of obedience, he promised everlasting happiness, and warned of death for disobedience.

Propositions

I. God's covenant with man is twofold, a covenant of works and one of grace: the first before the fall, and the second after it.

II. The covenant of works was confirmed by a twofold sacrament: the tree of life and the tree of knowledge of good and evil, both of which were located in the midst of paradise.

III. Their purpose was twofold: (1) That man's obedience might be put to the proof, by his eating or abstaining; (2) that the first might signify eternal happiness for those who obeyed, and the second, the loss of the highest good and the coming of the greatest evil for those who disobeyed.

IV. Therefore, the tree of life is so called for its sacramental meaning, not because life-giving power was in it.

V. Likewise, the tree of the knowledge of good and evil has its name because it signifies the highest good and evil, and because of the event associated with it.

For through it man learned how much good he lost, and what evil he brought upon himself.

Chapter XXI: The Covenant of Grace

(I)

1. The result and benefit of calling is the external fellowship [*communio*] of the covenant of grace, and of the church.

2. The external fellowship of the covenant of grace is that those who are called are considered a people of the covenant and of God.

3. This is said by analogy; actually, some are really people of God, and some only in external profession.

4. Both the giving [*oblatio*] and the sealing [*obsignatio*] of the covenant of grace must be considered.

5. The giving of the covenant of grace is the act by which God promises himself as a father in Christ to the elect, if they live in filial obedience.

Propositions

I. This is not to be understood as that universal covenant which God made with all creatures, not as the covenant of works with our first parents, but as the covenant that God made with us, out of pure mercy, after the fall. . . .

III. The efficient cause [of the covenant of grace] is the entire Holy Trinity, in particular [*singulariter*] Christ the God-man, the angel of the covenant. . . .

IV. The content [*materia*] of the covenant of grace is the agreement between two parties, God and man. God promises to be our God in Christ the Lord; man, in return, promises obedience of faith and life.

V. The form of the covenant consists of mutual obligation, but relations between unequals; the promise and obligation of God is free, whereas that of man is a debt and requirement.

VI. The purpose of the offering of the covenant is, like that of common calling, the glory of God and the salvation of the elect.

VII. The subject or object to whom the covenant is offered is all who are called, but strictly speaking [*proprie*] it is only the elect.

The covenant is offered to all who are called, but only the elect enjoy the promises of the covenant.

VIII. The administration of the covenant of grace is to be seen in its adjuncts.

IX. This administration is distinguished, with respect to time, into the old and the new covenant or testament.

X. The old testament is the covenant of grace, as administered until the time of the manifestation of Christ.

XI. There were three forms under which it was administered: the first for the period from Adam to Abraham, the second for that from Abraham to Moses, and the third for that from Moses to Christ. . . .

XIV. The new testament is the covenant of grace as administered after the coming of Christ.

XV. The old and new testaments are the same in substance; Christ is the testator of both, both have the same promise of grace in him, and in each is the same requirement of obedience of faith and life.

XVI. Therefore, those who teach that there are real differences between the old and the new testaments, such as the difference between the covenant of works and that of faith, or between law and gospel, are wrong; each testament or covenant is a covenant of grace. And each one presents law and gospel.

William Ames: Puritan Development of Covenant Theology

Given its dynamic sense of the movement of God in the history of salvation, Puritan theology naturally resonated with the theme of covenant. Thus for William Ames the duality of the covenant is not static but works itself out in a progressive movement from the covenant of works to a covenant of grace. The covenant of works is a "transaction" that lies broken through human disobedience; the covenant of grace is a "testament" that is fulfilled in the free promise of God. Again, the works/grace dichotomy does not parallel the differences between the Old and New Testaments, which are distinguished in administration but not in content.

SOURCE

William Ames, *Medulla SS. Theologiae* (1623, 1629), Book I, chap. 10, pars. 1, 3, 9–13; chap. 24, pars. 10–12; ET: "Special Government of Intelligent Creatures," and "The Application of Christ," in Ames, *Marrow*, 110–11, 150.

BIBLIOGRAPHY

Jens G. Møller, "The Beginnings of Puritan Covenant Theology," *Journal of Ecclesiastical History* 24 (1973): 23–32. Leonard J. Trinterud, "The Origins of Puritanism," *Church History* 20 (1951): 37–57. John von Rohr, "Covenant and Assurance in Early English Puritanism," *Church History* 34 (1965): 195–203.

Special Government of Intelligent Creatures

1. Special government is God's government of rational creatures in a moral way. . . .

3. This special government does not exclude the basic government of the reasonable creature, which is common to all creatures, but it is rather added to it. . . .

9. From this special way of governing rational creatures there arises a covenant between God and them. This covenant is, as it were, a kind of transaction of God with the creature whereby God commands, promises, threatens, fulfills; and the creature binds itself in obedience to God so demanding. Deut. 26:16–19, *This day the Lord your God commands you . . . this day you have demanded a guarantee from the Lord [a Iehova stipulatus es sponsionem hodie] . . . the Lord demanded a guarantee from you this day . . . to make you high . . . so that you be a holy people.*

10. This way of entering into covenant is not between those who are equal before the law but between lord and servant. It, therefore, rightly pertains to the government. It is very rightly called the covenant not of man but of God, who is the author and chief executor. Deut. 8:18, *That he may confirm his covenant.*

11. In this covenant the moral deeds of the intelligent creature lead either to happiness as a reward or to unhappiness as a punishment. The latter is deserved, the former not.

12. The proper difference, therefore, between a good work and sin is that a good work expects happiness from someone else as a reward. On the other hand, when this is lacking, evil works become supremely evil.

13. Hence arises the force and reason of conscience which is an intelligent creature's self-judgment in his subjection to God's judgment. . . .

The Application of Christ

10. The application by which God fulfills with greatest firmness what was contained in a covenant formerly made and broken is called in the Scriptures the *New covenant*, Heb. 8:8, 10; *A covenant of life, salvation, and grace*, Rom. 4:16; Gal. 3:18. In the same sense it is also called the *Gospel*, Rom. 1:16; *The good word of God*, Heb. 6:5; *A faithful saying and worthy of all acceptation*, 1 Tim. 1:15; *A good doctrine*, 1 Tim. 4:6; *The word of life*, Phil. 2:16; *The word of reconciliation*, 2 Cor. 5:19; *The gospel of peace*, Eph. 2:17 and 6:15; *The gospel of salvation. The word of truth*, Eph. 1:13; *The arm of God*, Isa. 53:1; *The fragrance of life to life*, 2 Cor. 2:16.

11. It is called a covenant because it is a firm promise. In the Scriptures every firm determination, even though pertaining to lifeless things,

is called a covenant. Jer. 33:20, 25, *My covenant with the day and my covenant with the night. . . . If my covenant be not with day and night, if I appoint not the statutes of heaven and earth.*

12. Yet because it is a free gift and confirmed by the death of the giver, it is more properly called a testament, not a covenant, Heb. 9:16. This sense is not found in a firm determination, which is not so properly called a testament as a covenant. . . .

Johannes Cocceius: Covenant as the Foundation of a Systematic Theology

Johannes Cocceius through his careful exegetical work carried covenant theology to new heights of systematization. According to Cocceius, the covenant of works established in Adam before the fall was a one-sided (*monopleuric*) promise by which God inscribed on Adamic humanity the law of nature, which required humanity to respond in the obedience of works to God's precepts. This universal covenant exists only by virtue of God's decision to strike the bargain (*ex pacto*) and so does not render God indebted to humanity in any way; on the other hand, if one obeys, one can expect God to fulfill the divine end of the bargain.

The covenant of works was undone by a series of five modifications; these were set in motion in Genesis but fulfilled in the new dispensation of Jesus Christ. First, the covenant is breached by human sin. Second, in an eternal, intertrinitarian pact between the Father and the Son, God decides to institute the covenant of grace: a new covenant, unbreakable, and sealed in the "suretyship" of Jesus Christ (on this, see the section on atonement, pp. 228–32, below). Third, the new covenant of grace is promulgated in the Old Testament (its first economy) in which circumcision and passover prefigure salvation through the death of Christ (its second economy). Fourth, death is imposed under the old economy, which in the new economy of Christ is carried out through justification and sanctification. Fifth, all vestiges of the covenant of works are removed through the resurrection of the body.[26]

This covenant theology shifted attention away from God's pretemporal decisions and toward the need for obedience and the unfolding of God's saving works in history.

SOURCES

Johannes Cocceius, **(A)** "De Foedere in Genere," chap. 1, *Summa Doctrinae de Foedere & Testamento Dei* (1648), pp. 45–46; ET: "The Covenant in General," trans. Mary Beaty.

26. See Barth, *Church Dogmatics* IV/1, pp. 59–66.

(B) "De foedere gratiae," chap. XLI, *Summa Theologiae* (1662), pp. 248–50; ET: "The Covenant of Grace," trans. Mary Beaty.

BIBLIOGRAPHY

Johannes Cocceius, "De Foedere operum & legali justitia," c. XXII, *Summa Theologiae* (1662), pp. 205–8. Idem, "De foedere gratiae," c. XLI, *Summa Theologiae* (1662), pp. 248–50. Idem, "De fine foedere gratiae, Gloria Dei," c. IX, *Summa Doctrinae de Foedere & Testamento Dei* (1648), pp. 79–80.
See the bibliography on p. 10.

A. THE COVENANT IN GENERAL

Some derive covenant (*foedus*) from striking (*feriendum*), others from faith (*fides*), still others from other sources. It is not unsatisfactory to take it from "that which is faithful" (*fidens*) or from trust (*fiducia*). But since we are concerned with the covenant of God of which there is notification in the scriptures, it does not so much matter that you know what the Latin word means as that you know the meaning of the Hebrew word for which the Latin is used.

Covenant (Heb. *berith*) is more commonly and suitably taken from ברת (to choose) than from ברא (to cut) as Grotius thinks. This is the term for an agreement of peace and friendship either before a war when affairs are still unresolved, or when the rights of one party have been violated by the other, or even after a war. In any agreement there is choice (αἵρεσις and *electio*) of conditions by each of the two parties. In an agreement on friendship, one of the contracting parties chooses and embraces the other with love and much good will and zeal. Abraham made such a covenant at Mamre with Eshcol and Aner (Gen. 14:13), and the seventy elders [i.e., authors of the Septuagint] call them "confederates." Likewise with Abimelech (Gen. 21:31), so also Isaac (Gen. 26:28, 29). The law of the Israelites forbids making such a covenant with the Amorites (Exod. 34:12, 13, 15; Deut. 7:2).

Jonathan had a covenant of mutual love and concern with David (1 Smyr. 18:3). Hence there is a "covenant of peace" (ברית שלום; Isa. 54:10), and it comes for the sake of peace (Zech. 11:10; Dan. 9:27)....

In a covenant there is not only precept but promise. God makes a covenant by setting forth the law and the promise connected with the law, and so he invites both assent to the law and expectation of the promise. But when, as is clear, "to strike a covenant" (the Hebrew says "to cut a covenant," that is, to make a covenant by involving the cutting up of an animal) means "to promise," and when it means this absolutely, beyond the law or condition which is to be observed by the other party, then metaphor is mixed with synecdoche. For just as the author of a covenant is willing to be bound by broad conditions to fulfill his promises to the person who agrees to the covenant, so the person who promises plainly and simply gives to those to whom he makes the promise the right to expect that the promises will be fulfilled. In this example, only the word "to cut" is used (2 Chron. 7:18): "And I will establish the throne of your kingdom, as I have covenanted" (that is, promised) "with your father David, saying, 'There shall not fail you a man holding power in Israel.'" So Hag. 2:4–5 . . . ; 2 Sam. 23:5. . . .

Covenant sometimes means an irrevocable gift, as in Num. 18:19. . . .

Covenant (διαθήκη) often is used more broadly among the Greeks living abroad and the Hellenistic Jews . . . , for it is also used for συνθήκη, a pact. Nevertheless, it also corresponds to the Hebrew *berith* (ברית) in the meaning of "testamentary disposition," which is closer to the Greek (namely, Gal. 3:15, and more clearly Heb. 9:16; cf. Heb. 8:10). . . .

God's covenant with man differs from the covenant that men make with one another, for men make a covenant concerning mutual benefits, while God makes a covenant concerned with his own. The "Covenant of God" is nothing except a divine declaration of the method of perceiving the love of God and of obtaining union and communion with him. If man uses this method he is in God's friendship, or, the Creator is his and God is his in a particular way (Gen. 17:7). There is one spirit with God (1 Cor. 6:17); there is one with him (John 17:21); there is his מיד אלהים, "familiar commerce with God" (Ps. 25:14; cf. Job 29:4; John 14:23).

The person who is outside the covenant is ἄθεος, "without God" (Eph. 2:12). . . .

Up to this point, therefore, the covenant of God with man is one-sided, since the plan and disposition concerning the method of perceiving God's love and his benefits belong to God alone, in almost the same manner as victors are accustomed to make arrangements concerning the vanquished, masters concerning their slaves . . . and parents their children. Nonetheless not every covenant of God is one-sided to such an extent that all stipulation is absent from one of the two parties, as when God makes a covenant with the day and the night, binding himself with a decree to preserve the distinction between day and night (Jer. 33:20; Gen. 8:22).

The covenant of God becomes two-sided or mutual when man, clinging close to God according to the law of the covenant, binds himself as it were by an agreement, by the force of the divine disposition, to be responsible for love and benefits. . . .

By assenting we glorify God, and we give him an abundant opportunity of glorying in us, just as God, by his promises, gives to those agreeing an opportunity of glorying in him. . . .

To those who have turned to him in faith, he gives the power of coming to him, so that before God their deeds may become manifest as if by a witness and exemplar, and so that they may stipulate from him remission of sin and all blessing. This stipulation is nothing except "certainty and the assurance of hope" (Heb. 6:11; 10:23). For, as obedience lies in agreement to the command of God, so also it lies in agreement to his promise or in stipulating in return for the promised blessings. Indeed, hope is extraordinary obedience in a particular covenant.

[There follow natural proofs of God's covenant with humanity through the evidence of conscience, the will, and temporal benefits, and demonstration that God's covenant binds the whole person, in body and spirit.]

God's covenant with man is twofold, from a diverse method of perceiving the love of God: of works and of grace. Scripture contrasts these two methods of attaining righteousness and thus all happiness, clearly indicating the contrast between works and faith. For faith, which is counted among works, should not be thought of as a work, since it is the equivalent of a powerful condition, without respect to persons, wrought by the suretyship achieved through the reconciliation of God, which has the word of "grace" attached to it and which faith receives as the cause of righteousness and from which it comes. . . . It is faith which believes it is true that "the one who has done those things will live in them." This pertains to the "covenant of works," but it does not justify. To have acted justifies at last. This faith condemns the man who has not acted, for the man who is condemned is forced to believe that he has been condemned. Therefore faith that justifies is "of the man who does not work" but who acknowledges that he is guilty and "believes in the God who justifies the wicked."

B. THE COVENANT OF GRACE

When a promise has been set forth by God or a testament issued, a "covenant of grace" has been set forth for sinful man. This is frequently mentioned in sacred literature and is called by its own name, *berith*, [or] *foedus*. For although, as we have taught above, that word bears the meaning of "testament," it does not for this reason lose its own meaning of a pact of peace and friendship in which there is a mutual choice and election of persons and an approving of conditions, such as those Modestinus (*De Excusationibus* 1.2, 1.6) calls choices, so that we relate the word ברה, "to choose." Even when this name is used for the testament of grace (as Jer. 31:31 and Isa. 55:3), it denotes the addition of certain blessings to be expected, coming from the proposal, and at the same time suggests a stipulation and an owed obedience and a consequent right of seeking those blessings. When this right has been obtained, the covenant is consummated.

The covenant which God makes with the sinner consists of these four [elements]: a stipulation or law-giving (Heb. 8:6) or παραγγίλια (1 Tim. 1:5; Acts 17:30; מצוא, Deut. 30:11, 12, 13, 14; cf. Rom. 10:6, 7, 8; ἐντολή, John 5:12, 14; 13:34; 1 John 2:3; 3:23); a conditional promise by which "obedience" is persuaded (Rom. 1:5) or "subjection," which is also called assent and agreement (2 Cor. 9:13; Heb. 3:1; 4:14; 10:23), in the sense that it is acquiescence in a law that has been passed as if [it is] just, holy, and good, or accommodated to attaining good. This acquiescence and obedience in a sinner is the third element required for joining a covenant, and they bring the fourth, namely, the sinner's right to claim, seek, and expect the promised blessing. From this he is and is called "righteous."

The covenant which God makes with a sinner is a covenant of grace. From this it follows that all parts of it are of pure grace and that nothing which partakes of the merit of works is to be mixed with it.

The law of this covenant is therefore not a law of works but a law of faith. For God stipulates faith, so that he may make a covenant with us from grace, and take us into friendship and communion. . . .

In this offered covenant there is also a stipulation not only of repentance in general but of the zeal for a good conscience in all things, a zeal for holiness. How could anyone believe the word by which God testifies to his love of mankind and not repent? The person who believes God judges that God is truthful, and loves the glory of the one promising sanctification and justification, desires to share with him, and expressly desires to be sanctified by him. Further, this person believes that God can do this (and so gives him glory for his power not less than that by which one believes that the sky and earth were drawn together by the divine Word) and wishes to act for the praise of glory [and] grace. Therefore that person yields himself to him and, in order to await all blessings from him, is eager to have a good conscience, lest his own heart should condemn him for neglecting such great salvation. From this it is clear that there is a stipulation of repentance in the stipulation of faith, or of conversion to God and zeal for keeping a good conscience.

We must notice carefully, however, that there is no stipulation of anything as a cause of righteousness and of life or, as we usually say, as a

condition from which hangs the right of hoping and seeking the promised blessing; in the very declaration of the plan or testament of God is
contained the fact that God has taken to himself the role of caring for us
and of giving righteousness and life. . . .

From this it is understood that salvation is in repentance alone and
that it consists of forsaking our own counsels and ways and consists of
faith in the Word of God by which he has revealed his counsel, and in
trust, and in love of him who offers himself a ransom for sinful man.

From all this it is apparent that through the offered covenant of grace
is shown the way of fleeing wrath and that the person who agrees to the
covenant receives the right of naming Jehovah as his God and of boasting in him and in the hope of the glory of God, and that he is free from
the fear of eternal damnation.

The person who is commanded to believe that the head of the serpent
is crushed by the divine will and grace cannot be left in fear of eternal
death because if eternal death were to be feared, then the power of the
serpent would not have been broken.

Again, it is clear that those who have fled the wrath have also received
and attained blessing, that is, the awarding of eternal life. Those who are
commanded to believe that sanctification is the work of God and who
have a heart purified through faith (Acts 15:9, and this for the reproach
of Satan) cannot doubt that all things have been prepared for them and
awarded not only for godliness but also for life in God (2 Pet. 1:3) and,
therefore, that they have received a blessing. For this reason Abraham
and his seed are given as an example of blessing, and those who believe
are said "to bless themselves" (Gen. 22:18), that is, to claim a blessing for
themselves, and to boast in God who is blessing them. For just as to
glory in God (Isa. 45:25) is to say about oneself this great and inestimable blessing, which is for God to be one's own, so "to bless oneself" in
him is to believe with trust and joy that the divine blessing has been
given and to affirm it before God and human beings in good conscience.
This excludes boasting in oneself and in anything of this world and in
any name, and it excludes the blessing of one who walks in his own
counsels (Deut. 29:19).

JOHN CALVIN: THE CALLING
OF ISRAEL

The church has always had to ponder the theological significance of Israel as
the bearer of the economy of grace prior to the advent of Jesus Christ. We
have already encountered Calvin's teaching on the unity of the Old and New

Testaments. Here Calvin reflects upon the priority of the Jews and the irrevocable nature of the calling issued to the true Israel of God.

SOURCES

(A) *Institutes* II.10.4, p. 431. **(B)** *Institutes* II.11.11–12, pp. 460–61. **(C)** *Commentary*: Romans 9:6 (1540); *CO* 49; ET: In Calvin, *Romans*, 197-98. **(D)** *Commentary*: Romans 11:25–26 (1540); *CO* 49; ET: In Calvin, *Romans*, 254-55.

BIBLIOGRAPHY

Hendrikus Berkhof, *Christian Faith: An Introduction to the Study of the Faith*, trans. Sierd Woudstra (Grand Rapids: Wm. B. Eerdmans, 1979), 221–65.

A. THE OLD TESTAMENT LOOKS TO JESUS CHRIST

[T]he Old Testament was established upon the free mercy of God, and was confirmed by Christ's intercession. For the gospel preaching, too, declares nothing else than that sinners are justified apart from their own merit by God's fatherly kindness; and the whole of it is summed up in Christ. Who, then, dares to separate the Jews from Christ, since with them, we hear, was made the covenant of the gospel, the sole foundation of which is Christ? Who dares to estrange from the gift of free salvation those to whom we hear the doctrine of the righteousness of faith was imparted? Not to dispute too long about something obvious—we have a notable saying of the Lord: "Abraham rejoiced that he was to see my day; he saw it and was glad" [John 8:56]. And what Christ there testified concerning Abraham, the apostle shows to have been universal among the believing folk when he says: "Christ remains, yesterday and today and forever" [Heb. 13:8]. Paul is not speaking there simply of Christ's everlasting divinity but of his power, a power perpetually available to believers.

B. ISRAEL, SET APART BY GOD

[U]ntil the advent of Christ, the Lord set apart one nation within which to confine the covenant of his grace. "When the Most High gave to the nations their inheritance, when he separated the sons of Adam," says Moses, "his people became his possession; Jacob was the cord of his inheritance" [Deut. 32:8–9]. Elsewhere he addresses the people as follows: "Behold, to the Lord your God belong heaven and . . . earth with all that is in it. Yet he cleaved only to your fathers, loved them so that he chose their descendants after them, namely, you out of all peoples" [Deut. 10:14, 15 p.; cf. Vg.]. He, therefore, bestowed the knowledge of his name solely upon that people as if they alone of all men belonged to him. He lodged his covenant, so to speak, in their bosom; he manifested the presence of his majesty to them; he showered every privilege upon them. But—to pass over the remaining blessings—let us consider the one in question. In communicating his Word to them, he joined them to himself, that he might be called and esteemed their God. In the meantime, "he allowed all other nations to walk" in vanity [Acts 14:16], as if they had nothing whatsoever to do with him. Nor did he give them the sole remedy for their deadly disease—the preaching of his Word. Israel was then the Lord's darling son; the others were strangers. Israel was recognized and received into confidence and safekeeping; the others were left to their own darkness. Israel was hallowed by God; the others were profaned. Israel was honored with God's presence; the others were excluded from all approach to him. "But when the fullness of time came" [Gal. 4:4] which was appointed for the restoration of all things, he was revealed as the reconciler of God and men; "the wall" that for so long had confined God's mercy within the boundaries of Israel "was broken down" [Eph. 2:14]. "Peace was announced to those who were far off, and to those who were near" [Eph. 2:17] that together they might be reconciled to God and welded into one people [Eph. 2:16]. Therefore there is now no difference between Jew and Greek [Gal. 3:28], between circumcision and uncircumcision [Gal. 6:15], but "Christ is all in all" [Col. 3:11; cf. Vg.]. "The nations have been made his inheritance, and the ends of the earth his property" [Ps. 2:8 p.], that "he may have unbroken dominion from sea to sea, and from the rivers even to the ends of the earth" [Ps. 72:8 p.; cf. Zech. 9:10]. . . .

The calling of the Gentiles, therefore, is a notable mark of the excellence of the New Testament over the Old.

C. NOT ALL ARE OF ISRAEL

When, in short, the whole people are called the inheritance and the peculiar people of God, what is meant is that they have been chosen by the Lord when the promise of salvation has been offered to them and confirmed by the symbol of circumcision. Since, however, many of them reject this adoption by their ingratitude, and thus in no degree enjoy its benefits, another difference arises among them with regard to the fulfilment of the promise. To prevent anyone from thinking it strange that this fulfilment of the promise was not evident in very many of the Jews,

Paul therefore denies that they were included in the true election of God.

We may, if it is preferred, put it in a different way: "The general election of the people of Israel does not prevent God from choosing for Himself by His secret counsel those whom He pleases." God's condescension in making a covenant of life with a single nation is indeed a remarkable illustration of undeserved mercy, but His hidden grace is more evident in the second election, which is restricted to a part of the nation only.

When Paul says that *they are not all Israel, which are of Israel,* and that *because they are Abraham's seed* they are not all children, he is using a figure of speech known as paronomasia. In the first clause he includes all the descendants, in the second he refers only to the true sons, who have not fallen from their position.

D. YET A MYSTERY:
ALL ISRAEL SHALL BE SAVED

And so all Israel shall be saved. Many understand this of the Jewish people, as if Paul were saying that religion was to be restored to them again as before. But I extend the word *Israel* to include all the people of God, in this sense, "When the Gentiles have come in, the Jews will at the same time return from their defection to the obedience of faith. The salvation of the whole Israel of God, which must be drawn from both, will thus be completed, and yet in such a way that the Jews, as the first born in the family of God, may obtain the first place." I have thought that this interpretation is the more suitable, because Paul wanted here to point to the consummation of the kingdom of Christ, which is by no means confined to the Jews, but includes the whole world. In the same way, in Gal. 6.16, he calls the Church, which was composed equally of Jews and Gentiles, the Israel of God, setting the people, thus collected from their dispersion, in opposition to the carnal children of Abraham who had fallen away from faith.

3

CREATION, FALL, PROMISE

CREATION AND THE HUMAN CREATURE

Creation

Huldrych Zwingli: The Contingency of Creation

God as Maker of Heaven and Earth brought into being everything that is out of nothing (*ex nihilo*); creation is completely dependent upon God for its existence. Zwingli's sermon on providence is cast in a highly philosophical mode of analysis to render intelligible the Christian conviction about the contingency of creation. One should note that Zwingli's philosophical arguments are more intricate than the short summary paragraph reproduced here.

SOURCE

Huldrych Zwingli, *De Providentia Dei* (first preached as a sermon at the Marburg Colloquy, October, 1529; revised and published, 1530), in *Sämtliche Werke* 6.3.64–230 = SS 4:79–144; ET: "On the Providence of God," in Zwingli, *Works* 2:140–41.

Having learned [in the philosophical arguments previously advanced] . . . that to have had a beginning is of the nature of the finite, and never to have had a beginning is of the nature of the infinite, that, accordingly there is only one single being that is infinite and, properly speaking, eternal, and having seen that the universe is finite and created, and not eternal, [therefore] the philosophers should open their eyes and see that the universe is finite and created and not eternal. Whether [the universe] be enduring, this is not the place to discuss, because we are seeking [here] for the beginnings, not the endings, of things, and because the divine scriptures satisfy the faithful upon this point, namely that the world shall pass away. Since, then . . . the universe had a beginning, it is evident that our mother earth is not of eternal existence nor lasting by nature, unless . . . you [erroneously] understand nature to be the Deity. . . . Nor does the earth come from itself. It must have come into being and have been produced out of nothing.

John Calvin: The Goodness of Creation

Calvin's reverent statement that in a sense "nature is God" is quoted often but seldom in its full context. Calvin is arguing that the "forces" or "powers" of nature should never be confused with the transcendent God from whom they derive. Moreover, as one contemplates the created order, one is led to marvel at God's work as Creator and Sustainer and to perceive that God has ordered all things for our good.

SOURCES

(A) *Institutes* I.5.5, pp. 56–58 (edited). (B) *Institutes* I.14.20–22, pp. 179–82.

BIBLIOGRAPHY

Susan E. Schreiner, *The Theater of His Glory: Nature and the Thought of John Calvin*, Studies in Historical Theology 3 (Durham, N.C.: Labyrinth, 1989).

A. DO NOT CONFUSE THE CREATURE
WITH THE CREATOR

Some persons, . . . , babble about a secret inspiration that gives life to the whole universe, but what they say is not only weak but completely profane. Vergil's famous saying pleases them:

> First of all, an inner spirit feeds
> Sky, earth, and watery fields, the shining orb
> Of moon, and Titan's star; and mind pervades
> Its members, sways all the mass, unites
>
> With its great frame. Thence come the race of man
> And beast, the life of winged things, strange shapes
> That ocean bears beneath his glassy floor.
> Of fire the vigor, and divine the source
> Of those life-seeds.[1]

As if the universe, which was founded as a spectacle of God's glory, were its own creator! For thus the same author has elsewhere followed the view common to Greeks and Latins alike:

The bees, some teach, received a share of mind,
Divine, ethereal draught. For God, men say,
Pervades all things, the earth, expanse of seas
And heaven's depth. From him the flocks and herds,
Men and beasts of every sort, at birth
Draw slender life; yea, unto him all things
Do then return; unmade, are then restored;
Death has no place; but still alive they fly
Unto the starry ranks, to heaven's height.[2]

See, of what value to beget and nourish godliness in men's hearts is that jejune speculation about the universal mind which animates and quickens the world! This shows itself even more clearly in the sacrilegious words of the filthy dog Lucretius which have been deduced from that principle.[3] This is indeed making a shadow deity to drive away the true God, whom we should fear and adore. I confess, of course, that it can be said reverently, provided that it proceeds from a reverent mind, that nature is God; but because it is a harsh and improper saying, since nature is rather the order prescribed by God, it is harmful in such weighty matters, in which special devotion is due, to involve God confusedly in the inferior course of his works.[4]

Let us therefore remember, whenever each of us contemplates his own nature, that there is one God who so governs all natures that he would have us look unto him, direct our faith to him, and worship and call upon him. For nothing is more preposterous than to enjoy the very remarkable gifts that attest the divine nature within us, yet to overlook the Author who gives them to us at our asking.

1. Vergil, *Aeneid* VI. 724–730 (translation adapted from H. R. Fairclough in LCL Vergil I. 556 f.).

2. Vergil, *Georgics* IV. 219–227 (translation adapted from H. R. Fairclough in LCL Vergil I. 210 ff.).

3. Lucretius, *De rerum natura* i. 54–79 (LCL edition, pp. 6 f.).

4. These sentences reflect statements of Lactantius.

B. THE SPIRITUAL LESSONS OF CREATION

Meanwhile let us not be ashamed to take pious delight in the works of God open and manifest in this most beautiful theater. For, as I have elsewhere said, although it is not the chief evidence for faith, yet it is the first evidence in the order of nature, to be mindful that wherever we cast our eyes, all things they meet are works of God. . . .

Therefore, to be brief, let all readers know that they have with true faith apprehended what it is for God to be Creator of heaven and earth, if they first of all follow the universal rule, not to pass over in ungrateful thoughtlessness or forgetfulness those conspicious powers which God shows forth in his creatures, and then learn so to apply it to themselves that their very hearts are touched. The first part of the rule is exemplified when we reflect upon the greatness of the Artificer who stationed, arranged, and fitted together the starry host of heaven in such wonderful order that nothing more beautiful in appearance can be imagined; who so set and fixed some in their stations that they cannot move; who granted to others a freer course, but so as not to wander outside their appointed course; who so adjusted the motion of all that days and nights, months, years, and seasons of the year are measured off; who so proportioned the inequality of days, which we daily observe, that no confusion occurs. It is so too when we observe his power in sustaining so great a mass, in governing the swiftly revolving heavenly system, and the like. For these few examples make sufficiently clear what it is to recognize God's powers in the creation of the universe. . . .

There remains the second part of the rule, more closely related to faith. It is to recognize that God has destined all things for our good and salvation but at the same time to feel his power and grace in ourselves and in the great benefits he has conferred upon us, and so bestir ourselves to trust, invoke, praise, and love him. Indeed, as I pointed out a little before, God himself has shown by the order of Creation that he created all things for man's sake. . . .

To conclude once for all, whenever we call God the Creator of heaven and earth, let us at the same time bear in mind that the dispensation of all those things which he has made is in his own hand and power and that we are indeed his children, whom he has received into his faithful protection to nourish and educate. We are therefore to await the fullness of all good things from him alone and to trust completely that he will never leave us destitute of what we need for salvation, and to hang our hopes on none but him! We are therefore, also, to petition him for whatever we desire; and we are to recognize as a blessing from him, and thankfully to acknowledge, every benefit that falls to our share. So, invited by the great sweetness of his beneficence and goodness, let us study to love and serve him with all our heart.

Francis Hutcheson: The Order of Creation

Francis Hutcheson (1694–1746), a licensed Presbyterian preacher and the son and grandson of Irish Presbyterian ministers, was a pivotal figure in the philosophy of aesthetics and morality. According to Hutcheson, human beings have an internal "aesthetic sense" by which to perceive the harmony and beauty of the world. This harmony reflects God's "benevolence," which is defined largely in terms of bringing about the good of human beings. Similarly human beings possess an innate "moral sense" by which to perceive virtue or vice. Virtue and vice, in turn, are defined in reference to promoting the happiness of human beings. In the passage below, Hutcheson reflects upon God's reasons for making the universe operate according to general physical laws.

While Hutcheson's philosophy exhibits certain traditional Christian themes, it reflects at the same time a critical anthropocentric shift away from classic Reformed theology and toward eighteenth-century Deism. Rather than classic Christian ethics, which centers upon the need for transforming grace and the virtue of "charity," moralists like Hutcheson affirmed the inherent "benevolence" of most human beings. And instead of the classic Christian vision of humanity being lifted up into the purposes of God, the purposes of God are now subtly being reduced to the purposes of humanity. Hutcheson's reflections, while they represented a prevailing intellectual and cultural shift in British philosophy, were not accepted by many of his contemporary Reformed divines, who brought him to trial for teaching tenets contrary to the Westminster Confession.

SOURCE

Francis Hutcheson, *Inquiry into the Original of Our Ideas of Beauty and Virtue* (London, 1725; 4th ed., 1738), Part I, "Inquiry Concerning Beauty, Order, Harmony, Design," sec. 8, art. 3.

BIBLIOGRAPHY

A critical edition of Part I is available: *Francis Hutcheson: An Inquiry Concerning Beauty, Order, Harmony, Design*, edited with introduction and notes by Peter Kivy (The Hague: Martinus Nijhoff, 1973). Selections also appear in L. A. Selby-Bigge, *British Moralists*, 2 vols. (Oxford, 1897).

Charles Taylor, *Sources of the Self: The Making of the Modern Identity* (Cambridge: Harvard University Press, 1989), esp. part 3. Basil Willey, *The English Moralists* (New York: W. W. Norton, 1964).

What reason might influence the Deity, whom no diversity of operation could distract or weary, to choose to operate by simplest means and general laws, and to diffuse uniformity, proportion, and similitude through all the parts of nature which we can observe?, perhaps there may be some real excellence in this manner of operation, and in these forms, which we know not. But this we may probably say, that since the divine goodness . . . has constituted our sense of beauty as it is at present, the same goodness might have determined the Great Architect to adorn this stupendous theatre in a manner agreeable to the spectators, and that part which is exposed to the observation of men so as to be pleasant to them, especially if we suppose that he designed to discover himself to them as wise and good, as well as powerful; for thus he has given them greater evidences through the whole earth of his art, wisdom, design, and bounty, than they can possibly have for the reason, counsel, and good-will of their fellow creatures, with whom they converse, with full persuasion of these qualities in them about their common affairs.

As to the operations of the Deity by general laws, there is still a farther reason from sense superior to these already considered, even that of virtue, or the beauty of action, which is the foundation of our greatest happiness. For were there no general laws fixed to the course of nature, there could be no prudence or design in men, no rational expectation of effects from causes, no schemes of action projected, or any regular execution. If, then, according to the frame of our nature, our greatest happiness must depend upon our actions, as it may perhaps be made appear it does, the universe must be governed not by particular wills but by general laws upon which we can found our expectations and project our schemes of action. Nay farther, though general laws did ordinarily obtain, yet if the Deity usually stopped their effects whenever it was necessary to prevent any particular evils, this would effectually and justly supersede all human prudence and care about actions, since a superior mind did thus relieve men from their charge.

Isaac Watts: The Power of God in Creation

SOURCE
Isaac Watts, Hymn: "I Sing the Mighty Power of God" (1709).

I sing the mighty power of God,
    That made the mountains rise;
That spread the flowing seas abroad,
    And built the lofty skies.
I sing the wisdom that ordained
    The sun to rule the day;
The moon shines full at His command,
    And all the stars obey.

I sing the goodness of the Lord,
  That filled the earth with food;
He formed the creatures with His word,
  And then pronounced them good.
Lord, how Thy wonders are displayed,
  Where'er I turn my eye:
If I survey the ground I tread,
  Or gaze upon the sky!

John Calvin: Angels, Good and Bad

Angels are created beings, distinct from God, who are wholly spiritual, lacking bodies, and who minister at the command of God. Evil angels were created good but became corrupted and now seek to thwart the reign and work of God. Through Christ, their defeat and ultimate impotence is assured.

SOURCE

Institutes I.14.5–19, pp. 165–79 (edited).

BIBLIOGRAPHY

Barth, *Church Dogmatics* III/3. § 51.

A. GOOD ANGELS

One reads here and there in Scripture that angels are celestial spirits whose ministry and service God uses to carry out all things he has decreed [e.g., Ps. 103:20–21]. Hence, likewise, this name has been applied to them because God employs them as intermediary messengers to manifest himself to men. The other names by which they are called have also been taken for a like reason. They are called "hosts" [Luke 2:13] because, as bodyguards surround their prince, they adorn his majesty and render it conspicuous; like soldiers they are ever intent upon their leader's standard, and thus are ready and able to carry out his command. . . . Likewise, on this account they are more than once called gods [e.g., Ps. 138:1], because in their ministry as in a mirror they in some respect exhibit his divinity to us.

But Scripture strongly insists upon teaching us what could most effectively make for our consolation and the strengthening of our faith: namely, that angels are dispensers and administrators of God's beneficence toward us. For this reason, Scripture recalls that they keep vigil for our safety, take upon themselves our defense, direct our ways, and take care that some harm may not befall us. . . .

141

Yet this point, which some restless men call in question, ought to be held certain: that angels are "ministering spirits" [Heb. 1:14], whose service God uses for the protection of his own, and through whom he both dispenses his benefits among men and also carries out his remaining works. Indeed, it was the opinion of the Sadducees of old [Acts 23:8] that by angels nothing was meant but either the impulses that God inspires in men or those examples of his power which he puts forth. But so many testimonies of Scripture cry out against this nonsense that it is a wonder such crass ignorance could be borne with in that people. . . .

So, then, whatever is said concerning the ministry of angels, let us direct it to the end that, having banished all lack of trust, our hope in God may be more firmly established. . . .

Farewell, then, to that Platonic philosophy of seeking access to God through angels, and of worshiping them with intent to render God more approachable to us. This is what superstitious and curious men have tried to drag into our religion from the beginning and persevere in trying even to this day.

B. BAD ANGELS

The fact that the devil is everywhere called God's adversary and ours also ought to fire us to an unceasing struggle against him. For if we have God's glory at heart, as we should have, we ought with all our strength to contend against him who is trying to extinguish it. If we are minded to affirm Christ's Kingdom as we ought, we must wage irreconcilable war with him who is plotting its ruin. . . .

Yet, since the devil was created by God, let us remember that this malice, which we attribute to his nature, came not from his creation but from his perversion. Therefore, lest we ourselves linger over superfluous matters, let us be content with this brief summary of the nature of devils: they were when first created angels of God, but by degeneration they ruined themselves, and became the instruments of ruin for others. . . .

But because that promise to crush Satan's head [Gen. 3:15] pertains to Christ and all his members in common, I deny that believers can ever be conquered or overwhelmed by him. Often, indeed, are they distressed, but not so deprived of life as not to recover; they fall under violent blows, but afterward they are raised up; they are wounded, but not fatally; in short, they so toil throughout life that at the last they obtain the victory.

The Human Creature

Huldrych Zwingli: Humanity, Known Only Through God

Even as God can be known only through God (pp. 73–75, above), so too humanity—the real truth about humanity—may be known only through the revelation of God.

SOURCE

Huldrych Zwingli, *Commentarius de vera et falsa religione* (1525); ET: *Commentary on True and False Religion*, in Zwingli, *Works* 3:75–76.

BIBLIOGRAPHY

Recall the opening lines of the *Institutes* (pp. 2–4, above), and see *Institutes* II.1.1–3, pp. 241–44.

To know man is as toilsome as to catch a cuttlefish, for as the latter hides himself in his own blackness in order not to be caught, so does man, as soon as he sees one is after him, stir up such sudden and thick clouds of hypocrisy that no Lynceus, no Argus, can discover him. Not only that biting critic Momus complained of this, but the divine herald of the Gospel, Paul, understood it so well that in 1 Cor. 2:11 he speaks on this wise: "For who among men knoweth the things of a man, save the spirit of the man, which is in him?" Though he says this only for the purpose of illustration, he really holds it as established that the human heart hides its purposes with such zeal and so many wiles that no one can have knowledge of them but itself; for unless this were his view, he could not logically draw the conclusion he is trying to prove in the passage. And Jeremiah says of this fleer from the light and this wiggler of ours, chap. 17:9, "The heart of man is wicked and unsearchable. Who can know it? I, the Lord, who search the heart and try the reins."

From this testimony it becomes manifest that man cannot be known by man.

Jonathan Edwards: Humanity, the Pinnacle of Creation

While humanity holds a place in the order of things clearly subordinate to the purposes and glory of God, nonetheless in Reformed piety God has shown favor to humanity in making men and women the apex of the created order.

143

SOURCE

Jonathan Edwards, "Concerning God's Moral Government," *Remarks on Important Theological Controversies*, in Edwards, *Works* (1834) 2:511–12.

God is most concerned about the state and government of that which is highest in his creation, and which he values most; and so he is principally concerned about the ordering [of] the state of mankind, which is a part of the creation that he has made superior, and that he values most: and therefore, in like manner, it follows, that he is principally concerned about the regulation of that which he values most in men, *viz.* what appertains to his intelligence and voluntary acts. If there be any thing in the principal part of the creation, that the Creator values more than other parts, it must be that wherein it is above them, or, at least, something wherein it differs from them. But the only thing wherein men differ from the inferior creation, is intelligent perception and action. This is that in which the Creator has made man to differ from the rest of the creation, and by which he has set him over it, and by which he governs the inferior creatures, and uses them for himself; and therefore it must needs be, that the Creator should be chiefly concerned that the state of mankind should be regulated according to his will, with respect to what appertains to him as an intelligent, voluntary creature. Hence it must be, that God does take care that a good moral government should be maintained over men; that his intelligent, voluntary acts should be all subject to rules; and that with respect to them all, he should be the subject of judicial proceeding.

John Calvin: Humanity, the Image of God

For Calvin the rational soul is the seat of the image of God. While a complete view of Calvin's anthropology would necessitate reviewing texts ranging over his entire corpus, the passage below sketches the qualitative endowments of the soul which enable it to enter into relationship with God.

SOURCE

Institutes I.15.2–7, pp. 184–95 (edited).

BIBLIOGRAPHY

John Calvin, *Psychopannychia* (1534; published, 1542), *CO* 5. Critical edition: *Psychopannychia*, ed. W. Zimmerli (Leipzig, 1932); ET: In *Tracts and Treatises*, 3 vols., trans. Henry Beveridge (Edinburgh, 1844; reprint: with introduction by Thomas F. Torrance, Grand Rapids: Wm. B. Eerdmans, 1958), 2:414–90.

Roy W. Battenhouse, "The Doctrine of Man in Calvin and Renaissance Platonism," *Journal of the History of Ideas* 9 (1948): 447–71. Mary Potter Engel, *John Calvin's Perspectival Anthropology*, AAR Academy Series 52 (Atlanta: Scholars Press, 1988), chap. 2. Thomas F. Torrance, *Calvin's Doctrine of Man* (Grand Rapids: Wm. B. Eerdmans, 1957).

[T]hat man consists of a soul and a body ought to be beyond controversy. Now I understand by the term "soul" an immortal yet created essence, which is his nobler part. Sometimes it is called "spirit." For even when these terms are joined together, they differ from one another in meaning; yet when the word "spirit" is used by itself, it means the same thing as soul. . . . Surely the conscience, which, discerning between good and evil, responds to God's judgment, is an undoubted sign of the immortal spirit. For how could a motion without essence penetrate to God's judgment seat, and inflict itself with dread at its own guilt? For the body is not affected by the fear of spiritual punishment, which falls upon the soul only; from this it follows that the soul is endowed with essence. Now the very knowledge of God sufficiently proves that souls, which transcend the world, are immortal, for no transient energy could penetrate to the fountain of life.

In short, the many pre-eminent gifts with which the human mind is endowed proclaim that something divine has been engraved upon it; all these are testimonies of an immortal essence. For the sense perception inhering in brute animals does not go beyond the body, or at least extends no farther than to material things presented to it. But the nimbleness of the human mind in searching out heaven and earth and the secrets of nature, and when all ages have been compassed by its understanding and memory, in arranging each thing in its proper order, and in inferring future events from past, clearly shows that there lies hidden in man something separate from the body. With our intelligence we conceive the invisible God and the angels, something the body can by no means do. We grasp things that are right, just, and honorable, which are hidden to the bodily senses. Therefore the spirit must be the seat of this intelligence. . . .

Now, unless the soul were something essential, separate from the body, Scripture would not teach that we dwell in houses of clay [Job 4:19]. . . .

[L]et us, therefore, hold—as indeed is suitable to our present purpose—that the human soul consists of two faculties, understanding and will. Let the office, moreover, of understanding be to distinguish between objects, as each seems worthy of approval or disapproval; while that of the will, to choose and follow what the understanding pronounces good, but to reject and flee what it disapproves.

Humanity, Fallen and Sinful

Original Sin and the Character of Sin in General

HEINRICH BULLINGER: ORIGINAL SIN AND ACTUAL SIN

Heinrich Bullinger has bequeathed to us a fine summary of Reformed teaching on sin in this sermon. It is Augustinian in its acceptance of original, hereditary sin and its rejection of Pelagianism.[1] The complete sermon took over two hours to preach and contained an exhaustive analysis of various kinds of actual sin. A representative extract appears here.

SOURCE

Heinrich Bullinger, "Of Sin," in *Decades* 2:358–73, 384–432 (edited).

Sin is the natural corruption of mankind, and the action which ariseth of it contrary to the law of God, whose wrath, that is, both death and sundry punishments, it bringeth upon us. . . .

[T]he nature of man was good. For it is an accidental quality that happened to man either in, or immediately after, his fall, and not a substantial property, to have his nature so spotted with corruption as now it is. Now we, being born in sin of sinful progenitors, have sin by descent as our natural property. . . .

[T]his evil doth by descent flow from our first parents into all their posterity, so that at this day sin doth not spring from elsewhere but of ourselves, that is to say, of our corrupt judgment, depraved will, and the suggestion of the devil. For the root of evil is yet remaining in our flesh by reason of that first corruption: which root bringeth forth a corrupt branch in nature like unto itself: which branch Satan even now, as he hath done always, doth by his sleights, subtleties, and lies, cherish, tend, and tender, as an imp of his own planting; and yet notwithstanding he laboureth in vain, unless we yield ourselves to his hands to be framed as he listeth. . . .

[S]in is the corruption of the good nature made by God, and not a creature created by God either in or with man. God created man good:

---

1. Those unfamiliar with these debates may consult J. Patout Burns, trans. and ed., *Theological Anthropology*, Sources of Early Christian Thought (Philadelphia: Fortress, 1981).

but man, being left to his own counsel, did through the persuasion of Satan, by his own action and depraved will, corrupt the goodness that God created in him: so now that sin is proper to man, I mean, man's corrupt action against the law of God, and not a creature created in him of God. . . .

And now among all these definitions I wish you, dearly beloved, to consider of this also: Original sin is the inheritably descending naughtiness or corruption of our nature, which doth first make us endangered to the wrath of God, and then bringeth forth in us those works which the scripture calleth the works of the flesh. Therefore this original sin is neither a deed, nor a work, nor a thought; but a disease, a vice, a depravation, I say, of judgment and concupiscence; or a corruption of the whole man, that is, of the understanding, will, and all the power of man; out of which at last do flow all evil thoughts, naughty words, and wicked deeds.

Thus sin taketh beginning at and of Adam; and for that cause it is called the inheritably descending naughtiness and corruption of our nature. . . .

Let us now see what and how great the hereditary naughtiness or corruption of our nature is, and what power it hath to work in man. Our nature verily, as I shewed you above, was before the fall most excellent and pure in our father Adam: but after the fall it did by God's just judgment become corrupt and utterly naught, which is in that naughtiness by propagation, or *ex traduce*, derived into all us which are the posterity and offspring of Adam; as both experience and the thing itself do evidently declare, as well in sucklings or infants as those of riper years. For even very babes give manifest tokens of evident depravation so soon as they once begin to be able to do anything; yea, before they can perfectly sound any one syllable of a whole word. All our understanding is dull, blunt, gross, and altogether blind in heavenly things. Our judgment in divine matters is perverse and frivolous. For there arise in us most horrible and absurd thoughts and opinions touching God, his judgments, and wonderful works. Yea, our whole mind is apt and ready to errors, to fables, and our own destruction: and when as our judgments are nothing but mere folly, yet do we prefer them far above God's wisdom, which we esteem but foolishness in comparison of our conceits and corrupt imaginations; for he lied not which said: "The natural man perceiveth not the things of the Spirit of God; for they are foolishness unto him; neither can he know them, because they are spiritually discerned" [1 Cor. ii. 14]. Now Paul calleth him the natural man, which liveth naturally by the vital spirit, and is not regenerate by the Holy

Ghost: and since we are all such, we are therefore wholly overcome and governed of *philautia*, that is, too great a self-love and delight in ourselves, whereby all things that we ourselves do work do highly please us; looking still very busily to our own selves and our commodity, when in the meantime we neglect all others, yea, rather do afflict them. Neither did Plato unadvisedly esteem that vice of self-love to be the very root of every evil. Furthermore, our whole will is led captive by concupiscence, which, as a root envenomed with poison, infecteth all that is in man, and doth incline, draw on, and drive men to things carnal, forbidden, and contrary to God, to the end that he may greedily pursue them, put all his delight in them, and content himself with them. Moreover there is in us no power or ability to do any good: for we are slow, sluggish, and heavy to goodness; but lively, quick, and ready enough to any evil or naughtiness. And, that I may at last conclude, and briefly express the whole force and signification of our hereditary depravation and corruption; I say, that this depravation of our nature is nothing else but the blotting of God's image in us.

I have thus far spoken of original sin, of the native and hereditary corruption of our nature, which is the first part in the definition of sin. Here followeth now the latter part; to wit, the very action which ariseth of that corruption, the actual sin, I say, which is so called *ab actu*, that is, an act or a deed-doing. For insomuch as that corruption which is born together with and is hereditary in us doth not always lie hid, but worketh outwardly and sheweth forth itself, and doth at last bring forth an imp of her own kind and nature, which imp is actual sin; therefore we define actual sin to be an action, or work, or fruit, of our corrupt and naughty nature, expressing itself in thoughts, words, and works against the law of God, and thereby deserving the wrath of God. . . .

But here we must especially note in the definition of actual sin the very property or difference, whereby this action is discerned from all other actions, and whereby the most proper note of sin is made manifest. This action therefore, even as all sins else do, doth directly tend against God's law. But what the law of God is, I have in my former sermons at large declared. Verily, it is none other but the very will of God. Now the will of God is, that man should be like unto his image, that is, that he should be holy, innocent, and so consequently saved. . . .

[S]ins do arise by steps, and increase by circumstances. For first, there is a hidden sin, contained in the very affection or desire of man. But I have already told you, that affections and desires are of two sorts; to wit, natural affections, which are not repugnant to the law of God; of which sort are the love of children, parents, and wife, and the desire of meat, drink, and sleep: although I know and do not deny but that sometimes those affections are defiled with the original spot. Again, there are carnal desires or affections in men, directly contrary to the will of God. Those affections are nourished and do increase by vain thoughts and carnal delights increasing in thy bosom; and at last they break out into the sin of the mouth, yea, after that, to the deed-doing, or actual sin itself.

JONATHAN EDWARDS: ORIGINAL SIN EXPLAINED

Written in response to John Taylor's "semi-Pelagian" or "Arminian" arguments in *Scripture-Doctrine of Original Sin* (1740), Edwards's *Original Sin* attempts to explain the pervasiveness of human depravity from the standpoint of the human "constitution" as part of "the established course of nature." For Edwards the question why contemporary human beings should bear responsibility for Adam's sin is no more difficult philosophically than the question why human beings should bear responsibility for their own past acts. The philosophical problem of defending Adam's status as head of the entire race is of the same class as defending the unity and integrity of the self over time. Edwards refers the ultimate answer to these questions to the will of God. But he also attempts to make the unity of the race and the character of the self intelligible by employing the vocabulary of "disposition," the "religious affections," and "principles of the heart," which he draws from experience and which we shall meet again later (pp. 257–59).

SOURCE

Jonathan Edwards, *The Great Christian Doctrine of Original Sin* .... (1758), in Edwards, *Works* (Yale) 3:381–86.

BIBLIOGRAPHY

Conrad Cherry, *The Theology of Jonathan Edwards: A Reappraisal* (Garden City, N.Y.: Doubleday, 1966; reprint: Bloomington: Indiana University Press, 1990), 196–202. Robert Jenson, *America's Theologian: A Recommendation of Jonathan Edwards* (New York: Oxford University Press, 1988), 141–53. Perry Miller, *Jonathan Edwards* (New York: W. Sloane, 1949), 265–82. For a nineteenth-century critique, see Charles Hodge, *Systematic Theology*, 3 vols. (Grand Rapids: Wm. B. Eerdmans, 1989), 2:216–27.

The case with man was plainly this: when God made man at first, he implanted in him two kinds of principles. There was an *inferior* kind, which may be called *natural*, being the principles of mere human nature; such as self-love, with those natural appetites and passions, which belong to the nature of man, in which his love to his own liberty, honor and pleasure, were exercised: these when alone, and left to themselves, are what the Scriptures sometimes call *flesh*. Besides these, there were *superior* principles, that were spiritual, holy and divine, summarily comprehended in divine love; wherein consisted the spiritual image of God, and man's righteousness and true holiness; which are called in Scripture the *divine nature*. These principles may, in some sense, be called *supernatural*,[1] being (however concreated or connate, yet) such as are above those principles that are essentially implied in, or necessarily resulting from, and inseparably connected with, *mere human nature;* and being such as immediately depend on man's union and communion with God, or divine communications and influences of God's spirit: which though withdrawn, and man's nature forsaken of these principles, human nature would be human nature still; man's nature as such, being entire without those divine principles, which the Scripture sometimes calls *spirit*, in contradistinction to *flesh*. . . .

These divine principles thus reigning, were the dignity, life, happiness, and glory of man's nature. When man sinned, and broke God's Covenant, and fell under his curse, these superior principles left his heart: for indeed God then left him; that communion with God, on which these principles depended, entirely ceased; the Holy Spirit, that divine inhabitant, forsook the house. Because it would have been utterly improper in itself, and inconsistent with the covenant and constitution God had established, that God should still maintain communion with man, and continue, by his friendly, gracious vital influences, to dwell with him and in him, after he was become a rebel, and had incurred God's wrath and curse. Therefore immediately the superior divine principles wholly ceased; so light ceases in a room, when the candle is withdrawn: and thus man was left in a state of darkness, woeful corruption and ruin; nothing but flesh, without spirit. The inferior principles of self-love and natural appetite, which were given only to serve, being alone, and left to themselves, of course became reigning principles; having no superior principles to regulate or control them, they became absolute masters of the heart. The immediate consequence of which was a *fatal catastrophe*, a turning of all things upside down, and the succession of a state of the most odious and dreadful confusion. Man did immediately set up himself, and the objects of his private affections and appetites as supreme; and so they took the place of God. . . .

And as Adam's nature became corrupt, without God's implanting or infusing any evil thing into his nature; so does the nature of his *posterity*. God dealing with Adam as the head of his posterity (as has been shewn) and treating them as one, he deals with his posterity as having *all sinned in him*. And therefore, as God withdrew spiritual communion and his vital gracious influence from the common head, so he withholds the same from all the members, as they come into existence. . . .

'Tis agreeable to the established order of nature, that the good qualities wanting in the tree, should also be wanting in the branches and fruit. 'Tis agreeable to the order of nature, that when a particular person is without good moral qualities in his heart, he should continue without 'em, till some new cause or efficiency produces them: and 'tis as much agreeable to an established course and order of nature, that since Adam, the head of the race of mankind, the root of that great tree with many branches springing from it, was deprived of original righteousness, the branches should come forth without it. Or, if any dislike the word "nature" as used in this last case, and instead of it choose to call it a "constitution," or established order of successive events, the alteration of the name won't in the least alter the state of the present argument. Where the name "nature" is allowed without dispute, no more is meant than an established method and order of events, settled and limited by divine wisdom. . . .

That we may proceed with the greater clearness in considering the main objections against supposing the guilt of Adam's sin to be imputed to his posterity, I would premise some observations with a view to the right stating of the doctrine of the imputation of Adam's first sin; and then shew the *reasonableness* of this doctrine, in opposition to the great clamor raised against it on this head.

I think, it would go far towards directing us to the more clear and distinct conceiving and right stating of this affair, if we steadily bear this in mind; that God, in each step of his proceeding with Adam, in relation to the covenant or constitution established with him, looked on his posterity as being one with him. (The propriety of his looking upon them so, I shall speak to afterwards.) And though he dealt more immediately with Adam, yet it was as the head of the whole body, and the root of the whole tree; and in his proceedings with him, he dealt with all the branches, as if they had been then existing in their root.

From which it will follow, that both guilt, or exposedness to punishment, and also depravity of heart, came upon Adam's posterity just as they came upon him, as much as if he and they had all coexisted, like a tree with many branches; allowing only for the difference necessarily resulting from the place Adam stood in, as head or root of the whole.

1. To prevent all cavils, the reader is desired particularly to observe, in what sense I here use the words, "natural" and "supernatural": not as epithets of distinction between that which is concreated or connate, and that which is extraordinarily introduced afterwards, besides the first state of things, or the order established originally, beginning when man's

nature began; but as distinguishing between what belongs *to*, or flows *from*, that nature which man has, merely *as* man, and those things which are *above* this, by which one is denominated, not only a *man*, but a truly *virtuous, holy*, and *spiritual* man; which, though they began, in Adam, as soon as humanity began, and are necessary to the perfection and well being of the human nature, yet are not essential to the constitution of it, or necessary to its being: inasmuch as one may have everything needful to his being *man* exclusively of them. If in thus using the words, "natural" and "supernatural," I use them in an uncommon sense, 'tis not from any affectation of singularity, but for want of other terms, more aptly to express my meaning. [This footnote is crossed out from the MS.]

Total Depravity

JOHN CALVIN: DEPRAVITY TOTAL IN EXTENT

For Calvin, contrary to popular stereotype, humanity did not wholly lose the divine image in the fall; nor did the fall wholly eradicate the effectiveness of human reason. The image is obscured but not eliminated. Human depravity is "total" in *extent* but not in *degree*. It corrupts *all* human faculties equally; but it does *not* corrupt them so completely as to obliterate them. Regarding "earthly" things, for instance, reason gets along rather well; but as to "heavenly" things, namely, the things of God, God's purposes, and our salvation, we are in radical need of grace.

SOURCE

Institutes II.1.9, II.2.12–13, 17–18, pp. 252–53, 270–72, 276–78 (edited).

[A]ll parts of the soul were possessed by sin after Adam deserted the fountain of righteousness. For not only did a lower appetite seduce him, but unspeakable impiety occupied the very citadel of his mind, and pride penetrated to the depths of his heart. Thus it is pointless and foolish to restrict the corruption that arises thence only to what are called the impulses of the senses; or to call it the "kindling wood" that attracts, arouses, and drags into sin only that part which they term "sensuality." In this matter Peter Lombard has betrayed his complete ignorance. For, in seeking and searching out its seat, he says that it lies in the flesh, as Paul testifies; yet not intrinsically, but because it appears more in the flesh. [Lombard, *Sentences*, II. xxx. 7f. and xxxi. 2–4 (MPL 192, 722, 724).]

And, indeed, that common opinion which they have taken from Augustine pleases me: that the natural gifts were corrupted in man through sin, but that his supernatural gifts were stripped from him. For by the latter clause they understand the light of faith as well as righteousness, which would be sufficient to attain heavenly life and eternal bliss. Therefore, withdrawing from the Kingdom of God, he is at the same time deprived of spiritual gifts, with which he had been furnished for the hope of eternal salvation. From this it follows that he is so banished from the Kingdom of God that all qualities belonging to the blessed life of the soul have been extinguished in him, until he recovers them through the grace of regeneration. Among these are faith, love of God, charity toward neighbor, zeal for holiness and for righteousness. All these, since Christ restores them to us, are considered adventitious, and beyond nature: and for this reason we infer that they were taken away. On the other hand, soundness of mind and uprightness of heart were withdrawn at the same time. This is the corruption of the natural gifts. For even though something of understanding and judgment remains as a residue along with the will, yet we shall not call a mind whole and sound that is both weak and plunged into deep darkness. And depravity of the will is all too well known.

Since reason, therefore, by which man distinguishes between good and evil, and by which he understands and judges, is a natural gift, it could not be completely wiped out; but it was partly weakened and partly corrupted; so that its misshapen ruins appear. John speaks in this sense: "The light still shines in the darkness, but the darkness comprehends it not" [John 1:5]. In these words both facts are clearly expressed. First, in man's perverted and degenerate nature some sparks still gleam. These show him to be a rational being, differing from brute beasts, because he is endowed with understanding. Yet, secondly, they show this light choked with dense ignorance, so that it cannot come forth effectively. . . .

To perceive more clearly how far the mind can proceed in any matter according to the degree of its ability, we must here set forth a distinction. This, then, is the distinction: that there is one kind of understanding of earthly things; another of heavenly. I call "earthly things" those which do not pertain to God or his Kingdom, to true justice, or to the blessedness of the future life; but which have their significance and relationship with regard to the present life and are, in a sense, confined within its bounds. I call "heavenly things" the pure knowledge of God, the nature of true righteousness, and the mysteries of the Heavenly Kingdom. The first class includes government, household management, all mechanical skills, and the liberal arts. In the second are the knowledge of God and of his will, and the rule by which we conform our lives to it.

THE REMONSTRANCE VERSUS THE SYNOD OF DORT

Having studied with Theodore Beza in Geneva, Jacob Arminius constructed his theology according to a broadly Reformed pattern, even though he sought simultaneously to subject that pattern to fundamental transformation.[2] In keeping with Protestant and Reformed doctrine, Arminius affirmed a generic belief in human depravity; but he conceived depravity not as a determinative corruptness but only as an "inclination to sin," inherited from Adam to be sure, but leaving human beings with a significant degree of freedom to choose. Arminius thought of original sin as a "bias" to sin, and not as a positive propensity that leaves one powerless not to sin (the Augustinian *non posse non peccare*); actual sin is a yielding to that bias on the basis of choice, and it is one's own choice for which one is responsible. Depravity could not be "total," said Arminius, or human beings would cease to be free and responsible. And in that case, they would retain neither their created "natural inclination" and "capacity" for salvation nor their ability to "cooperate" with God's grace.

The Synod of Dort rejected Arminius's view of sin, although the nuances that distinguish the Remonstrance from Dort on the topic of sin can be appreciated fully only when compared with their differing views on grace. They agreed that at the crucial point of turning to God, grace was necessary. They differed over how grace operates (see pp. 94–99, above).

SOURCES

(A) *Articuli Arminiani sive Remonstrantia* (1610) [Dutch: *De Remonstrantie en het Remonstrantisme*], Article III; ET: *The Five Arminian Articles* (1610), in Schaff, *Creeds* 3:546–47. **(B)** *Canones Synodi Dordrechtanae* (1618–19), Third and Fourth Heads of Doctrine, Articles I–IV; ET: "Of the Corruption of Man, his Conversion to God, and the Manner thereof," *Canons of the Synod of Dort*, Third and Fourth Heads of Doctrine, in Schaff, *Creeds* 3:582–84.

BIBLIOGRAPHY

Compare John Calvin, Commentary: Romans:7:14–25 (1540) = *Calvin's New Testament Commentaries* 8:146–55, with Jacob Arminius, *A Dissertation on the True and Genuine Sense of the Seventh Chapter of the Epistle to the Romans* (posthumously published, Leiden, 1613), in Arminius, *Works* 2:488–683. Arminius believes Paul speaks in this passage of an unregenerate person; Calvin insists the struggle depicted is that of the regenerate Christian.

2. One may gain a sense of Arminius's constructive systematic theology (as distinct from the controversial positions he took in addressing disputed theological questions) by consulting his classroom lectures and public addresses: *The Private Disputations of James Arminius, D.D. On the Principal Articles of the Christian Religion* . . . . and *Disputations on Some of the Principal Subjects of The Christian Religion*, in Arminius, *Works* 2:318–469, 2:77–317.

A. THE ARMINIAN REMONSTRANCE

ART. III. That man has not saving grace of himself, nor of the energy of his free will, inasmuch as he, in the state of apostasy and sin, can of and by himself neither think, will, nor do any thing that is truly good (such as saving Faith eminently is); but that it is needful that he be born again of God in Christ, through his Holy Spirit, and renewed in understanding, inclination, or will, and all his powers, in order that he may rightly understand, think, will, and effect what is truly good, according to the Word of Christ, John xv. 5: "Without me ye can do nothing."

B. THE SYNOD OF DORT

Third and Fourth Heads of Doctrine

Of the Corruption of Man, his Conversion to God,
and the Manner thereof.

ART. I. Man was originally formed after the image of God. His understanding was adorned with a true and saving knowledge of his Creator, and of spiritual things; his heart and will were upright, all his affections pure, and the whole Man was holy; but revolting from God by the instigation of the devil, and abusing the freedom of his own will, he forfeited these excellent gifts, and on the contrary entailed on himself blindness of mind, horrible darkness, vanity, and perverseness of judgment; became wicked, rebellious, and obdurate in heart and will, and impure in [all] his affections.

ART. II. Man after the fall begat children in his own likeness. A corrupt stock produced corrupt offspring. Hence all the posterity of Adam, Christ only excepted, have derived corruption from their original parent, not by imitation, as the Pelagians of old asserted, but by the propagation of a vicious nature [in consequence of a just judgment of God].

ART. III. Therefore all men are conceived in sin, and are by nature children of wrath, incapable of any saving good, prone to evil, dead in sin, and in bondage thereto; and, without the regenerating grace of the Holy Spirit, they are neither able nor willing to return to God, to reform the depravity of their nature, nor to dispose themselves to reformation.

ART. IV. There remain, however, in man since the fall, the glimmerings of natural light, whereby he retains some knowledge of God, of natural things, and of the difference between good and evil, and discovers some regard for virtue, good order in society, and for maintaining an orderly

155

external deportment. But so far is this light of nature from being sufficient to bring him to a saving knowledge of God, and to true conversion,
that he is incapable of using it aright even in things natural and civil.
Nay farther, this light, such as it is, man in various ways renders wholly
polluted, and holds it [back] in unrighteousness; by doing which he
becomes inexcusable before God.

JONATHAN EDWARDS: SINNERS IN THE HANDS
OF AN ANGRY GOD

This is the sermon which over the years has formed the notorious stereotype
of Edwards as a backward, unenlightened, hellfire-and-brimstone preacher.
Edwards was far from unenlightened, but he did believe in human depravity
and the need for grace. The point of the sermon, preached at Enfield, Connecticut, in 1741, is that but for the hand of God which graciously upholds us
we would all sink from the weight of sin.

SOURCE

Jonathan Edwards, Sermon: "Sinners in the Hands of an Angry God" (Enfield, Conn.,
1741), in Edwards, *Works* (1834) 2:9–10.

The bow of God's wrath is bent, and the arrow made ready on the
string, and justice bends the arrow at your heart, and strains the bow,
and it is nothing but the mere pleasure of God, and that of an angry God,
without any promise or obligation at all, that keeps the arrow one
moment from being made drunk with your blood. Thus all you that
never passed under a great change of heart, by the mighty power of the
Spirit of God upon your souls; all you that were never born again, and
made new creatures, and raised from being dead in sin, to a state of new,
and before altogether unexperienced, light and life, are in the hands of
an angry God. However you may have reformed your life in many things,
and may have had religious affections, and may keep up a form of religion
in your families and closets, and in the house of God, it is nothing but his
mere pleasure that keeps you from being this moment swallowed up in
everlasting destruction. However unconvinced you may now be of the truth
of what you hear, by and by you will be fully convinced of it. Those that are
gone from being in the like circumstances with you, see that it was so with
them; for destruction came suddenly upon most of them; when they
expected nothing of it, and while they were saying, Peace and safety: now
they see, that those things on which they depended for peace and safety,
were nothing but thin air and empty shadows.

The God that holds you over the pit of hell, much as one holds a spider, or some loathsome insect, over the fire, abhors you, and is dreadfully provoked: his wrath towards you burns like fire; he looks upon you as worthy of nothing else, but to be cast into the fire; he is of purer eyes than to bear to have you in his sight; you are ten thousand times more abominable in his eyes, than the most hateful venomous serpent is in ours. You have offended him infinitely more than ever a stubborn rebel did his prince: and yet, it is nothing but his hand that holds you from falling into the fire every moment. It is to be ascribed to nothing else, that you did not go to hell the last night; that you was suffered to awake again in this world, after you closed your eyes to sleep. And there is no other reason to be given, why you have not dropped into hell since you arose in the morning, but that God's hand has held you up. There is no other reason to be given why you have not gone to hell, since you have sat here in the house of God, provoking his pure eyes by your sinful wicked manner of attending his solemn worship. Yea, there is nothing else that is to be given as a reason why you do not this very moment drop down into hell.

O sinner! consider the fearful danger you are in: it is a great furnace of wrath, a wide bottomless pit, full of the fire of wrath, that you are held over in the hand of that God, whose wrath is provoked and incensed as much against you, as against many of the damned in hell. You hang by a slender thread, with the flames of divine wrath flashing about it, and ready every moment to singe it, and burn it asunder; and you have no interest in any Mediator, and nothing to lay hold of to save yourself, nothing to keep off the flames of wrath, nothing of your own, nothing that you ever have done, nothing that you can do, to induce God to spare you one moment.—

THE PSALTER: PSALM 6, "REPROVE ME NOT"

SOURCE

The Scottish Psalter (1623), based on Psalm 6.

Lord in thy wrath reprove me not,
  though I deserve thine ire:
Nor yet correct me in thy rage,
  O Lord, I thee desire.
For I am weak, therefore, O Lord,
  of mercy me forbear:
And heal me, Lord, for why thou knowest,
  my bones do quake for fear.

Freedom and Bondage of the Will

JOHN CALVIN: REAFFIRMING THE AUGUSTINIAN DOCTRINE

The Reformed tradition affirms freedom of the will, but it sees humanity exercising that freedom persistently and unalterably in contravention of God's command. For Calvin the sinful exercise of will is not the fault of God, since the will is free from external compulsion. It is a "voluntary will": its acts are genuine expressions of the self. The will is also free in its power of exercising contrary choice, which is to say, it possesses genuine "free choice" (*liberum arbitrium*): it may choose x or y in any given circumstance. Nevertheless, Calvin, along with Augustine, believes that what a person actually will choose in a given circumstance cannot help but reflect that person's essential character. There is a "necessity of the will" which, since the character of an unregenerate person is radically flawed, renders a person powerless not to sin (*non posse non peccare*). In this condition, only a fundamental conversion of the whole person, the will as well as every other faculty, can place one in a position to please God; and this is possible only through grace.

SOURCES

(A) John Calvin, *Responsio contra Pighium de libero arbitrio, CO* 6, 279–80; ET: *The Response to Pighius*, trans. Mary Beaty. **(B)** *Institutes* II.2.1, 5–6, 7, 10, 26, pp. 255, 262, 264.

BIBLIOGRAPHY

John H. Leith, "The Doctrine of the Will in the *Institutes of the Christian Religion*," in *Reformation Perennis: Essays on Calvin and the Reformation in Honor of Ford Lewis Battles*, ed. Brian A. Gerrish (Pittsburgh: Pickwick, 1981).

A. FROM *THE RESPONSE TO PIGHIUS*

First [Pighi] defines the force and idea of the noun [choice]. He wishes to have "choice" accepted for election or, more suitably, for the will itself, and in his interpretation that is called "free" which is independent or has power of itself to do whatever it does in such a way that it does not do it out of necessity but has the power not to do it.

As to the word [choice], I still profess what I bore witness to in my *Institutes*, that I am not so scrupulously exact in words that I would want to stir up any argument over that one, provided that the meaning of the subject matter remains sound.

If freedom is contrasted with constraint, I acknowledge and constantly assent that choice is free, and I consider that anyone who feels otherwise is a heretic. If choice should be called free, I say, in the sense that it is not forced or violently drawn about by external motion but is acted upon of its own accord, I make no objection. When they commonly conceive something else entirely, however, when they hear or read this adjective applied to a man's will, this displeases me.

If indeed they are referring to ability . . . and power, then as soon as the will is called free you could not prevent this fanciful idea from coming into many people's minds: the will therefore has good and evil under its power so that it may choose one or the other from its own strength.

I do not, therefore, quarrel uselessly over one small word, but I believe I have just cause to wish the word removed from our midst, since a major part of virtually the world dashes itself against it so dangerously.

The word does not even seem to accord entirely well with the usage of scripture. Freedom and servitude are opposites to one another, and the person who uses one in speaking denies the other. Therefore, if a man's will is enslaved it cannot properly be called free at the same time.

Now let us hear what the Holy Spirit declares. I will be content with one passage, because the question is not about the subject itself but only about the noun used for it. When Paul describes the condition of the saints, he bears witness that they are captives, held bound under the chains of sin to the extent to which they have not yet been set free through the Spirit of God (Rom. 7:23), and when he speaks of man's nature he says that it is sold under sin (Rom. 7:14). If the saints are slaves to the extent to which they are still abandoned to themselves and their own nature, what must we say of men in whom only nature flourishes and rules? If there is only half freedom after rebirth, what is there except full servitude in the first birth of the flesh? Paul has said this very thing before, for he gives thanks to God in the sixth chapter because the Romans have been freed from sin by which they were enslaved before (Rom. 6:17). We see that he judges that the whole person is in the power of slavery before rebirth, not just the remnants of the flesh.

The person who asserts, therefore, that there is free choice is using language different from that used by the Holy Spirit. Nonetheless, if learned men agree about the meaning, I put up with their using that word. I do not even prohibit its use by the people provided that the designated subject is well explained. If this cannot be accomplished, I warn my readers at this point that they should pay more attention to the subject than to the noun used for it.

Since Pighi cunningly and continually confuses constraint . . . with necessity, and since it is of the greatest importance to the question before us to grasp and carefully recall the distinction between them, it is appropriate to observe how these four differ among themselves: the will is either free or slave, or spontaneous or constrained. They commonly understand (and Pighi also defines it this way) that the will is free which has in its power the choice of good or evil. No will can be constrained since the one is inconsistent with the other, but for the sake of teaching we must say what that means, so that constraint may be understood. Therefore we call a will constrained when it is bent to this side or that not of its own accord nor by inner movement of its choice, but when it is carried violently about by external movement. We call the will spontaneous which bends itself of its own accord wherever it is led; it is not snatched along or dragged against its will.

Finally, that will is enslaved which, on account of corruption, is held captive under the command of evil desires so that it can choose nothing except evil even if it is acting freely and of its own accord and is not impelled by external movement.

In accordance with these definitions we concede that a man has choice and that it is spontaneous, so that if he does something evil he should impute it to himself and his own voluntary choice. We reject constraint and violence since they are inconsistent with the nature of the will, and we deny that the will is free because, on account of the depravity born in a person, it is carried toward evil out of necessity and can seek only evil. From this we may gather how great the difference is between necessity and constraint.

We do not say that a man is dragged along toward sin against his will but that, since his will is corrupt, he is held captive under the yoke of sin and therefore wills to do evil out of necessity. Where there is servitude there is necessity.

Whether the servitude is voluntary or constrained is of the greatest importance. We have stated that the necessity for sinning is nowhere other than in the corruption of the will. From this it follows that the will is spontaneous. You see now that the spontaneous and the necessary can meet. Pighi craftily tries to hide this when he judges that a person is free . . . if he does not act (whether well or badly) out of necessity.

B. FROM THE *INSTITUTES*

We have now seen that the domination of sin, from the time it held the first man bound to itself, not only ranges among all mankind, but also completely occupies individual souls. It remains for us to investigate more closely whether we have been deprived of all freedom since we have been reduced to this servitude; and, if any particle of it still survives, how far its power extends. But in order that the truth of this question may be more readily apparent to us, I shall presently set a goal to which the whole argument should be directed. The best way to avoid error will be to consider the perils that threaten man on both sides. (1) When man is denied all uprightness, he immediately takes occasion for complacency from that fact; and, because he is said to have no ability to pursue righteousness on his own, he holds all such pursuit to be of no consequence, as if it did not pertain to him at all. (2) Nothing, however slight, can be credited to man without depriving God of his honor, and without man himself falling into ruin through brazen confidence. Augustine points out both these precipices.

Here, then, is the course that we must follow if we are to avoid crashing upon these rocks: when man has been taught that no good thing remains in his power, and that he is hedged about on all sides by most miserable necessity, in spite of this he should nevertheless be instructed to aspire to a good of which he is empty, to a freedom of which he has been deprived. . . .

Now in the schools three kinds of freedom are distinguished: first from necessity, second from sin, third from misery. The first of these so inheres in man by nature that it cannot possibly be taken away, but the two others have been lost through sin. I willingly accept this distinction, except in so far as necessity is falsely confused with compulsion. . . .

If this be admitted, it will be indisputable that free will is not sufficient to enable man to do good works, unless he be helped by grace, indeed by special grace, which only the elect receive through regeneration. For I do not tarry over those fanatics who babble that grace is equally and indiscriminately distributed. . . .

Man will then be spoken of as having this sort of free decision, not because he has free choice equally of good and evil, but because he acts wickedly by will, not by compulsion. Well put, indeed, but what purpose is served by labeling with a proud name such a slight thing? A noble freedom, indeed—for man not to be forced to serve sin, yet to be such a willing slave that his will is bound by the fetters of sin! Indeed, I abhor contentions about words, with which the church is harassed to no purpose. But I have scrupulously resolved to avoid those words which signify something absurd, especially where pernicious error is involved.

JONATHAN EDWARDS: DEFENDING THE AUGUSTINIAN DOCTRINE

Edwards's philosophical defense of the Augustinian doctrine of freedom and bondage of the will rests on the insight that "the will is as the greatest apparent good." By this Edwards means that a person's exercise of freedom is always an expression of innate motive and of one's perception of what would be most desirable, all things considered. The power of choice reflects the very heart of the person; it is not merely an exercise of a detached and reified faculty called a "will."[3] When Arminians engage in reified talk of the will as the agent of choice rather than the person who is choosing, argues Edwards, they are speaking about a fiction.

SOURCE

Jonathan Edwards, *A Careful and Strict Enquiry into . . . Freedom of the Will . . . .* (1754), in Edwards, *Works* (Yale) 1:144, 150, 159, 160, 163.

BIBLIOGRAPHY

For the reception of Edwards's treatment in American theology, see Allen C. Guelzo, *Edwards on the Will: A Century of American Theological Debate* (Middletown, Conn.: Wesleyan University Press, 1989).

I have rather chosen to express myself thus, that the will always *is* as the greatest apparent good, or as what appears most agreeable, is, than to say that the will is *determined* by the greatest apparent good, or by what seems most agreeable; because an appearing most agreeable or pleasing to the mind, and the mind's preferring and choosing, seem hardly to be properly and perfectly distinct. If strict propriety of speech be insisted on, it may more properly be said, that the voluntary action which is the immediate consequence and fruit of the mind's volition or choice, is determined by that which appears most agreeable, than the preference or choice itself; but that the act of volition itself is always determined by that in or about the mind's view of the object, which causes it to appear most agreeable. I say, in or about the mind's view of the object, because what has influence to render an object in view agreeable, is not only what appears in the object viewed, but also the manner of the view, and the state and circumstances of the mind that views. . . .

A thing is said to be necessary, when we can't help it, let us do what we will. So anything is said to be impossible to us, when we would do it, or would have it brought to pass, and endeavor it; or at least may be supposed to desire and seek it; but all our desires and endeavors are, or would be vain. And that is said to be irresistible, which overcomes all our opposition, resistance, and endeavor to the contrary. And we are to

---

3. Edwards's implicit rejection of "faculty" psychology is one aspect of his relatively "modern" way of conceptualizing Christian anthropology.

be said unable to do a thing, when our supposable desires and endeavors to do it are insufficient. . . .

We are said to be *naturally* unable to do a thing, when we can't do it if we will, because what is most commonly called nature don't allow of it, or because of some impeding defect or obstacle that is extrinsic to the will; either in the faculty of understanding, constitution of body, or external objects. *Moral* inability consists not in any of these things; but either in the want of inclination; or the strength of a contrary inclination; or the want of sufficient motives in view, to induce and excite the act of the will, or the strength of apparent motives to the contrary. . . .

To give some instances of this moral inability: A woman of great honor and chastity may have a moral inability to prostitute herself to her slave. A child of great love and duty to his parents, may be unable to be willing to kill his father. A very lascivious man, in case of certain opportunities and temptations, and in the absence of such and such restraints, may be unable to forbear gratifying his lust. A drunkard, under such and such circumstances, may be unable to forbear taking of strong drink. A very malicious man may be unable to exert benevolent acts to an enemy, or to desire his prosperity: yea, some may be so under the power of a vile disposition, that they may be unable to love those who are most worthy of their esteem and affection. A strong habit of virtue and great degree of holiness may cause a moral inability to love wickedness in general, may render a man unable to take complacence in wicked persons or things; or to choose a wicked life, and prefer it to a virtuous life. And on the other hand, a great degree of habitual wickedness may lay a man under an inability to love and choose holiness; and render him utterly unable to love an infinitely holy Being, or to choose and cleave to him as his chief good. . . .

The plain and obvious meaning of the words "freedom" and "liberty," in common speech, is power, opportunity, or advantage, that anyone has, to do as he pleases. Or in other words, his being free from hindrance or impediment in the way of doing, or conducting in any respect, as he wills.[1] And the contrary to liberty, whatever name we call that by, is a person's being hindered or unable to conduct as he will, or being necessitated to do otherwise.

If this which I have mentioned be the meaning of the word "liberty," in the ordinary use of language; as I trust that none that has ever learned to talk, and is unprejudiced, will deny; then it will follow, that in propriety of speech, neither liberty, nor its contrary, can properly be ascribed to any being or thing, but that which has such a faculty, power or property, as is called "will." For that which is possessed of no such thing as will, can't have any power or opportunity of doing according to its will, nor be necessitated to act contrary to its will, nor be restrained from acting agreeably to it. And therefore to talk liberty, or the contrary, as belonging to the very will itself, is not to speak good sense; if we judge of sense, and nonsense, by the original and proper signification of words. For the will itself is not an agent that has a will: the power of choosing, itself, has not a power of choosing. That which has the power of volition or choice is the man or the soul, and not the power of volition itself. And he that has the liberty of doing according to his will, is the agent or doer who is possessed of the will; and not the will which he is possessed of. We say with propriety, that a bird let loose has power and liberty to fly; but not that the bird's power of flying has a power and liberty of flying. To be free is the property of an agent, who is possessed of powers and faculties, as much as to be cunning, valiant, bountiful, or zealous. But these qualities are the properties of men or persons; and not the properties of properties.

1. I say not only "doing," but "conducting": because a voluntary forbearing to do, sitting still, keeping silence, etc. are instances of persons' conduct, about which liberty is exercised; though they are not properly called "doing."

Humanity, Redeemed by God in Christ

JOHN CALVIN: RESTORATION OF THE PERFECT IMAGE OF GOD

While Reformed theology does not consider the image of God to have been annihilated as a result of the fall, the corruption of the image is so serious that complete knowledge of what it means to be a human being is now beyond our reach. Both the content of true humanity and the very knowledge of that content are obtainable only through Jesus Christ. This does not mean that non-Christians are somehow less human than Christians and may thus be denied the fundamental respect which is owed to all human beings as creatures in the image of God, but what it does mean is that the humanity of all persons is truncated due to the fall and hence needs the restoration which only the grace of God in Jesus Christ can give.

SOURCE

Institutes I.15.4, II.6.1, p. 189.

BIBLIOGRAPHY

T. F. Torrance, *Calvin's Doctrine of Man*, an excellent exposition of the image of God in Calvin.

[I]t seems that we do not have a full definition of "image" if we do not see more plainly those faculties in which man excels, and in which he ought to be thought the reflection of God's glory. That, indeed, can be nowhere better recognized than from the restoration of his corrupted nature. There is no doubt that Adam, when he fell from his state, was by this defection alienated from God. Therefore, even though we grant that God's image was not totally annihilated and destroyed in him, yet it was so corrupted that whatever remains is frightful deformity. Consequently, the beginning of our recovery of salvation is in that restoration which we obtain through Christ, who also is called the Second Adam for the reason that he restores us to true and complete integrity. For even though Paul, contrasting the life-giving spirit that the believers receive from Christ with the living soul in which Adam was created [1 Cor. 15:45], commends the richer measure of grace in regeneration, yet he does not remove that other principal point, that the end of regeneration is that Christ should reform us to God's image. Therefore elsewhere he teaches that "the new man is renewed . . . according to the image of his Creator" [Col. 3:10]. With this agrees the saying, "Put on the new man, who has been created according to God" [Eph. 4:24, Vg.].

Now we are to see what Paul chiefly comprehends under this renewal. In the first place he posits knowledge, then pure righteousness and holiness. From this we infer that, to begin with, God's image was visible in the light of the mind, in the uprightness of the heart, and in the soundness of all the parts. For although I confess that these forms of speaking are synecdoches, yet this principle cannot be overthrown, that what was primary in the renewing of God's image also held the highest place in the creation itself. To the same pertains what he teaches else-where, that "we . . . with unveiled face beholding the glory of Christ are being transformed into his very image" [2 Cor. 3:18].

JONATHAN EDWARDS: GOD GLORIFIED IN MAN'S DEPENDENCE

Even at the point of the redemption and exaltation of humanity, classical Reformed theology focuses its gaze on the glory of God. This sermon was preached on July 8, 1731, as a "public lecture" to a distinguished group of Bostonians at the First Congregational Church.

SOURCE

Jonathan Edwards, Sermon: "God Glorified in the Work of Redemption, by the Great-ness of Man's Dependence upon him, in the Whole of it" (Boston, 1731), in Edwards, *Works* (1834) 2:4–7.

BIBLIOGRAPHY

Perry Miller, *Jonathan Edwards*, 3–40.

Doctrine

1. The redeemed have all from the *grace* of God. It was of mere grace that God gave us his only-begotten Son. The grace is great in proportion to the excellency of what is given. . . .

The grace of God in bestowing this gift is most free. It was what God was under no obligation to bestow. He might have rejected fallen man, as he did the fallen angels. It was what we never did any thing to merit; it was given while we were yet enemies, and before we had so much as repented. It was from the love of God who saw no excellency in us to attract it; and it was without expectation of ever being requited for it. . . .

Man hath now a greater dependence on the grace of God than he had before the fall. He depends on the free goodness of God for much more than he did then. Then he depended on God's goodness for conferring the reward of perfect obedience; for God was not obliged to promise and bestow that reward. But now we are dependent on the grace of God for much more; we stand in need of grace, not only to bestow glory upon us, but to deliver us from hell and eternal wrath. . . .

And as we are dependent on the goodness of God for more now than under the first covenant, so we are dependent on a much greater, more free and wonderful goodness. We are now more dependent on God's arbitrary and sovereign good pleasure. We were in our first estate dependent on God for holiness. We had our original righteousness from him; but then holiness was not bestowed in such a way of sovereign good pleasure as it is now. Man was created holy, for it became God to create holy all his reasonable creatures. It would have been a disparagement to the holiness of God's nature, if he had made an intelligent creature unholy. But now when a fallen man is made holy, it is from mere and arbitrary grace; God may for ever deny holiness to the fallen creature if he pleases, without any disparagement to any of his perfections.

And we are not only indeed more dependent on the grace of God, but our dependence is much more conspicuous, because our own insufficiency and helplessness in ourselves is much more apparent in our fallen and undone state, than it was before we were either sinful or miserable. . . .

2. We receive all from the *power* of God. Man's redemption is often spoken of as a work of wonderful power as well as grace. . . . Yea, it is a more glorious work of power than mere creation, or raising a dead body to life, in that the effect attained is greater and more excellent. That holy

and happy being, and spiritual life, which is produced in the work of conversion, is a far greater and more glorious effect than mere being and life. . . .

Secondly, They are also dependent on God for all, as they have all *through* him. God is the medium of it, as well as the author and fountain of it. All we have, wisdom, the pardon of sin, deliverance from hell, acceptance into God's favour, grace and holiness, true comfort and happiness, eternal life and glory, is from God by a Mediator; and this Mediator is God; which Mediator we have an absolute dependence upon, as he through whom we receive all. So that here is another way wherein we have our dependence on God for all good. God not only gives us the Mediator, and accepts his mediation, and of his power and grace bestows the things purchased by the Mediator; but he the Mediator is God.

Our blessings are what we have by purchase; and the purchase is made of God, the blessings are purchased of him, and God gives the purchaser; and not only so, but God is the purchaser. Yea God is both the purchaser and the price; for Christ, who is God, purchased these blessings for us, by offering up himself as the price of our salvation. . . .

Thirdly, The redeemed have all their good *in God.* We not only have it of him, and through him, but it consists in him; he is all our good.—The good of the redeemed is either objective or inherent. By their objective good, I mean that extrinsic object, in the possession and enjoyment of which they are happy. Their inherent good is that excellency or pleasure which is in the soul itself. With respect to both of which the redeemed have all their good in God, or which is the same thing, God himself is all their good.

1. The redeemed have all their *objective* good in God. God himself is the great good which they are brought to the possession and enjoyment of by redemption. He is the highest good, and the sum of all that good which Christ purchased. . . .

2. The redeemed have all their *inherent* good in God. Inherent good is twofold; it is either excellency or pleasure. These the redeemed not only derive from God, as caused by him, but have them in him. They have spiritual excellency and joy by a kind of participation of God. They are made excellent by a communication of God's excellency. God puts his own beauty, *i.e.* his beautiful likeness, upon their souls.

Jonathan Edwards: God's End in Creating the World

Reformed theology has spoken in one voice in affirming that God's primary end in creating the world was to further God's own glory. This was not thought to entail "egoism" on God's part, because God is the most excellent being and because the happiness and enjoyment of God's creatures are included as components of this goal. Jonathan Edwards explains this using the conceptuality of God's communicative disposition, which we met previously in Edwards's theology of the trinitarian nature of God (pp. 69–72, 82–84, above).

SOURCE

Jonathan Edwards, *Dissertation I: Concerning the End for which God Created the World* (1753–54; posthumously published, 1788), in Edwards, *Works* (Yale) 8:528–35 (edited).

BIBLIOGRAPHY

Samuel Hopkins, "The Decrees of God," *System of Doctrines* (1792), in *The Works of Samuel Hopkins*, 3 vols. (Boston, 1865), 1:72–73. Hopkins is replicating the Edwardsian theology in the next generation.

The communication of [God's] knowledge is chiefly in giving the knowledge of himself: for this is the knowledge in which the fullness of God's understanding chiefly consists. And thus we see how the manifestation of God's glory to created understandings, and their seeing and knowing it, is not distinct from an emanation or communication of God's fullness, but clearly implied in it.

Again, the communication of God's virtue or holiness is principally in communicating the love of himself (which appears by what has before been observed). And thus we see how, not only the creature's seeing and knowing God's excellence, but also supremely esteeming and loving him, belongs to the communication of God's fullness. And the communication of God's joy and happiness consists chiefly in communicating to the creature that happiness and joy, which consists in rejoicing in God and in his glorious excellency; for in such joy God's own happiness does principally consist. . . .

Thus we see that the great and last end of God's works which is so variously expressed in Scripture, is indeed but *one*; and this *one* end is most properly and comprehensively called, "the glory of God"; by which name it is most commonly called in Scripture. And is fitly compared to an effulgence or emanation of light from a luminary, by which this glory of God is abundantly represented in Scripture. Light is the external expression, exhibition and manifestation of the excellency of the luminary, of the sun for instance: it is the abundant, extensive emanation and communication of the fullness of the sun to innumerable beings that partake of it. . . .

The emanation or communication of the divine fullness, consisting in the knowledge of God, love to God, and joy in God, has relation indeed both to God and the creature: but it has relation to God as its fountain, as it is an emanation from God; and as the communication itself, or thing communicated, is something divine, something of God, something of his internal fullness; as the water in the stream is something of the fountain; and as the beams are of the sun. And again, they have relation to God as they have respect to him as their object: for the knowledge communicated is the knowledge of God; and so God is the object of the knowledge: and the love communicated, is the love of God; so God is the object of that love: and the happiness communicated, is joy in God; and so he is the object of the joy communicated. In the creature's knowing, esteeming, loving, rejoicing in, and praising God, the glory of God is both exhibited and acknowledged; his fullness is received and returned. Here is both an *emanation* and *remanation*. The refulgence shines upon and into the creature, and is reflected back to the luminary. The beams of glory come from God, and are something of God, and are refunded back again to their original. So that the whole is *of* God, and *in* God, and *to* God; and God is the beginning, middle and end in this affair. . . .

And though the emanation of God's fullness which God intended in the creation, and which actually is the consequence of it, is to the creature as its object, and the creature is the subject of the fullness communicated, and is the creature's good; and was also regarded as such, when God sought it as the end of his works: yet it don't [*sic*] necessarily follow, that even in so doing, he did not make himself his end. It comes to the same thing. God's respect to the creature's good, and his respect to himself, is not a divided respect; but both are united in one, as the happiness of the creature aimed at is happiness in union with himself. The creature is no further happy with this happiness which God makes his ultimate end than he becomes one with God. The more happiness the greater union: when the happiness is perfect, the union is perfect. And as the happiness will be increasing to eternity, the union will become more and more strict and perfect; nearer and more like to that between God the Father and the Son; who are so united, that their interest is perfectly one. If the happiness of the creature be considered as it will be, in the whole of the creature's eternal duration, with all the infinity of its progress, and infinite increase of nearness and union to God; in this view, the creature must be looked upon as united to God in an infinite strictness. . . .

God aims at that which the motion or progression which he causes aims at, or tends to. If there be many things supposed to be so made and appointed, that by a constant and eternal motion, they all tend to a certain center; then it appears that he who made them and is the cause of their motion, aimed at that center, that term of their motion to which they eternally tend, and are eternally, as it were, striving after. And if God be this center, then God aimed at himself. And herein it appears that as he is the first author of their being and motion, so he is the last end, the final term, to which is their ultimate tendency and aim.

PROVIDENCE
In General
John Calvin

Providence is the exercise of divine power to preserve, maintain, and rule all that God created. To God, therefore, all things owe both their existence and their sustenance. For Calvin, and Reformed theology in general, this means that every event occurs under the mighty hand of God: "not a drop of rain falls" apart from God's will. God is actively at work in the lives of all people, and especially the elect, to accomplish the divine purposes in creation and redemption.

SOURCES

(A) *Institutes* I.16.1–2, I.17.2, pp. 197–99, 212 (edited). **(B)** *Contre la secte phantastique et furieuse des Libertins que se nomment Spirituelz* (1545); *CO* 7:145–252. For a fine translation of the entire work, see *Treatise Against the Libertines* (1545), in *Treatises Against the Anabaptists and Against the Libertines*, trans. and ed. Benjamin Wirt Farley (Grand Rapids: Baker, 1982), 242–49 (edited). In the translation below, we have drawn together the three major points of the chapter: CO 7: 186–92.

A. PROVIDENCE PERCEIVED BY FAITH
AND AN OBJECT OF PIETY

[T]o make God a momentary Creator, who once for all finished his work, would be cold and barren, and we must differ from profane men especially in that we see the presence of divine power shining as much in the continuing state of the universe as in its inception. For even though the minds of the impious too are compelled by merely looking upon earth and heaven to rise up to the Creator, yet faith has its own peculiar way of assigning the whole credit for Creation to God. To this pertains that saying of the apostle's to which we have referred before, that only "by faith we understand that the universe was created by the word of

God" [Heb. 11:3]. For unless we pass on to his providence—however we may seem both to comprehend with the mind and to confess with the tongue—we do not yet properly grasp what it means to say: "God is Creator." Carnal sense, once confronted with the power of God in the very Creation, stops there, and at most weighs and contemplates only the wisdom, power, and goodness of the author in accomplishing such handiwork. (These matters are self-evident, and even force themselves upon the unwilling.) It contemplates, moreover, some general preserving and governing activity, from which the force of motion derives. In short, carnal sense thinks there is an energy divinely bestowed from the beginning, sufficient to sustain all things.

But faith ought to penetrate more deeply, namely, having found him Creator of all, forthwith to conclude he is also everlasting Governor and Preserver—not only in that he drives the celestial frame as well as its several parts by a universal motion, but also in that he sustains, nourishes, and cares for, everything he has made, even to the least sparrow [cf. Matt. 10:29]. . . .

That this difference may better appear, we must know that God's providence, as it is taught in Scripture, is opposed to fortune and fortuitous happenings. Now it has been commonly accepted in all ages, and almost all mortals hold the same opinion today, that all things come about through chance. What we ought to believe concerning providence is by this depraved opinion most certainly not only beclouded, but almost buried. Suppose a man falls among thieves, or wild beasts; is shipwrecked at sea by a sudden gale; is killed by a falling house or tree. Suppose another man wandering through the desert finds help in his straits; having been tossed by the waves, reaches harbor; miraculously escapes death by a finger's breadth. Carnal reason ascribes all such happenings, whether prosperous or adverse, to fortune. But anyone who has been taught by Christ's lips that all the hairs of his head are numbered [Matt. 10:30] will look farther afield for a cause, and will consider that all events are governed by God's secret plan. . . .

Therefore no one will weigh God's providence properly and profitably but him who considers that his business is with his Maker and the Framer of the universe, and with becoming humility submits himself to fear and reverence. Hence it happens that today so many dogs assail this doctrine with their venomous bitings, or at least with barking: for they wish nothing to be lawful for God beyond what their own reason prescribes for themselves.

B. THREEFOLD GOVERNANCE OF
THE WORLD

As to God's governance of the world, I say that God has three modes of operation. . . .

First, there is a universal operation whereby God accompanies all creatures in keeping with the propriety and condition bestowed upon them at the time of creating them. This accompanying is none other than the "order of nature." . . .

The second mode by which God works in creatures is by making them serve the divine goodness, justice, and counsel. [This second mode] works according to God's will to aid the servants of God, to punish evildoers, and to put the patience of the faithful to the test, or to admonish them with God's fatherly kindness. . . .

The third mode of God's operation rests in the governing of the faithful, living and reigning in them by the Holy Spirit. Since we are under the corruption of original sin, we are as dry ground which can yield no good fruit at all. Our perspective is perverted, our will heedless of God, inclined and set upon evil, our whole nature, in a word, is treacherous. In this condition we have the power neither to engage in right conduct nor, as Paul would say (2 Cor. 3:5), to think a single good thought. Instead, all our sufficiency must come from God.

Isaac Watts and William Cowper

There is perhaps no better way to illustrate providence as an everyday feature of the Reformed way of life than through hymnody. We have already encountered the hymns of Isaac Watts (pp. 56–57, 140–41). William Cowper (1731–1800), an English lawyer and later assistant to the pastor and composer John Newton, was subject to serious incidents of suicidal depression and hallucinations and was for a season confined to an asylum. The hymn below, one of Cowper's most popular, first appeared in the "Olney Collection," which he published with John Newton; it was composed during the onset of an episode of mental illness.

SOURCES

(A) Isaac Watts, Hymn: "O God, Our Help in Ages Past" (1719). (B) William Cowper, Hymn: "God Moves in a Mysterious Way" (1774; published in the "Olney Collection," 1779).

BIBLIOGRAPHY

M. J. Quinlin, *William Cowper: A Critical Life* (Minneapolis: University of Minnesota Press, 1953).

A. ISAAC WATTS, "O GOD, OUR HELP IN AGES PAST"

O God, our Help in ages past,
    Our Hope for years to come,
Our shelter from the stormy blast,
    And our eternal Home:

Before the hills in order stood,
    Or earth received her frame,
From everlasting Thou art God,
    To endless years the same. . . .

O God, our Help in ages past,
    Our Hope for years to come,
Be Thou our Guard while life shall last,
    And our Eternal Home.

B. WILLIAM COWPER: "GOD MOVES IN A MYSTERIOUS WAY"

God moves in a mysterious way
    His wonders to perform;
He plants His footsteps in the sea,
    And rides upon the storm.

Deep in unfathomable mines
    Of neverfailing skill
He treasures up His bright designs,
    And works His sovereign will.

Ye fearful saints, fresh courage take;
    The clouds ye so much dread
Are big with mercy, and shall break
    In blessings on your head.

Blind unbelief is sure to err,
    And scan His work in vain;
God is His own Interpreter,
    And He will make it plain.

Preservation, Concurrence, and Government

Rendering the doctrine of providence comprehensible led seventeenth- and eighteenth-century Reformed theology into a number of technical distinctions. Preservation (*conservatio*) and concurrence (*concursus*) signal God's general maintenance of creation. Governance (*gubernatio*) goes a step further and indicates that God not only accompanies but also directs and rules over all events. In William Ames's explanation of this distinction, he conceives of conservation as a continuation of the act of creation (*continuata creatio*), a belief that emphasizes God's intimate involvement in history against any who would see God as only a passive onlooker.

In the covenant theology of Johannes Cocceius, we confront an elaboration of "continual creation" explained in biblical perspective. Similarly, Jonathan Edwards defends "continual creation" in a philosophically radical form whereby in each moment the created order is completely dependent upon God's creative action. By Edwards's day, "continual creation" stood in sharp contrast to the increasingly influential philosophy of Deism, which held that God created the world and then left it to operate in accordance with the established laws of nature without divine intervention. Some Reformed theologians have criticized Edwards's position for its failure to distinguish God's *creating* from God's *upholding* of the world and for its so-called occasionalism by which it seems to remove the independent integrity of mundane causes, thereby locating all efficiency of causation in God.[4]

At stake in this debate is the synthesizing of two equally important Reformed convictions: the sovereignty of God in all things and the fundamental distinction between the Creator and the creature. Reformed orthodoxy, represented here by François Turretin, tries to strike a middle ground between Deism and continual creation by holding together the "influx" of God into creaturely events and the integrity of creaturely causation. The precise mode of "concurrence" and "governance," however, remains beyond the comprehension of human minds. Much is on the line here, for those who deny God's governance of the world in order to shield God from blame for evil risk eliminating God's responsibility for the good as well.

SOURCES

(A) William Ames, *Medulla SS. Theologiae* (1623, 1629), Book I, chap. 9, pars. 14–19; ET: "Providence," and "Special Government of Intelligent Creatures," in Ames, *Marrow*,

---

4. For a critique of Edwards, see Hodge, *Systematic Theology* 1:577–81. For the argument that Edwards does indeed maintain an independent integrity for creation, see Sang Hyun Lee, *The Philosophical Theology of Jonathan Edwards* (Princeton: Princeton University Press, 1988), esp. chap. 3.

108–11. **(B)** Johannes Cocceius, "De Providentia Dei," c. XXVIII, *Summa Theologiae* (1662), pp. 217–20; trans. Mary Beaty. **(C)** Jonathan Edwards, *Original Sin* (1758), in Edwards, *Works* (Yale) 3:400–404. **(D)** François Turretin, *Institutio theologiae elencticae* (Geneva, 1688), Locus 6, qs. 5, 6, 7 (edited). This translation is a reworking of the nineteenth-century translation by George Musgrave Giger; it has been edited both to clarify meaning and to conform with modern English usage and style.

BIBLIOGRAPHY

An important recent examination of these issues is Kathryn Tanner, *God and Creation in Christian Theology: Tyranny or Empowerment?* (Oxford: Basil Blackwell, 1988).

A. WILLIAM AMES:
DISTINCTION BETWEEN
PRESERVATION AND GOVERNMENT

14. The providence of God is either conservational or governmental.

15. Conservation is God's making all things, universal and particular, to persist and continue in essence and existence as well as in their powers, Ps. 104:19, 20; Acts 17:28; Heb. 1:3. This is suitably called by the Schoolmen, "God's holding in his hand," because by this power God sustains all things as if with his hand.

16. Conservation necessarily comes between creation and the government of things created, because whatever is created is for some end and use to which it ought to be directed and governed. But it cannot reach this end or be directed towards it, unless it be continued and maintained in its being.

17. God's conservation is necessary for the creature because the creature depends in every way upon the creator—not only for its creation, but also for its being, existence, continuance, and operation. Every creature would return to that state of nothing whence it came if God did not uphold it; and the cessation of divine conservation would, without any other operation, immediately reduce every creature to nothing. Ps. 104:29, *If thou hide thy face, they are troubled; if thou take away their breath, they die and return to their dust.*

18. Some things—subject only to God—are conserved directly. This conservation is the same as creation, except that creation has a certain newness which conservation lacks and creation lacks a preceding existence which conservation implies. Conservation is nothing else than a continued creation, so to speak, and therefore it is joined with creation. Neh. 9:6, *Thou hast made . . . and thou preservest all things.*

19. Government is the power whereby God directs and leads all his creatures to their proper end. Ps. 29:10, *The Lord sits as king forever.*

B. JOHANNES COCCEIUS:
PRESERVATION AS "CONTINUAL CREATION"

[T]he conservation of the world does not exist without creation properly speaking. However many things come into being and however they are created, God creates that which the parents bring forth. Whatever is in the things which are brought forth is there because of God's call and command. To create is nothing other than to produce some new thing by means of a word.

Indeed, if new individual things did not arise every day, the groups of beings by which the world is adorned would perish as the individuals pass away, and thus the world would cease to be a habitation, especially of humankind for whose sake it was created, and so it would be in vain.

Therefore the creation of new individuals in every species is part of the conservation of the world and of the species in it. From this it is clear that the people are crazy who think that God takes forethought for groups of beings but does not extend it to the smallest single individuals or beings. Even the hairs of our head are numbered, and lest you think that God is concerned for humankind but that other things are beyond his care, not even little sparrows fall to the ground or are captured without his willing it (Matt. 10:29, 39). Does he not gather the tears and sighings of the saints and store them up in his thoughts? (Ps. 56:[8]). Add to this Matt. 6:30, Luke 12:28, 1 Cor. 15:38, Job 37:6 and 38:28, Matt. 5:45, Pss. 104:30 and 147:15–18.

Pindar has beautifully described God's exact knowledge of all things, even the smallest.

> [T]hou who knowest the end supreme of all things, and all the ways that lead thereto, the number of the leaves that the earth putteth forth in spring, the number of sands that, in the sea and the rivers, are driven before the waves and the rushing winds, and that which is to be, and when it is to come,—all this thou clearly seest. But, if I must measure myself against one that is wise, I needs must speak. Thou camest to this glade to be her wedded lord, and thou shalt bear her over the sea to the choicest garden of Zeus, where thou shalt make her queen of a city, when thou hast gathered the island-folk around the plain-encircled hill. . . . (*Pythian Odes* IX)

These words, though magnificently spoken, are nonetheless surpassed by the bare simplicity of scripture (Acts 15:18): "All his works are known to God from the beginning of the world." That is, he has known and decreed and determined what he is going to do.

In conservation, what the scholastics call "concurrence" is noteworthy. This means the dependence of second causes upon the first cause in their actions, for a thing that does not exist of itself cannot act of itself. It is amazing that there is anything which at one time did not exist; more amazing that it also acts; most amazing that it acts freely and in such a way that it can do contrary things. Nevertheless, it is very clear that there is freedom in certain acting beings (which, in the writing of the apostles, not only "are moved" but also "live") and that they necessarily depend in their actions on the first cause and on the nod of its will.

The "how" of this dependence is as hidden from the creature as is the very method of creation. Only the Creator and Prime Mover can know this, for he alone knows himself and his own powers and riches. Wisdom is not found in any thing or any place. Destruction and death have heard his voice; they announce to us that God has prepared his ways and known his place [Job 28:23]; that is, no creature knows the mind of God and what it is fitting that God should do or not do, and how God directs all things so that, although creatures often oppose him, nonetheless nothing happens contrary to his will. Death itself and destruction itself show, as if witnesses of it, that wisdom is with God. For, since all things are from nothing and cannot exist except by the divine will, no one can doubt that God has made all things beautifully from the beginning in his own time. Death also, by which people return to their dust, is a witness that God hates sins and has prepared something better for those who seek him. Therefore Psalm 139 bears witness properly that the knowledge of God and his work are omnipresent for a man—"You know my sitting down and my rising up and you understand my thoughts afar off" (that is, from long before; thus Isa. 25:1: "your counsels of old"; 22:11: "fashioned long ago"). "You are acquainted with all my ways. There is not a word in my tongue but, lo, O Lord, you know it altogether. You have beset me behind and before and you lay your hand on me. Knowledge is wonderful for me; it is sublime, I am not able to attain it. . . . I shall take the wings of the Dawn and dwell in the uttermost part of the sea; even there your hand leads me and your right hand holds me" (Ps. 139: 2–6, 9–10). However, just as we properly leave to God full knowledge of this part of providence, so it is for us to acknowledge for God's glory those things which have been manifested and revealed.

The same action and work, although it is of the second cause and is said to be of it and carries its name, nevertheless also depends on the first cause, not only remotely, as far as the essence and faculty of the second cause is [remote] from the first cause . . . but very closely and immediately, so that every movement of a created being depends on the first cause in particular. [See] Isa. 26:12, . . . Rom. 12:6, . . . Jer. 1:5. . . .

In such a way a person presupposes in God the nod of his will and the arranging and determining of his counsel with which he wishes an act to concur. While—just imagine—he has determined to grant to creatures who are free and not yet strong but are changing that they may also freely abuse the life and action which he has given and will give to them. By this means, concurrence hastens ahead, for this counsel exists before the action of the creature, and the efficacy of it accompanies the creature's action in time with it, as it were, but accompanies it as the efficacy of the first cause.

"Permission" is present with providence in sin. This is not concession, through the removal of an obstructing law, nor is it a ceasing from placing moral impediments or difficulties of acting (for often a sin is committed when the deed or certainty of the desire is struggling against all impediments), but it includes negation of that action by which God brings it about that his precepts are obeyed by the creature, with the providing of concurrence to the free action of the creature.

The Jesuits make up an "indifferent concurrence," placed in man's power, not influencing for good or bad effect before the will influences. Those are pure chimeras. For by this falsehood God is imagined to concur when it is uncertain whether anything should take place; to concur with both things and with neither and with one or the other; not to concur with the will of the man, to concur before he concurs, and to concur when the man has influenced him, and to depend on the man's influence and to be changed at the same time not only as regards knowledge but as regards his decree. For if concurrence is so entirely indifferent, God will not know ahead of time what a creature will do, but when the creature has wished and done that which has been permitted him, then finally God will know it and finally, after the creature's will has been seen and known, will resolve absolutely a thing which he did not decree from the beginning except conditionally. To pass on, in the same way man—even a sinner—becomes the master and cause of his own life and salvation. This is not the place to deal with that.

It is clear enough to one looking at the plan for the ages that God made in Christ, by which he determined to expiate and remit sins (Eph. 1:4; 3:11), that God has the determining will to which also a sinner is subjected, so that he cannot sin in everything and, by sinning, exceed the limitation of God and cannot sin of his own accord and freely when he is allowed, depending on the nod, or if you please, the certain concurrence of the first cause. For one who has decided to remit sins has decided also to permit them. And he who has determined to expiate them through his Son has known that what he was permitting would take place. And he who chose a certain and particular people to save before the foundations of the world were laid down, has not failed to know of their sins.

C. JONATHAN EDWARDS:
A RADICALIZED "CONTINUAL CREATION"

God's *preserving* created things in being is perfectly equivalent to a *continued creation*, or to his creating those things out of nothing at *each moment* of their existence. If the continued existence of created things be wholly dependent on God's preservation, then those things would drop into nothing, upon the ceasing of the present moment, without a new exertion of the divine power to cause them to exist in the following moment. If there be any who own, that God preserves things in being, and yet hold that they would continue in being without any further help from him, after they once have existence; I think, it is hard to know what they mean. To what purpose can it be, to talk of God's preserving things in being, when there is no need of his preserving them? Or to talk of their being dependent on God for continued existence, when they would of themselves continue to exist, without his help; nay, though he should wholly withdraw his sustaining power and influence?

It will follow from what has been observed, that God's upholding created substance, or causing its existence in each successive moment, is altogether equivalent to an *immediate production out of nothing*, at each moment, because its existence at this moment is not merely in part from God, but wholly from him; and not in any part, or degree, from its antecedent existence. For the supposing, that its antecedent existence *concurs* with God in *efficiency*, to produce some part of the effect, is attended with all the very same absurdities, which have been shown to attend the supposition of its producing it wholly. Therefore the antecedent existence is nothing, as to any proper influence or assistance in the affair: and consequently God produces the effect as much from *nothing*, as if there had been nothing *before*. So that this effect differs not at all from the first creation, but only *circumstantially*; as in first creation there had been no such act and effect of God's power before; whereas, his giving existence afterwards, *follows* preceding acts and effects of the same kind, in an established order.

Now, in the next place, let us see how the consequence of these things is to my present purpose. If the existence of created substance, in each successive moment, be wholly the effect of God's immediate power, in that moment, without any dependence on prior existence, as much as the first creation out of nothing, then what exists at this moment, by this power, is a *new effect;* and simply and absolutely considered, not the same with any past existence, though it be like it, and follows it according to a certain established method. And there is no identity or oneness in the case, but what depends on the *arbitrary* constitution of the Creator; who by his wise sovereign establishment so unites these successive new effects, that he *treats them as one,* by communicating to them like properties, relations, and circumstances; and so, leads us to regard and treat them as one. When I call this an arbitrary constitution, I mean, that it is a constitution which depends on nothing but the divine will; which *divine will* depends on nothing but the *divine wisdom.* In this sense, the whole course of nature, with all that belongs to it, all its laws and methods, and constancy and regularity, continuance and proceeding, is an *arbitrary constitution.* In this sense, the continuance of the very being of the world and all its parts, as well as the manner of continued being, depends entirely on an arbitrary constitution: for it don't all *necessarily* follow, that because there was sound, or light, or color, or resistance, or gravity, or thought, or consciousness, or any other dependent thing the last moment, that therefore there shall be the like at the next. All dependent existence whatsoever is in a constant flux, ever passing and returning; renewed every moment, as the colors of bodies are every moment renewed by the light that shines upon them; and all is constantly proceeding from God, as light from the sun. "In him we live, and move, and have our being."

Thus it appears, if we consider matters strictly, there is no such thing as any identity or oneness in created objects, existing at different times, but what depends on *God's sovereign constitution.* And so it appears, that the objection we are upon, made against a supposed divine constitution, whereby Adam and his posterity are viewed and treated as one, in the manner and for the purposes supposed, as if it were not consistent with truth, because no constitution can make those to be one, which are not one; I say, it appears that this objection is built on a false hypothesis: for it appears, that a *divine constitution* is the thing which *makes truth,* in affairs of this nature. The objection supposes, there is a oneness in created beings, whence qualities and relations are derived down from past existence, distinct from, and prior to any oneness that can be supposed to be founded on divine constitution. Which is demonstrably false; and sufficiently appears so from things conceded by the adversaries themselves: and therefore the objection wholly falls to the ground.

D. FRANÇOIS TURRETIN:
CONTINENTAL ORTHODOX DOCTRINE
OF CONCURRENCE AND GOVERNANCE,
NECESSITY AND CONTINGENCY

God Governs as Well as Concurs in the
Creaturely Occurrences

Because God is the Regulator and Lord of the world, and consequently of all that exists or is done in it, nothing is done merely by conservation or a general concourse. This is so because [for God] to "regulate" is to "preside over," [and] he who presides rules by a destined order which embraces both the settling of the end and the ordination of the means. Thus because he is the Lord of singular [occurrences], God holds subject to his sway all and every motion, action, and event, external and internal, good and bad.

As the creature derives its *being* from God, so also it ought to derive its *working*, for the mode of working follows the mode of being; for these walk side by side. Now every creature depends upon God for its being and therefore also in its operation. But if God by his providence is occupied only with the conservation of things, or with a general and indifferent concourse determined [solely] by secondary causes, then the creature in its working will not depend upon God; instead, God will rather depend upon the creature: first cause will be rendered secondary, and secondary, first; secondary cause will no longer be subordinate but coordinate and independent. . . .

If only a general concourse of God is granted, in vain is he prayed to for anything, because he can neither avert evil nor confer good. . . . Nor is it any use to give thanks for blessings procured through free agencies; nor to trust and hope in God or patiently submit our wills to his, because if God only "concurs," the good or evil which we hope or fear can as well happen as not happen. . . .

On the grounds of a general and indifferent concourse, God will be no more the cause of good than of evil . . . [and all would be determined merely by human will]. . . .

Finally if general and indifferent concourse is posited [without governance], then (1) the decree of God would be rendered uncertain and prescience fallible, because both would depend on the mutable will of human beings; (2) the operations of the will would be withdrawn from the dominion of God . . . ; (3) the creature would act more than God . . . ; and (4) the special reason of piety, situated in the dependence of our will upon the will of God would be subverted. . . .

There Is Not Only a Particular and Simultaneous but Also a Previous Concourse of God

Previous concourse (*precursus*) is the action of God by which, flowing into causes and their principles, he excites and previously moves creatures to action, and directs to the doing of a particular thing. Simultaneous concourse, however, is that by which God produces the action of the creature as to its being or substance, by which he is supposed to flow together with creatures into their actions and effects but not into the creatures themselves. Although indeed they do not differ really but only in [human] reason (because the simultaneous concourse is nothing else than continued previous concourse which not only flows into the causes themselves that it may work *in them* but into the effect itself so as to act *with them*) yet they can be considered distinctly. . . .

[We may explain this as follows:] Predetermination does not destroy but conserves the liberty of the will, because by it God does not compel rational creatures nor make them act by a physical or brute necessity, but he only effects this: that they, both indeed consistently with themselves and in accordance with their own nature (that is, from preference and spontaneously) are so determined by God that they also determine themselves. . . .

The necessity carried into things by predetermination is not destructive of liberty, because it is not *consequent* [i.e., does not make the cause itself or the effect to be necessary] but is *of consequence*, which means it only secures the action of a cause of this kind and indeed [does so] agreeably to the cause itself [which maintains itself] spontaneously and willingly. Whence these two can at the same time be true, a person wills spontaneously and yet with respect to providence (or premotion) that person cannot help willing; this is so because the premotion of God is such that it takes place in accordance with the nature of things, and does not take away from secondary causes the mode of operation proper to each. . . .

Although creatures are instruments of God which he uses for the execution of their own works, creatures [nonetheless] do not cease to possess a proper influx [over their works] and to hold *the relation of proper causes*, not indeed with respect to God but to the remaining causes subordinate to God. Nor is it absurd that there should be two totally acting causes of the same numerical effect of a different order, since the action of both causes is only one, by which they concur to the same effect.

Although the premotion of God is extended to evil actions, it does not on that account make God guilty of the fault, or the author of sin, because it only pertains to actions inasmuch as they are *material* and *entative*, not however as they are *moral*; that is, premotion goes to the *substance* of the act but not to its wickedness. . . .

How Can Concursus Be Reconciled with Free Will?

How [concourse and free will] can consist with each other, no mortal can in this life perfectly understand. Nor should this [mystery] seem surprising to us, since God has a thousand ways, incomprehensible to us, of concurring with our will, insinuating himself into us, and turning our hearts, so that even as we perform freely what we will, we still do nothing besides the will and determination of God. . . .

The true method of harmonizing these two things must . . . be sought . . . from the order of the causes themselves. . . . First, the concourse of providence and of free will is not of collateral and equal causes but of causes unequal and subordinate . . . , the one universal and hyperphysical . . . the other particular and physical. . . . Second, God so concurs with second causes that although he previously moves and predetermines them by a motion, not general only but also special, still he moves them according to their own nature and does not deprive them of their own proper mode of operating. . . . Third, since providence does not concur with the human will either by *coaction*, compelling the unwilling will, nor by *determining it physically*, as a brute and blind thing lacking judgment, but since it concurs with it *rationally* by turning the will in a manner suitable to itself, it follows that the will may determine itself as the proximate cause of its own actions, by the proper judgment of reason and the spontaneous willful election; hence, concourse does no violence to our will but rather kindly cherishes it. . . . Fourth, God so concurs with the human will as still to determine it differently in good and evil. For in the good actions, God so previously moves the will as to be the author of them, not only in the genus of nature but also according to their moral goodness by determining the will, not only as to the *thing* . . . but also as to the *mode*, that what is done should be done well, partly by giving to it good qualities through special help or supernatural grace, partly by exciting them when given, helping and educing action through cooperation. . . . In evil action, however, God so concurs as neither to effect, assist, nor approve them but to permit and efficaciously direct them, not by infusing wickedness but by so determining rational creatures physically to the substance of the act in the genus of being that they, when left to themselves . . . move and determine themselves. . . . Whence the guilt rests upon them alone from which God is forthwith free.

Miracles

The providential relationship between God and the world naturally raises the question of divine miracles. Some brief statements are provided below, together with the judgment shared by the majority of the Reformed in this period that the apostolic age of miracles has ceased. It should be noted that the language of "intervention" by God is absent from the definition of Peter Martyr. The conceptuality of an "intervention" into a mechanical "system," which came into prominence in the wake of Deism and Newtonian physics, pits God against God's own creative and sustaining purposes.

Peter Martyr Vermigli (1500–1562) was an influential Italian theologian about whom more is said below (pp. 321–22, 351 n.4). Caspar Olevianus, who was born in Treves in 1536 and died in Herborn in 1587, assisted Zacharias Ursinus in the drafting of the Heidelberg Catechism (pp. 4–6, 37–39, 59).

SOURCES

(A) Peter Martyr Vermigli, *Loci Communes* (London, 1576); ET: In Heppe, *Reformed Dogmatics*, 264. (B) Caspar Olevianus, *De Substantia Foederis Gratuiti inter Deum et electos itemque de mediis, quibus ea ipsa substantia nobis communicatur, libri duo* (Geneva, 1585); ET: In Heppe, *Reformed Dogmatics*, 265. (C) Westminster Confession of Faith (1647), chap. 5, par. 3, in Leith, *Creeds*, 200. (D) Jonathan Edwards, "1 Cor. 13:8–12," *Notes on the Bible*, in Edwards, *Works* (1834) 2:800.

BIBLIOGRAPHY

The most important philosophical treatments in this period which question the traditional view of miracles are David Hume, *Enquiry Concerning Human Understanding* (1748), Section X. Matthew Tindal, *Christianity as old as the Creation, or the Gospel a Republication of the Religion of Nature* (1730). John Toland, *Christianity Not Mysterious* (1696). Benedict [Baruch] Spinoza, *Tractatus Theologico-Politicus* (1670).

A. PETER MARTYR VERMIGLI:
DEFINITION

A miracle is a difficult and unusual work of divine force, surpassing every power of created nature, made public in order to fill those who perceive it with astonishment and to confirm faith in the words of God.

B. CASPAR OLEVIANUS:
THE PERFECT MIRACLE

[T]he supreme miracle is the sending of the gospel offering the Father's love, surpassing all the miracles from the beginning of the world, whereby he gives the son as a [sacrifice] for us and the head of the church by faith in himself.

C. WESTMINSTER CONFESSION: FREEDOM OF GOD

God, in his ordinary providence, maketh use of means, yet is free to work without, above, and against them, at his pleasure.

D. JONATHAN EDWARDS: THE CESSATION OF MIRACLES

1 Cor. xiii.8, 9, 10, 11, 12. "Charity never faileth: but whether there be prophecies, they shall fail;—For we know in part, and we prophesy in part. But when that which is perfect is come, then that which is in part shall be done away. When I was a child,—Now we see through a glass darkly," &c. There is a twofold failing or ceasing of those miraculous and other common gifts of the Spirit, both of which the apostle has doubtless respect to: one is their failing at the end of the present state of probation, or the present imperfect state of God's people in time, with respect to particular persons that have common gifts, at death, and with respect to the church of God collectively considered, at the end of the world; and the other is the failing of miraculous gifts in the church of Christ, even while yet remaining in its temporary and militant state, as they failed at or about the end of the apostolic age, that first and more imperfect, and less settled and established state of the christian church, before it was wholly brought out from under the Mosaic dispensation, wherein it was under tutors and governors, and before the canon of the Scripture was fully completed, and all parts of it thoroughly collected and established. Miraculous, and other common gifts of the Spirit, cease at the end of the imperfect state of the church: wherein the church knows in part, and is in a state of childhood in comparison of the more perfect state that follows. So there is a twofold perfect state of the church to answer them, wherein the church may be said to be in a state of manhood, with respect to the more imperfect state that they succeed. The first state of the church, in its first age on earth, before the canon of the Scripture was completed, &c. is its imperfect state, wherein the church knows in part, and is as a child, and speaks, and understands, and thinks as a child, and sees through a glass darkly, in comparison of the state of the church in its latter ages, wherein it will be in a state of

manhood, in a perfect state, and will see face to face in comparison of what it did in its first infant state; and so the gift of prophecy and tongues, &c. ceased at the end of the church's age of childhood, but charity remains when the elder age of the church comes, and when it shall put away childish things. That age shall be an age of love, but there shall be no miraculous gifts of the Spirit, as being needless, and more proper helps for the church in a state of infancy, than in that state of manhood.

Again, the church, all the while it remains in a militant state, is in an imperfect state, a state of childhood, sees through a glass darkly, thinks, speaks, and understands as a child, in comparison of what it will be in its heavenly and eternal state, when it shall be come to the measure of the stature of the fulness of Christ; when it shall see face to face, and know as it is known, then it shall put away such childish things, as the miraculous gifts of the Spirit, but love shall gloriously prevail. The world shall be a world of love. If we thus understand the apostle, it fully proves that the gifts of tongues, and miracles, &c. are not to be upheld in the church in the millennium.

Jonathan Edwards: The End of the Temporal World

Contrary to our own day in which contemplating the termination of the earth causes some to doubt God's provision for human beings, Jonathan Edwards looked at the same empirical evidence and saw in it only another confirmation of the glory and power of God and the certainty of life eternal.

SOURCE

Miscellany 867, in *The Philosophy of Jonathan Edwards from His Private Notebooks*, transcribed and edited by Harvey Townsend (Eugene: University of Oregon Press, 1955), 263–65.

World Will Come To An End

867. Christian religion. Immortality of the soul. A future state. That this world will come to an end. The natural world, which is in such continual labor, as is described in the first chapter of Ecclesiastes, constantly going round in such revolutions, will doubtless come to an end. These revolutions are not for nothing. There is some great event and issue of things that this labor is for, some grand period aimed at. Does God make the world restless, to move and revolve in all its parts,

to make no progress, to labor with motions so mighty and vast, only to come to the same place again, to be just where it was before? Doubtless some end is nearer approached to by these revolutions. Some great end is nearer to an accomplishment after a thousand revolutions are finished than when there was only one finished or before the first revolution began. . . .

Corollary 1. This is a confirmation of a future state; for if these revolutions have not something in another state that is to succeed this that they are subservient to, then they are in vain. If anything of this world is to remain after the revolutions of this world are at an end, doubtless it will be that part of this world that is the end of all the rest, or that creature for which all the rest is made. And that is man. . . .

Corollary 2. This confirms the divinity of the Christian revelation, which gives this account of things: that this world is to come to an end; it is to be destroyed; that the revolutions of the world have an appointed period; and that man, the end of this lower world, is to remain in being afterwards; and gives a most rational account of the good period, design, and issue of all things worthy of the infinite wisdom and majesty of God.

Is God the Author of Sin?[5]

Wolfgang Musculus:
Adam's Fall Foreseen

The logic of the Reformed doctrine of election left theologians with the obligation to show that God did not cause the fall. Wolfgang Musculus (1497–1563) states below the standard position that God foresaw humanity's fall in Adam but did not cause it to occur. Adam had been created good but fell into sin of his own accord. Hence humanity has only itself—not God—to blame for its predicament.

Musculus was professor of theology at Bern, Switzerland, from 1559 until his death, having previously been converted to the Reformation faith through reading Luther and spending time in both Augsburg and Strasbourg.

SOURCE

Wolfgang Musculus, *Loci communes sacrae theologiae* (1560), pp. 620–21; ET: In Heppe, *Reformed Dogmatics*, 303–4.

---

5. Reformed theologians, along with all Augustinians, face perplexities in relating divine sovereignty to the presence of evil in the world. For a standard treatment, see G. R. Evans, *Augustine on Evil* (Cambridge: Cambridge University Press, 1982).

God's ways are not like men's ways, so that it must be thought that it happened to Him, as it usually comes to us every day: our plans and acts promptly fall out far otherwise than we had intended. He created man in His image, upright and unimpaired. Who so senseless as to say that He had not foreseen what would happen to man by the serpent's persuasion? All therefore generally agree, and rightly, in this, that Adam's sin had been foreseen and foreknown from eternity. Thus the lapse of the human race did not so occur as to be beyond the mind and intention of the Creator: which means that He is a sham creator in His work, as though the thing happened otherwise than He resolved. . . .

[I]t is I think pretty clear that God refused to establish man's felicity and salvation upon his first state and constitution such as it was, but established it on his (man's) restoration predestined in Christ the Son, and He so arranged, that he should be redeemed and preserved neither by his knowledge of Himself (whence He even forbade him to eat of the tree of the knowledge of good and evil) nor by the worthiness and merits of his own righteousness, but by the sole grace and mercy of his free election, when otherwise ready to perish, by the intervention of His Son. The universal fall of the human race served to illustrate this grace of election. By the fall, before he had acquired any offspring, Adam fell into sin; and the result is that no mortal can be saved except by God's mercy. In the next place also the wretchedness, corruption and perdition, which overtaking this lapse of our first parents now holds the whole human race, renders the power and might of divine providence much more splendid, while through Christ we are more happily restored after the fall than we had been when created, before we fell: just as on the day of resurrection, when we shall be raised from the dust of the earth and the corruptible shall put on incorruption and the mortal immortality, the might of God's power will be declared much more gloriously, than if we were living for ever in this life devoid of corruption and death.

Pierre du Moulin:
The Character of God

In his rejection of the Arminian claim that the Reformed doctrine makes God the author of sin, du Moulin argues that God's actions are intrinsically just, for they are always circumscribed by God's character.

SOURCE

Pierre du Moulin, *Anatome Arminianismi* (1619), chap. 3; ET: "That God Is Not the Author of Sin," *Anatomy of Arminianism*, 7–8.

God is in no way the author or instigator of sin. . . . For God is not only just but also justice itself: And it is as impossible that he who is justice itself should sin or be the author of sin as that whiteness should black the wall or heat make one cold. Neither does God [merely do that which is] just but therefore the thing is just because God does it. And surely that idle device of some is to be hissed at, who say that God, though he enforces men to sin yet himself does not sin [inasmuch as God is bound by no law and] there [can be] no sin where there is no law. I confess indeed that God [breaks] no law: And yet it is certain that he can do nothing that is contrary to his own nature. God cannot lie because he is truth itself. God cannot sin because he is perfect righteousness itself. . . .

Jonathan Edwards: God Both Is and Is Not the Author of Evil

This passage denies Arminian charges that Edwards's view of freedom of the will (pp. 161–64, above) makes God the author of evil. In Edwards's radical view of divine sovereignty, God does bear responsibility for ordering the world in such a way as to permit evil. But it is still human beings who bear moral responsibility for the evil which they choose.

SOURCE

Jonathan Edwards, *Freedom of the Will* (1754), in Edwards, *Works* (Yale) 1:399.

BIBLIOGRAPHY

Jonathan Edwards, "Concerning the Divine Decrees in General and Election in Particular" (n.d.), *Remarks on Important Theological Controversies*, in Edwards, *Works* (1834) 2:529.

Again, if it will *follow at all*, that God is the author of sin, from what has been supposed of a sure and infallible connection between antecedents and consequents, it will *follow because of this*, viz. that for God to be the author or orderer of those things which he knows beforehand, will infallibly be attended with such a consequence, is the same thing in effect, as for him to be the author of that consequence. But if this be so, this is a difficulty which equally attends the doctrine of Arminians themselves; at least, of those of them who allow God's certain foreknowledge of all events. For on the supposition of such a foreknowledge, this is the case with respect to every sin that is committed: God knew, that if he ordered and brought to pass such and such events, such sins would infallibly follow. . . .

Therefore this supposed difficulty ought not to be brought as an objection against the scheme which has been maintained, as *disagreeing* with the Arminian scheme, seeing 'tis no difficulty owing to such a *disagreement;* but a difficulty wherein the Arminians share with us. That must be unreasonably made an objection against our differing from them, which we should not escape or avoid at all by agreeing with them.

And therefore I would observe,

II. They who object, that this doctrine makes God the author of sin, ought distinctly to explain what they mean by that phrase, "the author of sin." I know, the phrase, as it is commonly used, signifies something very ill. If by "the author of sin," be meant the sinner, the agent, or actor of sin, or the *doer* of a wicked thing; so it would be a reproach and blasphemy, to suppose God to be the author of sin. In this sense, I utterly deny God to be the author of sin; rejecting such an imputation on the most High, as what is infinitely to be abhorred; and deny any such thing to be the consequence of what I have laid down. But if by "the author of sin," is meant the permitter, or not a hinderer of sin; and at the same time, a disposer of the state of events, in such a manner, for wise, holy and most excellent ends and purposes, that sin, if it be permitted or not hindered, will most certainly and infallibly follow: I say, if this be all that is meant, by being the author of sin, I don't deny that God is the author of sin (though I dislike and reject the phrase, as that which by use and custom is apt to carry another sense), it is no reproach for the most High to be thus the author of sin. This is not to be the *actor* of sin, but on the contrary, of *holiness*. What God doth herein, is holy; and a glorious exercise of the infinite excellency of his nature. And I don't deny, that God's being thus the author of sin, follows from what I have laid down; and I assert, that it equally follows from the doctrine which is maintained by most of the Arminian divines.

GOSPEL AND LAW

Gospel and law in Reformed theology form two distinct but inseparable aspects of the one revelation of God. We have already observed this pattern of distinction within unity in the section on covenant. We shall encounter it yet again when we turn to the relationship of justification and sanctification.

The Reformed way of relating gospel and law is often used to distinguish Reformed theology from Lutheran theology. For Martin Luther, even though gospel and law are both considered part of the one Word of God, the chief task of a theologian is to refine one's ability to distinguish law from gospel, letter from spirit, works from faith.[6] While the Reformed recognize the importance of these distinctions, especially in covenant theology with its unfolding of the historical economy of the covenant of works and of grace, the Reformed were more concerned to comprehend the law as a positive form of God's grace. The sentiment from Psalm 19—that the law of the Lord is perfect, converting the soul, making the simple wise—is a bedrock conviction of Reformed piety. The rigor of the law, including its ceremonial prescriptions under the Old Testament dispensation, has been removed as a result of the gospel of Christ. But the gospel indicative, the liberation Christ has achieved for sinful humanity, creates an ethical imperative that includes obedience to God's commands.

This is nowhere better illustrated than in the Reformed teaching on the "uses of the law." The first use is the theological use whereby the law convicts us of sin. For Luther, this was the law's primary, although not exclusive, function. The second use, also affirmed by Luther, is the civil use according to which the law restrains social evil. The third use of the law is that by which believers are instructed in living unto righteousness. There are hints of this use in Luther, and Luther's successor Philipp Melanchthon is responsible for bringing it to the fore in sixteenth-century theological discussion. But for the Reformed, the third use is the *primary* use of the law; and this is an affirmation difficult for any good Lutheran to make.

Huldrych Zwingli: The Eternal Will of God

SOURCE

Huldrych Zwingli, *Commentarius de vera et falsa religione* (1525); ET: "The Law," *Commentary on True and False Religion*, in Zwingli, *Works* 3:137.

The Law is nothing else than the eternal will of God. For I shall say nothing here of civil laws or ceremonial laws, because they have to do

---

6. For a summary of the historical Lutheran view during this period, see Heinrich Schmid, *The Doctrinal Theology of the Evangelical Lutheran Church*, 3d ed., rev., trans. Charles A. Hay and Henry E. Jacobs (Philadelphia, 1889; reprint: Minneapolis: Augsburg, 1961), 508–20. For a Lutheran systematic view of the issue, see vol. 1 of Helmut Thielicke, *Theological Ethics*, 3 vols., ed. William H. Lazereth (Philadelphia: Fortress, 1966). Lutheran theology, with the primacy it lends to "justification by faith" apart from works of the law, launches a radical critique of all legalism in theology. The prominence Calvin gives to law has led one historian to label him a "crypto-Catholic." See Steven Ozment, *The Age of Reform: 1250–1550: An Intellectual and Religious History of Late Medieval and Reformation Europe* (New Haven and London: Yale University Press, 1980), chap. 11. Calvin does not, however, depart from Luther in his insistence that righteousness comes from grace alone.

with the outer man, and I am now talking of the inner man. Besides, these laws vary according to the exigencies of the times, as we often see in the case of civil laws; and ceremonial laws were abolished altogether by Christ, for they were made to be amended at some time, as was also done at the proper time, Heb. 9:10. But the divine laws, which have to do with the inner man, are eternal. The law will never be abrogated that you are to love your neighbor as yourself; and theft, false witness, murder, etc., will always be regarded as crimes. And that the Law is the eternal or permanent will of God is proved by what is written in Rom. 2:14 of those without the Law: namely, that they show the law has been published in their hearts, in that they do the things which the law commands, though the tablets of the law have not been set up before them. But none writes in the heart save God alone. Likewise, through the Law comes the knowledge of sin, Rom. 7:7, and, "where no law is, there is no transgression," Rom. 4:15. We are forced to admit, therefore, that the Law proceeded from God; for of ourselves we should not know what sin was unless God had manifested in His word what should be done and what not done. The Law, therefore, is nothing else than teachings as to the will of God, through which we understand what He wills, what He wills not, what He demands, what He forbids.

John Calvin: One Shall Be Blessed by Doing

SOURCE

John Calvin, Commentary: James 1:25 (1551); *CO* 55; ET: In *Calvin's New Testament Commentaries* 3: 273–74, trans. A. W. Morrison.

> But he that looketh into the perfect law, the law of liberty, and so continueth, being not a hearer that forgetteth, but a doer that worketh, this man shall be blessed in his doing. (James 1:25)

Being concerned with the Jews, he takes the word *Law*, so familiar to them, as suggesting the whole doctrine of God. But his reasons for speaking of the *perfect law, the law of liberty,* have eluded exegetes, who have failed to observe the contrast he makes, with reference to other passages of Scripture. As long as the Law is preached by man's outward utterance, and not written in the heart with the finger and Spirit of God, it is a dead letter, it is like a lifeless corpse. The Law may reasonably be held to be impaired, until it finds a place in the heart. The same argument applies to its lack of freedom. Divorced from Christ, it bears children unto bondage (Gal. 4:24), and it can only affect us with profound apprehension and fear (Rom. 8:15). But the Spirit of regeneration, printing its message on our inmost being, confers in like manner the grace of adoption. It is as though James had said, "Do not make a slavish thing of the Law's teaching, but rather a thing of liberty; don't be tied to the apron-strings, but reach out with it to perfection; you must receive it with whole-hearted affection, if you aim to find a godly and holy life." Further we may see from the witness of Jeremiah (31:33), and many others, that the re-fashioning which the Law of God will give us is a blessing of the new covenant. From this it follows that it could not be found, until the coming of Christ. He alone is the accomplished perfection of the Law. Hence James' addition of *liberty*, inseparably attached, for Christ's Spirit never gives us new birth without equally giving testimony and pledge to our adoption, so as to set our hearts free from fear and alarm. . . . [W]hen he adds, *this man shall be blessed in his doing*, he means that the blessing lies in the action itself, not merely in the empty sound.

John Calvin: The Unity of Gospel and Law

SOURCE

Institutes II.9.4, III.17.3–5, pp. 426–27, 805.

We refute those who always erroneously compare the law with the gospel by contrasting the merit of works with the free imputation of righteousness. This is indeed a contrast not at all to be rejected. For Paul often means by the term "law" the rule of righteous living by which God requires of us what is his own, giving us no hope of life unless we completely obey him, and adding on the other hand a curse if we deviate even in the slightest degree. This Paul does when he contends that we are pleasing to God through grace and are accounted righteous through his pardon, because nowhere is found that observance of the law for which the reward has been promised. Paul therefore justly makes contraries of the righteousness of the law and of that of the gospel [Rom. 3:21 ff.; Gal. 3:10 ff.; etc.]

But the gospel did not so supplant the entire law as to bring forward a different way of salvation. Rather, it confirmed and satisfied whatever the law had promised, and gave substance to the shadows. When Christ says, "The Law and the Prophets were until John" [Luke 16:16; cf. Matt. 11:13], he does not subject the patriarchs to the curse that the slaves of the law cannot escape. He means: they had been trained in rudiments only, thus remaining far beneath the height of the gospel teaching. Hence Paul, calling the gospel "the power of God unto salvation for every believer" [Rom. 1:16 p.], presently adds: "The Law and the Prophets bear witness to it" [Rom. 3:21]. And at the end of the same letter, although he teaches that "the preaching of Jesus Christ is the revelation of the mystery kept in silence through times eternal" [Rom. 16:25 p.], he qualifies this statement by adding an explanation, teaching that he was "made known through the prophetic writings" [Rom. 16:26 p.]. From this we infer that, where the whole law is concerned, the gospel differs from it only in clarity of manifestation. Still, because of the inestimable abundance of grace laid open for us in Christ, it is said with good reason that through his advent God's Heavenly Kingdom was erected upon earth [cf. Matt. 12:28]. . . .

What then? Have the promises been given only to vanish without bearing fruit? I declared just above that this was not my meaning. I say, indeed, that the promises have no beneficent effect upon us so long as they have reference to the merits of works, and consequently, if considered in themselves, they are in a sense abolished.

But when the promises of the gospel are substituted, which proclaim the free forgiveness of sins, these not only make us acceptable to God but also render our works pleasing to him. And not only does the Lord adjudge them pleasing; he also extends to them the blessings which under the covenant were owed to the observance of his law. I therefore admit that what the Lord has promised in his law to the keepers of righteousness and holiness is paid to the works of believers, but in this repayment we must always consider the reason that wins favor for these works.

Now we see that there are three reasons. The first is: God, having turned his gaze from his servants' works, which always deserve reproof rather than praise, embraces his servants in Christ, and with faith alone intervening, reconciles them to himself without the help of works. The second is: of his own fatherly generosity and loving-kindness, and without considering their worth, he raises works to this place of honor, so that he attributes some value to them. The third is: he receives these very works with pardon, not imputing the imperfection with which they are all so corrupted that they would otherwise be reckoned as sins rather than virtues. . . .

Zacharius Ursinus: The Differences
Between Gospel and Law

SOURCE

Zacharius Ursinus, *Explicationum catecheticarum* (1594), commentary on q. 92; ET: "In What Does the Law Differ from the Gospel?" in Ursinus, *Commentary*, 497–98.

The exposition of this question is necessary for a variety of considerations, and especially that we may have a proper understanding of the law and the gospel, to which a knowledge of that in which they differ greatly contributes. According to the definition of the law, which says, that it promises rewards to those who render perfect obedience; and that it promises them freely, inasmuch as no obedience can be meritorious in the sight of God, it would seem that it does not differ from the gospel, which also promises eternal life freely. Yet notwithstanding this seeming agreement, there is a great difference between the law and the gospel. They differ,

1. *As to the mode of revelation peculiar to each.* The law is known naturally: the gospel was divinely revealed after the fall of man. 2. *In matter or doctrine.* The law declares the justice of God separately considered: the gospel declares it in connection with his mercy. The law teaches what we ought to be in order that we may be saved: the gospel teaches in addition to this, how we may become such as the law requires, viz.: by faith in Christ. 3. *In their conditions or promises.* The law promises eternal life and all good things upon the condition of our own and perfect righteousness, and of obedience in us: the gospel promises the same blessings upon the condition that we exercise faith in Christ, by which we embrace the obedience which another, even Christ, has performed in our behalf; or the gospel teaches that we are justified freely by faith in Christ. With this faith is also connected, as by an indissoluble bond, the condition of new obedience. 4. *In their effects.* The law works wrath, and is the ministration of death: the gospel is the ministration of life and of the Spirit. (Rom. 4:15; 2 Cor. 3:7)

Westminster Confession: Moral Law
versus Ceremonial Law

SOURCE

"Of the Law," Westminster Confession of Faith (1646), chap. 19, in Schaff, *Creeds* 3:640–43.

1. God gave to Adam a law, as a covenant of works. . . .

2. This law, after his Fall, continued to be a perfect rule of righteousness. . . .

3. Besides this law, commonly called moral, God was pleased to give to the people of Israel, as a Church under age, ceremonial laws, containing several typical ordinances, partly of worship, prefiguring Christ, his graces, actions, sufferings, and benefits; and partly holding forth divers instructions of moral duties. All which ceremonial laws are now abrogated under the New Testament.

4. To them also, as a body politic, he gave sundry judicial laws, which expired . . . [other] than the general equity thereof may require.

5. The moral law doth forever bind all, as well justified persons as others, to the obedience thereof; and that not only in regard of the matter contained in it, but also in respect of the authority of God the Creator who gave it. Neither doth Christ in the gospel any way dissolve, but much strengthen, this obligation.

John Calvin: Three Uses of the Law

SOURCE

Institutes II.7.6–16, pp. 354–61 (edited).

But to make the whole matter clearer, let us survey briefly the function and use of what is called the "moral law." Now, so far as I understand it, it consists of three parts.

The first part is this: while it shows God's righteousness, that is, the righteousness alone acceptable to God, it warns, informs, convicts, and lastly condemns, every man of his own unrighteousness. For man, blinded and drunk with self-love, must be compelled to know and to confess his own feebleness and impurity. . . .

The law is like a mirror. In it we contemplate our weakness, then the iniquity arising from this, and finally the curse coming from both—just as a mirror shows us the spots on our face. For when the capacity to follow righteousness fails him, man must be mired in sins. After the sin forthwith comes the curse. Accordingly, the greater the transgression of which the law holds us guilty, the graver the judgment to which it makes us answerable. . . .

The wickedness and condemnation of us all are sealed by the testimony of the law. Yet this is not done to cause us to fall down in despair or, completely discouraged, to rush headlong over the brink—

provided we duly profit by the testimony of the law. It is true that in this way the wicked are terrified, but because of their obstinacy of heart. For the children of God the knowledge of the law should have another purpose. The apostle testifies that we are indeed condemned by the judgment of the law, "so that every mouth may be stopped, and the whole world may be held accountable to God" [Rom. 3:19]. He teaches the same idea in yet another place: "For God has shut up all men in unbelief," not that he may destroy all or suffer all to perish, but "that he may have mercy upon all" [Rom. 11:32]. This means that, dismissing the stupid opinion of their own strength, they come to realize that they stand and are upheld by God's hand alone; that, naked and empty-handed, they flee to his mercy, repose entirely in it, hide deep within it, and seize upon it alone for righteousness and merit. For God's mercy is revealed in Christ to all who seek and wait upon it with true faith. In the precepts of the law, God is but the rewarder of perfect righteousness, which all of us lack, and conversely, the severe judge of evil deeds. But in Christ his face shines, full of grace and gentleness, even upon us poor and unworthy sinners. . . .

Yet this first function of the law is exercised also in the reprobate: For, although they do not proceed so far with the children of God as to be renewed and bloom again in the inner man after the abasement of their flesh, but are struck dumb by the first terror and lie in despair, nevertheless, the fact that their consciences are buffeted by such waves serves to show forth the equity of the divine judgment. For the reprobate always freely desire to evade God's judgment. Now, although that judgment is not yet revealed, so routed are they by the testimony of the law and of conscience, that they betray in themselves what they have deserved. . . .

The second function of the law is this: at least by fear of punishment to restrain certain men who are untouched by any care for what is just and right unless compelled by hearing the dire threats in the law. But they are restrained, not because their inner mind is stirred or affected, but because, being bridled, so to speak, they keep their hands from outward activity, and hold inside the depravity that otherwise they would wantonly have indulged. Consequently, they are neither better nor more righteous before God. Hindered by fright or shame, they dare neither execute what they have conceived in their minds nor openly breathe forth the rage of their lust. Still, they do not have hearts disposed to fear and obedience toward God. Indeed, the more they restrain themselves, the more strongly are they inflamed; they burn and boil within, and are ready to do anything or burst forth anywhere—but for the fact that this dread of the law hinders them. Not only that—but so wickedly do they also hate the law itself, and curse God the Lawgiver, that if they could, they would most certainly abolish him, for they cannot bear him either when he commands them to do right, or when he takes vengeance on the despisers of his majesty. All who are still unregenerate feel—some more obscurely, some more openly—that they are not drawn to obey the law voluntarily, but impelled by a violent fear do so against their will and despite their opposition to it.

But this constrained and forced righteousness is necessary for the public community of men, for whose tranquillity the Lord herein provided when he took care that everything be not tumultuously confounded. . . .

There are two kinds of men whom the law leads by its tutelage to Christ.

Of the first kind we have already spoken: because they are too full of their own virtue or of the assurance of their own righteousness, they are not fit to receive Christ's grace unless they first be emptied. Therefore, through the recognition of their own misery, the law brings them down to humility in order thus to prepare them to seek what previously they did not realize they lacked.

Men of the second kind have need of a bridle to restrain them from so slackening the reins on the lust of the flesh as to fall clean away from all pursuit of righteousness. . . .

The third and principal use, which pertains more closely to the proper purpose of the law, finds its place among believers in whose hearts the Spirit of God already lives and reigns. For even though they have the law written and engraved upon their hearts by the finger of God [Jer. 31:33; Heb. 10:16], that is, have been so moved and quickened through the directing of the Spirit that they long to obey God, they still profit by the law in two ways.

Here is the best instrument for them to learn more thoroughly each day the nature of the Lord's will to which they aspire, and to confirm them in the understanding of it. It is as if some servant, already prepared with all earnestness of heart to commend himself to his master, must search out and observe his master's ways more carefully in order to conform and accommodate himself to them. And not one of us may escape from this necessity. For no man has heretofore attained to such wisdom as to be unable, from the daily instruction of the law, to make fresh progress toward a purer knowledge of the divine will.

Again, because we need not only teaching but also exhortation, the servant of God will also avail himself of this benefit of the law: by frequent meditation upon it to be aroused to obedience, be strengthened in it, and be drawn back from the slippery path of transgression. In this way the saints must press on; for, however eagerly they may in accordance with the Spirit strive toward God's righteousness, the listless flesh always so burdens them that they do not proceed with due readiness. The law is to the flesh like a whip to an idle and balky ass, to arouse it to work. Even for a spiritual man not yet free of the weight of the flesh the law remains a constant sting that will not let him stand still.

4

JESUS CHRIST

THE PERSON OF THE MEDIATOR

Just as in its trinitarian doctrine, so too in its doctrine of the person of Christ, classical Reformed theology intends to be thoroughly Nicene and Chalcedonian.[1] Jesus Christ is God incarnate, true God and true human being, one person possessing two natures. One of these natures is of the same reality as God, the other of the same reality as human beings—including, that is, a true body and a "rational soul," yet kept free from sin by the power of God.

In Chalcedonian Christology, the two natures belong together "without confusion, transmutation, division, or contrast."[2] In its appropriation of this formula, Reformed theology has characteristically sought to carve out a clear and genuine distinction (though not separation) between Christ's divine and human natures. Hence as one would expect, Reformed teaching on the person of Christ reflects the Reformed penchant for discriminating between God and creation which we observed in its doctrine of God. So prominently did this conviction about distinguishing God and the creature display itself in the early Reformed christologies that Reformed theologians found themselves having to deflect the charge of Nestorianism, the error of not merely distinguishing but also separating the two natures of Christ.

This issue of the two natures led the Reformed into a dispute with the Lutherans over three related issues.[3] While these controversies may seem

1. For an early summary of Reformed teaching in the light of the early christological debates, see Second Helvetic Confession (1566), chap. 11. For the classical christological statements, see Leith, *Creeds*, 28–36, 45–56. See also J.N.D. Kelly, *Early Christian Doctrines*, rev. ed. (New York: Harper & Row, 1978), chaps. 6, 9–12.
2. See Leith, *Creeds*, 35–36.
3. For the Lutheran position, see Heinrich Schmid, *The Doctrinal Theology of the Evangelical Lutheran Church*, 3d ed., rev., trans. Charles A. Hay and Henry E. Jacobs (Philadelphia, 1889; reprint: Minneapolis: Augsburg, 1961), secs. 31–33.

overly abstract, they were situated and played themselves out practically in two distinct theologies of the Lord's Supper. The first issue centered on the meaning of "the Word made flesh." For the Lutherans the Word, or λόγος, was completely incarnate in Jesus Christ. But for the Reformed the λόγος in its union with the human nature of Jesus did not exhaust itself but maintained an "extra" or transcendent dimension throughout Jesus' earthly life. Although given the term *extra Calvinisticum* by polemical opponents of Reformed theology, the doctrine had ample precedent in the medieval church.[4]

The second issue was over the communication of the properties (*communicatio idiomatum*). The two camps agreed that a communion of the divine and human natures occurred in the incarnation. Where they differed was over the unique properties (*idiomata*) of the two natures. Were the respective properties—divine properties such as omniscience and eternity, and human properties such as finitude and mortality—communicated between the two natures in an essential way, as the Lutherans insisted, or, as the Reformed maintained, did they retain their individual integrity in the incarnation? According to the Reformed, the properties of the two natures were indeed "attributable" to Christ's person "concretely," but there was no "communication" between the properties of the two natures in the sense of a confusion or commingling. The Reformed considered an assertion of anything more than attribution to constitute an unwarranted speculation into the mystery of the incarnation.

Just as the properties could not be commingled in the person of Christ, said the Reformed, neither could the divine and human elements be conjoined in a confused manner in the sacrament. The divine attribute which the Lutherans most wished to apply to the Lord's Supper was omnipresence, which leads us to the third issue, the ubiquity of the body. The Lutheran ubiquitarians held that Christ's body after the resurrection and ascension was in some sense all-present, which in turn provided a metaphysical ground for their view of the presence of Christ's body in the Supper. The Reformed, on the other hand, read scripture to say that the glorified body was located in heaven. Accordingly, the "real" presence of the body in the Lord's Supper must be mediated in such a way as to preserve the transcendence of Christ's resurrected body.

The following statements seek not to reproduce a complete portrait of the historic doctrine of the person of Christ but merely to highlight some of the distinctive traits of classical Reformed christology.

---

4. See E. David Willis, *Calvin's Catholic Christology: The Function of the So-Called Extra Calvinisticum in Calvin's Theology* (Leiden: E. J. Brill, 1966), esp. chaps. 1 and 2.

Huldrych Zwingli: Distinguishing the Two Natures of Christ

The first passage, taken from Zwingli's *Exposition*, gives a succinct statement of the two natures of Christ and their interrelations. In the second passage, drawn from one of Zwingli's exchanges with Luther, Zwingli coins the word "alloiosis" (ἀλλοίωσις, meaning "exchange") for the rhetorical device of referring by implication the properties of either the divine or human nature to the other. The human properties of hungering, suffering, and dying, for example, and the divine properties of forgiving, performing miracles, and ascending to heaven are not mixed but are predicated by alloiosis to the divine-human person. Similarly, in Zwingli's teaching on the sacraments, Christ's body is "signified" but does not literally become the bread of the Lord's Supper.

SOURCES

(A) Huldrych Zwingli, *Fidei expositio* (1536), in *SS* chap. 2; ET: "Of the Lord Christ," *Exposition of the Christian Faith*, in *Zwingli and Bullinger*, 251–53. **(B)** Huldrych Zwingli, *Amica exegesis* (1527), in *Sämtliche Werke* 5:562–758; ET: "On the *Alloiosis* of the Two Natures in Christ," *Friendly Exegesis, That Is, Exposition of the Eucharist to Martin Luther* (1527), in Zwingli, *In Search of True Religion*, 320–22 (edited).

BIBLIOGRAPHY

Walther Köhler, *Zwingli und Luther: Ihr Streit über das Abendmahl nach seinen politischen und religiösen Beziehung*, 2 vols. (Leipzig, 1953). W. P. Stephens, *The Theology of Huldrych Zwingli* (Oxford: Clarendon, 1989), chap. 4.

A. THE TWO NATURES OF CHRIST

We believe and teach that this Son of God, who is of God, so took to himself the nature of man that his divine nature was not destroyed or changed into that of man: but that each nature is present truly, properly and naturally: his divine nature has not in any way been diminished so as not to be truly, properly and naturally God. Nor has his human nature passed into the divine so that he is not truly, properly and naturally man, except in so far as he is without the propensity to sin. According to his divine nature, in every respect he is God with the Father and the Holy Spirit, not forfeiting any of the divine attributes by the assumption of human weakness. And according to his human nature he is in every way man, having all the properties which belong to the true and proper nature of man save only the propensity of sin, and not lacking any of them by reason of union with the divine nature.

Hence the attitudes and properties of both natures are reflected in all his words and works, so that the pious mind is able to see without difficulty which is to be accredited to each, although everything is rightly ascribed to the one Christ. It is quite correct to say that Christ hungered, for he is both God and man: yet he did not hunger according to his divine nature. It is quite correct to say that Christ healed all manner of sickness and all manner of disease: yet if you consider it more closely, this is something which concerns the divine power and not the human. But the difference of natures does not involve a division of the person any more than when we say that a man thinks and yet also sleeps. For although the power of thought belongs only to the mind and the need of sleep to the body, yet the man does not consist of two persons, but one. For the unity of the person continues in spite of the diversity of the natures.

And everywhere we confess that God and Man are one Christ, just as man subsists of a reasonable soul and an earthly body, as St. Athanasius taught. But Christ assumed the nature of man into the hypostasis or person of the Son of God.

B. "ALLOIOSIS" OF THE TWO NATURES

Alloiosis, then, so far as our subject is concerned, is that leap or transition or, if you prefer, interchange, by which when, speaking of one of Christ's natures, we use the terms that apply to the other. For instance, when Christ says, "My flesh is truly meat," [Jn. 6:55] the word flesh properly applies to his human nature, but by exchange it is used in this place of his divine nature. For in that he is the Son of God he is the food of the soul. For he says, "It is the Spirit that enlivens." [Jn. 6:63] Again, when he says that the son of the householder was slain by the husbandmen, though "son of the householder" is a characterization of his divinity, [cf. Mt. 21:33ff.] he uses it in reference to his human nature—for by virtue of that he could die, but not by any means of virtue of his divine nature.

When, I say, what applies to one of the natures is predicated of the other, this is alloiosis or exchange or change of attributes. It is so essential to know this and keep it in mind that one who disregards it or does not know it defiles not only the Gospel of John but also the others with extraordinary errors. The reason why they were all so much given to the use of this exchange or alloiosis of attributes is this: when he who is from all eternity Son of God put on humanity, he was made Son of Man also, not in the sense that he who was Son of God lost the lot or condition of being divine, or was transmuted into the position of man, nor in the sense that he turned human into divine nature, but in the sense that God and a human being became one Christ, who, in that he is the Son of God, is the life of all (for all things were made by him [Jn. 1:3]) and in that he is a human being, is the offering through which the eternal righteousness, which is also his righteousness, is reconciled.

These two natures, however, he joined and united into one substance or person in such a way that they still always retain each its own character, with the one exception that the tendency to sin is utterly foreign to his humanity. . . .

We say, therefore, that God who made the humanity he put on was made human, meaning that human nature was put on by the Son of God. This Athanasius confesses, "Not by the turning of divinity into flesh," he says, "but by the putting of humanity upon God." Yet no one is offended by the sharing of qualities when it is said, "God was made human," meaning "the human was made God," or "was taken upon the person of the Son of God." See what an inoffensive union! But see at the same time how we must not confuse the understanding of the properties, even if we interchange the names!—John 3:13: "No person has ascended up to heaven but he that came down from heaven, even the Son of Man which is in heaven. And as Moses lifted up the serpent, even so must the Son of Man be lifted up, so that whoever believes in him should have, etc." We have here "the Son of Man" twice, but not as a typification of the same nature. The Son of Man is lifted up and fixed upon the cross, and the Son of Man is in heaven though he had not yet ascended. His divine nature, therefore, by which he is forever with the Father, is called the Son of Man exactly as his human nature is called God when we say that God was born of the virgin. It was in virtue of his divinity, then, not in virtue of his humanity, that he was the Son of Man in heaven with the Father who never abandoned him.—Jn. 5:17: "My Father continuously works and I work." Here "I" is said of Christ, but it applies only to his superior nature, which performs miracles and works all things equally with the Father. But a little later, when he says, "Truly, truly, I say to you, the Son can do nothing of himself, but what he sees the Father doing," [Jn. 5:19] he calls the assumed human being "the Son," and declares that he can perform no miracles. I would not contend with those who perhaps not impiously, but inopportunely, would say that "Son" is put here for the divine nature also, in the sense that the Son works nothing which the Father does not work with him.

John Calvin and Theodore Beza:
The *Extra Calvinisticum* and the
Location of Christ's Body

We begin with Calvin's brief statements of the "extra" dimension from the *Institutes*, the first from the conclusion of his Christology and the second from an explication of the sacraments. Then, the significance and rationale for this Reformed teaching is explained in a straightforward way in a section from Theodore Beza's little book of Christian questions and answers.

SOURCES

(A) *Institutes* II.13.4, IV.17.30, pp. 481, 1403. **(B)** Beza, *Questions and Responses*, qs. 36–47, 49–51, pp. 12–16, 18–19.

BIBLIOGRAPHY

Heiko Oberman, "The `Extra' Dimension in the Theology of Calvin," *Journal of Ecclesiastical History* 21 (1970): 43–64. E. David Willis, *Calvin's Catholic Christology: The Function of the So-Called Extra Calvinisticum in Calvin's Theology* (Leiden: E. J. Brill, 1966).

A. JOHN CALVIN

1. *Extra* dimension in Christology.

They thrust upon us as something absurd the fact that if the Word of God became flesh, then he was confined within the narrow prison of an earthly body. This is mere impudence! For even if the Word in his immeasurable essence united with the nature of man into one person, we do not imagine that he was confined therein. Here is something marvelous: the Son of God descended from heaven in such a way that, without leaving heaven, he willed to be borne in the virgin's womb, to go about the earth, and to hang upon the cross; yet he continuously filled the world even as he had done from the beginning!

2. *Extra* dimension in the Sacraments.

There is a commonplace distinction of the schools to which I am not ashamed to refer: although the whole Christ is everywhere, still the whole of that which is in him is not everywhere. And would that the Schoolmen themselves had honestly weighed the force of this statement. For thus would the absurd fiction of Christ's carnal presence have been obviated. Therefore, since the whole Christ is everywhere, our Mediator is ever present with his own people, and in the Supper reveals himself in a special way, yet in such a way that the whole Christ is present, but not in his wholeness. For, as has been said, in his flesh he is contained in heaven until he appears in judgment.

B. THEODORE BEZA

Q36 However, why did He ascend into the heavens, rather than abide with us?

A36 With His body He did indeed depart from us among whom He was, above all the heavens where formerly He had no body. He did this, not only so that, while triumphing over His captive enemies, He might begin the possession of the heavenly kingdom as the first one who rose from the dead, but also so that He might instruct us to strive for that location where He has prepared a place for us. Meanwhile, He is very present by His own Spirit, governing the Church as the head over the members joined to it.

Q37 Therefore, He changed locations, so that He departed to where there is no place.

A37 Yes, He changed His location, as history testifies, and as the fact that He has a body, albeit glorified, demands. But He changed locations according to that nature which is physically restricted, yet not so that He might desert us (for He is still present with us with His full power, since He is truly God, and Christ is one person, both God and man at the same time), but so that He might teach us to withdraw from the earth to seek heavenly things. Moreover, that you say there is no place where He ascended is an empty description. Let it suffice, that the Godhead alone is infinite; all other things, whether in heaven, or above the heavens, or in the earth, or below it (and even though His body is glorified, it is still truly a human body), are by its nature finite and physically limited. How they are contained in that eternal glory will be clearer to us when we also go there.

Q38 In this way you appear to divide Christ, or to make two Christs, one here, the other there.

A38 I do not divide Christ, but I remove the confusion of the natures, when I say that He is departed according to His flesh. Yet that which is according to His deity is present, and if He is considered as a whole thing, that is, as a whole person, both God and man are present.

Q39 What does His sitting at the right hand of the Father show?

A39 That He is elevated into the high position of glory which is above every name, with the reality of his flesh not laid aside, but all infirmity; with the flesh already fully glorified by the deity dwelling in it, yet not absorbed into His essence nor into His essential properties; and with Him governing and administrating with full justice all things in heaven and on earth (except Him who subjects all things to Him).

Q40 What do you mean by "essential properties"?
A40 That which, when removed, by necessity causes the thing to be no longer what it was. Thus, for example, the body, with quantity removed, necessarily ceases to be a body.

Q41 And yet God is omnipotent.
A41 Who denies this?

Q42 Therefore, He is able to cause one and the same body to be in many places at the same time, or somewhere to be as in a place and not as in a place at the same time, but by some incomprehensible manner.
A42 That God is able to make it happen so that something that is, is not anymore, just as He made it happen so that something which was not, is, no one, unless He is insane, doubts, since it is so obvious that He is able to change the forms and qualities of things at will. But to make it happen so that something is and is not at the same time, or is such and is not such at the same time, God is not able to do, because He is not able to lie. Indeed, to not be able to lie is not a weakness, but is a sign of invariable strength.

Q43 You conclude, then, that Christ, touching His humanity, is now away from us.
A43 Altogether, and, indeed, by as much space as that which is above the heavens (where that flesh is exalted) is away from the earth (where we are).

Q44 Still, He said that He was presently in heaven, even while speaking to Nicodemus on the earth.
A44 That, as well as other things of this type, are understood in reference to the communication of idioms.

Q45 What are "idioms"?
A45 That which the dialectics call proper to the fourth mode: of which manner is (for example) infinity in the divine nature, and quantity in all things created, especially, bodily things.

Q46 Then this communication is false, since an idiom of this type ceases to be an idiom, as soon as it becomes common.

A46 This latter point I simply concede, but not the first one.

Q47 But these two things seem to cohere absolutely.

A47 Then understand it in this way: there remains of each nature in Christ, Godhead and manhood, their own essential properties, so as we have said, they are incommunicable; because unless we say this, infinite absurdities and certainly impieties follow. For the Godhead would be transformed into the manhood by those properties of the human nature which it receives into itself, and contrawise, the humanity, by the communication of the properties of the Godhead, would become a certain fictitious Godhead, so that Christ could not be said to be true God or true man, and likewise He would not be a saviour for us. Therefore, there is neither any communication of natures or essential properties, and how false and impious are those declarations, "The flesh is Godhead, the Godhead is flesh." Likewise are these statements false and impious, "The flesh of Christ is everywhere," or, "Christ is ubiquitous according to the flesh," or, "Christ is not ubiquitous according to His Godhead." And these, therefore, are most false, "The Godhead was crucified," or, "The Godhead died; the flesh of Christ is infinite." However, although these natures might be unique with their own essential, incommunicable properties, as I have said, nevertheless, they are united to so great an extent, that they are as one and the same substance, or constitute one person.

Q49 Why, then, do you call it the communication of idioms, if there is no real communication of natures and essential properties.

A49 We do not call the communication of properties the personal union itself, or the form of this union, but the proclamation, as the dialectics say, which is on account of the personal union of the two natures, in which an essential property or operation that agrees to one nature is attributed to the person concretely, and not abstractly. Moreover, since this proclamation is true, it is necessary that it be based on truth, nevertheless, in the same way, namely, in respect to the whole person considered concretely.

Q50 Again, therefore, you conclude that Christ, touching His flesh, truly and really has migrated from the earth above all the heavens, and thus is now absent from us who are in the earth.

A50 Yes, although I believe that Christ as man is most present with us, but in another regard, that is, inasmuch as this same man is also God. Yes, if you are willing, I will even concede that the humanity of Christ is also present, but in another regard, that is, not in and of itself in its essence, but inasmuch as it is joined to the omnipresent Word by hypostatic union. Therefore, it is indeed present in the Table itself.

Q51 **What advantage is Christ for us now, if we are deserted by Him?**

A51 Indeed, He never deserted us, since now, according to His own glorified flesh, He administers all things in heaven and on earth, with the name which is above every name received from the Father. Moreover, relying on this His power, He quickens His Church in this world by His mysterious and unspeakable power, and cherishes, and governs it, and at the same time reigns in the midst of all His enemies. Moreover, in heaven He intercedes all the while before the Father, until the ultimate enemy, clearly death, is utterly destroyed.

Jonathan Edwards: The Excellency of Christ

In this sermon Jonathan Edwards treats the traditional doctrine of the two natures of Christ with his characteristic originality and passion. Edwards considers the convergence in Christ's person of the divine and human properties, in all their distinctiveness, a most telling indicator of Christ's uniqueness as Mediator. The reader should note that "excellency" has a specific metaphysical meaning in Edwards's vocabulary, signifying the height of beauty, proportion, and relationality.

SOURCE

Jonathan Edwards, Sermon: "The Excellency of Christ," in Edwards, *Works* (1834) 1:681–82 (edited).

BIBLIOGRAPHY

Richard R. Niebuhr, " 'Being Is Proportion,' Jonathan Edwards' Philosophy of Excellency," in R. R. Niebuhr, *Streams of Grace: Studies of Jonathan Edwards, Samuel Taylor Coleridge, and William James* (Kyoto, Japan: Doshisha University Press, 1983), 12–38.

II. There do meet in the person of Christ such really diverse excellencies, which otherwise would have been thought utterly incompatible in the same subject; such as are conjoined in no other person whatever, either divine, human, or angelical; and such as neither men nor angels would ever have imagined could have met together in the same person, had it not been seen in the person of Christ. I would give some instances.

1. In the person of Christ do meet together infinite *glory* and lowest *humility*. Infinite glory, and the virtue of humility, meet in no other person but Christ. They meet in no created person; for no created person has infinite glory; and they meet in no other divine person but Christ. For though the divine nature be infinitely abhorrent to pride, yet humility is not properly predicable of God the Father, and the Holy Ghost, that exists only in the divine nature; because it is proper excellency only of a created nature; for it consists radically in a sense of a comparative lowness and littleness before God, or the great distance between God and the subject of this virtue; but it would be a contradiction to suppose any such thing in God.

But in Jesus Christ, who is both God and man, those two diverse excellencies are sweetly united. He is a person infinitely exalted in glory and dignity. Phil. ii. 6. "Being in the form of God, he thought it not robbery to be equal with God." There is equal honour due to him with the Father. John v. 23—"That all men should honour the Son, even as they honour the Father." God himself says to him, "Thy throne, O God, is for ever and ever," Heb. i. 8. And there is the same supreme respect and divine worship paid to him by the angels of heaven, as to God the Father, (ver. 6.) "Let all the angels of God worship him."

But however he is thus above all, yet he is lowest of all in humility. There never was so great an instance of this virtue among either men or angels, as Jesus. None ever was so sensible of the distance between God and him, or had a heart so lowly before God, as the man Christ Jesus. . . .

2. In the person of Christ do meet together infinite *majesty* and transcendent *meekness*. These again are two qualifications that meet together in no other person but Christ. Meekness, properly so called, is a virtue proper only to the creature: we scarcely ever find meekness mentioned as a divine attribute in Scripture; at least not in the New Testament; for thereby seems to be signified, a calmness and quietness of spirit, arising from humility in mutable beings that are naturally liable to be put into a ruffle by the assaults of a tempestuous and injurious world. But Christ being both God and man, hath both infinite majesty and superlative meekness. . . .

3. There meet in the person of Christ the deepest *reverence* towards God and *equality* with God. Christ, when on earth, appeared full of holy reverence towards the Father. He paid the most reverential worship to him, praying to him with postures of reverence. . . .

4. There are conjoined in the person of Christ infinite *worthiness* of good, and the greatest *patience* under sufferings of evil. He was perfectly innocent, and deserved no suffering. He deserved nothing from God by any guilt of his own; and he deserved no ill from men. Yea, he was not only harmless and undeserving of suffering, but he was infinitely worthy; worthy of the infinite love of the Father, worthy of infinite and eternal happiness, and infinitely worthy of all possible esteem, love, and service from all men. And yet he was perfectly patient under the greatest sufferings that ever were endured in this world. . . .

5. In the person of Christ are conjoined an exceeding spirit of *obedience*, with supreme *dominion* over heaven and earth. Christ is the Lord of all things in two respects: he is so, as God-man and Mediator; and thus his dominion is appointed, and given him of the Father. Having it by delegation from God, he is as it were the Father's vicegerent. But he is Lord of all things in another respect, *viz.* as he is (by his original nature) God. . . .

6. In the person of Christ are conjoined absolute *sovereignty* and perfect *resignation*. This is another unparalleled conjunction. Christ, as he is God, is the absolute sovereign of the world; the sovereign disposer of all events. The decrees of God are all his sovereign decrees; and the work of creation, and all God's works of providence, are his sovereign works. It is he that worketh all things according to the counsel of his own will. . . .

7. In Christ do meet together *self-sufficiency*, and an entire *trust* and reliance on God; which is another conjunction peculiar to the person of Christ. As he is a divine person, he is self-sufficient, standing in need of nothing. All creatures are dependent on him, but he is dependent on none, but is absolutely independent. His proceeding from the Father, in his eternal generation or filiation, argues no proper dependence on the *will* of the Father; for that proceeding was natural and *necessary*, and not arbitrary. But yet Christ entirely trusted in God: his enemies say that of him, "He trusted in God that he would deliver him," Matt. xxvii. 43. And the apostle testifies, 1 Pet. ii. 23. "That he committed himself to God."

THE WORK OF CHRIST
John Calvin:
Penal Substitutionary Atonement

The uniqueness of the person of Christ pays dividends in the work of Christ: Christ's divine nature enables him to pay the penalty for sin; his human nature enables him to do so on humanity's behalf. This is in keeping with Anselmic teaching on the work of Christ, but it conceives the satisfaction of Christ less as payment of a debt and more as payment of a penalty, to satisfy justice and the demands of the law and to redeem humanity from the power of sin and death into which their sin had enslaved them.[5]

SOURCE

Institutes II.12.2–3, p. 466.

BIBLIOGRAPHY

John Calvin, *The Deity of Christ, and Other Sermons*, trans. Leroy Nixon (Grand Rapids: Wm. B. Eerdmans, 1950). Paul van Buren, *Christ in Our Place: The Substitutionary Character of Calvin's Doctrine of Reconciliation* (Grand Rapids: Wm. B. Eerdmans, 1957).

[I]t was also imperative that he who was to become our Redeemer be true God and true man. It was his task to swallow up death. Who but the Life could do this? It was his task to conquer sin. Who but very Righteousness could do this? It was his task to rout the powers of world and air. Who but a power higher than world and air could do this? Now where does life or righteousness, or lordship and authority of heaven lie but with God alone? Therefore our most merciful God, when he willed that we be redeemed, made himself our Redeemer in the person of his only-begotten Son [cf. Rom. 5:8]. . . .

The second requirement of our reconciliation with God was this: that man, who by his disobedience had become lost, should by way of remedy counter it with obedience, satisfy God's judgment, and pay the penalties for sin. Accordingly, our Lord came forth as true man and took the person and the name of Adam in order to take Adam's place in obeying the Father, to present our flesh as the price of satisfaction to God's righteous judgment, and, in the same flesh, to pay the penalty that we had deserved. In short, since neither as God alone could he feel death, nor as man alone could he overcome it, he coupled human nature with divine that to atone for sin he might submit the weakness of the one to death; and that, wrestling with death by the power of the other nature, he might win victory for us. Those who despoil Christ of either his divinity or his humanity diminish his majesty and glory, or obscure his goodness. On the other hand, they do just as much wrong to men whose faith they thus weaken and overthrow, because it cannot stand unless it rests upon this foundation.

5. Cf. Anselm, *Cur Deus Homo?* The Latin edition of Anselm's works is in *Patrologia Latina*, ed. J. P. Migne, 221 vols. (Paris, 1844–64), vols. 117, 119; ET: *St. Anselm: Basic Writings*, 2d ed., trans. S. N. Deane (LaSalle, Ill.: Open Court, 1962), 171–288.

Offices of Christ as Prophet, Priest, and King

John Calvin

"Jesus Christ, our Prophet, Priest, and King," constitutes one of the standard Reformed rubrics for explaining the work of Christ. Although the offices are distinct, they form three interconnected aspects of the unitary work of Christ as Mediator. The three offices are biblically based and were mentioned by theologians prior to Calvin, but Calvin was the first to develop them into a comprehensive way of describing Christ's reconciling work.

SOURCE

Institutes II.15.1–6, pp. 494–503 (edited).

[I]n order that faith may find a firm basis for salvation in Christ, and thus rest in him, this principle must be laid down: the office enjoined upon Christ by the Father consists of three parts. For he was given to be prophet, king, and priest. Yet it would be of little value to know these names without understanding their purpose and use. The papists use these names, too, but coldly and rather ineffectually, since they do not know what each of these titles contains. . . .

The Meaning of the Prophetic Office for Us

Now it is to be noted that the title "Christ" pertains to these three offices: for we know that under the law prophets as well as priests and kings were anointed with holy oil. Hence the illustrious name of "Messiah" was also bestowed upon the promised Mediator. As I have elsewhere shown, I recognize that Christ was called Messiah especially with respect to, and by virtue of, his kingship. Yet his anointings as prophet and as priest have their place and must not be overlooked by us. Isaiah specifically mentions the former in these words: "The Spirit of the Lord Jehovah is upon me, because Jehovah has anointed me to preach to the humble, . . . to bring healing to the brokenhearted, to proclaim liberation to the captives . . . , to proclaim the year of the Lord's good pleasure," etc. [Isa. 61:1–2; cf. Luke 4:18]. We see that he was anointed by the Spirit to be herald and witness of the Father's grace. And that not in the common way—for he is distinguished from other teachers with a similar office. On the other hand, we must note this: he received anointing, not only for himself that he might carry out the office of teaching, but for his whole body that the power of the Spirit might be present in the continuing preaching of the gospel. This, however, remains certain: the perfect doctrine he has brought has made an end to all prophecies. . . .

The Kingly Office—Its Spiritual Character

I come now to kingship. It would be pointless to speak of this without first warning my readers that it is spiritual in nature. For from this we infer its efficacy and benefit for us, as well as its whole force and eternity. . . .

We have said that we can perceive the force and usefulness of Christ's kingship only when we recognize it to be spiritual. This is clear enough from the fact that, while we must fight throughout life under the cross, our condition is harsh and wretched. What, then, would it profit us to be gathered under the reign of the Heavenly King, unless beyond this earthly life we were certain of enjoying its benefits? For this reason we ought to know that the happiness promised us in Christ does not consist in outward advantages—such as leading a joyous and peaceful life, having rich possessions, being safe from all harm, and abounding with delights such as the flesh commonly longs after. No, our happiness belongs to the heavenly life! . . .

Thus it is that we may patiently pass through this life with its misery, hunger, cold, contempt, reproaches, and other troubles—content with this one thing: that our King will never leave us destitute, but will provide for our needs until, our warfare ended, we are called to triumph. Such is the nature of his rule, that he shares with us all that he has received from the Father. Now he arms and equips us with his power, adorns us with his beauty and magnificence, enriches us with his wealth. These benefits, then, give us the most fruitful occasion to glory, and also provide us with confidence to struggle fearlessly against the devil, sin, and death. Finally, clothed with his righteousness, we can valiantly rise above all the world's reproaches; and just as he himself freely lavishes his gifts upon us, so may we, in return, bring forth fruit to his glory. . . .

The Priestly Office: Reconciliation and Intercession

Now we must speak briefly concerning the purpose and use of Christ's priestly office: as a pure and stainless Mediator he is by his holiness to reconcile us to God. But God's righteous curse bars our access to him, and God in his capacity as judge is angry toward us. Hence, an expiation must intervene in order that Christ as priest may obtain God's favor for us and appease his wrath. Thus Christ to perform this office had to come forward with a sacrifice. For under the law, also, the priest was forbidden to enter the sanctuary without blood [Heb. 9:7], that believers might know, even though the priest as their advocate stood between them and God, that they could not propitiate God unless their sins were expiated [Lev. 16:2–3]. The apostle discusses this point at length in The Letter to the Hebrews, from the seventh almost to the end of the tenth chapter. To sum up his argument: The priestly office belongs to Christ alone because by the sacrifice of his death he blotted out our own guilt and made satisfaction for our sins [Heb. 9:22]. . . .

It follows that he is an everlasting intercessor: through his pleading we obtain favor. Hence arises not only trust in prayer, but also peace for godly consciences, while they safely lean upon God's fatherly mercy and are surely persuaded that whatever has been consecrated through the Mediator is pleasing to God. Although God under the law commanded animal sacrifices to be offered to himself, in Christ there was a new and different order, in which the same one was to be both priest and sacrifice. This was because no other satisfaction adequate for our sins, and no man worthy to offer to God the only-begotten Son, could be found. Now, Christ plays the priestly role, not only to render the Father favorable and propitious toward us by an eternal law of reconciliation, but also to receive us as his companions in this great office [Rev. 1:6]. For we who are defiled in ourselves, yet are priests in him, offer ourselves and our all to God, and freely enter the heavenly sanctuary that the sacrifices of prayers and praise that we bring may be acceptable and sweet-smelling before God. This is the meaning of Christ's statement: "For their sake I sanctify myself" [John 17:19]. For we, imbued with his holiness in so far as he has consecrated us to the Father with himself, although we would otherwise be loathsome to him, please him as pure and clean—and even as holy.

Westminster Shorter Catechism

This is an easily memorized statement of the work of Christ which has informed the piety of many Reformed lay people.

SOURCE
Westminster Shorter Catechism (1647), qs. 23–26, in Schaff, *Creeds* 3:680–81.

Q. 23: What offices doth Christ execute as our Redeemer?
A: Christ, as our Redeemer, executeth the offices of a Prophet, of a Priest, and of a King, both in his estate of humiliation and exaltation.

Q. 24: How doth Christ execute the office of a Prophet?

A: Christ executeth the office of a Prophet, in revealing to us by his Word and Spirit, the will of God for our salvation.

Q. 25: How doth Christ execute the office of a Priest?

A: Christ executeth the office of a Priest, in his once offering up of himself a sacrifice to satisfy divine justice, and reconcile us to God, and in making continual intercession for us.

Q. 26: How doth Christ execute the office of a King?

A: Christ executeth the office of a King, in subduing us to himself, in ruling and defending us, and in restraining and conquering all his and our enemies.

Humiliation and Exaltation of Christ

Westminster Larger Catechism

Reformed theological reflection on Christ's humiliation and exaltation are found in embryonic form in Calvin and become more highly systematized in the seventeenth century. The state of humiliation embraces such things as Christ's self-emptying in incarnation, his suffering and death, and the descent into hell. The exaltation includes the resurrection, the ascension, and the second coming. In Reformed dogmatics, the subject of both the humiliation and exaltation is thought to be the God-man. In keeping with the vexing questions about the relationship between the two natures, scholastic theologians differed over the relative degree of participation and agency in humiliation and exaltation between the divine and human natures and between the Father and the Son. In contrast to this sort of dispute, the Westminster Assembly was content to make the following simple scriptural affirmations.

SOURCE

Westminster Larger Catechism (1646), qs. 46–57, in *The Constitution of the Presbyterian Church (U.S.A.)*, Part I; *The Book of Confessions* 7.156–67.

BIBLIOGRAPHY

Institutes II.16.1–19, II.17.1–6, pp. 503–34.

Q. 46. What was the estate of Christ's humiliation?

A. The estate of Christ's humiliation was that low condition, wherein he, for our sakes, emptying himself of his glory, took upon him the form of a servant, in his conception and birth, life, death, and after his death until his resurrection.

Q. 47. How did Christ humble himself in his conception and birth?

A. Christ humbled himself in his conception and birth, in that, being from all eternity the Son of God in the bosom of the Father, he was pleased in the fullness of time to become the Son of man, made of a woman of low estate, and to be born to her, with divers circumstances of more than ordinary abasement.

Q. 48. How did Christ humble himself in his life?

A. Christ humbled himself in his life, by subjecting himself to the law, which he perfectly fulfilled, and by conflicting with the indignities of the world, temptations of Satan, and infirmities in his flesh; whether common to the nature of man, or particularly accompanying that his low condition.

Q. 49. How did Christ humble himself in his death?

A. Christ humbled himself in his death, in that having been betrayed by Judas, forsaken by his disciples, scorned and rejected by the world, condemned by Pilate, and tormented by his persecutors; having also conflicted with the terrors of death and the powers of darkness, felt and borne the weight of God's wrath, he laid down his life an offering for sin, enduring the painful, shameful, and cursed death of the cross.

Q. 50. Wherein consisted Christ's humiliation after his death?

A. Christ's humiliation after his death consisted in his being buried, and continuing in the state of the dead, and under the power of death till the third day, which hath been otherwise expressed in these words: "He descended into hell."

Q. 51. What was the estate of Christ's exaltation?

A. The estate of Christ's exaltation comprehendeth his resurrection, ascension, sitting at the right hand of the Father, and his coming again to judge the world.

Q. 52. How was Christ exalted in his resurrection?

A. Christ was exalted in his resurrection, in that, not having seen corruption in death (of which it was not possible for him to be held), and having the very same body in which he suffered, with the essential properties thereof (but without mortality and other common infirmities belonging to this life), really united to his soul, he rose again from the dead the third day by his own power; whereby he declared himself to be the Son of God, to have satisfied divine justice, to have vanquished death and him that had the power of it, and to be Lord of quick and dead. All which he did as a public person, the head of his Church, for their justification, quickening in grace, support against enemies, and to assure them of their resurrection from the dead at the last day.

Q. 53. How was Christ exalted in his ascension?

A. Christ was exalted in his ascension, in that having, after his resurrection, often appeared unto, and conversed with his apostles, speaking to them of the things pertaining to the Kingdom of God, and giving them commission to preach the gospel to all nations, forty days after his resurrection, he, in our nature, and as our head, triumphing over enemies, visibly went up into the highest heavens, there to receive gifts for men, to raise up our affections thither, and to prepare a place for us, where himself is, and shall continue till his second coming at the end of the world.

Q. 54. How is Christ exalted in his sitting at the right hand of God?

A. Christ is exalted in his sitting at the right hand of God, in that as God-man he is advanced to the highest favor with God the Father, with all fullness of joy, glory, and power over all things in heaven and earth; and doth gather and defend his Church, and subdue their enemies; furnisheth his ministers and people with gifts and graces, and maketh intercession for them.

Q. 55. How doth Christ make intercession?

A. Christ maketh intercession, by his appearing in our nature continually before the Father in heaven, in the merit of his obedience and sacrifice on earth, declaring his will to have it applied to all believers; answering all accusations against them; and procuring for them quiet of conscience, notwithstanding daily failings, access with boldness to the throne of grace, and acceptance of their persons and services.

Q. 56. How is Christ to be exalted in his coming again to judge the world?

A. Christ is to be exalted in his coming again to judge the world, in that he, who was unjustly judged and condemned by wicked men, shall come again at the last day in great power, and in the full manifestation of his own glory, and of his Father's, with all his holy angels, with a shout, with the voice of the archangel, and with the trumpet of God, to judge the world in righteousness.

Q. 57. What benefits hath Christ procured by his mediation?

A. Christ by his mediation hath procured redemption, with all other benefits of the covenant of grace.

The Genevan Church and Isaac Watts: Hymns

Hymnody has of course focused the attention of worshipers upon both the humiliation and exaltation in Christ's life in ways which relate them to the believer's own Christian experience.

SOURCES

(A) "I Greet Thee, Who My Sure Redeemer Art" (1545), trans. Elizabeth L. Smith (1868). From the church in Geneva but attributed in tradition to John Calvin. **(B)** Isaac Watts, "When I Survey the Wondrous Cross" (1707). **(C)** Isaac Watts, "Jesus Shall Reign Where'er the Sun" (1719).

A. GENEVA:

I greet Thee, who my sure Redeemer art,
  My only Trust and Saviour of my heart,
Who pain didst undergo for my poor sake;
  I pray thee from our hearts all cares to take.

Thou art the King of mercy and of grace,
  Reigning omnipotent in every place;
So come, O King, and our whole being sway;
  Shine on us with the light of Thy pure day.

B. ISAAC WATTS

When I survey the wondrous cross
  On which the Prince of glory died,
My richest gain I count but loss,
  And poor contempt on all my pride.

See, from His head, His hands, His feet,
  Sorrow and love flow mingled down:
Did e'er such love and sorrow meet,
  Or thorns compose so rich a crown?

C. ISAAC WATTS

Jesus shall reign where'er the sun
  Does his successive journeys run;
His Kingdom stretch from shore to shore,
  Till moons shall wax and wane no more.

Limited Atonement versus Universal Atonement

John Calvin: God's Love for the Human Race

Reformed theologians have not questioned whether the death of Christ could make sufficient satisfaction for the sins of all.[6] Where they have joined issue is over God's eternal purpose in Christ's death: did Christ die for all persons or only for the elect? The answer would seem to depend on how one interprets the question. At stake is the antinomy, intrinsic to the Reformed understanding of the gospel itself, between the reality and certainty of the salvation achieved by God in election and the contingency and integrity of the human appropriation of salvation by faith in Jesus Christ. The tension is reflected in this passage from Calvin's commentary on 1 Peter 3:9.

SOURCE

John Calvin, Commentary: 1 Peter 3:9; CO 55; ET: *The Epistle of Paul the Apostle to the Hebrews and The First and Second Epistles of St. Peter*, trans. William B. Johnston, *Calvin's New Testament Commentaries* 12:364.

["The Lord is not slack concerning his promise, as some count slackness; but is long-suffering toward you, not wishing that any should perish but that all should come to repentance." 1 Pet. 3:9]

This is His wondrous love towards the human race, that He desires all men to be saved, and is prepared to bring even the perishing to safety. We must notice the order, that God is preparing to receive all men into repentance, so that none may perish. These words indicate the means of obtaining salvation, and whoever of us seeks salvation must learn to follow in this way.

It could be asked here, if God does not want any to perish, why do so

---

6. Calvin quotes approvingly this classic formulation on the work of Christ (although he did not think it applicable to the passage in 1 John he happened to be exegeting): "Christ suffered sufficiently for the whole world but effectively only for the elect" (Commentary: 1 John 1:2, CR 55; ET: *Calvin's New Testament Commentaries* 5:244).

many in fact perish? My reply is that no mention is made here of the secret decree of God by which the wicked are doomed to their own ruin, but only of His loving-kindness as it is made known to us in the gospel. There God stretches out His hand to all alike, but He only grasps those (in such a way as to lead to Himself) whom He has chosen before the foundation of the world.

The Remonstrance versus the Synod of Dort

The Remonstrance, in challenging the predominant orthodox Reformed thinking, makes an unambiguous proclamation of the love of God in the fact that Christ died for all. The Synod of Dort, insisting not only on the mercy but also the justice of God, countered with the explanation that Christ's death is sufficient for all but efficient only for the elect.

SOURCES

(A) *Articuli Arminiani sive Remonstrantia* (1610) [Dutch: *De Remonstrantie en het Remonstrantisme*], Article II; ET: *The Five Arminian Articles* (1610), in Schaff, *Creeds* 3:546. **(B)** *Canones Synodi Dordrechtanae* (1618–19), Second Head of Doctrine, Articles III–VIII; ET: "Of the Death of Christ, and the Redemption of Men thereby," *Canons of the Synod of Dort*, in Schaff, *Creeds* 3:582–84.

BIBLIOGRAPHY

See materials on pp. 13, 94–97, 153–56, 222–24, 262–65, 288–91, 302–6.

A. THE REMONSTRANCE

ART. II. That, agreeably thereto, Jesus Christ, the Saviour of the world, died for all men and for every man, so that he has obtained for them all, by his death on the cross, redemption and the forgiveness of sins; yet that no one actually enjoys this forgiveness of sins except the believer, according to the word of the Gospel of John iii. 16: "God so loved the world that he gave his only-begotten Son, that whosoever believeth in him should not perish, but have everlasting life." And in the First Epistle of John ii. 2: "And he is the propitiation for our sins; and not for ours only, but also for the sins of the whole world."

B. THE SYNOD OF DORT

Second Head of Doctrine

Of the Death of Christ, and the Redemption of Men thereby.

ART. III. The death of the Son of God is the only and most perfect sacrifice and satisfaction for sin; is of infinite worth and value, abundantly sufficient to expiate the sins of the whole world.

ART. IV. This death derives its infinite value and dignity from these considerations; because the person who submitted to it was not only really man and perfectly holy, but also the only-begotten Son of God, of the same eternal and infinite essence with the Father and Holy Spirit, which qualifications were necessary to constitute him a Saviour for us; and because it was attended with a sense of the wrath and curse of God due to us for sin.

ART. V. Moreover the promise of the gospel is, that whosoever believeth in Christ crucified shall not perish, but have everlasting life. This promise, together with the command to repent and believe, ought to be declared and published to all nations, and to all persons promiscuously and without distinction, to whom God out of his good pleasure sends the gospel.

ART. VI. And, whereas many who are called by the gospel do not repent nor believe in Christ, but perish in unbelief; this is not owing to any defect or insufficiency in the sacrifice offered by Christ upon the cross, but is wholly to be imputed to themselves.

ART. VII. But as many as truly believe, and are delivered and saved from sin and destruction through the death of Christ, are indebted for this benefit solely to the grace of God given them in Christ from everlasting, and not to any merit of their own.

ART. VIII. For this was the sovereign counsel and most gracious will and purpose of God the Father, that the quickening and saving efficacy of the most precious death of his Son should extend to all the elect, for bestowing upon them alone the gift of justifying faith, thereby to bring them infallibly to salvation: that is, it was the will of God, that Christ by the blood of the cross, whereby he confirmed the new covenant, should effectually redeem out of every people, tribe, nation, and language, all those, and those only, who were from eternity chosen to salvation, and given to him by the Father; that he should confer upon them faith, which, together with all the other saving gifts of the Holy Spirit, he purchased for them by his death; should purge them from all sin, both original and actual, whether committed before or after believing; and having faithfully preserved them even to the end, should at last bring them free from every spot and blemish to the enjoyment of glory in his own presence forever.

John Owen and Richard Baxter:
The Extent of the Atonement

John Owen (1616–83) wrote his treatise *The Death of Death in the Death of Christ* (1647) to refute the position of John Cameron[7] and Moïse Amyraut, "hypothetical" or "conditional" universalism, a position we encountered earlier in the section on predestination (pp. 94–104). According to Amyraut, God desires all to be saved on the condition of faith and obedience. God's effectual calling is needed to supply this condition, however, and effectual calling occurs only in the elect. At the risk of oversimplifying, one may say that in Amyrauldian thought, election tends to serve redemption, whereas in the high Calvinist understanding, redemption tends to serve election.

Owen answered Cameron and Amyraut with an uncompromising state-ment of the exclusive divine agency in procuring salvation. He argued that since the achievement of salvation is solely attributable to the merciful and just power of God, and since many are not included among the elect, a universal atonement is a contradiction:

> It is in no way clear to me what glory redoundeth to the grace of God, what exaltation is given to the death of Christ, what encouragement to sinners in the things of God, by maintaining that our Saviour, in the intention and the designment of his Father, died for the redemption of millions for whom he purchased not one dram of saving grace, and concerning whom it was the purpose of God from eternity not to make out unto them effectually any of those means for a participation in the fruits of his death.[8]

The brief section presented below from Owen's lengthy and quite detailed treatise argues against conditional universalism on covenantal grounds.

Owen's fellow Englishman, Richard Baxter (1615–91), considered himself to be, like Owen, an adherent of the Calvinism of the Synod of Dort, including its view of limited atonement. Nevertheless, Baxter found Owen's position too harsh and believed it to be in jeopardy of making God the author of sin. Baxter criticized Owen in a work entitled *Aphorisms of Justification,* whereupon there ensued a minor pamphlet war focused on highly technical areas of scholastic theology. Baxter's own position seems to be close to that of Amyraut,

---

7. John Cameron (ca. 1579–1625) was a Scottish theologian who succeeded the high Calvinist Francis Gomarus (1563–1641) as theology professor at the Saumur Academy and had a great influence upon Moïse Amyraut.

8. John Owen, "To the Reader," *Of the Death of Christ, the Price He Paid, and the Purchase He Made,* in Owen, *Works* 10:433.

but he is not always free from ambiguity. Being more concerned with proclaiming the gospel in all its evangelical fullness than in achieving consistency
of technical expression, Baxter, toward the end of his life, expressed regret
over the whole debate. In keeping with this irenic sentiment, the excerpt from
Baxter below is from a pastoral tract which he wrote to assure potential
converts of the grace and wisdom of God.

SOURCES

(A) John Owen, *Salus Electorum, Sanguis Jesu; or, The Death of Death in the Death of
Christ: A Treatise of the Redemption and Reconciliation that is in the Blood of Christ.* . . .
(1647), in Owen, *Works* 10:237–39. (B) Richard Baxter, *A Call to the Unconverted to
Turn and Live.* . . . (1657), in *The Practical Works of Richard Baxter,* 4 vols. (London,
1838), 2:518–19.

BIBLIOGRAPHY

Richard Baxter, *Aphorisms on Justification.* Idem, *Universal Redemption of Mankind by
the Lord Jesus Christ Confession of Faith* (1655, posthumously published, 1694). Idem,
*Certain Disputations of Right to the Sacraments and the True Nature of Visible Christian-
ity* (1656). John Owen, Θεομαχια Αυτεξουσιαστικη, or *A Display of Arminianism.* . . .
(1642), in Owen, *Works* 10:1–137. Idem, *Of the Death of Christ.* . . . (1650), in Owen,
Works 10:428–79.

A. JOHN OWEN

Yea, every blessing of the new covenant being certainly common, and
to be communicated to all the covenantees, either faith is none of them,
or all must have it, if the covenant itself be general. But some may say
that it is true God promiseth to write his law in our hearts, and put his
fear in our inward parts; but it is upon condition. Give me that condition, and I will yield the cause. Is it if they do believe? Nothing else can
be imagined. That is, if they have the law written in their hearts (as every
one that believes hath), then God promiseth to write his law in their
hearts! Is this probable, friends? is it likely? I cannot, then, be persuaded
that God hath made a covenant of grace with all, especially those who
never heard a word of covenant, grace, or condition of it, much less
received grace for the fulfilling of the condition; without which the
whole would be altogether unprofitable and useless. . . .

Most apparent, then, it is that the new covenant of grace, and the
promises thereof, are all of them of distinguishing mercy, restrained
to the people whom God did foreknow; and so not extended universally to
all. Now, the blood of Jesus Christ being the blood of this covenant, and
his oblation intended only for the procurement of the good things
intended and promised thereby,—for he was the surety thereof, Heb. vii.

22, and of that only,—it cannot be conceived to have respect unto all, or any but only those that are intended in this covenant. . . .

Doth it become the wisdom of God to send Christ to die for men that they might be saved, and never cause these men to hear of any such thing; and yet to purpose and declare that unless they do hear of it and believe it, they shall never be saved? What wise man would pay a ransom for the delivery of those captives which he is sure shall never come to the knowledge of any such payment made, and so never be the better for it? Is it answerable to the goodness of God, to deal thus with his poor creatures? to hold out towards them all in pretence the most intense love imaginable, beyond all compare and illustration,—as his love in sending his Son is set forth to be,—and yet never let them know of any such thing, but in the end to damn them for not believing it? Is it answerable to the love and kindness of Christ to us, to assign unto him at his death such a resolution as this:—"I will now, by the oblation of myself, obtain for all and every one peace and reconciliation with God, redemption and everlasting salvation, eternal glory in the high heavens, even for all those poor, miserable, wretched worms, condemned caitiffs, that every hour ought to expect the sentence of condemnation; and all these shall truly and really be communicated to them if they will believe. But yet, withal, I will so order things that innumerable souls shall never hear one word of all this that I have done for them, never be persuaded to believe, nor have the object of faith that is to be believed proposed to them, whereby they might indeed possibly partake of these things?" Was this the mind and will, this the design and purpose, of our merciful high priest? God forbid. It is all one as if a prince should say and proclaim, that whereas there be a number of captives held in sore bondage in such a place, and he hath a full treasure, he is resolved to redeem them every one, so that every one of them shall come out of prison that will thank him for his good-will, and in the meantime never take care to let these poor captives know his mind and pleasure; and yet be fully assured that unless he effect it himself it will never be done. Would not this be conceived a vain and ostentatious flourish, without any good intent indeed towards the poor captives? Or as if a physician should say that he hath a medicine that will cure all diseases, and he intends to cure the diseases of all, but lets but very few know his mind, or any thing of his medicine; and yet is assured that without his relation and particular information it will be known to very few. And shall he be supposed to desire, intend, or aim at the recovery of all?

B. RICHARD BAXTER

But what is in the hearts of all men in the world, and consequently how they shall be used at last, he only that searcheth the heart can tell; and it is neither our duty nor our interest, nor possible to us, to know it of all particulars, much less to conclude, that none among them have such love, who believe him to be infinitely good, and to be to them a merciful, pardoning God. And we know withal, that all they that know not Jesus Christ, as this determinate person that was born of the Virgin Mary, suffered under Pontius Pilate, was crucified, dead, buried, rose again, &c. do yet receive all the foresaid mercies by him, and not by any other name or mediation, nor yet without his purchasing mediation. . . .

And if besides all the mercy that God showeth to others, he do antecedently and positively elect certain persons, by an absolute decree, to overcome all their resistances of his Spirit, and to draw them to Christ, and by Christ to himself, by such a power and way as shall infallibly convert and save them, and not leave the success of his mercy, and his Son's preparations, to the bare uncertainty of the mutable will of depraved man, what is there in this that is injurious to any others? or that representeth God unmerciful to any but such whose eye is evil because he is good, and as a free benefactor, may give more mercy to some than others of equal demerits? If they that hold no grace but what is universal, and left, as to the success, to the will of man, as the determining cause, do think that this is well consistent with the mercifulness of God; surely they that hold as much universal grace as the former, and that indeed all have so much, as bringeth and leaveth the success to man's will, and deny to no man any thing which the other give, do make God no less merciful than they, but more, if they moreover assert a special decree and grace of God, which with a chosen number, shall antecedently infallibly secure his ends in their repentance, faith, perseverance, and salvation. Is this any detraction from, or diminution of, his universal grace? or rather a higher demonstration of his goodness; as it is no wrong to man, that God maketh angels more holy, immutable, and happy. . . .

I conclude in general, that nothing is more sure, than that God is most powerful, wise, and good, and that all his works, to those that truly know them, do manifest all these in conjunction and perfect harmony; and that as to his decrees and providences, he is the cause of all good, and of no sin in act or habit, and that our sin and destruction is of ourselves, and of him is our holiness and salvation.

Herman Witsius:
Covenantal Theory

Seventeenth-century covenantal theology produced a distinctive mode of reflection on the work of Christ centered on the intertrinitarian covenant struck between the Father and the Son. We have already briefly sketched the reflections of the covenantal school of Johannes Cocceius, of which Herman Witsius was a prominent member (pp. 9–13, 40–41, 62–63, 65–66, 105–6, 126–31, 174, 176–79). According to Cocceius and Witsius, God had every right after the fall to condemn human beings but chose instead to create a new covenant, thus using the fall to reveal further depths of God's gracious mercy.

The center of this new covenant was a pact between the Father and Son in which the Son took on the obligations of the covenant of works. This intertrinitarian pact generated a multilateral "covenant of redemption" which in turn provided the basis for a unilateral "covenant of grace" between the triune God and the elect.[9] In this arrangement, Christ undertook the commitment of a "surety" to pay the legal obligations of elect sinners.[10] This commitment included Christ's assuming human nature and placing himself under the burden and penalties of the law. Implicit in Witsius's discussion is the distinction between Christ's active and passive obedience: by his active obedience Christ voluntarily entered into the obligations of the covenant of grace, including his submission to the requirements of the law; by his passive obedience Christ suffered the penalty of the law in his suffering and death, thus discharging the burden of his elect.

Reformed orthodoxy, steeped in the doctrine of justification by grace, insisted that God's foreknowledge of Christ's merit did not form the basis of election. In contrast, Cocceius and his school made a subtle step away from this doctrine by holding that the work of Christ effectuated election, although it is still the decision of God and not the works of human beings that grounds election and reconciliation.

---

9. Other covenant schemes portrayed the compact as sealed between the triune God and humanity in general, or, in keeping with "limited atonement," between God the Father and Christ as federal head of the elect. Thus the *Westminster Larger Catechism* explains: "The covenant of grace was made with Christ as the second Adam, and in him with all the elect as his seed" (q. 31).

10. Under the law of suretyship, a surety may make either an absolute or a conditional promise to make good the debtor's obligation. Under an absolute surety, the debtor's own burden as primary payor is immediately removed, whereas under a conditional surety the debtor still carries the responsibility until the surety performs. At stake in this distinction is *(a)* the "conditional" character of the covenant, which emphasizes the continued requirement of obedience rather than placing a more absolutist emphasis on election, and *(b)* the guilt of Israel under the old covenant: for Cocceius and his school, Christ's suretyship was conditional, and so while Israel received revelations from Christ, Israel's guilt could be completely removed only upon Christ's advent and atonement.

SOURCE

Herman Witsius, *De oeconomia foederium Dei cum hominibur libri quattuor* (1677), Book 1, Chapters 3–5; ET: "Of the Covenant Between the Father and the Son," in *The Oeconomy of the Covenants, Between God and Man* 1:226–92 (edited, with revised orthography and punctuation).

BIBLIOGRAPHY

Johannes Cocceius, "De pacto Dei Patris, etc.," Caput V, *Summa Doctrinae de Foedere & Testamento Dei* (1648), pp. 60–71. See also the bibliographies on pp. 10 and 106.

When I speak of the compact between the Father and the Son, I thereby understand the will of the Father giving the Son to be the Head and Redeemer of the elect; and the will of the Son presenting himself as a Sponsor or Surety for them; in all which the nature of the compact and agreement consists. The scripture represents the Father in the economy of our salvation as demanding the obedience of the Son even unto death and for it promising him that name which is above every name, even that he should be head of the elect in glory: but the Son as presenting himself to do the will of the Father, acquiescing in the promise, and in fine, requiring the kingdom and glory promised to him. . . .

[There follows scriptural exegesis of Luke 22:29, Heb. 7:22, Gal. 3:16–17, Ps. 119:22, Zech. 6:13, and answers to objections; then Witsius draws upon numerous other scriptural passages to explain the component parts of the covenant and invokes theologians such as Cocceius, Arminius, and Ames on behalf of his interpretation.]

I consider three periods, as it were, of this compact [between Father and Son]. Its commencement is to be sought in the eternal counsel of the Trinity: in which the Son of God was constituted by the Father with the approbation of the Holy Spirit, the Saviour of mankind; on this condition, that in the fullness of time, he should be made of a woman and made under law; which the Son undertook to perform. Peter has a view to this when he says that Christ was foreordained before the foundation of the world [1 Pet. 1:20]. . . . [Discussion of other passages follows.]

The second period of this covenant I place in that intercession of Christ by which, immediately upon the fall of man, he offered himself to God, now offended by sin, actually to perform those things to which he had engaged himself from eternity, saying, "Thou hast given them to me, I will make satisfaction for them": and so making way for the word of

229

grace to be declared to and the covenant of grace to be made with them. Thus Christ was actually constituted Mediator and declared as such immediately after the fall; and having undertaken the Suretyship, he began to [perform] many things belonging to the offices of the Mediator. As a Prophet, and the interpreter of the divine will, he even then, by the Spirit, revealed those things which relate to the salvation of the elect, and by his ministers published them [i.e., in the Old Testament]. Nay, he himself sometimes appeared in the character of an angel instructing his people in the counsel of God. As a King, he gathered his church and formed to himself a people, in whom he might reign by his Word and Spirit. . . . As a Priest, he took upon himself the sins of the elect, to be expiated by the sacrifice of his body, which was to be fitted for him in the fullness of time. In virtue of this, as being a faithful Surety, he likewise interceded for the elect by declaring his will that they might be taken into favor. . . .

The third period of the compact is that when on his assuming human nature he suffered his ears to be bored [cf. Ps. 40:7; Heb. 10:5],[11] that is, engaged himself as a voluntary servant to God, from love to his Lord and Father and to his spouse the church, and his spiritual children . . . which he solemnly testified by his circumcision on the eighth day after his birth, whereby he made himself a debtor to do the whole law. . . .

The Son, as precisely God, neither was nor could be subject to any law . . . , that being the nature of the Godhead. . . . Nor is it any objection to this that the Son from eternity undertook [Suretyship] for men and thereby came under a certain peculiar relation to those that were to be saved. For that engagement . . . was nothing but the most glorious act of the divine will of the Son. . . . And by undertaking to perform this obedience in the human nature in its proper time, the Son, as God, did no more subject himself to the Father than the Father subjected himself to the Son, [in the Father's] owing that reward of debt which he promised [the Son] a right to claim. All these things are to be conceived of in a manner becoming God. . . .

As a man, [Christ] was doubtless subject to the moral law . . . but also [as] an Israelite . . . he was . . . subject to the ceremonial and political laws . . . [even though] Christ declared himself "greater than the temple" and "Lord of the Sabbath" . . . [and] as the Son of God . . . exempted from paying tribute. . . . Certainly as God and the Son of God, he was Lord of the law, the Lawgiver himself, who on account of his divine

11. A Hebrew servant, after serving his appointed time, could voluntarily remain in the service of his master for life, the mark of which service was the piercing of the ear—ED.

nature had authority to dispense with precepts of a mutable and positive institution. . . . But Christ did not think it proper to insist on this his right; but rather to behave as a servant of rulers [Isa. 49:7].

But further as Mediator and Surety he is under the law . . . as enjoining the condition of perfect obedience . . . [and] . . . as binding to the penalty due to the sins of the elect, which he had taken upon himself. . . . [In addition,] the Son of God was, in virtue of the compact, subject to the curse of the law being made a curse for us [Gal. 3:16]. . . . [And] as the human nature does not, without the divine complete the person of the Mediator, the Mediator as such does not seem to have undertaken subjection to the law without bringing his divine nature likewise to share therein. . . . In order to remove this difficulty, we are accurately to distinguish between both natures, considered separately, and the person of [the] God-man, consisting of both natures united. It was proper that both natures should act suitably to themselves and their distinct properties. . . . The human nature [then] was really and properly subject to the law: nay, from the hypostatical union there was superadded a certain peculiar obligation upon the human nature of Christ considered in relation to the Suretyship to be undertaken for us as his brethren. . . .

[Then follows a lengthy discourse on the two natures and the person of Christ.]

Christ therefore is called our Surety because he engaged to God to make satisfaction for us. Which satisfaction is not to be understood in the Socinian sense, as if . . . Christ most perfectly fulfilled [merely] *the will* of God. . . . But it consists in this, that Christ [on our behalf and in our] stead did, both by doing and suffering [i.e., active and passive obedience], satisfy divine justice both the legislatory, the retributive, and vindictive, the most perfect manner fulfilling all the righteousness of the law. . . . [Witsius then gives a "Suretyship" interpretation of Psalm 40] [T]herefore Christ offered himself, in order to accomplish that will of God, by which we are sanctified, both by fulfilling all righteousness prescribed by the law, and by undergoing the guilt of our sins that he might atone for them as an expiatory sacrifice. . . .

[Then ensues a discussion of the character of Christ's suretyship and the justice of God in requiring it.]

But we must proceed a step further, and affirm that the obedience of Christ was accomplished by him [on our behalf] in order thereby to obtain for us a right to eternal life. The law, which God will have secured inviolable admits none to glory but on condition of perfect obedience. This none was ever possessed of but Christ who bestows it freely on his own people. . . .

231

Nor ought it to appear strange that obedience of Christ is sufficient to acquire to them a right to eternal life; even though it became [Christ] as man to yield obedience for himself. For we are here to consider the dignity of the person obeying, who, being man in such a manner as at the same time to be the eternal and infinite God, is much more excellent than all the elect taken together; and therefore his obedience is deservedly esteemed of such value that it may be imputed to all for obtaining a right to a blessed immortality. And though the divinity in the abstract did not obey, yet he who did is God; and thus the divinity of the person contributes very much to the dignity of the obedience. . . . [B]ut since he became man on our account, he also performed that obedience [on our behalf]. . . . [Thus] we ourselves are under no necessity of obeying, because no demand can be made on the principal debtor for [that which] the Surety has performed [on his behalf].

Hugo Grotius and Jonathan Edwards, Jr.: Governmental Theories

The governmental theory of the Dutch Reformed jurist Hugo Grotius (Huig de Groot) (1583–1645) draws upon political terminology to explain Christ's atoning work. God is not so much a creditor who may remit an obligation at will as a beneficent and just "governor." Such a governor punishes not for retribution but in accordance with desert and for the deterrence of future crime. In acting in the best interests of his subjects, therefore, a governor may mitigate the full rigor of the law but must not abrogate the law itself for fear of anarchy. By analogy, Christ's death was a vicarious sacrifice which was necessary to display divine justice but which occurred as a result of divine clemency and not of vengeance. While most Calvinists have considered Grotius's view heterodox, it was drafted to defend the sacrificial nature of Christ's death against the Socinian theory that viewed Christ as merely an exemplar of true obedience.

Jonathan Edwards, Jr. (1745–1801) offers a similar view, but one based not as much upon jurisprudential analogies as upon cosmic imagery of the universe as a single system under God. This imagery builds upon the metaphysical and ethical system of Jonathan Edwards, Sr., for whom true virtue is a "consent to being in general."

SOURCES

(A) Hugo Grotius, *Defensio fidei catholicae: de satisfactione Christi adversus Faustum socinum senensem* (1617), ed. Edwin Rabbie, trans. Hotze Mulder (Assen/Maastrict: Van Gorcum, 1990); *Opera Theologica*, vol. 1, ed. the Grotius Institute of the Royal

Netherlands Academy of Arts and Sciences, 115–17, 133, 135, 137, 139, 143 (edited). This is a critical edition with Latin and English appearing on alternate pages. **(B)** Jonathan Edwards, Jr., *Thoughts on the Atonement* (n.d.), in Jonathan Edwards, Jr., *Works* 1:493–507 (edited).

BIBLIOGRAPHY

Robert L. Ferm, *A Colonial Pastor: Jonathan Edwards the Younger: 1745–1801* (Grand Rapids: Wm. B. Eerdmans, 1976). R. S. Franks, *A History of the Doctrine of the Work of Christ: In Its Ecclesiastical Development* (London and New York: Hodder & Stoughton, 1918).

On Grotius, see also the introductions and bibliographies in Grotius, *Defensio fidei catholicae*, ed. Rabbie.

A. HUGO GROTIUS

So, to sum up what has been said up to this point: since Scripture says that Christ was "chastised" by God (i.e., punished), that "Christ bore our sins" (i.e., the punishment of sins), "was made sin" (i.e., subjected to the punishment of sins), "was made a curse in the eyes of God" or "into a curse," i.e., liable to the penalty of the law; since, furthermore, the suffering of Christ itself, full of tortures, bloody, ignominious, is a most appropriate matter of punishment; since, moreover, Scripture says that this was inflicted on him by God "on account of our sins" (i.e., our sins so deserving), since death itself is said to be the "wages," i.e., the punishment of sin, certainly it can by no means be doubted that with regard to God the suffering and death of Christ had the character of a punishment, nor are we to listen to the interpretations of Socinus, which depart from the perpetual use of the words without example, especially when no reason prevents us from retaining the received meaning of the words, as will be demonstrated more clearly below. There is, therefore, a punishment, in God actively, in Christ passively; yet in the passion of Christ there is also a certain action, namely the voluntary endurance of the suffering of punishment. . . .

The end of the matter under discussion, according to the intention of God and Christ, which posited in the act may also be called its effect, is twofold: namely, the demonstration of divine justice, and the remission of sins with respect to us, i.e., our impunity. For if one takes the exaction of punishment impersonally, its end is the demonstration of divine justice; but if personally, i.e., why was Christ punished, the end is that we might achieve impunity. . . .

We now have an understanding of the state of the controversy and have established from places in Scripture the doctrine on which the faith of the church rests; now, to dispel the objections which Socinus' intelligence, or, to speak more truthfully, abuse of his intelligence, dictated to him, we must in the first place understand the role or the function of God in the matter with which we are dealing. Socinus admits that we are dealing with liberation from punishment; we add that we are also dealing with the infliction of punishment. As a result, God must here be considered as a ruler throughout. For to inflict punishment, or to liberate from punishment someone whom you can punish—which Scripture calls "justify"—, is the exclusive prerogative of the ruler as such, as it is of the father in a family, of the king in a state, and of God in the universe. . . .

But although in the place cited above Socinus regards God as the highest sovereign, yet he often ascribes to him a far different position in this situation, viz. that of an offended party. Now, he wants every offended party to be the creditor of the punishment, and in this to have the same right as other creditors in things due to them, a right for which he often even uses the term "ownership"; therefore, he repeats very frequently that God must here be regarded as an offended party, as a creditor, as an owner, putting forward these three notions as if they amount to the same. Since this error of Socinus' is spread very widely through his whole treatise and may almost be said to be in this matter his fundamental mistake, it ought to be carefully refuted.

To do this, let the first assertion be the following: punishment is not an act which falls within the competence of the offended party as such. This can be proved to be so, because otherwise every offended party would itself have the right of inflicting punishment, which appears to be false from the fact that we have proved that punishment is an act of the superior authority, which Socinus himself admits, when he says that God must here be seen as a sovereign. This entails another very strong argument: if God punishes as a sovereign, then he also revokes punishment as a sovereign, not as an offended party. . . .

It is a traditional principle that no one is fit to be the judge in his own cause, but this principle is not one of natural, but of positive law, and consequently not universal either. For it clearly does not apply to the highest rulers, by which term I also refer to parents, as far as the care of their families is concerned. . . .

Let the second assertion be the following: by nature, the offended party as such has no right in punishment. This goes a little further than the first assertion. For there we denied that the act of punishing is within the right of the offended party; here we deny not only that he has any right to perform the act himself, but also to oblige someone else to perform it; i.e., in punishment the offended party is not really a creditor, which, yet, Socinus upholds and often repeats as if it were beyond doubt. By "creditor" I do not mean here, in the strict sense according to the origin of the word, someone who put his faith in someone else, but more generally, according to the legal definition: creditors are those to whom anything is due for any reason whatsoever. . . .

Let the third assertion be the following: the right of punishment in the ruler is neither the right of absolute ownership nor a personal right. This is proved, in the first place, from the final cause, which usually best distinguishes the faculties. For the right of absolute ownership, as well as a personal right, is secured for the sake of him who has this right, but the right of punishment does not exist for the sake of him who punishes, but for the sake of a community. For all punishment has as its goal the common good, viz. the preservation of order and an example, so that the desirability of punishment has no justification except this cause, whereas the right of ownership and a personal right are in themselves desirable. In this vein, God himself says that he does not derive pleasure from the punishment of those who are punished. Again, it is never contrary to justice to waive the right of ownership or a personal right, because it is the nature of ownership that one may use it or not use it. But to let certain sins go unpunished (as, for instance, of those who do not repent) would be unjust in a ruler, even in God, as Socinus admits. The right of punishment is, therefore, not the same as the right of ownership or a personal right. Moreover, no one is said to be just or is praised for his justice, because he uses his right of property or because he calls in a debt. But any ruler, and also God himself, is said to be just or is praised for his justice, because he does not remit punishments but severely exacts them: 'just art thou, Lord, in judging thus' (Apoc. 16:5); this has been proved in several places above. Again, diversity of virtues arises from diversity of objects. Now, the virtue by which we waive our right of ownership or our personal right is called liberality, not clemency; but that virtue by which impunity is granted is not called liberality, but clemency.

B. JONATHAN EDWARDS, JR.

When Christ is said to be *sacrificed for us,* it must mean, that he was substituted and died in our stead, to make atonement for us *really,* as the ancient sacrifices did *typically.* . . .

If then Christ did die, not as a martyr, and to establish and confirm the gospel, but as a substitute to atone for the sins of his people; let us now inquire, whether this measure were necessary, and for what reason it was necessary.

1. We may argue the necessity of it from the very fact itself. We cannot imagine, that either God the Father or his Son Jesus Christ, would ever have consented to the death of Christ, for the end before mentioned, unless it had been of absolute necessity.

2. We argue the necessity of Christ's death and atonement from several declarations of scripture. "Other foundation can no man lay, than that is laid; which is Jesus Christ." "There is no other name under heaven, given among men, whereby we must be saved; neither is there salvation in any other." "Thus it behoved Christ to suffer," Luke 24:46. "If there had been a law given, which could have given life, verily righteousness should have been by the law," Gal. 3:12. "If righteousness come by the law, then Christ is dead in vain," Chap. 2:21. With the same force may we argue, that if righteousness come by the mere sovereign goodness of God, without an atonement, then Christ is dead in vain. . . .

3. The necessity of Christ's death and atonement may be argued from rational considerations. If repentance, including reformation, be all that is necessary to pardon and acceptance with God, then the glory of God, and the good and prosperity of his kingdom require no more. Whatever these require, and nothing more, is necessary in order to pardon. But the kingdom of God is the universe taken as a system; and the declarative glory of God is the highest perfection, good or prosperity of this system.

If, therefore, the good of the universal system require no more, in order to the pardon of the sinner, than his bare repentance and reformation, then the glory of God requires no more. Again, if the good of the universe require no more, then justice requires no more. For, whenever a crime is committed against any community, and the government of it, if there be no substitution of atonement, the crime deserves just such a punishment as the public good requires. The requirement of the public good is the exact measure of justice in this case. Now, therefore, if the public good of the universe require no more of the sinner, in order to pardon, than that he repent and reform, this is all that justice requires of him, and he justly deserves no other punishment than this. Now, this is no punishment at all, no evil, but an invaluable good. Therefore sin, by which he deserves no more, is no moral evil, no crime at all; which is absurd, and consequently the principle from which it follows, viz. that repentance and reformation are all that is necessary to pardon and acceptance with God, is absurd also.

But if we allow that sin is a crime or moral evil, it deserves punishment, and the general good of the universe requires that punishment,

236

and consequently does not admit, that the sinner be acquitted from it, but in consequence of something done or suffered, which, to the purpose of supporting the dignity of law and government, and so, of securing the general good, is equivalent to the punishment of the sinner according to law; and this is the very atonement for which we plead.

5
THE HOLY SPIRIT
AND THE CHRISTIAN LIFE

THE PERSON AND WORK OF
THE HOLY SPIRIT

The person and work of the Holy Spirit is key to the general cogency and inner coherence of Reformed theology. On the one hand, Reformed Christianity ascribes salvation to grace alone, grounded in the eternal election of God. On the other hand, believers must actively embrace salvation through faith and are called to express that faith outwardly in the Christian life. It is God the Holy Spirit, the "Lord and Giver of life" (*Westminster*), who makes the link between these two affirmations.

John Calvin

Calvin is preeminently a theologian of the Holy Spirit. The first selection on the person of the Spirit is from Calvin's discussion of the Trinity; the second on the Spirit's work comes from the opening portion of his treatment of the Christian life. The chief work of the Spirit toward humanity is the creation of faith, which is more than blind trust in a God who may or may not save; it is instead a confidence born of grasping God's beneficence toward us in Christ.

SOURCES

(**A**) *Institutes* I.13.14, pp. 138–39. (**B**) *Institutes* III.1.1–2, 3, 7, pp. 537–39, 541, 551.

BIBLIOGRAPHY

On the topics in this chapter, especially as they pertain to Calvin, see John Leith, *John Calvin's Doctrine of the Christian Life* (Louisville, Ky.: Westminster/John Knox, 1989). Lucien Joseph Richard, *The Spirituality of John Calvin* (Atlanta: John Knox, 1974). Ronald S. Wallace, *Calvin's Doctrine of the Christian Life* (Edinburgh: Oliver & Boyd, 1959; reprint: Tyler, Tex.: Geneva Divinity School Press, 1982).

A. THE DEITY OF THE HOLY SPIRIT

[W]hat Scripture attributes to [the Spirit] and we ourselves learn by the sure experience of godliness is far removed from [creatureliness]. For it is the Spirit who, everywhere diffused, sustains all things, causes them to grow, and quickens them in heaven and in earth. Because he is circumscribed by no limits, he is excepted from the category of creatures; but in transfusing into all things his energy, and breathing into them essence, life, and movement, he is indeed plainly divine.

Again, if regeneration into incorruptible life is higher and much more excellent than any present growth, what ought we to think of him from whose power it proceeds? Now, Scripture teaches in many places that he is the author of regeneration not by borrowing but by his very own energy; and not of this only, but of future immortality as well. In short, upon him, as upon the Son, are conferred functions that especially belong to divinity. [1 Cor. 2:10, Rom. 11:34, 1 Cor. 12:10, Ex. 4:11, 1 Cor. 6:11, 1 Cor. 12:11, 12:4.]

B. THE WORK OF THE HOLY SPIRIT
AND FAITH

We must now examine this question. How do we receive those benefits which the Father bestowed on his only-begotten Son—not for Christ's own private use, but that he might enrich poor and needy men? First, we must understand that as long as Christ remains outside of us, and we are separated from him, all that he has suffered and done for the salvation of the human race remains useless and of no value for us. Therefore, to share with us what he has received from the Father, he had to become ours and to dwell within us. For this reason, he is called "our Head" [Eph. 4:15], and "the first-born among many brethren" [Rom. 8:29]. We also, in turn, are said to be "engrafted into him" [Rom. 11:17], and to "put on Christ" [Gal. 3:27]; for, as I have said, all that he possesses is nothing to us until we grow into one body with him. It is true that we obtain this by faith. Yet since we see that not all indiscriminately embrace that communion with Christ which is offered through the gospel, reason itself teaches us to climb higher and to examine into the secret energy of the Spirit, by which we come to enjoy Christ and all his benefits. . . .

[T]he Holy Spirit is the bond by which Christ effectually unites us to himself. To this, also, pertains what we taught in the previous book concerning his anointing.

But, in order to get a clearer notion of this matter, so well worth investigating, we must bear in mind that Christ came endowed with the Holy Spirit in a special way: that is, to separate us from the world and to gather us unto the hope of the eternal inheritance. Hence he is called the "Spirit of sanctification" [cf. 2 Thess. 2:13; 1 Peter 1:2; Rom. 1:4] because he not only quickens and nourishes us by a general power that is visible both in the human race and in the rest of the living creatures, but he is also the root and seed of heavenly life in us. . . .

Further, God the Father gives us the Holy Spirit for his Son's sake, and yet has bestowed the whole fullness of the Spirit upon the Son to be minister and steward of his liberality. For this reason, the Spirit is sometimes called the "Spirit of the Father," sometimes the "Spirit of the Son." Paul says: "You are not in the flesh, but in the spirit, if indeed the Spirit of God dwells in you. But if anyone does not have the Spirit of Christ, he is not his" [Rom. 8:9, cf. Vg.]. . . .

But faith is the principal work of the Holy Spirit. Consequently, the terms commonly employed to express his power and working are, in large measure, referred to it because by faith alone he leads us into the light of the gospel, as John teaches: to believers in Christ is given the privilege of becoming children of God, who are born not of flesh and blood, but of God [John 1:12–13]. . . .

Now, the knowledge of God's goodness will not be held very important unless it makes us rely on that goodness. Consequently, understanding mixed with doubt is to be excluded, as it is not in firm agreement, but in conflict, with itself. Yet far indeed is the mind of man, blind and darkened as it is, from penetrating and attaining even to perception of the will of God! And the heart, too, wavering as it is in perpetual hesitation, is far from resting secure in that conviction! Therefore our mind must be otherwise illumined and our heart strengthened, that the Word of God may obtain full faith among us. Now we shall possess a right definition of faith if we call it a firm and certain knowledge of God's benevolence toward us, founded upon the truth of the freely given promise in Christ, both revealed to our minds and sealed upon our hearts through the Holy Spirit.

The Heidelberg Catechism

The comfort offered to the believer in Christ, a central theme of Heidelberg, is made applicable through the work of the Spirit.

SOURCE

Catechismus oder Christlicher Unterricht. . . . (1563) = *Der Heidelberger Katechismus,* q. 53; ET: Heidelberg Catechism, in Cochrane, *Confessions,* 314.

Q. 53: What do you believe concerning "the Holy Spirit"?

A: First, that, with the Father and the Son, he is equally eternal God; second, that God's Spirit is also given to me, preparing me through a true faith to share in Christ and all his benefits, that he comforts me and will abide with me forever.

UNION WITH CHRIST

Herman Witsius: Faith, the Fount of the Spiritual Life

If union with Christ is made possible through the Spirit's sovereign work, it must nonetheless be appropriated by believers through the faith which inaugurated the true spiritual life. Witsius offers an exposition of faith completely orthodox in content but woven in the rich language of piety that characterized the late-seventeenth-century Dutch Reformed.

SOURCE

Herman Witsius, *De oeconomia foederium Dei cum hominibur libri quattuor* (1677), Book 3, Chapter 4, Section 7; ET: "Of Faith," *The Oeconomy of the Covenants between God and Man* 2:73–91 (edited).

The principal act of spiritual life, which is implanted in the elect by regeneration, and the source of all subsequent vital operation, is true Faith in God through Christ. . . . Now it is not any one particular act or habit of soul, nor ought it to be restricted to any one particular faculty thereof; but it is a certain complex thing, consisting of various acts, which without confusion pervade, and by a sweet conjunction mutually prompt and assist one another: it imports change of the whole man; is the spring of the whole spiritual life, and, in fine, the holy energy and activity of the whole soul towards God in Christ. . . .

The first thing which faith either comprehends or presupposes is the knowledge of things to be believed. . . . And all should strive to have their faith as little implicit and as much distinct as possible; as becometh those who are filled with all knowledge [Rom. 15:14]. . . .

To this must be joined assent, which is the second act of faith, whereby a person receives and acknowledges as truths those things which he knows. . . . This assent is principally founded on the infallible veracity of God who testifies of himself and of his Son. . . . There may at times be waverings, staggerings, and even inclinations to unbelief, in the best of

believers, especially when they are subject to some violent temptation . . .
but these are certain defects of faith, arising from the weakness of the
flesh. . . .

That which follows this assent [thirdly] is the love of truth. . . . For
since there is a clear manifestation of the glory of God in saving
truths . . . it is not possible but the believing soul viewing these amiable
perfections of the Deity in those truths should break out into a flame of
love to them. . . .

Hence arises a fourth act of faith, a hunger and thirst after Christ. . . .
This hunger and thirst are followed by a receiving of Christ the Lord for
justification, sanctification, and so for complete salvation, which is the
fifth and indeed the formal and principal act of faith. . . .

[Now] because the soul, thus apprehending Christ for salvation, does
at the same time recline and stay itself upon him, therefore this act of
faith is explained by this metaphor also [in scripture: viz. Ps. 77:6; Isa.
48:2; Isa. 1:10; 10:20; 2 Chron. 16:7, 8; Num. 11:12; Isa. 40:4; 46:12;
40:11; Deut. 1:31; 33:27]. . . . Moreover, when the believing soul so
receives Christ and leans upon him, it not only considers him as a
Saviour but also as a Lord. . . . Nor does Christ offer himself as
a husband to the soul upon any other condition but this, that he
acknowledge him as his Lord. And when the soul casts himself upon
Jesus, he at the same time renounces his own will and surrenders himself up to the will of Jesus, to be carried whithersoever he pleaseth.
Hence there is also in faith a humble surrender and giving up one's self,
whereby the believer, as in duty bound, yields himself and all that is his
to Christ, who is freely given him. "I am my beloved's, and my beloved is
mine" [Song of Songs 6:3]. . . .

Hence . . . the soul now obtains trust and confidence, tranquility, joy,
peace, and bold defiance to all enemies and dangers whatever, a glorying
in the Lord, a glorying in adversity. . . .

[In sum,] faith comprehends the knowledge of the mystery of God
and of Christ in the light of grace, the truth of which mystery the
believer acknowledges with full assent of mind, on the authority and
testimony of God: And not only so, but he is also in love with that truth,
exults therein, and glorifies God; he likewise ardently desires communion with Christ; that the things which are true in Christ may be also
true to him for salvation; wherefore, when Christ is offered to him by the
Word and Spirit, he receives him with the greatest complacency of soul,
leans and rests upon him, and gives and surrenders himself to him;
which done he glories that Christ is now his own, and most sweetly
delights in him, reposing himself under the shadow of the tree of life,

and satiating himself with its most delicious fruits. This is the faith of God's elect, an invaluable gift, the bond of our union with Christ, the scale of paradise, the key of the ark of the covenant, with which its treasures are unlocked, the never-ceasing fountain of a holy, quiet, and blessed life.

JUSTIFICATION BY GRACE THROUGH FAITH

Huldrych Zwingli: Early Statement of the Reformed Gospel

The Sixty-Seven Articles constitutes one of Zwingli's earliest manifestos on the Reformation faith, written for the so-called First Zurich Disputation in 1523 after he had renounced his papal pension (1520), resigned his commission as "people's priest" (1522), and begun to incorporate Luther's central reformation insights.[1] Zwingli begins straightaway with a summary of the gospel which he has been preaching in Zurich. He clearly proclaims scripture alone, grace alone, Christ alone, and salvation by faith.[2] Since the polemical context of Zwingli's articles was a public debate to defend himself before the city council on the content of his preaching, Zwingli was not trying to encapsulate his theology in complete and systematic form. In his later work, *On True and False Religion*, Zwingli places the gospel, including justification, not at the beginning of the work but at the climax of a discussion of God, Christ, and religion. The Sixty-Seven Articles could be considered the first Reformed confessional statement. Here are the opening sixteen articles.

---

1. Zwingli always asserted his independence from Luther, claiming that he began to "preach the gospel" of the Reformation faith in 1516; but it is unclear from the extant evidence just what that gospel was. Zwingli's conviction about the primacy of scripture and trusting God in Christ no doubt began independently of Luther, but Zwingli's overall theology was refined as a result of his engagement with Luther, especially on justification. Zwingli seems to have received significant clarification from Luther perhaps as early as 1519, but certainly after Luther's writings of 1520. For various perspectives on Zwingli's "breakthrough" to reform, see Jacques Courvoisier, *Zwingli, A Reformed Theologian* (Richmond, Va.: John Knox Press, 1963); Walther Köhler, *Huldrych Zwingli* (Stuttgart: Koehler Verlag, 1952; rev. ed., Zurich: Benzigeon, 1984); Gottfried W. Locher, *Zwingli's Thought: New Perspectives* (Leiden: E. J. Brill, 1981); idem, *Huldrych Zwingli in neuer sicht* (Zurich, 1969), on reformation experience as early as 1516; Arthur Rich, *Die Anfange der Theologie Huldrych Zwinglis* (Zurich: Zwingli Verlag, 1949), on Zwingli's acquisition of central reformation insights from Luther after 1520; H. Schmid, *Zwingli's Lehre von der göttlichen und menschlichen Gerechtigkeit* (Zurich: Zwingli Verlag, 1959), esp. 27–45.

2. The statement seems implicitly to mean "by faith *alone*," but the qualifier is admittedly absent. For an interpretation that considers justification by faith *alone* to be absent, see Ulrich Gäbler, *Huldrych Zwingli: His Life and Work*, trans. Ruth C. L. Gritsch (Philadelphia: Fortress, 1986), chap. 5.

SOURCE

Huldrych Zwingli, *Sieben und Sechzig Schlussreden* (1523), in *Sämtliche Werke* 1:470.14–471.7; ET: Sixty-seven Articles, arts. 1–16, in Cochrane, *Confessions*, 36–37.

BIBLIOGRAPHY

For Zwingli's commentary on the Sixty-Seven Articles, see *Sämtliche Werke* 2:14–457; ET: In *Huldrych Zwingli: Writings,* vol. 1: *The Defense of the Reformed Faith,* ed. E. J. Furcha (Allison Park, Penna.: Pickwick, 1984).

The following . . . articles and opinions, I, Huldreich Zwingli, confess that I preached in the venerable city of Zurich on the basis of the Scripture which is called *theopneustos* [i.e., inspired by God], and I offer to debate and defend them; and where I have not now correctly understood the said Scripture, I am ready to be instructed and corrected, but only from the aforesaid Scripture.

I

All who say that the Gospel is nothing without the approbation of the Church err and slander God.

II

The sum of the Gospel is that our Lord Jesus Christ, the true Son of God, has made known to us the will of His heavenly Father, and by his innocence has redeemed us from death and reconciled us unto God.

III

Therefore Christ is the only way to salvation for all who ever lived, do live or ever will live.

IV

He who seeks or points to another door errs—yea, is a murderer of souls and a robber.

V

Therefore all who regard another doctrine as equal to or higher than the Gospel err and do not know what the Gospel is.

VI

For Christ Jesus is the leader and captain whom God has promised and given to the whole human race:

VII

That He [Christ] might be the eternal salvation and the Head of all believers, who are His body, which, however, is dead and can do nothing without Him.

VIII

From this it follows, first, that all who live in the Head are His members and children of God. And this is the Church or fellowship of the saints, the bride of Christ, *ecclesia catholica*.

IX

Secondly, that, just as the members of a physical body can do nothing without the guidance of the head, so now in the body of Christ no one can do anything without Christ, its Head.

X

Just as that man is demented whose members operate without his head, lacerating, wounding and harming himself, so also are the members of Christ demented when they undertake something without Christ, their Head, tormenting and burdening themselves with foolish ordinances.

XI

Therefore we perceive that the so-called clerical traditions with their pomp, riches, hierarchy, titles and laws are a cause of all nonsense, because they are not in agreement with Christ, the Head.

XII

Thus they continue to rant and rave, not out of concern for the Head (for that is what is being striven for now by the grace of God) but because they are not permitted to rave on and instead are required to listen to the Head alone.

XIII

When we listen to the Head, we acquire a pure and clear knowledge of the will of God, and we are drawn to Him by His Spirit and are conformed to Him.

XIV

Hence all Christians should do their utmost that everywhere only the Gospel of Christ be preached.

XV

For our salvation is based on faith in the Gospel and our damnation on unbelief; for all truth is clear in Him.

XVI

In the Gospel we learn that human doctrines and traditions are of no avail to salvation.

The First Confession of Basel: Spread of the Reformed Gospel

Reform began in earnest in Basel in 1522 under the leadership of John Oecolampadius (1482–1531) and was officially in place by 1529. The First

Confession of Basel may have originated with a confession drafted by Oeco-lampadius, but in any event it was completed by his successor Oswald Myco-nius in 1532 and was made official in 1534. It proclaims justification by faith but urges the need for faith to issue forth in works, a characteristic stance of Reformed theology.

SOURCE

Confessio Fidei Basileensis prior (January 21, 1534) (originally adopted as *Bekanntnuss unseres heiligen Christlichen Glaubens wie es die Kylch zu Basel halt*); Latin: Niemeyer, *Collectionem Confessionum*, 85ff.; ET: The First Confession of Basel (1534), in Cochrane, *Confessions*, 94–95.

BIBLIOGRAPHY

Another early Reformed statement on justification may be found in The Tetrapolitan Confession of 1530, written by Martin Bucer (Bützer) and Wolfgang Capito; in Cochrane, *Confessions*, 57–60.

Concerning Faith and Works

We confess that there is forgiveness of sins through faith in Jesus Christ the crucified. Although this faith is continually exercised, signal-ized, and thus confirmed by works of love, yet do we not ascribe to works, which are the fruit of faith, the righteousness and satisfaction for our sins. On the contrary, we ascribe it solely to a genuine trust and faith in the shed blood of the Lamb of God. For we freely confess that all things are granted to us in Christ, Who is our righteousness, holiness, redemption, the way, the truth, the wisdom and the life. Therefore the works of believers are not for the satisfaction of their sins, but solely for the purpose of showing in some degree our gratitude to the Lord God for the great kindness He has shown us in Christ.

Heinrich Bullinger: Development of the Reformed Gospel

In this sermon from Bullinger's *Decades*, published in 1549, the Reformed understanding of justification has now reached a state of advanced clarity, thanks to its assimilation of the essentials of Luther's theology. In a subtle transformation of Luther's theology, however, Bullinger makes clear the Reformed emphasis on the need for works to follow from faith. This shift parallels the Reformed focus upon law which we have previously seen in chapter 3, pages 190–99.

SOURCE

Heinrich Bullinger, "That the Faithful Are Justified by Faith Without the Law and Works," in *Decades* 1:112–14, 120–21 (edited).

God hath appointed, that whosoever doth believe in Christ, being cleansed from his sins, shall be made heir of life everlasting.

This will I make more evident yet, by declaring how that faith alone, that is, that faith for itself, and not for any works of ours, doth justify the faithful. For itself I say, not in respect that it is in us a quality of the mind, or our own work in ourselves; but in respect that faith is the gift of God's grace, having in it a promise of righteousness and life; and in respect that, naturally, of itself, it is a certain and undoubted persuasion resting upon God, and believing that God, being pacified by Christ, hath through Christ bestowed life and all good things on us. Therefore faith for Christ, and by the grace and promise of God, doth justify: and so faith, that is, that which we believe, and wherein our confidence is settled, God, I say, himself by the grace of God doth justify us through our redemption in Christ: so that now our own works or merits have no place left to them at all, I mean, in justification: for otherwise good works have their place in the faithful, as we in place convenient do mean to shew. For Paul, the teacher of the Gentiles, doth in the way of opposition compare Christ with Adam, and sheweth that of Adam, and so of our own nature and strength, we have nothing but sin, the wrath of God, and death. And this doth he shew under the name of Adam, to the intent that no man should seek for righteousness and life in the flesh. And again, on the other side, he declareth that we by Christ have righteousness, the grace of God, life, and the forgiveness of all our sins. In this opposition, he doth earnestly urge and often repeat this word, "of one," to no other end verily, but that we should understand, that faith alone doth justify.

To the Galatians he doth very evidently use this kind of argument. "To the last will and testament of a man, if it once be proved, nobody doth add or take any thing away." Reason therefore doth rightly require, that no man put to or take away any thing from the testament of God. But this is the testament which God confirmed; that his will is, to bestow the blessing upon Abraham's seed, not in many, or by many, but through one. "For he saith not, And to the seeds, as though he spake of many; but as speaking of one he saith, And to thy seed, that is, Christ." Therefore, it is a detestable thing to augment or diminish any thing in this testament of God. Christ alone is the only Saviour still: men can neither save themselves nor other.

Again, in the same epistle to the Galatians he saith: "We know that man is not justified by the works of the law, but by faith in Jesus Christ; insomuch as no flesh shall be justified by the works of the law."

Again, in the fourth chapter to the Romans he saith: "Therefore by faith is the inheritance given, that it might be by grace, that the promise might be sure to all the seed; not to that only that is of the law, but to that also that is of the faith of Abraham." He rehearseth here two causes, for which he attributeth justification to faith, and not to works. The first is, that justification may be of free gift, and that the grace of God may be praised. The latter is, that the promise and salvation may remain stedfast, and that it may come upon the Gentiles also: but it should not be given to the Gentiles, if it were due only to the law and circumcision, because the Gentiles lack them both. Finally, the hope of our salvation ought to be stedfastly established: but it should never be surely grounded, or safely preserved, if it were attributed to our own works or merits; for in them is always something wanting. But in God and in the merit of the Son of God can nothing be lacking. Therefore our salvation is surely confirmed, not to be doubted of, and assuredly certain, if that we seek for it by faith in the Son of God, who is our righteousness and salvation.

Moreover, whereas we say, that the faithful are justified by faith alone, or else by faith without works, we do not say, as many think we do, that faith is post alone, or utterly destitute of good works: for wheresoever faith is, there also it sheweth itself by good works; because the righteous cannot but work righteousness. But before he doth work righteousness, that is to say, good works, he must of necessity be righteous: therefore the righteous doth not attain to righteousness that goeth before by works that follow after.

John Calvin: The Reformed Relation
Between Justification and Sanctification

Calvin is acutely aware of the interplay between justification and sanctification, Christ for us and Christ in us. Justification, consisting in the forgiveness of sins and the imputation of Christ's righteousness to sinners, is for Calvin the "main hinge" on which the Christian life turns. But forgiveness of sins is only one part of the complete experience of salvation, which also includes a transformed self and the renewal of the whole of life. Forgiveness without renewal leads to the ethical impotence of antinomianism, or lawlessness;

while concentrating on renewal without justification results in "works righteousness." Thus to assure that the Reformation's emphasis on justification would not be misunderstood, Calvin placed his discussion of justification well after his treatment of the transformation of the self in "regeneration," or sanctification. Nevertheless, the tactical priority given to regeneration should not obscure the irrevocable character for Calvin of God's forgiveness as the basis of Christian living.

SOURCES

(A) *Institutes* III.1.1, pp. 592–93. **(B)** *Institutes* III.11.1–2, pp. 725–27. **(C)** *CO* 40:439.

BIBLIOGRAPHY

John Leith, *John Calvin's Doctrine of the Christian Life*. Karl Barth, *Church Dogmatics* IV/2, pp. 509–11.

A. THE RELATION OF FORGIVENESS AND RENEWAL

Even though we have taught in part how faith possesses Christ, and how through it we enjoy his benefits, this would still remain obscure if we did not add an explanation of the effects we feel. With good reason, the sum of the gospel is held to consist in repentance and forgiveness of sins [Luke 24:47; Acts 5:31]. Any discussion of faith, therefore, that omitted these two topics would be barren and mutilated and well-nigh useless. Now, both repentance and forgiveness of sins—that is, newness of life and free reconciliation—are conferred on us by Christ, and both are attained by us through faith. As a consequence, reason and the order of teaching demand that I begin to discuss both at this point. However, our immediate transition will be from faith to repentance. For when this topic is rightly understood it will better appear how man is justified by faith alone, and simple pardon; nevertheless actual holiness of life, so to speak, is not separated from free imputation of righteousness. Now it ought to be a fact beyond controversy that repentance not only constantly follows faith, but is also born of faith. For since pardon and forgiveness are offered through the preaching of the gospel in order that the sinner, freed from the tyranny of Satan, the yoke of sin, and the miserable bondage of vices, may cross over into the Kingdom of God, surely no one can embrace the grace of the gospel without betaking himself from the errors of his past life into the right way, and applying his whole effort to the practice of repentance. There are some, however, who suppose that repentance precedes faith, rather than flows from it, or is produced by it as fruit from a tree. Such persons have never known the power of repentance, and are moved to feel this way by an unduly slight argument.

B. JUSTIFICATION BY FAITH

Christ was given to us by God's generosity, to be grasped and possessed by us in faith. By partaking of him, we principally receive a double grace: namely, that being reconciled to God through Christ's blamelessness, we may have in heaven instead of a Judge a gracious Father; and secondly, that sanctified by Christ's spirit we may cultivate blamelessness and purity of life. Of regeneration, indeed, the second of these gifts, I have said what seemed sufficient. The theme of justification was therefore more lightly touched upon because it was more to the point to understand first how little devoid of good works is the faith, through which alone we obtain free righteousness by the mercy of God; and what is the nature of the good works of the saints, with which part of this question is concerned. Therefore we must now discuss these matters thoroughly. And we must so discuss them as to bear in mind that this is the main hinge on which religion turns, so that we devote the greater attention and care to it. For unless you first of all grasp what your relationship to God is, and the nature of his judgment concerning you, you have neither a foundation on which to establish your salvation nor one on which to build piety toward God. But the need to know this will better appear from the knowledge itself.

But that we may not stumble on the very threshold—and this would happen if we should enter upon a discussion of a thing unknown—first let us explain what these expressions mean: that man is justified in God's sight, and that he is justified by faith or works. He is said to be justified in God's sight who is both reckoned righteous in God's judgment and has been accepted on account of his righteousness. Indeed, as iniquity is abominable to God, so no sinner can find favor in his eyes in so far as he is a sinner and so long as he is reckoned as such. Accordingly, wherever there is sin, there also the wrath and vengeance of God show themselves. Now he is justified who is reckoned in the condition not of a sinner, but of a righteous man; and for that reason, he stands firm before God's judgment seat while all sinners fall. If an innocent accused person be summoned before the judgment seat of a fair judge, where he will be judged according to his innocence, he is said to be "justified" before the judge. Thus, justified before God is the man who, freed from the company of sinners, has God to witness and affirm his righteousness. In the same way, therefore, he in whose life that purity and holiness will be found which deserves a testimony of righteousness before God's throne will be said to be justified by works, or else he who, by the wholeness of his works, can meet and satisfy God's judgment. On the contrary, justified by faith is he who, excluded from the righteousness of works, grasps the righteousness of Christ through faith, and clothed in it, appears in God's sight not as a sinner but as a righteous man.

Therefore, we explain justification simply as the acceptance with which God receives us into his favor as righteous men. And we say that it consists in the remission of sins and the imputation of Christ's righteousness.

C. FAITH AND WORKS

Faith without works justifies, although this needs prudence and a sound interpretation: for this proposition, that faith without works justifies, is true and yet false, according to the different senses that it bears. The proposition that faith without works justifies by itself is false, because faith without works is void. But if the clause "without works" is joined with the word "justifies," the proposition is true, since faith cannot justify when it is without works because it is dead, and a mere fiction. He who is born of God is just, as John says (1 John 5:18). Thus faith can be no more separated from works than the sun from its heat; yet faith justifies without works, because works form no reason for our justification; but faith alone reconciles us to God and causes him to love us, not in ourselves but in his only-begotten Son.

Jonathan Edwards: Justification and the Great Awakening

Edwards preached his sermon series on justification in 1734. It was soon followed by the first revival in the town of Northampton, in which over three hundred persons experienced a profoundly moving religious transformation. The revival lasted into the year 1735 and was the precursor to a later, more widespread phenomenon throughout New England. In this passage, Edwards seeks to clarify the assertion of the New England theology which conceived faith as the "condition" of the covenant. Faith is the instrumental means to union with Christ but is not of itself the cause. Edwards is resolute in ascribing salvation entirely to the work of God.

SOURCE

Jonathan Edwards, *Justification by Faith Alone* (1734; published 1738), in Edwards, *Works* (1834) 1:622–28.

BIBLIOGRAPHY

Conrad Cherry, *The Theology of Jonathan Edwards: A Reappraisal* (Garden City, N.Y.: Doubleday, 1966; reprint: Bloomington: Indiana University Press, 1990). This is the definitive work on "faith" in Edwards.

1. How justification is by *faith*.—Here the great difficulty has been about the import and force of the particle *by*, or what is that influence that faith has in the affair of justification that is expressed in Scripture by being justified by faith.

Here, if I may humbly express what seems evident to me, though faith be indeed the condition of justification so as nothing else is, yet this matter is not clearly and sufficiently explained by saying that faith is the condition of justification; and that because the word seems ambiguous, both in common use, and also as used in divinity. In one sense, Christ alone performs the condition of our justification and salvation; in another sense, faith is the condition of justification; in another sense, other qualifications and acts are conditions of salvation and justification too. . . .

But I humbly conceive we have been ready to look too far to find out what that influence of faith in our justification is, or what is that dependence of this effect on faith, signified by the expression of being justified by faith, overlooking that which is most obviously pointed forth in the expression, viz. that (there being a mediator that has purchased justification) faith in this mediator is that which renders it a meet and suitable thing, in the sight of God, that the believer, rather than others, should have this purchased benefit assigned to him.—There is this benefit purchased, which God sees it to be a more meet and suitable thing that it should be assigned to some rather than others, because he sees them differently qualified; that qualification wherein the meetness to this benefit, as the case stands, consists, is that in us by which we are justified. If Christ had not come into the world and died, &c. to purchase justification, no qualification whatever in us could render it a meet or fit thing that we should be justified. But the case being as it now stands, viz. that Christ has actually purchased justification by his own blood for infinitely unworthy creatures, there may be certain qualifications found in some persons, which, either from the relation it bears to the mediator and his merits, or on some other account, is the thing that in the sight of God renders it a meet and condecent thing, that they should have an interest in this purchased benefit, and of which if any are destitute, it renders it an unfit and unsuitable thing that they should have it. The wisdom of God in his constitutions doubtless appears much in the fitness and beauty of them, so that those things are established to be done that are fit to be done, and that those things are connected in his constitution that are agreeable one to another. So God justifies a believer according to his revealed constitution, without doubt, because he sees something in this qualification that, as the case stands, renders it a fit thing that such should be justified; whether it be because faith is the instrument, or as it were the hand, by which he that has purchased justification is apprehended and accepted or because it is the acceptance itself, or whatever else. To be justified, is to be approved of God as a proper subject of pardon, with a right to eternal life; and therefore, when it is said that we are justified by faith, what else can be understood by it, than that faith is that by which we are rendered approvable, fitly so, and indeed, as the case stands, proper subjects of this benefit?

This is something different from faith being the *condition* of justification, though inseparably connected with justification. So are many other things besides faith; and yet nothing in us but faith renders it meet that we should have justification assigned to us; as I shall presently show in answer to the next inquiry, viz.

2. How this is said to be by faith *alone*, without any manner of virtue or goodness of our own. This may seem to some to be attended with two difficulties, viz. how this can be said to be by faith alone, without any virtue or goodness of ours, when faith itself is a virtue, and one part of our goodness, and is not only some manner of goodness of ours, but is a very excellent qualification, and one chief part of the inherent holiness of a Christian? And if it be a part of our inherent goodness or excellency (whether it be this part or any other) that renders it a condecent or congruous thing that we should have this benefit of Christ assigned to us, what is this less than what they mean who talk of a merit of congruity? And moreover, if this part of our christian holiness qualifies us, in the sight of God, for this benefit of Christ, and renders it a fit or meet thing, in his sight, that we should have it, why should not other parts of holiness, and conformity to God, which are also very excellent, and have as much of the image of Christ in them, and are no less lovely in God's eyes, qualify us as much, and have as much influence to render us meet, in God's sight, for such a benefit as this? Therefore I answer,

When it is said, that we are not justified by any righteousness or goodness of our *own*, what is meant is, that it is not out of respect to the excellency or goodness of any qualifications or acts in us whatsoever, that God judges it meet that this benefit of Christ should be ours; and it is not, in any wise, on account of any excellency or value that there is in faith, that it appears in the sight of God a meet thing, that he who believes should have this benefit of Christ assigned to him, but purely from the relation faith has to the person in whom this benefit is to be had, or as it unites to that mediator, in and by whom we are justified.

John Newton: Amazing Grace

John Newton (1725–1807) had a conversion experience at sea while a young man, after which he became an evangelical. Under the guidance of the incomparable evangelist George Whitefield (1714–1770) and others, Newton embraced the Calvinist form of evangelicalism in the Church of England. This hymn has deeply influenced the piety of countless Christians from many different confessions.

SOURCE

John Newton, Hymn: "Amazing Grace—How Sweet the Sound" (1779).

Amazing grace—how sweet the sound
 That saved a wretch like me!
I once was lost, but now am found,
 Was blind, but now I see.

'Twas grace that taught my heart to fear,
 And grace my fears relieved;
How precious did that grace appear
 The hour I first believed!

REGENERATION AND SANCTIFICATION

In General

William Ames: The Place of Sanctification in the Christian Life

The aim of the Holy Spirit's work in the believer is a changed life. This changed life was at the heart of Puritan theology as exemplified here by William Ames.

SOURCE

William Ames, *Medulla SS. Theologiae* (1623, 1629), Book I, chap. 29, pars. 1–8; ET: "Sanctification," in Ames, *Marrow*, 167–68.

BIBLIOGRAPHY

In addition to the bibliographies herein on Ames, see G. F. Nuttall, *The Holy Spirit in Puritan Faith and Experience* (Oxford: Basil Blackwell, 1946).

1. The real change of state is an alteration of qualities in man himself. 2 Cor. 5:17, *Old things have passed away; all things are new.*

2. The change is not in relation or reason, but in genuine effects seen in degrees of beginning, progress, and completion. 2 Cor. 4:16, *The inner man is renewed day by day.*

3. This alteration of qualities is related to either the just and honorable good of sanctification, or the perfect and exalted good of glorification. Rom. 6:22, *You have your fruit in holiness and your end in everlasting life.*

4. Sanctification is the real change in man from the sordidness of sin to the purity of God's image. Eph. 4:22–24, *Put off that which pertains to the old conversation, that old man, corrupting itself in deceivable lusts, and be renewed in the spirit of your mind. Put on that new man who according to God is created to righteousness and true holiness.*

5. Just as in justification a believer is properly freed from the guilt of sin and has life given him (the title to which is, as it were, settled in adoption), so in sanctification the same believer is freed from the sordidness and stain of sin, and the purity of God's image is restored to him.

6. Sanctification is not to be understood here as a separation from ordinary use or consecration to some special use, although this meaning is often present in Scripture, sometimes referring to outward and sometimes to inward or effectual separation. If this meaning is taken, sanctification may relate to calling or that first rebirth in which faith is communicated as a principle of new life; a common confusion of regeneration and sanctification hereby arises. The term is rather to be understood as that change in a believer in which he has righteousness and indwelling holiness imparted to him. 2 Thess. 2:13, *Through sanctification of the Spirit.*

7. For God himself witnesses that holiness is a gift of inherent grace. Jer. 31:33, *I will put my law into their mind, and in their heart will I write it;* Ezek. 36:25, 27, *I will give you a new heart, and a new spirit will I put into the midst of you.*

8. Sanctification is distinguished from that change in a man which is linked to his calling in faith and repentance, for in the latter faith is not properly considered a quality but a relationship to Christ, nor is repentance considered a change of disposition (for then it would be the same as sanctification), but a change of the mind's purpose and intent. Sanctification involves a real change of qualities and disposition.

Jonathan Edwards: An Analysis of Sanctification in the Religious Affections

The theological question that most engaged Edwards during the revivals was, What is true religion? His answer was that true religion is centered principally in the "affections." These are not merely passing feelings or passions; rather, they make up the abiding disposition of the self, its essential character. The content of Christian affections consists in the love of God for God's own sake. In this way Edwards shifted theological inquiry into the arena of concrete human experience.[3] Whereas much of seventeenth-century orthodoxy labored over whether God loves the elect with or without conditions, Edwards turned the question around and asked whether believers place conditions on their love for God. Those who are truly converted love God not primarily to save their souls but because through grace they have perceived the excellency of God. This loving God for God's own sake did not mean the total *abolition* of self or of the desire for a holy sort of happiness; but it did mean the *subordination* of self to the greater glory of God. Edwards developed twelve "tests" to plumb the genuineness of the affections, the chief one being the fruit of Christian practice.

SOURCES

(A) Jonathan Edwards, *A Treatise Concerning Religious Affections* (1746), in Edwards, *Works* (Yale) 240–43, 246–53. **(B)** Jonathan Edwards, *Religious Affections* (Yale) 2:383–84.

BIBLIOGRAPHY

Jonathan Edwards, "Concerning Faith," *Remarks on Important Theological Controversies*, in Edwards, *Works* (1834) 2:578–82. Idem, *Charity and Its Fruits* (1739), in Edwards, *Works* (Yale) 8:327–38.

3. In the terminology of the day, Edwards's method was "experimental." It was not, however, "empirical," if by that term is meant the grounding of authority solely in data derived from the senses.

A. SANCTIFICATION:
THE RELIGIOUS AFFECTIONS

The first objective ground of gracious affections, is the transcendently excellent and amiable nature of divine things, as they are in themselves; and not any conceived relation they bear to self, or self-interest.

I say that the supremely excellent nature of divine things, is the first, or primary and original objective foundation of the spiritual affections of true saints; for I do not suppose that all relation which divine things bear to themselves, and their own particular interest, are wholly excluded from all influence in their gracious affections. For this may have, and indeed has, a secondary and consequential influence in those affections that are truly holy and spiritual. . . .

'Tis unreasonable to think otherwise, than that the first foundation of a true love to God, is that whereby he is in himself lovely, or worthy to be loved, or the supreme loveliness of his nature. This is certainly what makes him chiefly amiable. What chiefly makes a man, or any creature lovely, is his excellency; and so what chiefly renders God lovely, and must undoubtedly be the chief ground of true love, is his excellency. God's nature, or the divinity, is infinitely excellent; yea 'tis infinite beauty, brightness, and glory itself. . . .

There is doubtless such a thing as a gracious gratitude, which does greatly differ from all that gratitude which natural men experience. It differs in the following respect. . . .

1. True gratitude or thankfulness to God for his kindness to us, arises from a foundation laid before, of love to God for what he is in himself; whereas a natural gratitude has no such antecedent foundation. The gracious stirrings of grateful affection to God, for kindness received, always are from a stock of love already in the heart, established in the first place on other grounds, viz. God's own excellency; and hence the affections are disposed to flow out, on occasions of God's kindness. The saint having seen the glory of God, and his heart overcome by it, and captivated into a supreme love to him on that account, his heart hereby becomes tender, and easily affected with kindnesses received. If a man has no love to another, yet gratitude may be moved by some extraordinary kindness; as in Saul towards David. But this is not the same kind of thing, as a man's gratitude to a dear friend, that his heart was before possessed with a high esteem of, and love to; whose heart by this means became tender towards him, and more easily affected with gratitude, and affected in another manner. Self-love is not excluded from a gracious gratitude; the saints love God for his kindness to them, "I love

the Lord, because he hath heard the voice of my supplication" (Ps. 116:1). But something else is included; and another love prepares the way, and lays the foundation, for these grateful affections. . . .

B. SANCTIFICATION:
THE FRUITS OF CHARITY

Gracious and holy affections have their exercise and fruit in Christian practice. I mean, they have that influence and power upon him who is the subject of 'em, that they cause that a practice, which is universally conformed to, and directed by Christian rules, should be the practice and business of his life.

This implies three things; (1) That his behavior or practice in the world, be universally conformed to, and directed by Christian rules. (2) That he makes a business of such a holy practice above all things; that it be a business which he is chiefly engaged in, and devoted to, and pursues with highest earnestness and diligence: so that he may be said to make this practice of religion eminently his work and business. And (3) That he persists in it to the end of life: so that it may be said, not only to be his business at certain seasons, the business of Sabbath days, or certain extraordinary times, or the business of a month, or a year, or of seven years, or his business under certain circumstances; but the business of his life; it being that business which he perseveres in through all changes, and under all trials, as long as he lives.

The necessity of each of these, in all true Christians, is most clearly and fully taught in the Word of God.

Mortification and Vivification
John Calvin

For Calvin, repentance contains two components: mortification and vivification, the death of the old sinful self and the birth of new life in the Holy Spirit.

SOURCE
Institutes III.3.3–9, p. 595.

BIBLIOGRAPHY
John Leith, *John Calvin's Doctrine of the Christian Life*.

Mortification [is] explain[ed] as sorrow of soul and dread conceived from the recognition of sin and the awareness of divine judgment. For when anyone has been brought into a true knowledge of sin, he then begins truly to hate and abhor sin; then he is heartily displeased with himself, he confesses himself miserable and lost and wishes to be another man. Furthermore, when he is touched by any sense of the judgment of God (for the one straightway follows the other) he then lies stricken and overthrown; humbled and cast down he trembles; he becomes discouraged and despairs. This is the first part of repentance, commonly called "contrition." "Vivification" [is understood] as the consolation that arises out of faith. That is, when a man is laid low by the consciousness of sin and stricken by the fear of God, and afterward looks to the goodness of God—to his mercy, grace, salvation, which is through Christ—he raises himself up, he takes heart, he recovers courage, and as it were, returns from death to life.

Richard Sibbes

Richard Sibbes (1577–1635) was a highly successful English preacher who deeply influenced Puritanism. *The Bruised Reed and Smoking Flax* (1630) is one of Sibbes's best-known works, made popular by Richard Baxter's acknowledgment of what he learned from it when his father gave it to him as a young boy. The theme of the work is the dying to self wrought by the Holy Spirit in conversion. The title derives from Matt. 12:20, "A bruised reed shall he not break, and smoking flax shall he not quench, till he send forth judgment into victory," which is in turn a quotation of one of the servant songs of Isaiah (Isa. 42:1–4).

SOURCE

Richard Sibbes, *The Bruised Reed and Smoking Flax* (1630), in *The Works of Richard Sibbes, D.D.* Nichol's Series of Standard Divines, 8 vols. (Edinburgh: James Nichol, 1862), 43–44.

BIBLIOGRAPHY

G. F. Nuttall, *The Holy Spirit in Puritan Faith and Experience.*

Those that Christ hath to do withal are Bruised.

This bruising is required [1] before conversion (1), that so the Spirit may make way for itself into the heart by leveling all proud, high thoughts, and that we may understand ourselves to be what indeed we are by nature. We love to wander from ourselves and to be strangers at home, till God bruiseth us by one cross or other, and then we *bethink ourselves,* and come home to ourselves with the prodigal (Luke xv.17.)

A marvellous hard thing it is to bring a dull and a shifting heart to cry with feeling for mercy. Our hearts, like malefactors, until they be beaten from all shifts, never cry for the mercy of the Judge. Again (2), this bruising maketh us set a high price upon Christ. The gospel is the gospel indeed then; then the fig-leaves of morality will do us no good. And (3) it maketh us more thankful, and (4) from thankfulness more fruitful in our lives; for what maketh many so cold and barren, but that bruising for sin never endeared God's grace unto them? Likewise (5), this dealing of God doth establish us the more in his ways, having had knocks and bruisings in our own ways. This is the cause oft of relapses and apostasies, because men never smarted for sin at the first; they were not long enough under the lash of the law. Hence this inferior work of the Spirit in *bringing down high thoughts*, 2 Cor. x.5, is necessary before conversion. And, for the most part, the Holy Spirit, to further the work of conviction, joineth some affliction, which, sanctified, hath a healing and purging power.

Nay, [2] after conversion we need bruising, that (1) reeds may know themselves to be reeds, and not oaks; even reeds need bruising, by reason of the remainder of pride in our nature, and to let us see that we live by mercy. And (2) that weaker Christians may not be too much discouraged when they see stronger shaken and bruised. Thus Peter was bruised when he wept bitterly, Matt. xxvi.75. This reed, till he met with this bruise, had more wind in him than pith. "Though all forsake thee, I will not," &c., Matt. xxvi.35. The people of God cannot be without these examples. The heroical deeds of those great worthies do not comfort the church so much as their falls and bruises do. Thus David was bruised, Ps. xxxii.3–5, until he came to a free confession, without guile of spirit; nay, his sorrows did rise in his own feeling unto the exquisite pain of breaking of bones, Ps. li.8. Thus Hezekiah complains that God had "broken his bones" as a lion, Isa. xxxviii.13. Thus the chosen vessel St Paul needed the messenger of Satan to buffet him, lest he should be lifted up above measure, 2 Cor. xii.7.

Hence we learn that we must not pass too harsh judgment upon ourselves or others when God doth exercise us with bruising upon bruising; there must be a conformity to our head, Christ, who "was bruised for us," Isa. liii.5, that we may know how much we are bound unto him. Profane spirits, ignorant of God's ways in bringing his children to heaven, censure broken-hearted Christians for desperate persons, whenas God is about a gracious good work with them. It is no easy matter to bring a man from nature to grace, and from grace to glory, so unyielding and untractable are our hearts.

Growth in Grace: Irresistible Grace and Perfection

John Calvin

Even though Reformed Christianity places a great premium upon the continual growth in grace which is sanctification, it has also insisted that perfection awaits eschatological fulfillment in glorification, the final phase of reconciliation with God (see pp. 381–84, below).

SOURCE

Institutes III.3.10–12, pp. 602–4.

Thus, then, are the children of God freed through regeneration from bondage to sin. Yet they do not obtain full possession of freedom so as to feel no more annoyance from their flesh, but there still remains in them a continuing occasion for struggle whereby they may be exercised; and not only be exercised, but also better learn their own weakness. In this matter all writers of sounder judgment agree that there remains in a regenerate man a smoldering cinder of evil, from which desires continually leap forth to allure and spur him to commit sin. They also admit that the saints are as yet so bound by that disease of concupiscence that they cannot withstand being at times tickled and incited either to lust or to avarice or to ambition, or to other vices. . . .

Accordingly, we say that the old man was so crucified [Rom. 6:6], and the law of sin [cf. Rom. 8:2] so abolished in the children of God, that some vestiges remain; not to rule over them, but to humble them by the consciousness of their own weakness. And we, indeed, admit that these traces are not imputed, as if they did not exist; but at the same time we contend that this comes to pass through the mercy of God, so that the saints—otherwise deservedly sinners and guilty before God—are freed from this guilt. And it will not be difficult for us to confirm this opinion, since there are clear testimonies to the fact in Scripture. What clearer testimony do we wish than what Paul exclaims in the seventh chapter of Romans? . . . Paul speaks there as a man reborn [Rom. 7:6]. . . .

Jacob Arminius, the Remonstrance, and the Synod of Dort

While Calvin appeals to the many nonregenerate as evidence for double predestination, Arminius points to the same empirical phenomenon to argue that God's grace could not be "irresistible." Moreover, he considers it an open question whether any believer could, by grace, reach perfection in this life. In its response to Arminius and the Remonstrance, the Synod of Dort upholds the sovereignty of God's work in regeneration as a comfort to believers; their salvation rests not at all on themselves, in which case it would be uncertain indeed, but solely on the invincible grace of God.

SOURCES

(A) Jacob Arminius, *Verklarung van Jacob Arminius* (1608), Article IV and VII; ET: in Arminius, *Works* 1:664, 672–91 (edited). **(B)** *Articuli Arminiani sive Remonstrantia* (1610) [Dutch: *De Remonstrantie en het Remonstrantisme*], Article IV; ET: *The Five Arminian Articles*, in Schaff, *Creeds* 3:547. **(C)** *Canones Synodi Dordrechtanae* (1618–19), Third and Fourth Heads of Doctrine, Articles XI–XVI; ET: "Of the Corruption of Man, his Conversion to God, and the Manner thereof," *The Canons of the Synod of Dort*, in Schaff, *Creeds* 3:590–92.

BIBLIOGRAPHY

See pp. 94–97, 153–56, 222–24, 288–91, 302–6.

A. JACOB ARMINIUS

IV. The Grace of God

. . . I am by no means injurious or unjust to grace, by attributing, as it is reported of me, too much to man's free-will: For the whole controversy reduces itself to the solution of this question, "Is the grace of God a certain irresistible force?" That is, the controversy does not relate to those actions or operations which may be ascribed to grace, (for I acknowledge and inculcate as many of these actions or operations as any man ever did,) but it relates solely to the mode of operation,— *whether it be irresistible or not:* With respect to which, I believe, according to the scriptures, that many persons resist the Holy Spirit and reject the grace that is offered. . . .

VII. The Perfection of Believers in this Life

Beside those doctrines on which I have treated, there is now much discussion among us respecting *the perfection of believers, or regenerate persons, in this life;* and it is reported, that I entertain sentiments on this subject, which are very improper, and nearly allied to those of the Pelagians, viz. "that it is possible for the regenerate in this life perfectly to keep God's precepts." To this I reply, though these might have been my sentiments, yet I ought not on this account to be considered a Pelagian, either partly or entirely,—provided I had only added that "they could do this *by the grace of Christ,* and *by no means without it.*" But while I never asserted, that *a believer could perfectly keep the precepts of Christ in this life*, I never denied it, but always left it as a matter which has still to be decided. For I have contented myself with those sentiments which St. Augustine has expressed on this subject, whose words I have frequently quoted in the University, and have usually subjoined, that I had no addition to make to them.

B. THE REMONSTRANCE

Art. IV. That this grace of God is the beginning, continuance, and accomplishment of all good, even to this extent, that the regenerate man himself, without prevenient or assisting, awakening, following and co-operative grace, can neither think, will, nor do good, nor withstand any temptations to evil; so that all good deeds or movements, that can be conceived, must be ascribed to the grace of God in Christ. But as respects the mode of the operation of this grace, it is not irresistible, inasmuch as it is written concerning many, that they have resisted the Holy Ghost. Acts vii., and elsewhere in many places.

C. THE SYNOD OF DORT

Art. XI. But when God accomplishes his good pleasure in the elect, or works in them true conversion, he not only causes the gospel to be externally preached to them, and powerfully illuminates their minds by his Holy Spirit, that they may rightly understand and discern the things of the Spirit of God, but by the efficacy of the same regenerating Spirit he pervades the inmost recesses of the man; he opens the closed and softens the hardened heart, and circumcises that which was uncircumcised; infuses new qualities into the will, which, though heretofore dead, he quickens; from being evil, disobedient, and refractory, he renders it good, obedient, and pliable; actuates and strengthens it, that, like a good tree, it may bring forth the fruits of good actions.

Art. XII. And this is the regeneration so highly celebrated in Scripture and denominated a new creation: a resurrection from the dead; a making alive, which God works in us without our aid. But this is nowise effected merely by the external preaching of the gospel, by moral suasion, or such a mode of operation that, after God has performed his part, it still remains in the power of man to be regenerated or not, to be converted or to continue unconverted; but it is evidently a supernatural work, most powerful, and at the same time most delightful, astonishing, mysterious, and ineffable; not inferior in efficacy to creation or the resurrection from the dead, as the Scripture inspired by the author of this work declares; so that all in whose hearts God works in this marvelous manner are certainly, infallibly, and effectually regenerated, and do actually believe. Whereupon the will thus renewed is not only actuated and influenced by God, but, in consequence of this influence, becomes itself active. Wherefore, also, man is himself rightly said to believe and repent, by virtue of that grace received.

ART. XIII. The manner of this operation can not be fully comprehended by believers in this life. Notwithstanding which, they rest satisfied with knowing and experiencing that by this grace of God they are enabled to believe with the heart and to love their Saviour.

Jean de Labadie

Jean de Labadie (1610–74), a Frenchman trained by Jesuits, began his ministry as a secular priest. Considering himself inspired by God, he traveled around, preaching discipleship and reform. Before long, having become enamored of Protestant doctrine, his preaching brought him into conflict with Catholic authorities and he was censured. Later, at a Carmelite retreat, Labadie was affected significantly by his reading of Calvin's *Institutes.* In 1660 he officially converted to the Reformed faith and soon turned the energies he had exerted trying to change Catholicism toward a similar "reform of the Reformed." In 1666, after a time as pastor and teacher in Montauban and Geneva, he moved to Holland with a small cadre of disciples and soon was appointed pastor at Middelbourg. Labadie's preaching was successful and attracted the admiration of leading Dutch Reformed leaders such as Gisburtus Voetius, Jacodus van Lodensteyn, and Anna Maria van Schuurman. Nevertheless, because of Labadie's emphasis on rigorism and asceticism, as well as his own personal quirks, his circle of devotees was destined to remain small.

The following passage comes from the first of two sermons entitled "The Apostolic Visitation of the Church," which Labadie preached upon commencing his pastorate in Middelbourg. He addresses himself to a Dutch society grown affluent through its thriving commerce but, at the same time, spiritually impoverished through worldly compromise.

While some within the Reformed tradition have considered Labadie an extremist, in his emphasis on sanctification he was mining a genuinely Reformed vein. Labadie died while still a member of the Reformed church, although his particular view of Christianity placed him constantly on the edge of separatism.

SOURCE

Jean de Labadie, *L'Arrivée apostolique aux eglises, représentée par celles de l'apostre Saint Paul, aux eglises de Rome & de Corinthe, A dessein, de les renouveller à repentance, & les ayder à se sanctifier de plus en plus* (Middelbourg: Jean Misson, 1667). The text below comes from the sermon "La venuë de S. Paul à l'eglise de Corinthe," pp. 98–101 (edited).

BIBLIOGRAPHY

Journal of Jasper Danckaerts, 1679–1680, Original Narratives of Early American History, ed. B. B. James and J. F. Jameson (New York: Charles Scribner's Sons, 1913). T. J. Saxby, *The Quest for the New Jerusalem: Jean de Labadie and the Labadists, 1610–1744* (Dordrecht, Boston, Lancaster: Martinus Nijhoff, 1987). See also pp. 14–16, above, and 298–99, 323–24, below.

We can no longer deny that [church and society] have left unprotected a very great number, so that all sorts of vices have entered into our souls: ambition and pride from the prosperity and good success [we have enjoyed] in our business affairs; avarice and the coveting of great wealth from this our prosperous commerce and general business dealings with people both here and abroad. . . .

But there is forgiveness [from God] so that one may fear [God] and neither desire to sin nor chance to die in his sins and [thus] perish [eternally]. For those who repent, shall live; and those who live by repentance and faith shall live yet again [eternally]. And they shall know [God's] mercy and grace in the outward justification of their sins and of [God's] empowerment [lit. "spirit"] and grace in the [inward] sanctification.

Work, O Lord, this twofold efficacy in your church and particularly make [your people] humble in their whole being, right now before your eyes. And let them groan sincerely at your feet, resolving themselves to fast this day from meat, and to fast from vice forever. Let them weep and abstain from ever committing any sin.

Convert us, therefore, indeed convert us. Strike our hearts, chastise us, and speak to us as is necessary: "Now you sin," but, "Sin no more." No more of malicious sin, nor of that sort of sin which attracts us to all manner of temporal or eternal evil.

O God of all good, who desires good for us and deploys the good on our behalf. O All Beneficent One, make us completely holy and lift us up, that rising to see your face we may partake of the full extent of your wisdom and the plenitude of your good.

JOHN CALVIN: CHRISTIAN FREEDOM

"God alone is Lord of the conscience."[4] This powerful Protestant affirmation of freedom, which relativizes and calls into question all authority save that of God alone, has had significant consequences for Reformed Christianity and for Western culture. Freedom flows directly from the experience of justification, as John Calvin makes clear in his explanation of this most fundamental feature of Protestantism.

SOURCE

Institutes III.19.1–7, pp. 833–39 (edited).

BIBLIOGRAPHY

See pp. 346–64, below. Jane Dempsey Douglass, *Women, Freedom, and Calvin* (Philadelphia: Westminster, 1985.)

We must now discuss Christian freedom. He who proposes to summarize gospel teaching ought by no means to omit an explanation of this topic. For it is a thing of prime necessity, and apart from a knowledge of it consciences dare undertake almost nothing without doubting; they hesitate and recoil from many things; they constantly waver and are afraid. But freedom is especially an appendage of justification and is of no little avail in understanding its power. . . .

Christian freedom, in my opinion, consists of three parts. The first: that the consciences of believers, in seeking assurance of their justification before God, should rise above and advance beyond the law, forgetting all law righteousness. . . .

The second part, dependent upon the first, is that consciences observe the law, not as if constrained by the necessity of the law, but that freed from the law's yoke they willingly obey God's will. . . .

The third part of Christian freedom lies in this: regarding outward things that are of themselves "indifferent," we are not bound before God by any religious obligation preventing us from sometimes using them and other times not using them, indifferently. And the knowledge of this freedom is very necessary for us, for if it is lacking, our consciences will have no repose and there will be no end to superstitions.

4. See "Of Christian Liberty and Liberty of Conscience," Westminster Confession of Faith (1647), chap. 20, in Schaff, *Creeds* 3:643–45.

CHRISTIAN VOCATION AND DISCIPLESHIP

John Calvin: We Are Not Our Own

Notwithstanding the importance of law in Calvin's theology, when he turns to the Christian life he urges a practice that transcends the law. In keeping with Paul's admonition in Romans 12, Christians are to give their all as living sacrifices.

SOURCE

Institutes III.7.1–2, pp. 689–90.

Even though the law of the Lord provides the finest and best-disposed method of ordering a man's life, it seemed good to the Heavenly Teacher to shape his people by an even more explicit plan to that rule which he had set forth in the law. Here, then, is the beginning of this plan: the duty of believers is "to present their bodies to God as a living sacrifice, holy and acceptable to him," and in this consists the lawful worship of him [Rom. 12:1]. From this is derived the basis of the exhortation that "they be not conformed to the fashion of this world, but be transformed by the renewal of their minds, so that they may prove what is the will of God" [Rom. 12:2]. Now the great thing is this: we are consecrated and dedicated to God in order that we may thereafter think, speak, meditate, and do, nothing except to his glory. For a sacred thing may not be applied to profane uses without marked injury to him.

If we, then, are not our own [cf. 1 Cor. 6:19] but the Lord's, it is clear what error we must flee, and whither we must direct all the acts of our life.

We are not our own: let not our reason nor our will, therefore, sway our plans and deeds. We are not our own: let us therefore not set it as our goal to seek what is expedient for us according to the flesh. We are not our own: in so far as we can, let us therefore forget ourselves and all that is ours.

Conversely, we are God's: let us therefore live for him and die for him. We are God's: let his wisdom and will therefore rule all our actions. We are God's: let all the parts of our life accordingly strive toward him as our only lawful goal [Rom. 14:8; cf. 1 Cor. 6:19]. O, how much has that man profited who, having been taught that he is not his own, has taken away dominion and rule from his own reason that he may yield it to God! For, as consulting our self-interest is the pestilence that most effectively leads to our destruction, so the sole haven of salvation is to be wise in nothing and to will nothing through ourselves but to follow the leading of the Lord alone.

Let this therefore be the first step, that a man depart from himself in order that he may apply the whole force of his ability in the service of the Lord. I call "service" not only what lies in obedience to God's Word but what turns the mind of man, empty of its own carnal sense, wholly to the bidding of God's Spirit. While it is the first entrance to life, all philosophers were ignorant of this transformation, which Paul calls "renewal of the mind" [Eph. 4:23]. For they set up reason alone as the ruling principle in man, and think that it alone should be listened to; to it alone, in short, they entrust the conduct of life. But the Christian philosophy bids reason give way to, submit and subject itself to, the Holy Spirit so that the man himself may no longer live but hear Christ living and reigning within him [Gal. 2:20].

John Bunyan: The Pilgrim's Progress

John Bunyan (1628–88) was a Calvinist preacher connected with an English Independent congregation who suffered imprisonment at Royalist hands from 1660 to 1672. Bunyan's *The Pilgrim's Progress* was one of the most important and widely read devotional classics that English Puritanism produced, and thus it provides a unique, if indirect, glimpse into Puritan religion as practiced by the ordinary believer. The poem tracks a Pilgrim named Christian in his journey from the City of Destruction to Mount Zion. In the following passage, Christian has stopped in a palace for the relief of godly sojourners, whereupon he is engaged in conversation by Piety, Prudence, and Charity.

SOURCE

John Bunyan, *The Pilgrim's Progress* (1678), Longman's English Classics Edition, ed. George Rice Carpenter (New York, 1905), 44–49.

BIBLIOGRAPHY

John Bunyan, *Grace Abounding to the Chief of Sinners* (1660). This is Bunyan's autobiography.

For the Puritans and their devotional practice, see C. L. Cohen, *God's Caress* (New York: Oxford University Press, 1986). N. Pettit, *The Heart Prepared* (New Haven: Yale University Press, 1966). G. S. Wakefield, *Puritan Devotion* (London: Epworth, 1957). O. Watkins, *The Puritan Experience* (London: Routledge & Kegan Paul, 1972).

PIETY. Come, good Christian, since we have been so loving to you to receive you into our house this night, let us, if perhaps we may better ourselves thereby, talk with you of all things that have happened to you in your pilgrimage.

CHR. With a very good will; and I am glad that you are so well disposed.

PIETY. What moved you at first to betake yourself to a pilgrim's life?

CHR. I was driven out of my native country by a dreadful sound that was in mine ears; to wit, that unavoidable destruction did attend me, if I abode in that place where I was.

PIETY. But how did it happen that you came out of your country this way?

CHR. It was as God would have it; for when I was under the fears of destruction, I did not know whither to go; but by chance there came a man, even to me, as I was trembling and weeping, whose name is Evangelist, and he directed me to the Wicket-gate, which else I should never have found, and so set me into the way that hath led me directly to this house.

PIETY. But did you not come by the house of the Interpreter?

CHR. Yes, and did see such things there, the remembrance of which will stick by me as long as I live, especially three things; to wit, how Christ, in despite of Satan, maintains his work of grace in the heart, how the man had sinned himself quite out of hopes of God's mercy, and also the dream of him that thought in his sleep the day of judgment was come.

PIETY. Why, did you hear him tell his dream?

CHR. Yes, and a dreadful one it was, I thought. It made my heart ache as he was telling of it; but yet I am glad I heard it.

PIETY. Was that all you saw at the house of the Interpreter?

CHR. No, he took me, and had me where he showed me a stately palace, and how the people were clad in gold that were in it, and how there came a venturous man, and cut his way through the armed men that stood in the door to keep him out, and how he was bid to come in and win eternal glory. Methought those things did ravish my heart. I would have stayed at that good man's house a twelvemonth, but that I knew I had farther to go.

PIETY. And what saw you else in the way?

CHR. Saw! Why, I went but a little further, and I saw One, as I thought in my mind, hang bleeding upon a tree; and the very sight of him made my burden fall off my back; for I groaned under a very heavy burden, but then it fell down from off me. It was a strange thing to me; for I never saw such a thing before. Yea, and while I stood looking up, (for then I could not forbear looking) three shining ones came to me. One of them testified that my sins were forgiven me; another stript me of my rags, and gave me this broidred coat which you see; and the third set the mark which you see in my forehead, and gave me this sealed roll (and with that he plucked it out of his bosom).

PIETY. But you saw more than this, did you not?

CHR. The things that I have told you were the best. Yet some other matters I saw, as, namely, I saw three men, Simple, Sloth, and Presumption, lie asleep, a little out of the way, as I came, with irons upon their heels. But do you think I could awake them? I also saw Formality and Hypocrisy come tumbling over the wall, to go, as they pretended, to Zion; but they were quickly lost, even as I myself did tell them, but they would not believe. But, above all, I found it hard work to get up this hill, and as hard to come by the lions' mouth; and, truly, if it had not been for the good man the porter, that stands at the gate, I do not know but that, after all, I might have gone back again. But I thank God I am here, and thank you for receiving of me.

Then Prudence thought good to ask him a few questions, and desired his answer to them.

PRU. Do you not think sometimes of the country from whence you came?

CHR. Yes, but with much shame and detestation. Truly, if I had been mindful of that country from whence I came out, I might have had opportunity to have returned; but now I desire a better country, that is, a heavenly one.

PRU. Do you not yet bear away with you some of the things that then you were conversant withal?

CHR. Yes, but greatly against my will; especially my inward and carnal cogitations, with which all my countrymen, as well as myself, were delighted. But now all those things are my grief; and might I but choose mine own things, I would choose never to think of those things more; but when I would be a-doing of that which is best, that which is worst is with me.

PRU. Do you not find sometimes as if those things were vanquished which at other times are your perplexity?

CHR. Yes, but that is but seldom; but they are to me golden hours in which such things happens to me.

PRU. Can you remember by what means you find your annoyances at times as if they were vanquished?

CHR. Yes, when I think what I saw at the cross, that will do it; and when I look upon my broidered coat, that will do it; and when I look into the roll that I carry in my bosom, that will do it; and when my thoughts wax warm about whither I am going, that will do it.

PRU. And what is it that makes you so desirous to go to Mount Zion?

CHR. Why, there I hope to see Him alive that did hang dead on the cross; and there I hope to be rid of all those things that to this day are in me an annoyance to me. There they say there is no death; and there I shall dwell with such company as I like best. For, to tell you the truth, I love Him because I was by him eased of my burden; and I am weary of my inward sickness. I would fain be where I shall die no more, and with the company that shall continually cry, *Holy, holy, holy.*

Then said Charity to Christian, Have you a family; are you a married man?

CHR. I have a wife and four small children.

CHAR. And why did you not bring them along with you?

CHR. Then Christian wept, and said, Oh, how willingly would I have done it! but they were all of them utterly averse to my going on pilgrimage.

CHAR. But you should have talked to them, and have endeavored to have shown them the danger of being behind.

CHR. So I did, and told them also what God had showed to me of the destruction of our city; but I seemed to them as one that mocked, and they believed me not.

CHAR. And did you pray to God that he would bless your counsel to them?

CHR. Yes, and that with much affection; for you must think that my wife and poor children were very dear unto me.

CHAR. But did you tell them of your own sorrow, and fear of destruction? for I suppose that destruction was visible enough to you.

CHR. Yes, over, and over, and over. They might also see my fears in my countenance, in my tears, and also in my trembling under the apprehension of the judgment that did hang over our heads; but all was not sufficient to prevail with them to come with me.

CHAR. But what could they say for themselves, why they came not?

CHR. Why, my wife was afraid of losing this world; and my children were given to the foolish delights of youth. So, what by one thing, and what by another, they left me to wander in this manner alone.

Philip Doddridge: Self-Examination

Philip Doddridge (1702–51) was pastor of an Independent congregation in Northampton, England, as well as the premier teacher in the nonconformist academy from 1729 on. Reformed in his theology, Doddridge nevertheless opposed the rigidity of high Calvinism. He was instrumental in promoting the theology of Richard Baxter. This selection comes from the end of a chapter that urges the believer to self-examination in order to determine whether she is experiencing genuine growth in grace.

SOURCE

Philip Doddridge, "The Christian Assisted in Examining into His Growth in Grace," chapter 26 of *The Rise and Progress of Religion in the Soul* (1745), in *The Works of Philip Doddridge, D.D.*, 5 vols. (London, 1803–5), 2:239–47 (edited).

BIBLIOGRAPHY

Philip Doddridge, *Practical Discourses* (London, 1742). G. F. Nuttall, ed., *Philip Doddridge, 1701–51: His Contribution to English Religion* (London: Independent Press, 1951).

10. Do you also advance in zeal and activity, for the service of God, and the happiness of mankind?—Does your love shew itself solid and sincere, by a continual flow of good works from it? Can you view the sorrows of others with tender compassion, and with projects and contrivances what you may do to relieve them? Do you feel in your breast, that you are more frequently devising liberal things, and ready to wave your own advantage or pleasure that you may accomplish them? Do you find your imaginations teeming (as it were) with conceptions and schemes, for the advancement of the cause and interest of Christ in the world, for the propagation of his Gospel and for the happiness of your fellow-creatures? And do you not only pray, but act for it; act in such a manner, as to shew that you pray in earnest, and feel a readiness to do what little you can in this cause, even though others, who might, if they pleased, very conveniently do a vast deal more, will do nothing?

11. And, not to enlarge upon this copious head, reflect once more how your affections stand, with regard to this world, and another?—Are you more deeply and practically convinced of the vanity of these things which are seen, and are temporal? Do you perceive your expectations from them, and your attachments to them, to diminish? You are willing to stay in this world, as long as your Father pleases; and it is right and well: but do you find your bonds so loosened to it, that you are willing, heartily willing, to leave it at the shortest warning; in that if God should see fit to summon you away on a sudden though it should be in the midst of your enjoyments, pursuant to expectations, and hopes, you would cordially consent to that to move; without saying, Lord, let me stay a little while longer to enjoy this or that agreeable entertainment, to finish this or that scheme? Can you think with an habitual calmness and hearty approbation, if such be the divine pleasure of waking the

more when you lie down on your bed, of returning home the more when you go out of your house? and yet, on the other hand, how great soever the burdens of life are, do you find a willingness to bear them, in submission to the will of your heavenly Father, though it should be to many future years, and though they should be years of far greater affliction, than you have ever yet seen? Can you say calmly and steadily, if not with such overflowings of tender affections as you could declare, "Behold, thy servant, thy child, is in thine hand, do with me as seemeth good in thy sight! My will is melted into thine; to be lifted up or laid down, to be carried out or brought in, to be here or there, in this or that circumstance, just as thou pleasest, and as shall best suit with thy great extensive plan, which it is impossible that I, or all the angels in heaven, should mend."

12. These, if I understand matters aright, are some of the most substantial evidences of growth and establishment in religion. Search after them: bless God for them, so far as you discover them in yourself; and study to advance in them daily, under the influences of divine grace, to which I heartily recommend you, and to which I intreat you frequently to recommend yourself.

Thomas Shepard: The Parable of the Ten Virgins

Thomas Shepard (1605–49) was perhaps the most influential New England preacher and teacher of his generation. Educated at Cambridge and somewhat of a miscreant in youth, he was converted under the preaching of the Cambridge covenant theologian John Preston (1587–1628). He fled to America in 1635. Shepard's *Parable of the Ten Virgins* was prepared posthumously from sermon notes. Based on Matt. 25:1–4, its theme is that true believers have been called out and are being prepared under the empowering of the covenant of grace to meet Christ. But among those awaiting Christ in the church visible, only some are wise and many are foolish and will be disappointed. The following passage considers the four things that put a soul in readiness to enjoy Christ.

SOURCE

Thomas Shepard, *The Parable of the Ten Virgins* (London, 1660), part 1, chap. 7, pp. 39–42 (edited with orthography and punctuation modified).

BIBLIOGRAPHY

J. A. Albro, *The Life of Thomas Shepard*, vol. 4 of *The Lives of the Chief Fathers of New England* (Boston, 1870). The standard work for this period is Perry Miller, *The New*

England Mind: The Seventeenth Century (Cambridge: Belknap Harvard University Press, 1939). For early American devotional practice, see C. E. Hambrick-Stowe, *The Practice of Piety* (Chapel Hill: University of North Carolina Press, 1982). See also N. Pettit, *The Heart Prepared.*

Concerning a Christian's Duty of being constantly and continually ready to meet Christ, and to enjoy Communion with him.

1. That which makes a Christian unready for [Christ] are those strong fears and jealousies and damping doubts of the love of Christ to him. The soul happily has made choice of him, is content with him, melts into wonderment and love to think that he should love him: what me? and Christ has writ him on . . . the palms of his Hands . . . [Isa. 49:14]. Is it possible? is it credible? one that has been so vile, one that still has such a Heart, for him to set his Heart on me? Surely no: hence the Soul is afraid to die, and desires too much to live still . . . [But on the other hand,] the soul is prepared and ready for him when he has some comfortable assurance of the love of Christ towards him, that it can say, if I live he loves me, tho' he kills me by Death, yet I know that he loves me: nay, then he loves me most, when he puts an end to my sins and to my sorrows too? And therefore now says as one ready to receive a Prince, now let him come or send for me when he will . . . [Rom. 8:28]. . . .

2. Then a man is unprepared for the Lord Jesus' coming, while he wants affections suitable to the majesty, and according to the love of the Lord Jesus: Suppose a woman knows her husband's love, yet if she has lost love to him . . . is she not [unfit] to appear before him . . . ? Have you not lost your love, your first love, or second love? You have love, is it not divided to other things, as wife, child, friends, hopes or provisions for them . . . ? Or if you do love him, 'tis with a carnal love, he has no more than a lust has had, and it may be not much, 'tis with a cold love; now you are unfit for him. . . . [1 Pet. 4:7]. Now therefore the soul is prepared to meet Christ when, if the soul has lost its affections, recovers them . . . and . . . breaks out with such love unto Christ as is fitting for him [2 Tim. 4:8]. . . .

3. Then a man is unready for Christ, while he neglects the work of Christ; for suppose a man has some inward love to Christ, yet neglects and has no heart to do the work of Christ: he is as yet no more fit to meet Christ than a steward who has had much betrusted him . . . and he has let all seasons go wherein he might have traded for him and gained somewhat to him. How can he appear before him when [there are] no

275

fair accounts to be seen? . . . Oh thus 'tis with many Christians; hence those sad alarms of conscience and shakings of God's Spirit. . . .

Now therefore then the soul is ready for the Lord when 'tis daily at it, finishing God's work . . . [Jn. 17:5]. Christ has given us our [life's] work, day's work, every hour's work; for Christ has ever employment; now tho' a soul may live long and cannot finish its [life's] work, yet if it finish its day's work, or hour's work, it may have comfort then if the Lord should come. . . .

4. Then is a man unready when having done his work he grows puffed up with it: for let all the three former be wrought in the soul, if now the soul be puffed up, thinks highly of itself, attributes anything to itself, . . . so he is too big for the Lord. . . . Now therefore when a Christian is ready to give all for free Grace, and to adore that, now he is ready for the Lord [Ps. 108:1]. . . . God's last end is to bring the soul to the praise of the riches of his grace, not only to enjoy God as [did] Adam. Now the great reason why Christ comes not to his people presently after they are espoused to him, 'tis to make them ready to attain that end. Hence he leaves sins, temptations, sorrows, desertions, on purpose, that they may at conclusion look back and see if ever saved, pardoned, it's grace. Now therefore when the soul is brought to do this, when he has this rent in his hand, now the Lord is ready to receive him, and it too, and he is prepared to the Lord. . . . So that you think you boast not, Oh the Lord sees you do, or have not hearts so enlarged towards grace as you should, it's certain you are yet unready then; but when empty, and poor, and cast down, and make an infinite matter of a small sin, and set a high price on a little love, much more on infinite, now you are prepared: Hence David falls a praising when near to death, and the Lord near to come to him.

Sarah Pierrepont Edwards:
A Personal Account

In January 1742 Sarah Pierrepont Edwards, a devout and pious woman born of a prestigious New England family, experienced a remarkable spiritual seizure marked by visions and fainting spells and also by an intense sense of joy, well-being, and divine favor. These occurred while her husband, Jonathan, was away on an extended preaching tour. A certain Mister Buell had assumed the Northampton pulpit and was enjoying more success at preaching revival than had Edwards. Upon his return, Edwards asked his wife to record the event, and he included it anonymously in his tract, *Some Thoughts on the Revival* (1742). This is a short portion of Sarah Edwards's recollections.

SOURCE

Sarah Pierrepont Edwards, "An Account of Her Solemn Self-Dedications" (1742), in Edwards, *Works* (1834) 1:lxii–lxiii, lxiv–lxv (edited).

BIBLIOGRAPHY

Elisabeth S. Dodds, *Marriage to a Difficult Man: The Uncommon Union of Jonathan and Sarah Edwards* (Philadelphia: Westminster, 1971).

About 11 o'clock, as I accidentally went into the room where Mr. Buell was conversing with some of the people, I heard him say, "that we, who are the children of God, should be cold and lifeless in religion!" and I felt such a sense of the deep ingratitude manifested by the children of God, in such coldness and deadness, that my strength was immediately taken away, and I sunk down on the spot. Those who were near raised me, and placed me in a chair; and from the fulness of my heart, I expressed to them, in a very earnest manner, the deep sense I had of the wonderful grace of Christ towards me, of the assurance I had of his having saved me from hell, of my happiness running parallel with eternity, of the duty of giving up all to God, and of the peace and joy inspired by an entire dependence on his mercy and grace. Mr. Buell then read a melting hymn of Dr. Watts's, concerning the loveliness of Christ, the enjoyments and employments of heaven, and the Christian's earnest desire of heavenly things; and the truth and reality of the things mentioned in the hymn, made so strong an impression on my mind, and my soul was drawn so powerfully towards Christ and heaven, that I leaped unconsciously from my chair. I seemed to be drawn upwards, soul and body, from the earth towards heaven; and it appeared to me that I must naturally and necessarily ascend thither. These feelings continued while the hymn was reading, and during the prayer of Mr. Christophers, which followed. After the prayer, Mr. Buell read two other hymns, on the glories of heaven, which moved me so exceedingly, and drew me so strongly heavenward, that it seemed as it were to draw my body upwards, and I felt as if I must necessarily ascend thither. At length my strength failed me, and I sunk down; when they took me up and laid me on the bed, where I lay for a considerable time, faint with joy, while contemplating the glories of the heavenly world. After I had lain a while, I felt more perfectly subdued and weaned from the world, and more fully resigned to God, than I had ever been conscious of before. I felt an entire indifference to the opinions, and representations, and conduct of mankind respecting me; and a perfect willingness, that God should employ some other instrument than Mr. Edwards, in advancing the work of grace in Northampton. I was entirely swallowed up in God, as my only portion, and his honour and glory was the object of my supreme desire and delight. At the same time, I felt a far greater love to the children of God, than ever before. I seemed to love them as my own soul; and when I saw them, my heart went out towards them, with an inexpressible endearedness and sweetness. I beheld them by faith in their risen and glorified state, with spiritual bodies re-fashioned after the image of Christ's glorious body, and arrayed in the beauty of heaven. The time when they would be so appeared very near, by faith it seemed as if it were present. This was accompanied with a ravishing sense of the unspeakable joys of the upper world. They appeared to my mind in all their reality and certainty, and as it were in actual and distinct vision; so plain and evident were they to the eye of my faith, I seemed to regard them as begun. These anticipations were renewed over and over, while I lay on the bed, from twelve o'clock till four, being too much exhausted by emotions of joy, to rise and sit up; and during most of the time, my feelings prompted me to converse very earnestly with one and another of the pious women, who were present, on those spiritual and heavenly objects, of which I had so deep an impression. A little while before I arose, Mr. Buell and the people went to meeting.

I continued in a sweet and lively sense of divine things, until I retired to rest. That night, which was Thursday night, Jan. 28, was the sweetest night I ever had in my life. I never before, for so long a time together, enjoyed so much of the light, and rest, and sweetness of heaven in my soul, but without the least agitation of body during the whole time. The great part of the night I lay awake, sometimes asleep, and sometimes between sleeping and waking. But all night I continued in a constant, clear, and lively sense of the heavenly sweetness of Christ's excellent and transcendent love, of his nearness to me, and of my dearness to him; with an inexpressibly sweet calmness of soul in an entire rest in him. . . .

My soul remained in a kind of heavenly elysium. So far as I am capable of making a comparison, I think that what I felt each minute, during the continuance of the whole time, was worth more than all the outward comfort and pleasure, which I had enjoyed in my whole life put together. It was a pure delight, which fed and satisfied the soul. . . .

This lively sense of the beauty and excellency of divine things continued during the morning, accompanied with peculiar sweetness and delight. To my own imagination, my soul seemed to be gone out of me to God and Christ in heaven, and to have very little relation to my body. God and Christ were so present to me, and so near me, that I seemed removed from myself. The spiritual beauty of the Father and the Saviour, seemed to engross my whole mind; and it was the instinctive feeling of my heart, "Thou art; and there is none beside thee." I never felt such an entire emptiness of self-love, or any regard to any private, selfish interest of my own. It seemed to me, that I had entirely done with myself.

CHRISTIAN MARRIAGE AND FAMILY

Protestantism forged a new positive theology of marriage and family life. Marriage and family were now seen to be a high calling, the norm of Christian living, in contrast to medieval Catholicism for which the monasteries offered the most noble form of Christian existence. The passage below from Martin Bucer (Bützer) (1491–1551), architect of reform in Strasbourg, is noteworthy for its belief that true marriage is not just a matter of formal agreement but requires a content of heartfelt love. Bucer figured prominently in John Milton's seventeenth-century reflections upon divorce. In the second passage, the jurist and ecumenist Hugo Grotius, one of the most liberal men of his age, includes the traditional Reformed rejection of adultery as one of the essentials upon which all Christians should agree. William Gouge (1578–1653), who was a participant at the Westminster Assembly, contributes our third selection on mutuality in marriage. The fourth set of texts comes from Richard Baxter (1615–91), perhaps the most prolific practical theologian of the seventeenth-century Puritans. Baxter and Gouge, while ensconced in the patriarchal assumptions of their day, were forward-looking nonetheless in their formal advocacy of equality and mutuality between the sexes.

SOURCES

(A) Martin Bucer, "Whether It May Be Permitted That the Promise of Marriage May Be Rescinded Before It Is Fulfilled," *De Regno Christi* (1550), in *Melanchthon and Bucer*, 324–26. (B) Hugo Grotius, *Meletius Sive De Iis Quae Inter Christianos Conveniunt Epistola/Meletius or Letter on the Points of Agreement Between Christians* (1611), trans. and ed. Guillaume H. M. Posthumus Meyjes (Leiden: E. J. Brill, 1988), 130–31; a critical edition with Latin and English text. (C) William Gouge, *Of Domesticall Duties*, Eight Treatises, 3d ed. (London: George Miller, 1634), 216 (orthography and punctuation edited). (D) Richard Baxter, "Mutual Duties of Husbands and Wives Toward Each Other," *Christian Directory* (1664–65), Part II, Christian Economics, chapter 7, sect. 11, in *The Practical Works of Richard Baxter*, 4 vols. (London, 1838), 1:431–38 (edited). (E) Richard Baxter, "Instruction of Children," *The Saint's Everlasting Rest* (1650), Part III, chap. 14, sect. 11, in *The Practical Works of Richard Baxter* 3:239–42 (edited).

BIBLIOGRAPHY

Primary Sources: Martin Bucer, "Marriage, Divorce, and Celibacy," from *Commentary on the Four Holy Gospels*, in *Common Places of Martin Bucer,* trans. and ed. D. F. Wright, Courtenay Library of Reformation Classics 4 (Appleford, Eng.: Sutton Courtenay Press, 1972), 403–7. John Milton, *The Doctrine and Discipline of Divorce Restor'd to the good of both Sexes* (London, 1644), available in various modern editions of Milton's prose works. See selections in Joyce L. Irwin, *Womanhood in Radical Protestantism: 1525–1675*, Studies in Women and Religion (New York and Toronto: Edwin Mellen, 1979).

Secondary Sources: Jane Dempsey Douglass, "Women and the Continental Reformation," in *Religion and Sexism: Images of Woman in the Jewish and Christian Traditions*, ed. Rosemary Radford Ruether (New York: Simon & Schuster, 1974), 293–317. Cornelia Niekus Moore, *The Maiden's Mirror: Reading Material for German Girls in the Sixteenth and Seventeenth Centuries*, Wolfenbütteler Forschungen Herausgegeben von der Herzog August Bibliotek 36 (Wiesbaden: Harrassowitz, 1987). François Wendel, *Le Mariage à Strasbourg à l'époque de la Réforme, 1520–1692* (Strasbourg, 1928).

A. MARTIN BUCER: TRUE MARRIAGE NEEDS TRUE ASSENT

Since it is already abundantly obvious that there are very often second thoughts about an agreement of matrimony and there are discovered just and honorable causes for withdrawing from this agreement, it certainly cannot be alien to the office of pious princes that they make possible for persons in such situations the same arrangement for withdrawing from a promised marriage as did pious emperors of old, especially when only a promise of matrimony and no carnal intercourse has been involved. As there is no true marriage without a true assent of hearts between those who make the agreement, it is appropriate for pious princes to take very special pains that no marriage take place among their subjects without this assent and love. For when the wedding feast has been celebrated and plenty of carnal intercourse thus enjoyed, it is the right time for the nuptial agreement to have its full confirmation.

B. HUGO GROTIUS: ABSTAIN FROM ADULTERY

Sexual intercourse out of wedlock is forbidden. In this respect the shortsightedness of all philosophers and legislators is amazing.

When a certain well-known man came out of a brothel, he said: well done!" in the hallowed words of Cato.

We had better listen to Epictetus: "abstain from sexual intercourse before marriage." And Dio Chrysostomus in one of his orations shows in an eminent way that promiscuity is only one step away from the brothel. If people would follow the lead of nature it would not be difficult to understand that sexuality has been instituted for the sake of progeny and that children should not be fathered without the intention to educate them well; and since this is incumbent on both parents, it requires that they should live constantly together. As to leisure and sleep, they should be enjoyed only in so far as it is proper and in the way that nature requires for relaxing body and mind.

C. WILLIAM GOUGE: MATRIMONIAL UNITY

The first, highest, chiefest, and most absolutely necessary common-mutual duty betwixt man and wife is *matrimonial unity*, whereby husband and wife do account one another to be *one flesh* and accordingly preserve the inviolable union whereby they are knit together. This is that duty which the Apostle enjoineth to husbands and wives in these words, "Let not the wife depart from her husband: Let not the husband put away his wife" [1 Cor. 7:10–11]. He there speaketh of renouncing each other and making the matrimonial bond frustrate and of no effect: which bond he would have to be kept firm and inviolable, and they *two* who are thereby made *one*, constantly to remain *one*, and not to make themselves *two* again. This *matrimonial unity* is so necessary as it may not be dis-united or dissolved, though one be a Christian, the other a pagan.

D. RICHARD BAXTER: MUTUALITY
IN MARRIAGE

O therefore resolve without delay, to live together as heirs of heaven, and to be helpers to each other's souls. To which end I will give you these following sub-directions, which if you will faithfully practice, may make you to be special blessings to each other.

Direct. I. If you would help to save each other's souls, you must each of you be sure that you have a care of your own; and retain a deep and lively apprehension of those great and everlasting matters, of which you are to speak to others. It cannot be reasonably expected that he should have a due compassion to another's soul, that hath none to his own; and that he should be at the pains that is needful to help another to salvation, that setteth so little by his own, as to sell it for the base and momentary ease and pleasure of the flesh. . . .

Direct. II. Take those opportunities which your ordinary nearness and familiarity affordeth you, to be speaking seriously to each other about the matters of God, and your salvation. When you lie down and rise together, let not your worldly business have all your talk; but let God and your souls have the first and the last, and at least the freest and sweetest of your speech, if not the most. . . .

Direct. IV. Watch over the hearts and lives of one another, and labour to discern the state of one another's souls, and the strength or weakness of each other's sins and graces, and the failings of each other's lives, that so you may be able to apply to one another the most suitable help. What you are unacquainted with, you cannot be very helpful in; you cannot cure unknown diseases; you cannot give wise and safe advice, about the state of one another's souls, if you are mistaken in them. God hath placed you nearest to each other, that you might have so much interest in each other, as to quicken you to a loving care, and so much acquaintance with each other, as to keep you from misunderstanding, and so from neglecting or deceiving one another. . . .

Direct. XIV. Join together in frequent and fervent prayer. Prayer doth force the mind into some composedness and sobriety, and affecteth the heart with the presence and majesty of God. Pray also for each other when you are in secret, that God may do that work which you most desire, upon each other's hearts.

Direct. XV. Lastly, Help each other by an exemplary life. Be that yourselves which you desire your husband or wife should be: excel in meekness, and humility, and charity, and dutifulness, and diligence, and self-denial, and patience, as far as you do excel in profession of religion.

E. RICHARD BAXTER: INSTRUCTION OF CHILDREN

3. Consider, How near your children are to you, and then you will perceive that from this natural relation also they have interest in your utmost help. Your children are, as it were, parts of yourselves; if they prosper when you are dead, you take it almost as if you lived and prospered in them. If you labour never so much, you think it not ill bestowed, nor your buildings or purchases too dear, so that they may enjoy them when you are dead; and should you not be of the same mind for their everlasting rest?

4. You will else be witnesses against your own souls; your great care, and pains, and cost for their bodies, will condemn you for your neglect of their precious souls. You can spend yourselves in toiling and caring

for their bodies, and even neglect your own souls, and venture them sometimes upon unwarrantable courses, and all to provide for your posterity; and have you not as much reason to provide for their souls? Do you not believe that your children must be everlastingly happy or miserable when this life is ended? and should not that be forethought in the first place? . . .

9. On the other side, do but think with yourselves, what a world of comfort you may have if you be faithful in this duty. First, If you should not succeed, yet you have freed your own souls; and though it be sad, yet not so sad, for you may have peace in your own consciences. Secondly, But if you do succeed, the comfort is unexpressible. For, 1. Godly children will be truly loving to yourselves that are their parents; when a little riches, or matters of this world, will oft make ungodly children to cast off their very natural affection. 2. Godly children will be most obedient to you; they dare not disobey and provoke you, because of the command of God, except you should command them that which is unlawful, and then they must obey God rather than men. 3. And if you should fall into want, they would be most faithful in relieving you, as knowing they are tied by a double bond, of nature and of grace. 4. And they will also be helpers to your souls, and to your spiritual comforts; they will be delighting you with the mention of heaven, and with holy conference and actions. . . .

10. Consider, further, that the very welfare of church and state lieth mainly on this duty of well educating children; and without this, all other means are like to be far less successful. I seriously profess to you, that I verily think all the sins and miseries of the land may acknowledge this sin for their great nurse and propagator. Oh, what happy churches might we have, if parents did their duties to their children!

11. I entreat you that are parents, also to consider what excellent advantages you have above all others for the saving of your children.

1. They are under your hands while they are young, and tender, and flexible; but they come to ministers when they are grown elder, and stiffer, and settled in their ways, and think themselves too good to be catechised, and too old to be taught. You have a twig to bend, and we an oak. You have the young plants of sin to pluck up, and we the deep-rooted vices. . . .

2. Consider, also, that you have the affections of your children more than any others. None in the world hath that interest in their hearts as you. . . .

6. Above all, you are ever with them, and so have opportunity as to know their faults, so to apply the remedy. You may be still talking

to them of the word of God, and minding them of their state and duty, and may follow and set home every word of advice, as they are in the house with you, or in the shop, or in the field at work. Oh, what an excellent advantage is this, if God do but give you hearts to use it!

WORSHIP AND PRAYER

In turning to worship and prayer, we do not take up a new and discrete subject matter but a mode of life which has been presupposed in all the theology that has gone before. Quite a bit of the material we have already encountered had worship and prayer as its focus: sermons, catechisms, devotional literature. Even the dogmatic treatises were designed to make pastors better equipped to proclaim the Word of God in worship.

Life in the Spirit is nurtured through regular worship and prayer. These consummate activities of the Christian life cannot be insulated from the works of the Spirit we have just previously explored: freedom, discipleship, and calling. Rather, worship and prayer are circumscribed both by these personal qualities and by the communal existence in the church, which is the subject of the next chapter.

The two statements below by Bullinger enunciate worship and prayer as heartfelt supplication. After this comes John Calvin's advice on the four rules of right prayer. Then follows a standard hymn of Reformed worship. The next statement, from the Westminster Confession, is less focused on worship as response and more designed to enjoin worship as a duty. Finally, the sketches of Reformed sanctuaries from the sixteenth to the eighteenth centuries give visual testimony to a theology and experience of worship as the believing community focusing together on the centrality of Word and Sacraments.

BIBLIOGRAPHY

Hughes Oliphant Old, *Worship, That Is Reformed According to Scripture*, Guides to the Reformed Tradition (Atlanta: John Knox, 1984). *Liturgies of the Western Church*, selected and introduced by Bard Thompson (Philadelphia: Fortress, 1961), chaps. 5–12.

Heinrich Bullinger: Adoration and Invocation

SOURCE

Heinrich Bullinger, "Of Adoring or Worshipping, of Invocating or Calling Upon, and of Serving the Only, Living, True, and Everlasting God," in *Decades* 4:199, 206.

ADORATION

[T]o adore is to reverence and respect God, to bequeath ourselves wholly unto him, and to cleave inseparably unto him, upon him only and alone to hang in all things, and to have recourse unto him in all our necessities whatsoever. Furthermore, the outward adoration doth immediately, when it is needful and ability granted, follow a mind rightly endued with true faith and holy fear of God. For adoration is two-fold, or of two sorts: one of the mind or spirit, which is inward, sound, sincere and true; another of the body, which is outward, unsound, counterfeit, and false, which may proceed from him in whom there is no sparkle of religion. True adoration is the fruit of true faith and holy fear of God; namely, a lowly or suppliant yielding and humble consecrating, whereby we bequeath ourselves, yield and submit ourselves, unto our God, whom as we understand to be our best and most merciful Father, so to be our most high and almighty God: upon him therefore alone we do wholly depend, and to him only we have respect: which also forthwith, so soon as occasion is ministered unto us, we express and testify by outward adoration.

INVOCATION

That invocation therefore or calling upon God, whereof at this time we entreat, is a lifting up of man's mind to God in great necessity or in some desire, and a most ardent craving of counsel and assistance by faith; and also a bequeathing or committing of ourselves into the protection of God, and as it were a betaking of ourselves to his sanctuary and only safeguard. In invocation therefore (true invocation, I mean) a faithful mind is first of all required, which doth acknowledge God to be the author and only giver of all good gifts; who is willing to hear them that call upon him, and is able to grant us all our requests and desires whatsoever. An uncessant and ardent petition or beseeching is also required.

John Calvin: Four Rules of Prayer
SOURCE
Institutes III.1.1–11, pp. 850–64 (edited).

It is, therefore, by the benefit of prayer that we reach those riches which are laid up for us with the Heavenly Father. For there is a communion of men with God by which, having entered the heavenly sanctuary, they appeal to him in person concerning his promises in order to experience, where necessity so demands, that what they believed was not vain, although he had promised it in word alone. Therefore we see that to us nothing is promised to be expected from the Lord, which we are not also bidden to ask of him in prayers. So true is it that we dig up by prayer the treasures that were pointed out by the Lord's gospel, and which our faith has gazed upon.

Now for framing prayer duly and properly, let this be the first rule: that we be disposed in mind and heart as befits those who enter conversation with God. This we shall indeed attain with respect to the mind if it is freed from carnal cares and thoughts by which it can be called or led away from right and pure contemplation of God, and then not only devotes itself completely to prayer but also, in so far as this is possible, is lifted and carried beyond itself.

Let this be the second rule: that in our petitions we ever sense our own insufficiency, and earnestly pondering how we need all that we seek, join with this prayer an earnest—nay, burning—desire to attain it. For many perfunctorily intone prayers after a set form, as if discharging a duty to God.

Now the godly must particularly beware of presenting themselves before God to request anything unless they yearn for it with sincere affection of heart, and at the same time desire to obtain it from him. Indeed, even though in those things which we seek only to God's glory we do not seem at first glance to be providing for our own need, yet it is fitting that they be sought with no less ardor and eagerness. When, for example, we pray that "his name be sanctified" [Matt. 6:9; Luke 11:2], we should, so to speak, eagerly hunger and thirst after that sanctification.

To this let us join a third rule: that anyone who stands before God to pray, in his humility giving glory completely to God, abandon all thought of his own glory, cast off all notion of his own worth, in fine, put away all self-assurance—lest if we claim for ourselves anything, even the least bit, we should become vainly puffed up, and perish at his presence. We have repeated examples of this submission, which levels all haughtiness, in God's servants; each one of whom, the holier he is, the more he is cast down when he presents himself before the Lord.

The fourth rule is that, thus cast down and overcome by true humility, we should be nonetheless encouraged to pray by a sure hope that our prayer will be answered.

Praising God in Song

SOURCE

Hymn: "All People That on Earth Do Dwell" (1561), from Psalm 100; ascribed to William Kethe.

All people that on earth do dwell,
 Sing to the Lord with cheerful voice;
Him serve with mirth, His praise forth tell,
 Come ye before Him and rejoice. . . .

O enter then His gates with praise,
 Approach with joy His courts unto;
Praise, laud, and bless His name always,
 For it is seemly so to do.

Westminster Confession: A Summary of Worship

SOURCE

"Of Religious Worship and the Sabbath Day," Westminster Confession of Faith (1645), chap. 21, in Schaff, *Creeds* 3:646–49.

V. The reading of the Scriptures with godly fear; the sound preaching; and conscionable hearing of the Word, in obedience unto God with understanding, faith, and reverence; singing of psalms with grace in the heart; as, also, the due administration and worthy receiving of the sacraments instituted by Christ; are all parts of the ordinary religious worship of God: besides religious oaths, vows, solemn fastings, and thanksgivings upon several occasions; which are, in their several times and seasons, to be used in an holy and religious manner.

VI. Neither prayer, nor any other part of religious worship, is now under the gospel, either tied unto or made more acceptable by any place in which it is performed, or towards which it is directed: but God is to be worshiped every where in spirit and truth; as in private families daily, and in secret each one by himself, so more solemnly in the public assemblies, which are not carelessly or willfully to be neglected or forsaken, when God, by his Word or providence, calleth thereunto.

VII. As it is of the law of nature, that, in general, a due proportion of time be set apart for the worship of God; so, in his Word, by a positive, moral, and perpetual commandment, binding all men in all ages, he hath particularly appointed one day in seven for a Sabbath, to be kept holy unto him: which, from the beginning of the world to the resurrection of Christ, was the last day of the week; and, from the resurrection of Christ, was changed into the first day of the week, which in Scripture is called the Lord's day, and is to be continued to the end of the world, as the Christian Sabbath.

VIII. This Sabbath is then kept holy unto the Lord, when men, after a due preparing of their hearts, and ordering of their common affairs beforehand, do not only observe an holy rest all the day from their own works, words, and thoughts, about their worldly employments and recreations; but also are taken up the whole time in the public and private exercises of his worship, and in the duties of necessity and mercy.

The Architecture of Worship

SOURCE

Plate 7, "The Reformation Builds New Sanctuaries," in André Biéler, *Architecture in Worship*, trans. Odette and Donald Elliott (Edinburgh and London: Oliver & Boyd, 1965), 66–67.

See page 289.

THE PERSEVERANCE OF THE SAINTS: THE REMONSTRANCE AND DORT

For Calvin, faith and assurance of God's grace were synonymous. Moreover, God's sovereignty in salvation meant that the God who began the good work would carry it through to completion (Philippians 1). Arminius, on the other hand, was impressed with the tangible evidence of many who seemed once to have believed but then fall away. The differing perspectives are illustrated here in the Remonstrance and Dort.

SOURCES

(A) *Articuli Arminiani sive Remonstrantia* (1610) [Dutch: *De Remonstrantie en het Remonstrantisme*], Article V; ET: *The Five Arminian Articles*, in Schaff, *Creeds* 3:548–49.
(B) *Canones Synodi Dordrechtanae* (1618–19), Fifth Head of Doctrine, Articles I–III, IX–X; ET: "Of the Perseverance of the Saints," *Canons of the Synod of Dort*, in Schaff, *Creeds* 3:584–85.

BIBLIOGRAPHY

See pp. 94–97, 153–56, 222–24, 262–65, 302–6.

Fig. 1. *Le Temple du Paradis at Lyons* (1564)

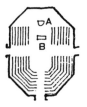

Fig. 2. *Le Grand Temple de la Rochelle* (1577) *by Philibert de l'Orme*

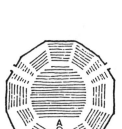

Fig. 3. *Le Temple de Rouen* (1601) *by Nicolas Genevais*

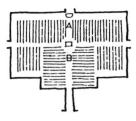

Fig. 4. *Le Temple de Charenton* (1623) *by Salomon de Brosse*

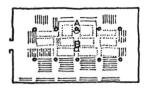

Fig. 5. *One of the Amsterdam sanctuaries* (1620–1631)

The seats indicated by dotted lines were removed when the Lord's Supper was celebrated.

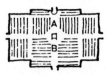

Fig. 6. *The church at Wadenswil* (1764)

Fig. 7. *The church at Horgen* (1780)

Fig. 8. *The church at Kloten* (1785)
(A) Pulpit (B) Communion Table

A. THE REMONSTRANCE

ART. V. That those who are incorporated into Christ by a true faith, and have thereby become partakers of his life-giving Spirit, have thereby full power to strive against Satan, sin, the world, and their own flesh, and to win the victory; it being well understood that it is ever through the assisting grace of the Holy Ghost; and that Jesus Christ assists them through his Spirit in all temptations, extends to them his hand, and if only they are ready for the conflict, and desire his help, and are not inactive, keeps them from falling, so that they, by no craft or power of Satan, can be misled nor plucked out of Christ's hands, according to the Word of Christ, John x.28: "Neither shall any man pluck them out of my hand." But whether they are capable, through negligence, of forsaking again the first beginnings of their life in Christ, of again returning to this present evil world, of turning away from the holy doctrine which was delivered them, of losing a good conscience, of becoming devoid of grace, that must be more particularly determined out of the Holy Scripture, before we ourselves can teach it with the full permission of our minds.

B. THE SYNOD OF DORT

ART. I. Whom God calls, according to his purpose, to the communion of his Son our Lord Jesus Christ, and regenerates by the Holy Spirit, he delivers also from the dominion and slavery of sin in this life; though not altogether from the body of sin and from the infirmities of the flesh, so long as they continue in this world.

ART. II. Hence spring daily sins of infirmity, and hence spots adhere to the best works of the saints, which furnish them with constant matter for humiliation before God, and flying for refuge to Christ crucified; for mortifying the flesh more and more by the spirit of prayer and by holy exercises of piety; and for pressing forward to the goal of perfection, till being at length delivered from this body of death, they are brought to reign with the Lamb of God in heaven.

ART. III. By reason of these remains of indwelling sin, and the temptations of sin and of the world, those who are converted could not persevere in a state of grace if left to their own strength. But God is faithful, who having conferred grace, mercifully confirms and powerfully preserves them therein, even to the end.

ART. IX. Of this preservation of the elect to salvation, and of their perseverance in the faith, true believers for themselves may and do obtain assurance according to the measure of their faith, whereby they arrive at the certain persuasion that they ever will continue true and living members of the Church; and that they experience forgiveness of sins, and will at last inherit eternal life.

ART. X. This assurance, however, is not produced by any peculiar revelation contrary to, or independent of the Word of God, but springs from faith in God's promises, which he has most abundantly revealed in his Word for our comfort; from the testimony of the Holy Spirit, witnessing with our spirit, that we are children and heirs of God (Rom. viii. 16); and, lastly, from a serious and holy desire to preserve a good conscience, and to perform good works. And if the elect of God were deprived of this solid comfort, that they shall finally obtain the victory, and of this infallible pledge or earnest of eternal glory, they would be of all men the most miserable.

6

THE CHURCH

THE CALLING AND MISSION OF THE CHURCH

John Calvin: The Priesthood of All Believers

For Protestants, the relation between God and humanity does not require the mediation of priests or ecclesiastical structures. All believers are themselves priests who may make intercession before God on their own behalf and for their fellow human beings. The Reformed appropriated this belief directly from Luther's Reformation theology.[1] Its effect was to relativize ecclesiastical structures and emphasize the responsibility of each believer for living unto righteousness.

SOURCES

(A) *Institutes* II.15.6, p. 502. **(B)** John Calvin, Commentary: 1 Peter 2:9; *CO* 55; ET: In *Calvin's New Testament Commentaries* 12:266.

A. FROM THE *INSTITUTES*

For we who are defiled in ourselves, yet are priests in him, offer ourselves and our all to God, and freely enter the heavenly sanctuary that the sacrifices of prayers and praise that we bring may be acceptable and sweet-smelling before God. . . . For we, imbued with his holiness in so far as he has consecrated us to the Father with himself, although we

---

1. For the classical statement of this doctrine, see Martin Luther, *Die Freiheit eines Christenmenschen* (1520), WA 7:49–73; ET: *The Freedom of a Christian*, trans. W. A. Lambert, revised by Harold J. Grimm, in *Career of the Reformer: I*, Luther's Works, 55 vols., ed. Jaroslav Pelikan and Helmut T. Lehmann (Philadelphia: Fortress, 1955–), 31:329–77. See also T. W. Manson, *Ministry and Priesthood, Christ's and Ours* (London: Epworth, 1958).

would otherwise be loathsome to him, please him as pure and clean—and even as holy.

B. FROM 1 PETER 2:9

In the words "a royal priesthood" there is a striking inversion of the words of Moses. He says, "a priestly kingdom," but the same thing is meant. What Peter means is this: Moses called your fathers a sacred kingdom, because the whole people enjoyed as it were a royal freedom, and from their body the priests were chosen; both dignities were therefore joined together; but now you are royal priests, and that in a more excellent way, because you are each consecrated in Christ to be both the associates of his kingdom, and partakers of his priesthood. Though the fathers had something like what you have, yet you far excel them. After the wall of partition has been pulled down by Christ, we are now gathered from every nation, and the Lord bestows these high titles on all whom He makes his people.

Heinrich Bullinger: The Church Universal

Heinrich Bullinger's description of the church displays with classic clarity the tension between the general and the particular in Reformed theology. The church has a universal embrace, containing all the elect in whatever place and from whatever time. But concurrently, as a people of the called and committed, the pure church includes only the "truly faithful and holy." This tension is an abiding one in Reformed theology and practice.

SOURCE

Bullinger, "Of the Holy Catholic Church," *Decades*, in *Zwingli and Bullinger*, 189–90, 292, 293.

The Church is the whole company and multitude of the faithful, as it is partly in heaven and partly remains still upon earth: and as it agrees plainly in unity of faith or true doctrine, and in the lawful partaking of the sacraments: for it is not divided, but united and joined together as it were in one house and fellowship.

This Church is usually called catholic, that is to say, universal. For it sends out its branches into all places of the wide world, in all times and all ages; and it comprehends generally all the faithful the whole world over. For the Church of God is not tied to any one region, nation, or kindred; to condition, age, sex, or kind: all the faithful generally and each one in particular, wherever they may be, are citizens and members of this Church. St. Paul the apostle says: "There is neither Jew nor Greek, neither bondman nor free, neither man nor woman: for ye be all one in Christ Jesus."

The Church is distinguished into the two parts, the Church triumphant and the Church militant. The Church triumphant is the great company of holy spirits in heaven, triumphing because of the victory which has now been won against the world, and sin and the devil, and enjoying the vision of God, in which there consists the fulness of all kinds of joy and pleasure, and concerning which they set forth God's glory and praise his goodness for ever. . . .

The Church militant is a congregation of men upon earth, professing the name and religion of Christ, and still fighting in the world against the devil, sin, the flesh and the world, in the camp and tents and under the banner of our Lord Christ. This Church again must be taken in two ways. For either it must be taken strictly, in which case it comprises only those who are not only called but are in actual fact the Church, the faithful and elect of God, lively members, knit unto Christ not merely with outward bands or marks but in spirit and faith, and often by the latter without the former, of which we shall speak later. This inward and invisible Church of God may well be termed the elect bride of Christ, known only to God, who alone knows who are his. . . .

Or the Church in the wider sense comprises not only those who are truly faithful and holy, but also those who although they have no true or unfeigned faith and are not clean and holy in the conversation of their lives do acknowledge and profess true religion together with true believers and holy men of God, approving and accepting virtues and reproving evil, and not as yet separating themselves from the unity of this holy Church militant. From this standpoint not even the wicked and hypocrites (as we find that there were in the Church of the time of Christ and the apostles, such as Judas, Ananias and Sapphira, Simon Magus, and also Demas, Hymenaeus, Alexander and many others) are excluded and put out of the Church, which Church may well be described as the outward and visible Church. But this Church again must be thought of either in respect of its individual parts or the whole. It has to be considered both generally and in particular. And the particular Church is that Church which consists of a certain number and is known by the name of some definite place: for it takes its name from the place, being called by the name of some city, like the churches of Zurich and Berne, etc. . . .

But as we began to say, the catholic Church of God has continued with us from age to age from the very first, and at this very time it is dispersed throughout the whole world, both visibly and invisibly; and the Lord's people and God's house shall remain upon the earth to the world's end. For there has never yet been any world, neither shall there be any age, in which God has not sanctified or will not sanctify some men to himself, in whom he may dwell, and that they shall be his flock and holy house; for the testimonies of the old-time prophets also record that the Church is perpetual. . . .

The Savoy Declaration: The Gathered Church

The Savoy Declaration, which consists in a modification of the Westminster Confession, is the principal statement of church polity for the Congregational wing of the Reformed tradition. In contrast to the republican philosophy of the Presbyterians, in which authority resides in the wider organization of the presbytery or classis, Savoy vests power democratically in each individual congregation. It also pushes Reformed theology more in the direction of a "pure" church.

SOURCE

"Of the Institution of Churches," The Savoy Declaration (1658), in Schaff, *Creeds* 3:724.

BIBLIOGRAPHY

G. F. Nuttall, *Visible Saints: The Congregational Way, 1640–1660* (Oxford: Basil Blackwell, 1957).

III. Those thus called (through the Ministry of the Word by his Spirit) he commandeth to walk together in particular Societies or Churches, for their mutual edification and the due performance of that public Worship which he requireth of them in this world.

IV. To each of these Churches thus gathered, according unto his mind declared in his Word, he hath given all that Power and Authority which is any way needful for their carrying on that Order in Worship and Discipline which he hath instituted for them to observe with Commands and Rules for the due and right exerting and executing of that Power.

V. These particular Churches thus appointed by the Authority of Christ, and intrusted with power from him for the ends before expressed, are each of them as unto those ends the seat of that Power which he is pleased to communicate to his Saints or Subjects in this World, so that as such they receive it immediately from himself.

Anna Maria van Schuurman:
The True Church

With its emphasis on sanctification, Reformed theology is naturally concerned with holy obedience. It has thus sought to strike a balance for the
church between being in the world yet not of the world, between embracing
all people and being a company of the committed.

The Labadists pushed the Reformed emphasis on holiness more radically
toward the sectarian alternative. They espoused a return to the purity of the
primitive church, and over the years they became increasingly separatist in
polity. The *Eukleria* of Anna Maria van Schuurman was among the most
important of the Labadist writings. Van Schuurman decries the vices of "Christendom" which, since Constantine, has entered into an unholy compromise
with worldly powers. The message here is that God is willing to pour out the
full measure of the Spirit upon any who will forsake the Babylonian captivity
of the church and make righteousness their aim.

The Labadists endured for about seventy years in the Netherlands and in
colonial Maryland. Notwithstanding the group's pure church ideal, many of
Labadie's followers remained within the Reformed church to work for evangelical renewal.

SOURCE

Anna Maria van Schuurman, *Eukleria, seu Melioris Partis Electio pars secunda,
Historiam vitae ejus usque ad mortem persequens* (Amsterdam: J. Van de Velde, 1684),
115–16, trans. Iain S. Maclean and W. S. Johnson.

BIBLIOGRAPHY

See pp. 14–16, 265–66, above, and 323–24, below. See also Ernst Troeltsch, *The Social
Teaching of the Christian Churches*, trans. Olive Wyon, 2 vols. (London: George Allen &
Unwin; New York: Macmillan, 1931; reprint: Louisville, Ky.: Westminster/John Knox,
1992). Note Troeltsch's discussion of the way in which Calvinism links up with sectarian
movements in the seventeenth century.

[I]t did not please the most wise God and most sovereign Lord of all
to dispense his gifts in such a manner that the churches closely succeeding that first Jerusalem church might obtain the abundance of the Holy
Spirit. And so that first grace [invested in the first Jerusalem church]
was gradually removed from degenerate "Christendom," so that it might
be given over to the "mystery of iniquity" and to the universal [spirit of]
anti-Christ. Particularly in the time of Constantine the Great (ca. 312)
the world crept into the church; or rather in its customary manner it
[the world] began to be let in to the church.

Even if we grant that "Christendom" is to be found indefinitely in the world, however, no one ought to think there is any age in which this prophecy is not being fulfilled among the truly faithful: "For as many as are sons of God are led by the Spirit of God," [Rom. 8:14] "And wherever two or three are gathered together, Christ is in the midst of them" [Matt. 18:20]. [This shall be accomplished] without fail through his Spirit, who is the light and leader of these [truly faithful] ones. [Conversely,] . . . "whoever does not have the Spirit of Christ, that one is not of him" [Rom. 8:9]. For that one is not a Christian, nor can that one be named "Christian" in any proper way. But by contrast, we [who are truly faithful] stand with the words of sacred scripture: that in those latter times, after the fall of Babylon and the binding of Satan, and after the entry of the Gentiles into the Kingdom of Christ, and, finally, after the conversion of all the Jews, [all] those universal and illustrious prophecies will be completely fulfilled, first from the Old Testament and then from the New. . . .

THE MARKS OF THE CHURCH

The Word Preached and the Sacraments Rightly Administered

Protestantism sought to place the church upon a different foundation than that which was perceived in Rome. As the Ten Theses of Berne, a 1528 Reformed confession, put it:

> The holy, Christian Church, whose only Head is Christ, is born of the Word of God, abides in the same, and does not listen to the voice of a stranger.[2]

Early Protestants believed a true church to exist in those places, but only those places, in which they found the gospel preached and the sacraments rightly administered.[3] In this pairing, the preaching of the Word held the primacy, for it was the "abiding mark" that rendered all else within the church intelligible. The harsh condemnation of "synagogues of the devil" in the Genevan Confession below is mitigated, but only somewhat, by Calvin's acknowledgment that vestiges of the church still exist among the Roman Catholics.

SOURCES

(A) French: *Confession de la Foy*; Latin: *Confessio Fidei* (1536), par. 10; *CO* 9:693–700, 5:355–362; ET: *The Genevan Confession*, in *Treatises* 31; see also *CO* 22:33–74. **(B)** *Institutes* IV.3.12, p. 1052.

2. The Ten Theses of Berne, in Leith, *Creeds*, 129.
3. Augsburg Confession (1530), article 7, in Schaff, *Creeds* 3:58–72.

A. GENEVAN CONFESSION

While there is one only Church of Jesus Christ, we always acknowl-edge that necessity requires companies of the faithful to be distributed in different places. Of these assemblies each one is called Church. But in as much as all companies do not assemble in the name of our Lord, but rather to blaspheme and pollute him by their sacrilegious deeds, we believe that the proper mark by which to discern the Church of Jesus Christ is that his holy gospel be purely and faithfully preached, pro-claimed, heard, and kept, that his sacraments be properly administered, even if there be imperfections and faults, as there always will be among men. On the other hand, where the Gospel is not declared, heard, and received, there we do not acknowledge the form of the Church. Hence the churches governed by the ordinances of the pope are rather syna-gogues of the devil than Christian churches.

B. JOHN CALVIN

However, when we categorically deny to the papists the title of *the* church, we do not for this reason impugn the existence of churches among them. Rather we are only contending about the true and lawful constitution of the church, required in the communion not only of the sacraments (which are the signs of profession) but also especially of doctrine.

Heinrich Bullinger: Outward and Inward Marks

This is a continuation of Bullinger's sermon encountered earlier (pp. 300–302). It is one of the finest sixteenth-century statements on the nature of the church.

SOURCE

Heinrich Bullinger, "Of the Holy Catholic Church," *Decades*, in *Zwingli and Bullinger*, 299–302, 304–305 (edited).

Now since we have said that the Church militant upon earth is marked by God with certain tokens and marks by which it may be known in this world, it follows that we must now speak of those outward marks of the Church of God. And there are two particular and principal marks, the sincere preaching of the Word of God, and the lawful partaking of the sacraments of Christ. There are some who add to these the study of godliness and unity, patience in affliction, and the calling on the name of God by Christ, but we include these in the two already mentioned. . . .

St. Paul writing to the Ephesians says: "Christ gave himself for the congregation, that he might sanctify it, and cleanse it in the fountain of water through the word." In this testimony of the apostle you have the marks of the Church, that is, the Word and the sacrament by which Christ makes to himself a Church. For with his grace he calls, with the blood of Christ he purifies: and he proclaims this by his Word to be received with faith, and seals it with sacraments, in order that the faithful should have no doubts concerning their salvation obtained through Christ. Now these things properly belong to the faithful and holy members. . . .

Now properly (as I said earlier) all these testimonies belong to the elect members of God, who are endued with faith and true obedience. They do not properly belong to hypocrites who are without faith and due obedience. Yet because these too hear the voice of the shepherd outwardly, and ensue virtue, and openly or outwardly are annexed to the elect and true believers in the partaking of the sacraments, indeed, to the true body of Christ, for the sake of the outward signs they are reckoned to be in the Church so long as they do not depart from it. On this point, for the sake of perspicuity, having treated of the marks of the Church, we must now add that it is as a common rule[1] that these marks declare and note the members of the Church. For there are certain special members who although they lack these marks are not excluded from the society and communion of the true Church of Christ. For it is most certain that there are many in the world who do not hear the ordinary preaching of God's Word, or come into the company of those that call upon God, or receive the sacraments: not because they despise them, or find pleasure in being absent from sermons and the preaching of God's Word[2] but because through necessity, such as imprisonment or sickness or the constraint of other evils, they cannot attain to that which they earnestly desire; and yet for all that they are true and lively members of Christ and of the catholic Church. In times past the Lord instituted or appointed to[3] the people of Israel a visible Church which he established by a certain law and set forth by visible signs. If any man despised this Church, or refused when he was able to hear the doctrine of the Church, or to enter in among the holy company and do sacrifice, or railed at it, or instead of the appointed order of worshipping God embraced some other kind, he was certainly not reckoned to be of the order and number of the people of God. And yet it is certain that there was an innumerable company of men dispersed throughout the whole world among the Gentiles who never did or could communicate with this visible company and congregation of God's people, and yet they were still holy members of this society and communion, and the friends of almighty God. . . . Therefore the Word and sacraments are by common decree the marks of the Church, but they do not separate or mark off from the communion and society of the faithful those believers who by some necessity are shut out from the visible company of the faithful. . . .

Apart from these outward marks of the Church which true believers have in common with hypocrites, there are certain inward marks which belong specially to the godly alone: or if you prefer, call them rather bonds or peculiar gifts. It is these which make the outward marks to be fruitful and make men worthy and acceptable in the sight of God if for some necessary cause the outward marks are absent. For without them no man can please God. Therefore in them we have the true mark[4] of God's children. They are the fellowship of God's Spirit, a sincere faith, and twofold charity, for by these the faithful, as true and lively members of Christ, are united and knit together, first to their head Christ, and then to all members of the body ecclesiastical. And the consideration of this point belongs chiefly to the knowledge of the true Church of God, which although it tolerates rotten members is not defiled by them through their outward conjunction, for by continual study it labours by all means to keep itself undefiled to God. And first of all the evangelical and apostolic doctrine teaches us that Christ is joined to us by his Spirit, and that we are tied to him in mind or spirit by faith, that he may live in us and we in him.

1. Lat. *lege communi.*
2. Lat. omits "and . . . God's Word."
3. Lat. *in populo.*
4. Lat. *typus.*

Jacob Arminius and Hugo Grotius: The Ecumenical Church

The unity of the church is guaranteed by God; but on a human level this unity is threatened by the church's bitter and often bloody fragmentation. In times of schism, ecclesiastical disorder, and religious wars, Reformed Christians concerned for the unity and peace of the church have sought irenic remedies. For example, Calvin considered the possibility of an ecumenical council.[4]

4. John Calvin, Letter to Thomas Cranmer (1552), in *Letters of John Calvin*, ed. Jules Bonnet, 4 vols. (Philadelphia, 1858), 2:345–48. See also *Calvin's Ecclesiastical Advice*, trans. Mary Beaty and Benjamin W. Farley (Louisville, Ky: Westminster/John Knox, 1991), 46–48, and sources cited therein.

Moreover, Pierre du Moulin, James I, and others collaborated at the Synod of Tonneins in 1614 to propose that the confessions of the Reformed churches be taken together to formulate one confession for all. Similarly, the liberal Calvinist John de Serres proposed an ecumenical council that would even include the Roman Catholics.[5]

Two figures who were to become casualties of religious infighting within the Reformed community proposed blueprints for dialogue and ecumenical tolerance just a few years prior to the rather intolerant Synod of Dort (1618–19). "On Reconciling Religious Dissensions" was Arminius's 1606 rectoral address at the University of Leyden. The "Meletius, or Letter on the Points of Agreement Between Christians," which was only discovered in 1984, was written by Hugo Grotius probably for The Hague Conference of 1611, a conference which called upon Remonstrants and Counter-Remonstrants to exercise mutual tolerance. Both Arminius and Grotius advocate humility, given the elusive nature of ascertaining truth, and they propose that the articles of religion to which one must subscribe be restricted to only those strictly necessary for salvation.

SOURCES

(A) Jacob Arminius, "On Reconciling Religious Dissensions Among Christians" (1606), in *Jacobi Arminii Orationes itemque tractatus*, 2d ed. (Leyden, 1613), 114–50; ET: In Arminius, *Works* 1:471–73 (edited). (B) Hugo Grotius, *Meletius Sive De Iis Quae Inter Christianos Conveniunt Epistola/Meletius or Letter on the Points of Agreement Between Christians* (1611), trans. and ed. Guillaume H. M. Posthumus Meyjes (Leiden: E. J. Brill, 1988), 133–34 (edited).

BIBLIOGRAPHY

John McNeill, *Unitive Protestantism* (Richmond, Va.: John Knox, 1974). R. Rouse and S. C. Neill, eds., *A History of the Ecumenical Movement* (Philadelphia: Westminster, 1967). See pp. 94–97, 153–56, 222–24, 262–65, 288–91, 302–6.

A. JACOB ARMINIUS

These necessary concessions we shall obtain from our minds without much difficulty, if the following four considerations become the objects of our sedulous attention:

FIRST. *How extremely difficult it is to discover the truth on all subjects, and to avoid error.*

---

5. See W. Brown Patterson, "James I and the Huguenot Synod of Tonneins of 1614," *Harvard Theological Review* 65 (1972) 241–70; idem, "Jean de Serres and the Politics of Religious Pacification, 1594–98," in *Church, Society and Politics*, ed. Derek Baker, Studies in Church History 12 (Oxford: Basil Blackwell, 1975), 223–44.

SECONDLY. That those who hold erroneous opinions have been induced through *ignorance* to adopt them, is far more probable, than that *malice* has influenced them to contrive a method of consigning themselves and other people to eternal destruction.

THIRDLY. It is possible that they who entertain these mistaken sentiments, are of the number of the elect, whom God, it is true, may have permitted to fall, but only with this design,—that he may raise them up with the greater glory. How then can we indulge ourselves in any harsh or unmerciful resolutions against these persons, who have been destined to possess the heavenly inheritance, who are our brethren, the members of Christ, and not only the servants but the sons of the Lord Most High?

LASTLY. Let us place ourselves in the circumstances of an adversary, and let him in return assume the character which we sustain; since it is as possible for us, as it is for him, to hold wrong principles. When we have made this experiment, we may be brought to think, that the very person whom we had previously thought to be in error, and whose mistakes in our eyes had a destructive tendency, may perhaps have been given to us by God, that out of his mouth we may learn the truth which has hitherto been unknown to us.

To these four reflections, let there be added, *a consideration of all those articles of religion respecting which there exists on both sides a perfect agreement.* These will perhaps be found to be so numerous and of such great importance, that when a comparison is instituted between them, and the others which may properly be made the subjects of controversy, the latter will be found to be few in number and of small consequence. This is the very method which a certain famous prince in France is reported to have adopted, when Cardinal Lorraine attempted to embroil the Lutherans, or those who adhered to the Augustan Confession, with the French Protestants, that he might interrupt and neutralize the salutary provisions of the Conference at Poissy, which had been instituted between the Protestants and the Papists.

But since it is customary after long and grievous wars, to enter into a truce, or a cessation from hostilities, prior to the conclusion of a treaty of peace and its final ratification; and, since, during the continuance of a truce, while every hostile attempt is laid aside, peaceful thoughts are naturally suggested, till at length a general solicitude is expressed with regard to the method in which a firm peace and lasting reconciliation may best be effected;—it is my special wish, that there may now be among us a similar cessation from the asperities of religious warfare, and that both parties would abstain from writings full of bitterness, from sermons remarkable only for the invectives which they contain, and from the unchristian practice of mutual anathematizing and execration. Instead of these, let the controversialists substitute *writings full of moderation,* in which the matters of controversy may, without respect of persons, be clearly explained and proved by cogent arguments: Let such sermons be preached as are calculated to excite the minds of the people to the love and study of truth, charity, mercy, long-suffering, and concord; which may inflame the minds both of Governors and people with a desire of concluding a pacification, and may make them willing to carry into effect such a remedy as is, of all others, the best accommodated to remove dissensions.

That remedy is, *an orderly and free convention of the parties that differ from each other:* In such an assembly, (called by the Greeks a *synod,* and by the Latins a *council,*) after the different sentiments have been compared together, and the various reasons of each have been weighed, in the fear of the Lord, and with calmness and accuracy, let the members deliberate, consult, and determine what the word of God declares concerning the matters in controversy, and afterwards let them by common consent promulge and declare the result to the Churches.

B. HUGO GROTIUS

Now when there is a fight over precepts, it hardly ever involves ethics—for these have definite and unequivocal rules—but deals with those matters which everybody establishes for himself for the sake of preserving order, and in which a short cut to concord is to leave every man to his own discretion. . . . Many controversies over dogmas are merely due to words which must be avoided for consensus to appear. With any further quarrels we have to check whether they concern matters which it is necessary to know. At this point we have, first of all, to correct the error that generally more dogmas are formulated than ethics require. Indeed it is impossible that everybody should agree about everything. Moreover, everybody sticks obstinately to what he has once learnt, however wrong. . . .

The remedy for this disease will therefore consist in limiting the number of necessary articles of faith to those few that are most self-evident; and to inquire into the other doctrinal points which lead to the perfection of pious wisdom without prejudice, preserving charity and under the guidance of the Holy Scriptures. Finally, if people err even on matters of some importance, the only thing we can do is not to accuse them with hateful incriminations for the results of their unintended error, but to relieve the misery of their ignorance by a kindly explanation. For if we have to forgive sins committed against rules that are known and understood, there surely is no reason not to forgive a sin committed in spite of oneself? Salvianus gave a memorable statement on this matter when he wrote about the most odious error of his time; what better way to conclude this discourse than by quoting his words: "Granted they are heretics, but they are so unwittingly. That is to say that they are heretics in our eyes, but not in theirs. For they so much believe themselves to be Catholics that they bring us into disrepute by calling us heretics. So what they are in our eyes, we are in theirs. [. . .] We have the truth, but they presume they have it. We honour God, but they are convinced that their creed is the right way to honour God. They do not observe their religious duties, but to them this is the highest religious duty. They are impious, but they think theirs is the true piety. So they do err, but they do so in good faith, not out of hatred of God but out of love for him, convinced that they honour and love the Lord. Although they do not have the right faith, yet they consider this the perfect love for God. Nobody except the Judge can know in what way they are to be punished for this erroneous belief on Judgement Day. I think that until that time God is patient with them, since He sees that though they do not have the right belief, their error results from a sincere conviction."

Discipline

Some Reformed theologians have added discipline as one of the marks of the church. The Scots Confession and the Belgic Confession are two prominent documents which take this position.

The Reformers had stressed subordination of discipline to the Word of God; this funded an evolution over the years toward relying more upon moral suasion than upon external coercion, although external constraint by no means disappeared during this period. John Cotton, early-seventeenth-century pastor of the First Church in Boston, held a democratic view of discipline as vesting in the people to govern themselves. There appears below a portion from his classic defense of the congregationalist system in colonial New England, *The Keyes of the Kingdom of Heaven.*

SOURCES

(A) French: *La Confession de foi des églises réformées Walonnes et Flammandes.* Latin: *Confessio Belgica* (Belgic Confession) (1561, rev. 1619), Art. 29; ET: "Of the Marks of the

True Church," in Schaff, *Creeds* 3:419–20 (contains both the original French text and ET); and in Cochrane, *Confessions*, 210–11. **(B)** "The Notes by which the True Kirk shall be Determined from the False," *The Confession of the Faith and Doctrine Believed and Professed by the Protestants of Scotland* (1560), Chapter 18, in Cochrane, *Confessions*, 176–77. **(C)** John Cotton, *The Keyes Of the Kingdom of Heaven, and Power thereof, according to the Word of God* (London, 1644); Boston: Tappan & Dennet, 1843), 20–21, 25 (orthography modified).

BIBLIOGRAPHY

Karl Barth, *The Knowledge of God and the Service of God According to the Teaching of the Reformation: Recalling the Scottish Confession of 1560*, The Gifford Lectures (1938), trans. J.L.M. Haire and Ian Henderson (London: Hodder & Stoughton, 1938). Martin Bucer, "The Ministry of the Discipline of Life and Manners," *De Regno Christi* (1550), in *Melanchthon and Bucer*, 240ff. *Institutes* IV.12.1–7, pp. 1229–35. John Knox, *History of the Reformation in Scotland*, 2 vols, ed. W. C. Dickinson (London: Thomas Nelson & Sons, 1949). Schaff, *Creeds* 1:502–8, 680–85.

A. THE BELGIC CONFESSION

The marks by which the true Church is known are these: If the pure doctrine of the gospel is preached therein; if she maintains the pure administration of the sacraments as instituted by Christ; if church discipline is exercised in punishing of sin; in short, if all things are managed according to the pure Word of God, all things contrary thereto rejected, and Jesus Christ acknowledged as the only Head of the Church. Hereby the true Church may certainly be known, from which no man has a right to separate himself.

B. THE SCOTS CONFESSION

The notes of the true Kirk, therefore, we believe, confess, and avow to be: first, the true preaching of the Word of God, in which God has revealed Himself to us, as the writings of the prophets and apostles declare; secondly, the right administration of the sacraments of Christ Jesus, with which must be associated the Word and promise of God to seal and confirm them in our hearts; and lastly, ecclesiastical discipline uprightly ministered, as God's Word prescribes, whereby vice is repressed and virtue nourished.

C. JOHN COTTON

The liberties of the Brethren, or of the Church consisting of them, are many and great.

1. The Church of Brethren hath the *power*, *privileges*, and *liberty* to choose their officers. . . .

2. It is the *privilege* or *liberty* the Church hath received to send forth one or more of their Elders, as the public service of Christ, and of the Church may require. . . .

3. The *Brethren* of the Church have the *power* and *liberty* of propounding any just exception against such as offer themselves to be admitted unto their communion, or unto the seals of it. . . .

4. As the *Brethren* have a *power* of order, and the *privilege* to expostulate with their Brethren, in case of private scandals, according to the rule, Matt. 18:15–16, so in case of public scandal, the whole Church of *Brethren* have *power* and *privilege* to join with the *Elders*, in inquiring, hearing, judging of public scandals; so as to bind notorious offenders and impenitents under censure, and to forgive the repentant. . . .

SACRAMENTS

Huldrych Zwingli and John Calvin on the Reformed Understanding of Sacraments

The Reformed tradition stood steadfast in its rejection of the Roman Catholic doctrine that the sacraments convey grace automatically in and of themselves (*ex opere operato*). In contrast, the Reformed asserted, as a logical extension of the belief in justification by grace through faith, that in the absence of faith there is no sacrament. But this did not mean that the sacraments were lacking in importance or that they were not attended by grace. The first selection is the list of the virtues of the sacraments prepared by Huldrych Zwingli, the second is an excerpt from Calvin's theology of sacraments.

SOURCES

(A) Huldrych Zwingli, *Fidei expositio* (1536) in *SS*; ET: "Of the Virtue of the Sacraments," *Exposition of the Christian Faith*, in *Zwingli and Bullinger*, 262–65. **(B)** *Institutes* IV.14.1–14, pp. 1277–90 (edited).

BIBLIOGRAPHY

For the sacraments in covenant theology, see Johannes Cocceius, "De Sacramentis Foederis gratiae," Caput LII, *Summa Theologiae* (1562), 278–79. The best contemporary statement of Reformed sacramental theology is Donald Baillie, *The Theology of the Sacraments* (New York: Charles Scribner's Sons, 1957). See also Ronald S. Wallace, *Calvin's Doctrine of Word and Sacrament* (Edinburgh: Oliver & Boyd, 1953; reprint: Tyler, Tex.: Geneva Divinity School Press, 1982).

A. HULDRYCH ZWINGLI: THE VIRTUE
OF THE SACRAMENTS

[U]nder the guise of piety we ought not to ascribe either to the Supper or to baptism anything that might jeopardize religion and truth. But does that mean that the sacraments have no virtue or power at all?

1. they are sacred and venerable things instituted and received by the great High Priest Christ himself. . . .

2. they testify to historical facts. . . .

3. they take the place and name of that which they signify. . . .

4. they represent high things. The value of all signs increases according to the value of that which they signify. . . .

5. the analogy between the signs and the things signified. . . .

6. the sacraments augment faith and are an aid to it. This is particularly true of the Supper. . . .

7. they act as an oath of allegiance. . . . So . . . the people of Christ are brought together as one body by the sacramental partaking of his body. . . .

(B) JOHN CALVIN: DEFINITION OF
THE SACRAMENTS

First, we must consider what a sacrament is. It seems to me that a simple and proper definition would be to say that it is an outward sign by which the Lord seals on our consciences the promises of his good will toward us in order to sustain the weakness of our faith; and we in turn attest our piety toward him in the presence of the Lord and of his angels and before men. Here is another briefer definition: one may call it a testimony of divine grace toward us, confirmed by an outward sign, with mutual attestation of our piety toward him.

Now, from the definition that I have set forth we understand that a sacrament is never without a preceding promise but is joined to it as a sort of appendix, with the purpose of confirming and sealing the promise itself, and of making it more evident to us and in a sense ratifying it. By this means God provides first for our ignorance and dullness, then for our weakness. Yet, properly speaking, it is not so much needed to confirm his Sacred Word as to establish us in faith in it. For God's truth is of itself firm and sure enough, and it cannot receive better confirmation from any other source than from itself. But as our faith is slight and feeble unless it be propped on all sides and sustained by every means, it trembles, wavers, totters, and at last gives way. Here our merciful Lord, according to his infinite kindness, so tempers himself to our capacity that, since we are creatures who always creep on the ground, cleave to the flesh, and, do not think about or even conceive of anything spiritual, he condescends to lead us to himself even by these earthly elements, and to set before us in the flesh a mirror of spiritual blessings. For if we were incorporeal (as Chrysostom says), he would give us these very things naked and incorporeal. Now, because we have souls engrafted in bodies, he imparts spiritual things under visible ones. Not that the gifts set before us in the sacraments are bestowed with the natures of the things, but that they have been marked with this signification by God. . . .

What our opponents commonly say is this: a sacrament consists of the word and the outward sign. For we ought to understand the word not as one whispered without meaning and without faith, a mere noise, like a magic incantation, which has the force to consecrate the element. Rather, it should, when preached, make us understand what the visible sign means. . . .

As to the confirmation and increase of faith (which I think I have already explained in clear terms), I should therefore like my readers to be reminded that I assign this particular ministry to the sacraments. Not that I suppose there is some secret force or other perpetually seated in them by which they are able to promote or confirm faith by themselves. Rather, I consider that they have been instituted by the Lord to the end that they may serve to establish and increase faith.

But the sacraments properly fulfill their office only when the Spirit, that inward teacher, comes to them, by whose power alone hearts are penetrated and affections moved and our souls opened for the sacraments to enter in. If the Spirit be lacking, the sacraments can accomplish nothing more in our minds than the splendor of the sun shining upon blind eyes, or a voice sounding in deaf ears. Therefore, I make such a division between Spirit and sacraments that the power to act rests with the former, and the ministry alone is left to the latter—a ministry empty and trifling, apart from the action of the Spirit, but charged with great effect when the Spirit works within and manifests his power.

From this something else follows; assurance of salvation does not depend upon participation in the sacrament, as if justification consisted in it. For we know that justification is lodged in Christ alone, and that it is communicated to us no less by the preaching of the gospel than by the seal of the sacrament, and without the latter can stand unimpaired.

Baptism

John Calvin: Baptism

Calvin's definition integrates baptism into his theology of reconciliation and the Christian life.

SOURCE

Institutes IV.15.1–6, pp. 1303–8.

Baptism is the sign of the initiation by which we are received into the society of the church, in order that, engrafted in Christ, we may be reckoned among God's children. Now baptism was given to us by God for these ends (which I have taught to be common to all sacraments): first, to serve our faith before him; secondly, to serve our confession before men. We shall treat in order the reasons for each aspect of its institution. Baptism brings three things to our faith which we must deal with individually. The first thing that the Lord sets out for us is that baptism should be a token and proof of our cleansing; or (the better to explain what I mean) it is like a sealed document to confirm to us that all our sins are so abolished, remitted, and effaced that they can never come to his sight, be recalled, or charged against us. For he wills that all who believe be baptized for the remission of sins [Matt. 28:19; Acts 2:38].

Accordingly, they who regarded baptism as nothing but a token and mark by which we confess our religion before men, as soldiers bear the insignia of their commander as a mark of their profession, have not weighed what was the chief point of baptism. It is to receive baptism with this promise: "He who believes and is baptized will be saved" [Mark 16:16].

Baptism also brings another benefit, for it shows us our mortification in Christ, and new life in him. Indeed (as the apostle says), "we have been baptized into his death," "buried with him into death, . . . that we may walk in newness of life" [Rom. 6:3–4]. By these words he not only exhorts us to follow Christ as if he had said that we are admonished through baptism to die to our desires by an example of Christ's death, and to be aroused to righteousness by the example of his resurrection. But he also takes hold of something far higher, namely, that through baptism Christ makes us sharers in his death, that we may be engrafted in it [Rom. 6:5, cf. Vg.].

Lastly, our faith receives from baptism the advantage of its sure testimony to us that we are not only engrafted into the death and life of

Christ, but so united to Christ himself that we become sharers in all his blessings. For he dedicated and sanctified baptism in his own body [Matt. 3:13] in order that he might have it in common with us as the firmest bond of the union and fellowship which he has deigned to form with us.

Herman Witsius: Infant Baptism

The basis for the Reformed practice of infant baptism is found in the prevenient action of God in the covenant. Who better then to explain the practice than one well-schooled in the seventeenth-century covenant theology, such as Herman Witsius? The practice is not merely an acquiescence in long-standing ecclesiastical tradition [infant baptism is well-documented from the second century on]; but here Witsius marshals the biblical basis for continuing to mark the children of believers with the sign of the covenant, in hopes that they too will one day own the covenant for themselves. Unlike Roman Catholic baptism, Reformed baptism is not thought to leave an indelible imprint on the soul; and unlike Anabaptist practice, the Reformed theology of baptism emphasizes not the faith of the believer—although for the Reformed, faith must surely be present—but the prevenient promise of God. Salvation rests not in the church's profession or practice but in the eternal will of God.

SOURCE

Herman Witsius, *De oeconomia foederium Dei cum hominibur libri quattuor* (1677), Book 4, Chapter 16; ET: "Of Baptism," *The Oeconomy of the Covenants Between God and Man* 3:409–14 (edited).

BIBLIOGRAPHY

Institutes IV.16.1–32, pp. 1324–59. John Calvin, *Brieve instruction pour armer tous bons fideles contre les erreurs de la secte commune des Anabaptistes* (Geneva, 1544), CO 7:49–142; ET: *Treatises Against the Anabaptists and Against the Libertines*, trans. and ed. Benjamin Wirt Farley (Grand Rapids: Baker, 1982), 44–158.

We readily acknowledge that there is no express and special command of God, or of Christ, concerning infant baptism: yet there are general commands from which this special command is deduced by evident consequence. For to begin with what is most general: God declared to Abraham that it was his constant and unchangeable will that the sign of the covenant should not be denied to those in covenant with him, when he said, Gen. 17:13, "And my covenant shall be in your flesh for an everlasting covenant." By these words he commands the sign of his covenant to be in the flesh of all the posterity of Abraham with which he has entered into a covenant of grace. From this injunction he infers (v. 14) the necessity of circumcision, because he gave it as a sign of the covenant. When therefore upon the change of the economy [of the covenants] he substituted in the place of circumcision another sign of the covenant, in consequence of that general command, all those in covenant are bound to take upon them the new sign. . . .

There is another command of Christ, Mt. 28:19, "Go ye therefore and (μαθητεύσατε) disciple all nations, baptizing them [in the name of the Father and the Son and the Holy Spirit."] There Christ commands disciples to be gathered into his school and sealed as persons in covenant with him with the seal of baptism. But it is evident when parents become the disciples of Christ their children are also accounted in the number of disciples. Just as among the Jews, together with the proselyte parents, their young children were initiated in the Jewish rites. It was not therefore necessary that Christ should expressly mention the baptism of infants. . . .

Peter supplies us with another argument, Acts 2:38, 39, "Be baptized every one of you in the name of Jesus Christ, for the remission of sins, and ye shall receive the gift of the Holy Spirit. For the promise is unto you, and to your children." . . . Who are we here to understand by the children who partake of the promise of grace, whether adults only actually called, who are capable of making a profession of faith, or also younger children and infants? The orthodox justly affirm the last: not only because mention simply is made of children without distinction of age; but also because God expressly promised to Abraham to be the God of his seed . . . [Gen. 17:7, 12]. We add that Christ permitted little children to come to him, laid his hands upon them, and declared, that of such was the kingdom of heaven, Mt. 16:13–15. But whom Matthew calls παιδία, "little children," Luke, chap. 18:15, calls βρέφη, "infants". . . [1 Pet. 2:2]. . . .

Let the fourth argument stand thus: It is unjustifiable to exclude from baptism those who are made partakers of the Holy Spirit [Acts 10:47]. . . . Even the children of believers have received the Holy Spirit: for otherwise they could neither be holy [1 Cor. 7:14] . . . nor be Christ's to whom none belongs who has not his Spirit [Rom 8:9], nor see the kingdom of heaven [Jn. 3:5]. . . .

Fifthly, they who belong to the church of God have a right to baptism. The reason is because baptism is the sign of association with and seal of initiation into the church [Acts 2:41 . . . Eph. 5:26]. . . . But that infants belong to the church appears from this, that when God commanded his church to be gathered together he did not suffer their "little ones, and those that sucked the breasts, to be absent [Dt. 29:10–11; Joel 2:16] and protests that "they were born unto him" [Ez. 16:20].

Sixthly, we argue from this, that baptism has succeeded in the [place] of circumcision. The apostle declares this, Col. 2:11–12 where he proves the abrogation of the ceremonial law, and especially of circumcision with respect to believers of the New Testament, from this consideration that the spiritual thing formerly signified and sealed by circumcision is now signified and sealed by baptism. . . .

Here certainly appears the extraordinary love of our God, in that as soon as we are born, and just as we come from our mother, he hath commanded us to be solemnly brought from her bosom, as it were, into his own arms. . . .

Lord's Supper

Huldrych Zwingli: Christ's "Sacramental" Presence in the Supper

Zwingli's theology of the presence of Christ in the Lord's Supper has been much maligned and misunderstood. In contrast to Calvin's affirmation of Christ's "real presence"[6] in the Supper, Zwingli is often accused of teaching a "real absence." This is a mistaken interpretation. Zwingli affirms wholeheartedly the presence of Christ in the Supper, and in his later theology he thinks of this not only as a "spiritual" presence in the hearts of believers but also as a "sacramental" presence which not only expresses faith but augments it as well: we "eat the body of Christ with the heart and the mind in conjunction with the sacrament." Precisely what this "sacramental" language means is debatable, but those who would impugn Zwingli for an impoverished view of the Supper should note that his theology of sacraments does contain a number of rich dimensions: it is a corporate act, by which believers remember Christ's sacrifice, offer thanksgiving for it, and are strengthened in their faith, whereby they confess their sins and pledge themselves, in ethical response to Christ's death, that they will engage in righteous activity in the world for the furtherance of God's reign.[7]

---

6. In actuality Calvin spoke little of "real" presence because he feared the term would be misunderstood in the Roman sense; instead, Calvin preferred to speak of a "true" presence (pp. 317–19, above).
7. Zwingli's sacramental theology evolved over an extended period of time. Zwingli leaned toward a "spiritual" view of eating and drinking in the Supper even prior to his elevation to the Gröstminster in 1518–19. During the so-called *First Disputation* in Zurich in 1523, Zwingli denied the repetition of Christ's sacrifice in the Roman Mass, holding rather that the Mass was a "memorial" to Jesus' suffering. At this time, however, Zwingli did not question whether the body and

SOURCE

Huldrych Zwingli, *Fidei expositio* (1531), in *SS*; ET: "The Presence of the Body of Christ in the Supper," *Exposition of the Christian Faith*, in *Zwingli and Bullinger*, 254–62.

BIBLIOGRAPHY

W. P. Stephens, *The Theology of Huldrych Zwingli* (Oxford: Clarendon, 1986), chaps. 9–11. B. A. Gerrish, "The Lord's Supper in the Reformed Confessions," *Theology Today* 23 (1966): 224–43.

To eat the body of Christ spiritually is equivalent to trusting with heart and soul upon the mercy and goodness of God through Christ, that is, to have the assurance of an unbroken faith that God will give us the forgiveness of sins and the joy of eternal salvation for the sake of his Son, who gave himself for us and reconciled the divine righteousness to us. For what can he withhold from us when he delivered up his only begotten Son?

If I may put it more precisely, to eat the body of Christ sacramentally is to eat the body of Christ with the heart and the mind in conjunction with the sacrament.

So then, when you come to the Lord's Supper to feed spiritually upon Christ, and when you thank the Lord for his great favour, for the redemption whereby you are delivered from despair, and for the pledge

blood were actually consumed (*The Defense of the Reformed Faith*, trans. E. J. Furcha, in vol. 1 of *Selected Writings of Huldrych Zwingli*, ed. H. Wayne Pipkin and Edward J. Furcha, Pittsburgh Theological Monographs [Allison Park, Penna.: Pickwick, 1984], 104). Later he moved toward a more resolutely symbolic view. In a November 1524 letter to Matthew Alber, Zwingli maintained that when Jesus says, "This is my body," in John 6, the word "is" means "signifies" (*Sämtliche Werke* 3:335–54; ET: *Selected Writings* 2:127–45). Zwingli would come to incorporate this exegesis into his later theology, and soon thereafter, in 1525, this move would precipitate a conflict with the Erasmian Catholic Joachim am Grüt before the city council. As a result of Zwingli's victory in this conflict, the Mass in Zurich was abolished and a form of the Supper thought to be more in accord with apostolic practice was instituted. (For Zwingli's exegetical arguments in response to am Grüt, see his *Subsidiary Essay on the Eucharist* [1525], *Sämtliche Werke* 4:458–504; ET: *Selected Writings* 2:187–231.) In accordance with the council's desires, the Supper was to be celebrated only four times a year.

After 1525 Zwingli engaged in a number of sacramental controversies with Luther and the Lutherans which culminated in the Marburg Colloquy in 1529. Again the presence of Christ's body and blood were at the heart of the dispute. Luther himself never wavered from a firm belief in the real presence of Christ's body and blood. Zwingli opposed Luther, although seldom by name, in a number of tracts and treatises prior to Marburg. In keeping with his zeal to preserve the separate integrity of God and humanity and each of Christ's two natures, Zwingli rejected the Lutheran doctrine of transubstantiation, as well as the belief in the ubiquity of Christ's body and "communication of attributes" (see pp. 201–6). The Reformed and Lutheran participants in the Colloquy (Zwingli himself was absent) failed to reach agreement, largely because of Zwingli's refusal to assent to the Lutheran language of "consubstantiation." After Marburg, Zwingli's writings contain more of the language of "sacrament" and "true presence," but he still maintained a considerable distance between himself and Luther (see his *Friendly Exegesis, Exposition of the Matter of the Eucharist to Martin Luther* [1527], in *Sämtliche Werke* 5:562-758; ET: *Selected Writings* 2:233–385).

whereby you are assured of eternal salvation, when you join with your brethren in partaking of the bread and wine which are the tokens of the body of Christ, then in the true sense of the word you eat him sacramentally. You do inwardly that which you represent outwardly, your soul being strengthened by the faith which you attest in the tokens.

But of those who publicly partake of the visible sacraments or signs, yet without faith, it cannot properly be said that they eat sacramentally. . . .

Now for some time there has been bitter contention amongst us as to what the sacraments or signs themselves either do or can do in the Supper. Our adversaries allege that the sacraments give faith, mediate the natural body of Christ, and enable us to eat it as substantially present. But we have good cause to think otherwise.

First, because no external things but only the Holy Spirit can give that faith which is trust in God. The sacraments do give faith, but only historical faith. All celebrations, monuments and statues give historical faith, that is, they remind us of some event, refreshing the memory like the feast of the passover amongst the Hebrews or the remission of debts at Athens, or it may be that they commemorate some victory like the stone at Ebenezer.

Now the Lord's Supper, too, does create faith in this way, that is, it bears sure witness to the birth and passion of Christ. But to whom does it bear witness? To believers and unbelievers alike. For whether they receive it or not, it testifies to all that which is of the power of the sacrament, the fact that Christ suffered. But only to the faithful and pious does it testify that he suffered for us. For it is only those who have been taught inwardly by the Spirit to know the mystery of the divine goodness who can know and believe that Christ suffered for us: it is they alone who receive Christ. For no one comes to Christ except the Father draw him. And Paul settles the whole dispute with a single word when he says: "Let a man examine himself and so let him eat of that bread and drink of that cup." Therefore if we are to examine ourselves before we come, it is quite impossible that the Supper should give faith: for faith must be present already before we come.

Second, we oppose the erroneous teaching of our adversaries when they argue that the natural body of Christ is presented to us in the symbols because that is the force and effect of the words: "This is my body." The argument is met by the words of Christ already adduced, which deny the continued presence of his body in the world. And if that was the force of the words, the body presented would be his passible body. For when he spoke the words he still had a mortal body: hence the disciples partook of his mortal body. For he did not possess two bodies, the one immortal and impassible, the other mortal. And if the apostles ate his mortal body, which do we eat? Naturally, the mortal body. But the body which once was mortal is now immortal and incorruptible.

Finally, we oppose our adversaries when they assert that it is the present, natural and essential body of Christ which is eaten: an assertion which is clean contrary to all religion. At the miraculous draught of fishes, when Peter became aware of the presence of Christ in divine power, he said, "Depart from me, for I am a sinful man, O Lord," for he was astonished. And do we desire to feed on his natural body like cannibals? As if anyone loved his children in such a way that he wished to devour and eat them. Or as if cannibals were not regarded as the most bestial of men. The centurion said: "I am not worthy that thou shouldest come under my roof." But Christ himself testified concerning him that he had not found so great faith, no, not in Israel. The greater and holier faith is, the more it is content to feed spiritually.

John Calvin: Christ's True Presence in the Supper

It is Calvin's—not Zwingli's—view of the Supper which has become normative for most Reformed Christians. Like Zwingli, Calvin thinks of the presence as a "visible sign" and maintains a certain reserve about Christ's presence as over against the Lutherans. But in contrast to Zwingli, Calvin wants to underscore the conviction that God truly effects in the believer the reality which is in the sacrament. The following brief passage is from a treatise Calvin wrote in French in 1540 during his sojourn at Strasbourg. During this time Calvin was especially concerned to negotiate a sacramental accord among the Reformed that would come down stronger on Christ's presence in the Supper than did Zwingli and forge a middle way between Luther and Rome.

SOURCE

John Calvin, *Petit traicté de la sainte cène de nostre Seigneur Jésus-Christ. Auquel est demonstrè la vraye institution, profit et utilité d'icelle* (Geneva, 1541); OS 1:503–30, pars. 12–15; ET: *Short Treatise on the Lord's Supper*, in *Calvin's Tracts and Treatises*, trans. Henry Beveridge, 3 vols. (Calvin Translation Society, 1849; reprint: Grand Rapids: Wm. B. Eerdmans, 1958), 2:170–72.

BIBLIOGRAPHY

Institutes IV.17–18, pp. 1359–1448. John Calvin, "A Communion Hymn," in *The Piety of John Calvin: An Anthology Illustrative of the Spirituality of the Reformer*, trans. and ed. Ford Lewis Battles, music ed. Stanley Tagg (Grand Rapids: Baker, 1978), 171. Brian A. Gerrish, "Gospel and Eucharist: John Calvin on the Lord's Supper," in idem, *The Old*

Protestantism and the New (Chicago: University of Chicago Press, 1982), 106–17. Killian McDonnell, *John Calvin, the Church, and the Eucharist* (Princeton: Princeton University Press, 1967). John Nevin, *The Mystical Presence: A Vindication of the Reformed or Calvinistic Doctrine of the Holy Eucharist* (1866); reissued as *The Mystical Presence and Other Writings on the Eucharist*, ed. Bard Thompson and George H. Bricker, Lancaster Series on the Mercersburg Theology 4 (Philadelphia and Boston: United Church Press, 1966).

12. How the Bread Is Called the Body, and the Wine the Blood of Christ.

We begin now to enter on the question so much debated, both anciently and at the present time—how we are to understand the words in which the bread is called the body of Christ, and the wine his blood. This may be disposed of without much difficulty, if we carefully observe the principle which I lately laid down, viz., that all the benefit which we should seek in the Supper is annihilated if Jesus Christ be not there given to us as the substance and foundation of all. That being fixed, we will confess, without doubt, that to deny that a true communication of Jesus Christ is presented to us in the Supper, is to render this holy sacrament frivolous and useless—an execrable blasphemy unfit to be listened to.

13. What Is Requisite in Order to Live in Jesus Christ.

Moreover, if the reason for communicating with Jesus Christ is to have part and portion in all the graces which he purchased for us by his death, the thing requisite must be not only to be partakers of his Spirit, but also to participate in his humanity, in which he rendered all obedience to God his Father, in order to satisfy our debts, although, properly speaking, the one cannot be without the other; for when he gives himself to us, it is in order that we may possess him entirely. Hence, as it is said that his Spirit is our life, so he himself, with his own lips, declares that his flesh is meat indeed, and his blood drink indeed. (John vi.55.) If these words are not to go for nothing, it follows that in order to have our life in Christ our souls must feed on his body and blood as their proper food. This, then, is expressly attested in the Supper, when of the bread it is said to us that we are to take it and eat it, and that it is his body, and of the cup that we are to drink it, and that it is his blood. This is expressly spoken of the body and blood, in order that we may learn to seek there the substance of our spiritual life.

317

14. How the Bread and Wine Are the Body of Jesus Christ.

Now, if it be asked whether the bread is the body of Christ and the wine his blood, we answer, that the bread and the wine are visible signs, which represent to us the body and blood, but that this name and title of body and blood is given to them because they are as it were instruments by which the Lord distributes them to us. This form and manner of speaking is very appropriate. For as the communion which we have with the body of Christ is a thing incomprehensible, not only to the eye but to our natural sense, it is there visibly demonstrated to us. Of this we have a striking example in an analogous case. Our Lord, wishing to give a visible appearance to his Spirit at the baptism of Christ, presented him under the form of a dove. St. John the Baptist, narrating the fact, says, that he saw the Spirit of God descending. If we look more closely, we shall find that he saw nothing but the dove, in respect that the Holy Spirit is in his essence invisible. Still, knowing that this vision was not an empty phantom, but a sure sign of the presence of the Holy Spirit, he doubts not to say that he saw it, (John i.32,) because it was represented to him according to his capacity.

15. The Sacrament Is Represented by Visible Signs.

Thus it is with the communion which we have in the body and blood of the Lord Jesus. It is a spiritual mystery which can neither be seen by the eye nor comprehended by the human understanding. It is therefore figured to us by visible signs, according as our weakness requires, in such manner, nevertheless, that it is not a bare figure but is combined with the reality and substance.

The Zurich Consent: A Reformed Ecumenical Compromise

The Zurich agreement on the Supper (*Consensus Tigurinus*) was an ecumenical compromise between the sacramental views of Calvin and Zwingli. It was worked out in 1549 primarily between Calvin and Bullinger and, upon its publication in 1551, was widely accepted by the Swiss churches.

SOURCE

Consensio mutua in re sacramentaria Tigurinæ Ecclesiæ et D. Calvini ministri Genevensis Ecclesiæ jam nunc ab ipsis authoribus edita (*Consensus Tigurinus*, 1549; published, Geneva and Zurich, 1551); *OS* 2:241–58; *CO* 7:689–748, pars. 6, 12, 16–18, 21–23; ET:

Mutual Consent of the Churches of Zurich, in *Calvin's Tracts and Treatises* 2:214, 216, 217, 218–19.

BIBLIOGRAPHY

Timothy George, "John Calvin and the Agreement of Zurich (1549)," in *John Calvin and the Church: A Prism of Reform*, ed. Timothy George (Louisville, Ky.: Westminster/John Knox, 1990).

6. The spiritual communion which we have with the Son of God takes place when he, dwelling in us by his Spirit, makes all who believe capable of all the blessings which reside in him. In order to testify this, both the preaching of the gospel was appointed, and the use of the sacraments committed to us, namely, the sacraments of holy Baptism and the holy Supper. . . .

12. Besides, if any good is conferred upon us by the sacraments, it is not owing to any proper virtue in them, even though in this you should include the promise by which they are distinguished. For it is God alone who acts by his Spirit. When he uses the instrumentality of the sacraments, he neither infuses his own virtue into them nor derogates in any respect from the effectual working of his Spirit, but, in adaptation to our weakness, uses them as helps; in such manner, however, that the whole power of acting remains with him alone. . . .

16. Besides, we carefully teach that God does not exert his power indiscriminately in all who receive the sacraments, but only in the elect. For as he enlightens unto faith none but those whom he hath fore-ordained to life, so by the secret agency of his Spirit he makes the elect receive what the sacraments offer.

17. By this doctrine is overthrown that fiction of the sophists which teaches that the sacraments confer grace on all who do not interpose the obstacle of mortal sin. For besides that in the sacraments nothing is received except by faith, we must also hold that the grace of God is by no means so annexed to them that whoso receives the sign also gains possession of the thing. For the signs are administered alike to reprobate and elect, but the reality reaches the latter only. . . .

18. It is true indeed that Christ with his gifts is offered to all in common, and that the unbelief of man not overthrowing the truth of God, the sacraments always retain their efficacy; but all are not capable of receiving Christ and his gifts. Wherefore nothing is changed on the part of God, but in regard to man each receives according to the measure of his faith. . . .

21. We must guard particularly against the idea of any local presence. For while the signs are present in this world, and seen by the eyes and handled by the hands, Christ, regarded as man, must be sought nowhere else than in heaven, and not otherwise than with the mind and eye of faith. Wherefore it is a perverse and impious superstition to inclose him under the elements of this world.

22. Those who insist that the formal words of the Supper—"This is my body; this is my blood," are to be taken in what they call the precisely literal sense, we repudiate as preposterous interpreters. For we hold it out of controversy that they are to be taken figuratively—the bread and wine receiving the name of that which they signify. Nor should it be thought a new or unwonted thing to transfer the name of things figured by metonomy to the sign, as similar modes of expression occur throughout the Scriptures, and we by so saying assert nothing but what is found in the most ancient and most approved writers of the Church.

23. When it is said that Christ, by our eating of his flesh and drinking of his blood, which are here figured, feeds our souls through faith by the agency of the Holy Spirit, we are not to understand it as if any mingling or transfusion of substance took place, but that we draw life from the flesh once offered in sacrifice and the blood shed in expiation.

Peter Martyr Vermigli: God's Visible Presence

The Italian reformer Peter Martyr Vermigli prepared this balanced statement of Christ's presence in the Supper for his Huguenot supporters at the Colloquy of Poissy (September 9 to October 9, 1561). This colloquy had been called by Catherine de' Medici to resolve the simmering conflict between Catholics and Protestants over the advance of Protestant doctrine in France. Theodore Beza and Vermigli led the Reformed delegation to the conference, which ended in a stalemate, a prelude to France's ensuing decades of civil war.

Peter Martyr's literary output consists of eucharistic writings and biblical commentaries, many of which were compiled as a collection of systematic theology, the *Loci communes*, or *Common Places*. Like Calvin, he sought a middle way between Roman and Lutheran views on the one hand and Zwinglian on the other.

SOURCE

Peter Martyr Vermigli, *Mémoires de Condé*, vol. 2 (London and Paris, 1740), 716–18; ET: *A Personal Confession at Poissy* (1561), trans. J. C. McLelland.

BIBLIOGRAPHY

Life, Early Letters and Eucharistic Writings of Peter Martyr, Courtenay Library of Reformation Classics (Appleford, Eng.: Sutton Courtenay, 1989). Marvin Walter Anderson, *Peter Martyr: A Reformer in Exile (1542–1562)* (Nieuwkoop: B. de Graaf, 1975). J. C. McLelland, *The Visible Words of God: An Exposition of the Sacramental Theology of Peter Martyr Vermigli, 1500–1562* (Edinburgh: Oliver & Boyd, 1957). Idem, ed., *Peter Martyr Vermigli and Italian Reform* (Waterloo, Ontario: Wilfrid Laurier University Press, 1980). D. Nugent, *Ecumenism in the Ages of the Reformation: The Colloquy of Poissy* (Cambridge: Harvard University Press, 1974).

On Beza, see Jill Raitt, *The Eucharistic Theology of Theodore Beza: Development of the Reformed Doctrine,* AAR Studies in Religion 4 (Chambersburg, Penna., 1972).

Since the promises of the New Testament are not at all empty, but full of efficacy and virtue, presenting us in truth with what they promise, and since a living faith makes us share in and enjoy what is offered us in them, we must believe and confess the presence of the Body of Jesus Christ in the Holy Supper. In it the substance of his flesh and blood is truly promised, offered and given us as the true meat and drink of the soul, following this most sacred Word: "Take, eat, this is my body; take, drink, this is my blood."

By his secret and ineffable operation, the Holy Spirit effects in us, here on earth, this communication and participation in his Body which dwells nowhere else than in heaven, divinely accommodating his grandeur to our capacity and bringing distant places together. By his power he unites heaven with earth, as if visibly, to place his royal throne in the midst of the Supper and to give himself more closely as food for our soul. In the same way, and yet incomprehensibly, by its wonderful property faith accommodates and raises our soul to heaven, giving it access and entrance to the throne of his Majesty. There we may taste and enjoy, and by this means be incorporated in him and among ourselves; so that in this eating, made bone of his bone and flesh of his flesh, we feel living within us the ransom and salvation he accomplished, with the co-ownership of all his wealth.

The creatures that are presented to us, bread and wine, sanctified by the Word and Prayer, remain to us only a sign, mark and visible witness of the thing signified—spiritual and invisible, without transformation, confusion or harm of the substance or anything else. For the sacred promise applies not to the bread but to the faithful; nor is the divine institution ordained for any nobility, favor, or reverence of creatures, still less to honor or adore them, but to this alone, to seek and to find Jesus Christ in the Supper, the true meat and substance of our souls, and to guide, comfort, and entertain the faithful, who are restored through their incorporation and communication with Jesus Christ and eternal life. Thus neither the bread nor the wine is transformed, but rather the faithful are here united, converted, and transformed in Christ by the sacred eating. There is not need to give us more than that, such as natural things, or any change or exchange or miraculous mixing of divine things with human. In this regard, the Holy Spirit is, with faith, the only means and eternal minister of this heavenly and spiritual participation and eating of the body and blood of Jesus Christ, and not bread and wine, corruptible creatures which are there only to serve as marks and signs to show the faithful that Jesus Christ is present at the Supper and gives himself to them. Thus creatures remain bare and stripped of all other substance: the most one finds in them is the simple analogy of material signs, bread and wine, with the thing signified, which is heavenly bread: Jesus Christ the only true meat, drink, nourishment and life of our souls.

Jacodus van Lodensteyn: Christ in the Inner-Room

A more mystical view of Christ's presence in the Supper arose among the seventeenth-century Reformed Pietists in the Netherlands. Jacodus van Lodensteyn (1620–77) was a prominent Dutch preacher, serving at Zoetermeer, Sluis, and, from 1653 on, in Utrecht, who sought reform of the practical life of piety. He had been a student of Voetius and of Cocceius and was intrigued by Jean de Labadie. Unlike Labadie, however, Lodensteyn and his followers had no interest in separating from the official church, seeking instead to abstain from the externals of church life and to intensify the inner life. The following is a sermon preached at the Lord's Supper on Song of Sol. 1:4, "The King carried her into his inner-room." In it Lodensteyn engages in a highly symbolic interpretation of the experience of the Lord's Supper. The "King" is Christ, the bride is the church, the inner-room is heaven. The communicant in the inner room is cleansed, fed, and is able to behold the glory of the Lord. While this mystical approach to the Christian life is not widespread among Reformed Christians, it has arisen throughout Christian history and is typical of the experience of late-seventeenth- and early-eighteenth-century Pietism.

SOURCE

Jacodus van Lodensteyn, Sermon 9, on Song of Sol. 1:4, "De Koning heeft my gebracht in sijne binnen-kameren," in *Geestelyke Opwekker voor het Onverloochende, Doode en*

Geestelose Christendom, X Predicatien (Amsterdam: Adrianus en Johannes Douci, 1732), trans. Iain S. Maclean.

BIBLIOGRAPHY

Cornelius Pieter van Andel, *Oontmoeting met Jacodus van Lodensteyn* (Campen: Kok, 1978). Peter C. Erb, ed., *Pietists: Selected Writings*, Classics of Western Spirituality (New York: Paulist, 1983). This volume notes the importance of Reformed Pietism but limits its selections largely to Lutheran Pietists. Wilhelm Goeters, *Die Vorbereitung des Pietismus in der Reformierten Kirche der Niederlande* (Leipzig and Utrecht, 1911). Heinrich Heppe, *Geschichte des Pietismus und der Mystik in der reformirten Kirche* (Leiden, 1879). F. Ernest Stoeffler, *The Rise of Evangelical Pietism*, Studies in the History of Religions 9 (Leiden: E. J. Brill, 1965).

The King bids us see there [in the inner-room] his beautiful and wonderful glory. And what is this? Is it priceless paintings, tapestries of houses or courts or costly ornaments? Oh not at all! All that is not to be found in the King's inner-room. What he bids us see is the King himself. For everything which is in the inner-room is nothing else but the king himself. There everything reflects DIVINITY. And that sight was so wonderful that we could see nothing else in the whole inner-room. For the God we saw included everything in himself. We saw him there clearly before us, and from close by, for we were with him in the inner-room. That which we now saw of the Godhead was nothing else than that he was revealed to us in his attributes and virtues. There we saw the glory of God in the face of Jesus Christ (2 Cor. 4:6). We saw the glory of Christ, who is the image of God (v. 4). We saw his righteousness, his mercy, his faithfulness, his truth, his love, there also that he loved us from eternity, his goodness, his friendship, his meekness, his humility and what other like things there were. And all this we see in him in the greatest perfection. Now when we saw all these things, we began to see the glory of this King. Then he became before us as a son (Ps. 84:12) who as swiftly as he arises the moon and the stars must disappear from sight. Likewise all earthly pleasures flee from our eyes, so that we see nothing else but the KING. We should also there at the table have seen the holy angels, who also are present there (Ps. 34:8; 1 Cor. 11:10; Heb. 1:14), but with our seeing the king, all that glory was also out of our sight. We saw ourselves no longer in the inner-room. That is to say, we sank away in our groundless nothingness. We melted and were consumed in ourselves and we said, with the man of God, Jacob: (Gen. 28:17) "How awesome is this place? This is nothing else but a house of God, and this is a gate of heaven (v. 16). Surely the Lord is in this place, and I did not know it." And this affecting of our hearts we can call loving God with our whole heart, and with our whole soul and with our whole mind (Matt. 22:37). We call God desirable, all and only for his own sake because he is such a glorious God.

We saw yet more in the inner-room and should have had yet much more to tell; but when we with our eyes beheld this son, our eyes became so blinded, that we again saw nothing but the King himself. Then we saw yet another thing: namely, in the reflection of the King we saw also our brothers and sisters. These we must necessarily see when we see the King; for they are members of Christ—they see the Head, they also see the members, because the members had put on Christ (Gal. 3:27). They were in him (John 15:5, 6, 7; Rom. 8:1; Phil. 3:9; 2 Cor. 5:17; 1 John 2:6). We saw how they in this their glory carried the Image of that King, adorned with fine shapes and so we saw again in them the King, or [should I say] them in the King.

CHRISTIAN MINISTRY

For Reformed theology, the strength and growth of the church rest squarely with the sovereign work of God. At the same time, however, Reformed Christians acknowledge that God works through the means of grace. The ministry is one of the most important of these means, and Reformed churches have always insisted on excellence in their church leaders in preaching, teaching, and pastoral care, as illustrated in these short selections. From Calvin we have three short extracts: (1) a statement of the functions of elders and deacons, (2) an excerpt from his discussion of the outer and inner call to ministry, and (3) a prayer for ministers and their mission. The mission of the ministry is amplified (4) through the nascent Reformed missionary zeal exhibited by Martin Bucer. The next selection (5) is a piercing address by William Ames to a young group of ministerial students in Franeker. We conclude (6) with the admonitions of Richard Baxter concerning the need for pastoral care.

SOURCES

(A) *Institutes* IV.3.4–9, p. 1061. (B) *Institutes* IV.3.4–9, pp. 1062–63 (edited). (C) Ford Lewis Battles, ed., *The Piety of John Calvin: An Anthology Illustrative of the Spirituality of the Reformer*, 120–21. (D) Martin Bucer, "Approved Evangelists Must Be Sent Out to All Parts of the Realm," *De Regno Christi* (1550), in *Melanchthon and Bucer*, 269–71. (E) William Ames, *Paraenesis ad Studiosos*, appended without pagination at the end of Ames, *De conscientia et eius jure vel casibus: libri quinque* (Amsterdam, 1630); ET: "An

Exhortation to the Students of Theology," delivered at Franeker in 1623, trans. Douglas Horton (1958), no pagination; an edited selection appears below. **(F)** Richard Baxter, "Oversight of the Flock," *Gildas Salvianus; The Reformed Pastor* (1656), Chapter II, in *The Practical Works of Richard Baxter*, 4 vols. (London, 1838), 4:379–84 (edited).

BIBLIOGRAPHY

Alexandre Ganoczy, *Calvin: théologien de l'église et du ministère* (Paris: Editions du Cerf, 1964). David D. Hall, *The Faithful Shepherd: A History of the New England Ministry in the Seventeenth Century* (Chapel Hill, N.C.: University of North Carolina Press, 1972). Elsie Anne McKee, *John Calvin On the Diaconate and Liturgical Almsgiving* (Geneva: Librairie Droz, 1984). Idem, *Diakonia in the Classical Reformed Tradition and Today* (Grand Rapids: Wm. B. Eerdmans, 1989).

A. JOHN CALVIN: ELDERS AND DEACONS

The elders

But in the letter to the Romans [Rom.12:7–8] and in the first letter to the Corinthians [1 Cor. 12:28], he lists others, as powers, the gift of healing, interpretation, government, and caring for the poor. Two of these I omit as being temporary, for it is not worthwhile to tarry over them. But two of them are permanent: government and caring for the poor.

Governors [1 Cor. 12:28] were, I believe, elders chosen from the people, who were charged with the censure of morals and the exercise of discipline along with the bishops. For one cannot otherwise interpret his statement, "Let him who rules act with diligence" [Rom. 12:8, cf. Vg.]. Each church, therefore, had from its beginning a senate, chosen from godly, grave, and holy men, which had jurisdiction over the correcting of faults. Of it we shall speak later. Now experience itself makes clear that this sort of order was not confined to one age. Therefore, this office of government is necessary for all ages.

The deacons

The care of the poor was entrusted to the deacons. However, two kinds are mentioned in the letter to the Romans: "He that gives, let him do it with simplicity; . . . he that shows mercy, with cheerfulness" [Rom. 12:8, cf. Vg.]. Since it is certain that Paul is speaking of the public office of the church, there must have been two distinct grades. Unless my judgment deceive me, in the first clause he designates the deacons who distribute the alms. But the second refers to those who had devoted themselves to the care of the poor and sick.

B. JOHN CALVIN: CALL TO THE MINISTRY

Outer and inner call

The treatment of this matter involves four points: that we may know (1) what sort of ministers they should be, (2) how, and (3) by whom they should be appointed, and (4) by what rite or ceremony they should be installed.

I am speaking of the outward and solemn call which has to do with the public order of the church. I pass over that secret call, of which each minister is conscious before God, and which does not have the church as witness. But there is the good witness of our heart that we receive the proffered office not with ambition or avarice, not with any other selfish desire, but with a sincere fear of God and desire to build up the church. That is indeed necessary for each one of us (as I have said) if we would have our ministry approved by God. . . .

To sum up, only those are to be chosen who are of sound doctrine and of holy life, not notorious in any fault which might both deprive them of authority and disgrace the ministry [1 Tim. 3:2–3; Titus 1:7–8]. The very same requirements apply to deacons and presbyters [1 Tim. 3:8–13].

C. JOHN CALVIN: PRAYER FOR MINISTERS

Also we pray Thee,
True Father and Savior,
For all those whom Thou hast ordained
By Thy believers
And to whom Thou hast committed
The care of souls
And the dispensing of Thy sacred gospel,
That Thou mayest lead them
And conduct them
By Thy Holy Spirit,
In order that they may be found
Faithful and loyal ministers
Of Thy glory,
Having always this end,
That all the poor wandering and lost sheep,
Being gathered and led back
To the Lord Jesus Christ,

Chief pastor and prince of bishops;
In order that, from day to day,
They may profit and grow in Him
Unto all righteousness and holiness.

D. MARTIN BUCER: PREACHING THE GOSPEL

Furthermore, since such great ignorance of the Kingdom of Christ holds sway over all everywhere, so that its power and its salutary effect upon its men and the fact that apart from it everything is harmful and destructive can hardly be explained, taught, or presented convincingly in one or two sermons, no matter how helpful and accurate they are, there must first be sent out to all the churches of the realm evangelists who are appropriately learned and motivated for the Kingdom of Christ. They must announce assiduously, zealously, and in a timely fashion to the people everywhere the good news of the Kingdom. And they should teach from the Gospel, with strength and energy, whatever pertains to the Kingdom of Christ and whatever it is necessary to believe and do for present and future happiness.

In delegating these men, utmost care will have to be taken that none are sent out except those from whose whole life and manner of devotion it is obvious that they are not in any way considering or seeking their own interests in this office but only those things which pertain to the glory of Christ and the repair of the churches. Therefore, it will not be sufficient at all to have heard from them only one or two worthy sermons, just as it will not be at all possible to judge someone suitable for this office from the fact that he seems skilled and acceptable at preaching. Their whole lives, their habits of behavior and special interests, must be inquired into and explored, to see how strong a talent and a will they have for restoring the Kingdom of Christ.

E. WILLIAM AMES: ADVICE TO STUDENTS
OF THEOLOGY

[T]hose whose names appear among the graduates of theology seldom if ever give thought to the proper end of theology. And how is it to be wondered at that those who never fix their eyes intently upon such an end never reach it?

What the purpose of the minister ought to be, the Apostle teaches in few words—I Timothy 4:16—to save himself and them that hear him—that is, living to God himself, to lead others to God, or to address and devote himself wholly to the glory of God and the edification of the church.

How far this kind of purpose is from the thoughts of the greater number of those who nowadays aspire to the ministry or educate themselves in the hope of it is too clear to require many words of description. Given the fact that hardly any of those who are born in noble families or expect from their parents means by which to live more amply enter divinity or ever consider the ministry for themselves, what other reason for this is there than that, given to worldly desires, they cannot encourage their crooked minds to pursue things which lack honor and great profit in this world, however heavenly and divine they may plainly be?

Jerome observes of a certain Roman patrician that he was accustomed to say jokingly to the blessed Damasus, "Make me bishop of the city of Rome and I shall become a Christian today." It is easy to guess that many of those who now shun the ministry and condemn it would immediately become ministers if they could be made abbots, bishops, cardinals, or pontiffs. But it were well for the ministry not to have anything in it which would lead to its surrounding itself with worldly properties in this way.

If only the minds of those who are studying to attain what they see neglected, not to say spurned, by others were of a different sort! But truly most of these seem ready to choose any other profession that pays well rather than the ministry if only they could get into it with the same ease; but since to their regret they cannot do so, they slip into the ministry as it were of necessity, according to the old proverb, "Those who cannot play the harp take to the fife." They therefore enter the profession just as others enter a business or a secular occupation—so that they may get a living for themselves. No one should be surprised that later they become useless weights to the church, time-servers and place-servers, seeking their own and not the things of God. The greater marvel is the grace and providence of God, by which it has come about that up till now the church has lived on, although burdened to an unhappy degree by men of this hireling kind.

Up to this point I have been speaking of our basic fault, from which others easily grow.

Most closely and deeply related to it is another—that to our studies we do not bring minds fitted for the divine discipline.

[T]here are students of many different subjects, but in the great company of such students, so called, few really study theology. For the ministry it is enough for many to run lightly through some imperfect syllabus. Although they plainly have the book with God's signature before them, they do not care to have it unlocked and opened to them.

Our ministers, however, think themselves to be quite prepared for all the parts of their office if they know only the doctrines—and would they knew them!

They do not, however, examine all of the doctrines—but only those brought into controversy and especially agitated. They are concerned to look only into those placed in Scripture which they see cited by others to support some generalization or polish off some argument. They devote no care to the thorough learning of languages. They regard logic as superfluous. They put their trust in the annotations, commentaries, and often even the fabrications of men. What a miserable fate for the churches—really to be deplored with tears by all good men—when those whom they would have as pastors think so little of them as to seem often to have in mind nothing but their own illusions! May this kind of irreligion be far from you, my dear young people—very far from you! Study the Scriptures diligently, while you have the opportune time. Study to understand them logically and clearly, so that you may have your wits exercised "to discern both good and evil" (Heb. 5:14). Study them for themselves, not only for bits of dogma to aid in controversy but for all the information and instruction they offer in the method and practice of the religious and virtuous life: that you may come out men of God made perfect unto all good works (2 Tim. 3:17). Almost all of you are quick in your studies, but you cannot afford to lose any part of your youth in troublesome and frivolous trifles. Let it therefore by your first and only care to make the Scriptures, clearly understood, your friend. They are the warp and woof of theology; and, as Clement of Alexandria warns, all your sermons should ἀναπνεῖν καὶ ζῆν—live and breathe—from them.

Among other authors, of whose support you ought sometimes to make use, those especially are to be selected and read often in whom runs the sap, the blood, of the Scriptures. These lead to the practice of the religious life. One must struggle not only to understand the Scriptures but also to reproduce them in some way, having it always firmly fixed in mind that theology is finally, truly, and usefully learned not when it settles down in the stomach of the intellect or memory but when it is carried over into the springs of action themselves, in the innermost center of the heart.

F. RICHARD BAXTER: DILIGENCE
IN PASTORAL CARE

III. The object of our pastoral care is, *all the flock*: that is, the church, and every member of it. It is considered by us, 1. In the whole body.

All the flock being thus known, must afterward be heeded. One would think all reasonable men should be satisfied of that, and it should need no further proof. Doth not a careful shepherd look after every individual sheep? and a good schoolmaster look to every individual scholar, both for instruction and correction? and a good physician look after every particular patient? and good commanders look after every individual soldier? Why then should not the teachers, the pastors, the physicians, the guides of the churches of Christ, take heed to every individual member of their charge? Christ himself, the great and good shepherd, and Master of the church, that hath the whole to look after, doth yet take care of every individual. In Luke xv. he tells us, that he is as the Shepherd that "leaveth the ninety and nine sheep in the wilderness, to seek after one that was lost;" or, as the "woman that lighteth a candle, and sweepeth the house, and searcheth diligently to find the *one* groat that was lost; and having found it, doth rejoice, and call her friends and neighbours to rejoice." And Christ telleth us, that "even in heaven there is joy over *one* sinner that repenteth."

(1.) We have many of our flock that are young and weak; though of long standing, yet of small proficiency or strength, Heb. v. 11, 12. And indeed it is the most common condition of the godly: most of them stick in weak and low degrees of grace; and it is no easy matter to get them higher. To bring them to higher and stricter opinions, is very easy; that is, to bring them from the truth into error, on the right hand as well as on the left: but to increase their knowledge and gifts is not easy; but to increase their graces is the hardest of all.

(2.) Another sort of converts that need our special help, are those that labour under some particular distemper, that keeps under their graces, and maketh them temptations and troubles to others, and a burden to themselves. For, alas! too many such there are! Some that are specially addicted to pride and some to worldliness, and some to this or that sensual desire; and many to frowardness and disturbing passions. It is our duty to set in for the assistance of all these, and partly by dissuasions and clear discoveries of the odiousness of the sin, and partly by suitable directions about the way of remedy to help them to a fuller conquest of their corruptions. We are leaders of Christ's army against the powers of darkness, and must resist all the works of darkness wherever we find them, though it be in the children of light.

(3.) Another sort that our work is about, is declining christians, that are either fallen into some scandalous sin, or else abate their zeal and diligence and show us that they have lost their former love. As the case of backsliders is very sad, so our diligence must be great for their recovery.

(4.) Another part of ministerial work is about those that are fallen under some great temptation. Much of our assistance is needful to our people in such a case; and therefore every minister should be a man that hath much insight into the tempter's wiles. We should know the great variety of them, and the cunning craft of all Satan's instruments that lie in wait to deceive, and the methods and devices of the grand deceiver. Some of our people lie under temptations to error and heresy, especially the young, unsettled, and most self-conceited; and those that are most conversant or familiar with seducers. Young, raw, ungrounded christians are commonly of their mind that have most interest in their esteem, and most opportunity of familiar talk to draw them into their way.

(5.) Another part of our work is to comfort the disconsolate, and to settle the peace of our people's souls, and that on sure and lasting grounds. To which end the quality of the complainants, and the course of their lives, had need to be known; for all people must have the like consolations that have the like complaints. But of this I have spoken already elsewhere; and there is so much said by many, especially Mr. Bolton in his "Instructions for Right Comforting," that I shall say no more.

(6.) The rest of our ministerial work is upon those that are yet strong; for they also have need of our assistance; partly to prevent their temptations and declinings, and preserve the grace they have; partly to help them for a further progress and increase; and partly to direct them in the improving of their strength for the service of Christ, and the assistance of their brethren.

7

POLITICS, SOCIETY, AND CULTURE

CHRISTIAN ETHICS

In the theology which has preceded, we have never been very far away from Christian ethics. The balanced relationship in Reformed thought between faith and works, gospel and law, justification and sanctification, the covenant of works and of grace—points to the Reformed insistence that the Christian life is not merely a matter of being saved *from* something but being saved *for* something. It is not only living under God's gracious favor but living under God's righteous command as well. The methodological division of theology into faith and observance made by several theologians in chapter 1 will now be given some content in this chapter. We cannot develop Reformed reflection on ethics, politics, society, and culture in any detail, but we do hope to illustrate briefly the important place these spheres have held in the tradition.

BIBLIOGRAPHY

Peter Barth, "Was ist reformierte Ethik?" *Zwischen den Zeiten* 10 (1932): 410–36. Ernst Troeltsch, *The Social Teaching of the Christian Churches*, trans. Olive Wyon, 2 vols. (London: George Allen & Unwin; New York: Macmillan, 1931; reprint: Louisville, Ky.: Westminster/John Knox, 1992).

In General

William Ames: True Religion

In Book II of *The Marrow of Theology*, Ames turns his attention to ethics. The following paragraphs show that true religion for Ames includes right action.

SOURCE

William Ames, *Medulla SS. Theologiae* (1623, 1629), Book II, chap. 4; ET: "Religion," in Ames, *Marrow*, 236–38 (edited).

1. Observance consists of either religion or justice.

2. This division is made by God in substance in the parts of the decalogue, as explained by Christ, Matt. 2:37. . . .

3. The Christian life has the same division, more frequently expressed as holiness and righteousness, Luke 1:75; Eph. 4:24. And this is the meaning of the division between love for God and love for neighbor.

4. We use the words religion and justice because religion is a most general word including all the duties which we owe to God. . . .

5. Religion is the observance whereby we do those things which directly pertain to God's honor. Rom. 1:21. . . .

6. Therefore the word is rightly said by some to be derived from *religare*, binding fast. . . .

7. Religion takes the first place in observance. First, obedience towards God must necessarily begin with God himself and with those attitudes and deeds by which we are carried towards him. 2 Cor. 8:5. . . . Second, justice towards men must be carried out by force and virtue of religion if it is to be true observance towards God. It would not be observance towards God unless it brought honor to God, and it would not bring honor to God unless it proceeded from a religious attitude. 1 Cor. 10:31. . . , Col. 3:17. . . , Col. 3:23. Third, religion commands the acts of justice and is not only the truly efficient but also the directing and ordering cause of them. James 1:26. . . . Fourth, religion is in a way the end of all acts of justice in that they open the way to an act of religion as something greater.

8. Justice itself is, therefore, sometimes called religion in the Scriptures. James 1:27. . . . Justice is not only an inseparable sign of true religion, but also something which must be done at the command of religion and have its beginning from it. . . .

13. The duties of religion should, therefore, be performed with more intensity and dedication than the duties of justice, for the rule, "Love with all your heart, all your soul, and all your mind (Matt. 22:37)," belongs properly to the former and not the latter. . . .

15. If the duties of piety and justice cannot be performed together in just and prudent balance, the duties of piety are to be preferred. Matt. 12:46–48; Luke 2:49. . . .

16. But a just balance is found when the greatest are given proportionally the most and the lesser less.

17. God is better worshipped with inward affection than outward deed. But men need the outward deed more. An outward work of religion may, therefore, sometimes be omitted in order that a necessary work of justice and mercy may be done. Matt. 12:1, 3, 4, 7, 10, 12. . . .

Cotton Mather: Essays to Do Good

Cotton Mather (1663–1728), who was among the most illustrious of early American preachers, provides an example of the Reformed preoccupation with godly action.

SOURCE

Cotton Mather, *Bonifacius: An Essay Upon the Good* (1710); reprint: The John Harvard Library; edited and introduction by David Levin (Cambridge: The Belknap Press of Harvard University Press, 1966), 18–20.

BIBLIOGRAPHY

See the recent collection of reprints in *Cotton Mather: Historical Writings*, A Library of American Puritan Writings, The Seventeenth Century, vol. 23, ed. Sacvan Bercovitch (New York: AMS 1991). Ralph and Louise Boas, *Cotton Mather: Keeper of the Puritan Conscience* (New York: Harper & Brothers, 1928). David Levin, *Cotton Mather: The Young Life of the Lord's Remembrancer, 1663–1703* (Cambridge: Harvard University Press, 1978). Richard Lovelace, *The American Pietism of Cotton Mather: Origins of American Evangelicalism* (Grand Rapids: Wm. B. Eerdmans, 1979). Robert Middlekauf, *The Mathers: Three Generations of Puritan Intellectuals, 1596–1728* (New York: Oxford University Press, 1971).

Our *obligations* to *do good* are infinite: they *do evil* against all *obligations*. The *compensations* made unto them who *do good*, are encouraging beyond all expression. . . .

To the title of GOOD WORKS there do belong, those *essays to do good*, which are now urged for. To produce them, the *first* thing, and indeed the ONE thing, that is *needful*, is, a glorious work of GRACE on the soul, renewing and quickening of it, and *purifying* of the sinner, and rendering him *zealous of good works*: a *workmanship* of God upon us, *creating* us over again, by JESUS CHRIST, *for good works*. And then, there is needful, what will necessarily follow upon such a *work*: that is, a *disposition to do good works* upon true, genuine, generous, and evangelical *principles*. Those *principles* are to be *stated*, before we can go any further; when they are *active*, we shall go a great deal further. . . .

It is in the first place, to be taken for granted: that the *end* for which we do *good works* must not be, to afford the matter of our *justification*, before the Law of the holy God. Indeed, no *good works* can be done by any man until he be *justified*. . . .

It is the *righteousness* of the *good works* done by our Saviour and *Surety*, not our own, that *justifies* us before God, and answers the demands of His Law upon us. We do by *faith* lay hold on those *good works* for our *justifying righteousness* before we arrive to do our own. 'Tis not our *faith* itself, either as doing of *good works*, or as being itself one of them, which entitles us to the *justifying righteousness* of our Saviour. But it is *faith*, only *as* renouncing of our own righteousness, and relying on that of our Saviour, provided for the *chief of sinners*, by which we are *justified*. Sir, all your attempts at *good works* will come to nothing, till a *justifying faith* in your Saviour, shall carry you forth unto them. . . .

The *rule*, by which we are to *glorify* God, is given us in the law of *good works*, which we *enjoy* (I will express it *so!*) in the *Ten Commandments*. It is impossible for us, to be released from all obligations to glorify God by a conformity to this *rule*; sooner shall we cease to be creatures. The *conformity* to that rule in the *righteousness*, which our Saviour by His obedience to it, has *brought in*, to *justify* us, has forever *magnified the Law, and made it honorable*. Though our Saviour has furnished us, with a perfect and spotless *righteousness*, when His obedience to the *Law*, is placed unto our account; yet it is a *sin* for us at all to fall short in our own obedience to the *Law:* we must always loathe and judge ourselves for the *sin*. We are not under the *Law* as a *covenant of works*. Our own exactness in doing of *good works*, is not now the *condition* of our *entering into life. Woe unto us if it were!* But still, the *Covenant of Grace* holds us to it, as our *duty*. . . .

It is to be feared, that we too seldom *inquire* after our OPPORTUNITIES TO DO GOOD. Our *opportunities to do good* are our TALENTS. An awful account must be rendered unto the great God, concerning our use of the TALENTS, wherewith He has entrusted us, in these precious *opportunities*. We do not *use* our *opportunities*, many times because we do not *know* what they are; and many times, the reason why we do not *know*, is because we do not *think*. Our *opportunities to do good*, lie by unregarded, and unimproved, and so 'tis but a mean account that can be given of them. . . .

You will doubtless find them, to be more than you were *aware* of. *Plain men dwelling in tents*, persons of a very *ordinary character*, may in a way of bright piety, prove persons of *extraordinary usefulness*. . . .

This then is the next PROPOSAL. Without abridging yourselves of your *occasional thoughts* on the question, often every day, *What good may I do?*, state a *time* now and then for more *deliberate thoughts* upon it. Can't you find a *time* (suppose once a week, yea, and how agreeably, on the *Lord's* day) to take that question into your consideration: WHAT IS THERE THAT I MAY DO, FOR THE SERVICE OF THE GLORIOUS LORD, AND FOR THE WELFARE OF THOSE, FOR WHOM I OUGHT TO BE CONCERNED? Having implored the *direction* of God, who is the *Father of Lights*, and the

Author and Giver of *good thoughts, consider* on the matter, in the various aspects of it. *Consider* till you have *resolved* on something. The *resolutions* which you *take up*, immediately *write down*. Examine what *precept* and what *promise*, you can find in the Word of God, that may countenance the intentions, in these your *memorials*. Look over the *memorials* at proper seasons afterwards, to see how far you have proceeded in the execution of them. The advantages of these *reserved* and *revised* MEMORIALS, no *rhetoric* will serve to commend them, no *arithmetic* to number them. There are some *animals*, of whom we say, "They do not know their own strength." *Christians*, why should you be *they*?

Let us descend unto PARTICULARS. But in doing so, let it not be imagined, that I pretend unto an enumeration of all the GOOD DEVICES, that are to be thought upon. Indeed, not a *thousandth* part of them, need or can be now enumerated. The *essay*, which I am now upon, is, only to dig open the several *springs* of *usefulness*; which having once begun to run, will spread into *streams*, which no *human foresight* can comprehend. *Spring up, O well!* . . .

Jonathan Edwards: Consent to Being in General

Works do not save but the saved perform good works. Yet what is the difference between the good works of the Christian and the deeds of those outside the faith? The answer for Edwards is that the deeds themselves may resemble one another but differ in both their source and goal. The source of true virtue is the heart converted by grace; the goal is the good of "Being in general," which for Edwards means the whole system of creation with God at its head. Edwards's achievement in this essay is to transpose the theology and ethics of salvation by grace into the vocabulary of the eighteenth-century philosophy.

SOURCE

Jonathan Edwards, *The Nature of True Virtue* (1753–54; posthumously published, 1788), in Edwards, *Works* (Yale) 8:539–40, 544–47 (edited).

BIBLIOGRAPHY

Roland André DeLattre, *Beauty and Sensibility in the Thought of Jonathan Edwards: An Essay in Aesthetics and Theological Ethics* (New Haven: Yale University Press, 1968). Douglas J. Elwood, *The Philosophical Theology of Jonathan Edwards* (New York: Columbia University Press, 1960). Clyde Holbrook, *The Ethics of Jonathan Edwards: Morality and Aesthetics* (Ann Arbor: University of Michigan Press, 1973). See also Norman Fiering, *Jonathan Edwards's Moral Thought and Its British Context* (Chapel Hill: University of North Carolina Press, 1981). Fiering mistakenly attempts to treat Edwards's ethics apart from his theology, but the book is very useful for placing Edwards in historical context.

[V]irtue is the beauty of those qualities and acts of the mind that are of a *moral* nature, i.e., such as are attended with desert or worthiness of *praise* or *blame*. Things of this sort . . . [belong] . . . to the *disposition* and *will*, or . . . to the *heart*. . . . [V]irtue is the beauty of the qualities and exercises of the heart, or those actions which proceed from them. So that when it is inquired, what is the nature of true *virtue*? this is the same as to inquire what that is which renders any habit, disposition, or exercise of the heart truly *beautiful*?

I use the phrase "true" virtue . . . because . . . there is a distinction to be made between some things which are truly virtuous, and others which only seem to be virtuous, through a partial and imperfect view of things; that some actions and dispositions appear beautiful, if considered partially and superficially . . . which would appear otherwise in a more extensive and comprehensive view. . . .

True virtue most essentially consists in benevolence to Being in general. Or perhaps to speak more accurately, it is that consent, propensity and union of heart to Being in general, that is immediately exercised in a general good will. . . .

[T]he primary object of virtuous love is Being, simply considered . . ., not in love to any particular beings, because of their virtue or beauty, nor in gratitude because they love us; but in a propensity and union of heart to Being simply considered; exciting "absolute Benevolence" (if I may so call it) to Being in general. I say true virtue "primarily" consists in this. For I am far from asserting that there is no true virtue in any other love than this absolute benevolence. . . .

The first object of virtuous benevolence is *Being*, simply considered: and if Being, *simply* considered, be its object, then Being *in general* is its object. . . . And it will seek the good of every *individual* being unless it be conceived as not consistent with the highest good of Being in general. . . .

And further, if Being, simply considered, be the first object . . . then that Being who has *most* of being, or has the greatest share of existence, other things being equal, so far as such a being is exhibited to our faculties or set in our view, will have the *greatest* share of the propensity and benevolent affection of the heart. . . .

The *second* object of virtuous propensity of heart is *benevolent* being. . . . When anyone under the influence of general benevolence sees another being possessed of the like general benevolence, this attaches his heart to him, and draws forth greater love to him, than merely his having existence. . . therefore he that is governed by love to Being in general, must of necessity have complacence [i.e., pleasure, approbation] in him, and the greater degree of benevolence to him, as it were out of gratitude

to him for his love to general existence, that his own heart is extended
and united to, and so looks on its interest as its own. . . .

The Ten Commandments

John Calvin: Three Rules for Interpreting the Decalogue

The law is the revelation of the will of God, but in its literal embodiment it
neither exhausts God nor the will of God. God's will transcends the law, and so
we must observe the full spirit and not the mere letter of the law. Calvin's
enunciation of rules for interpreting the Ten Commandments is in keeping
with this observation.

SOURCE

Institutes II.8.6–11, pp. 372–77 (edited).

BIBLIOGRAPHY

John Calvin's Sermons on the Ten Commandments, trans. Benjamin Wirt Farley (Grand
Rapids: Baker, 1978).

First, let us agree that through the law man's life is molded not only to
outward honesty but to inward and spiritual righteousness. Although no
one can deny this, very few duly note it. This happens because they do
not look to the Lawgiver, by whose character the nature of the law also is
to be appraised. . . .

When we say that this is the meaning of the law, we are not thrusting
forward a new interpretation of our own, but we are following Christ, its
best interpreter. The Pharisees had infected the people with a perverse
opinion: that he who has committed nothing by way of outward works
against the law fulfills the law. Christ reproves this most dangerous
error, and he declares an unchaste glance at a woman to be adultery
[Matt. 5:28]. He testifies that "anyone who hates his brother is a
murderer" [I John 3:15]. . . .

Let this be our second observation: the commandments and prohibitions always contain more than is expressed in words. . . .

Therefore, plainly a sober interpretation of the law goes beyond the
words; but just how far remains obscure unless some measure be set.
Now, I think this would be the best rule, if attention be directed to the
reason of the commandment; that is, in each commandment to ponder
why it was given to us. . . .

In the third place we ought to ponder what the division of the divine law into two Tables meant. This is impressively mentioned at various times with good reason, as all sane men will agree. And there is a ready reason for us not to remain uncertain on this matter. God has so divided his law into two parts, which contain the whole of righteousness, as to assign the first part to those duties of religion which particularly concern the worship of his majesty; the second, to the duties of love that have to do with men.

Surely the first foundation of righteousness is the worship of God. When this is overthrown, all the remaining parts of righteousness, like the pieces of a shattered and fallen building, are mangled and scattered.

Westminster Shorter Catechism: The Meaning of the Decalogue

In keeping with Calvin's counsel to follow the spirit rather than the letter of the law, Westminster offers a broad definition of the Decalogue's requirements. Note that the full text, which is not reproduced here, contains prohibitions and other remarks as well.

SOURCE

Westminster Shorter Catechism, qs. 46, 50, 54, 58, 64, 68, 71, 74, 77, 80 (1647), in Schaff, *Creeds* 3:684–94.

The First Commandment requireth us to know and acknowledge God to be the only true God, and our God; and to worship and glorify him accordingly. . . .

The Second Commandment requireth the receiving, observing, and keeping pure and entire all such religious worship and ordinances as God hath appointed in his Word. . . .

The Third Commandment requireth the holy and reverent use of God's names, titles, attributes, ordinances, Word, and works. . . .

The Fourth Commandment requireth the keeping holy to God such set times as he hath appointed in his Word; expressly one whole day in seven, to be a holy Sabbath to himself. . . .

The Fifth Commandment requireth the preserving the honor, and performing the duties, belonging to everyone in their several places and relations, as superiors, inferiors, or equals. . . .

The Sixth Commandment requireth all lawful endeavors to preserve our own life, and the life of others. . . .

The Seventh Commandment requireth the preservation of our own and our neighbor's chastity, in heart, speech, and behavior. . . .

The Eighth Commandment requireth the lawful procuring and furthering the wealth and outward estate of ourselves and others. . . .

The Ninth Commandment requireth the maintaining and promoting of truth between man and man, and of our own and our neighbor's good name, especially in witness-bearing. . . .

The Tenth Commandment requireth full contentment with our own condition, with a right and charitable frame of spirit toward our neighbor and all that is his. . . .

Herman Witsius: The Decalogue Neither a Covenant of Works nor of Grace

Some careless interpreters of the Reformed tradition equate the covenant of works with the Old Testament dispensation as a whole rather than with the prelapsarian covenant with Adam. Here Witsius interprets the Decalogue as, strictly speaking, neither a covenant of works nor a covenant of grace but a historical covenant which partakes of each.

SOURCE

Herman Witsius, *De oeconomia foederium Dei cum hominibur libri quattuor* (1677), Book 4, Chapter 4; ET: "Of the Decalogue," *The Oeconomy of the Covenants Between God and Man* 3:34–38 (edited, with orthography and punctuation revised).

The covenant made with Israel at Mount Sinai was not formally the covenant of works. 1. Because that cannot be renewed with the sinner, in such a sense as to say, "If, for the future, thou shalt perfectly perform every instance of obedience, thou shalt be justified by that, according to the covenant of works." For by this the pardon of former sins would be presupposed, which the covenant of works excludes. 2. Because God did not require perfect obedience from Israel as a condition of this covenant, as a cause of claiming the reward; but sincere obedience, as an evidence of reverence and gratitude. 3. Because it did not [include] Israel under the curse, in the sense peculiar to the covenant of works, where all hope of pardon was cut off, if they sinned but in the least instance.

However the carnal Israelites, not adverting to God's purpose or intention as they ought, mistook the true meaning of that covenant, embraced it as a covenant of works, and by it sought for righteousness. Paul declares this, Rom. 9:31–32. . . , Gal. 4:24–25. . . .

Nor was it formally a covenant of grace: because that requires not only obedience but also promises and bestows strength to obey. For thus the covenant of grace is made known, Jer. 32:39. . . , Jer. 31:31–33 . . . , Deut. 29:4.

What was it then? It was a *national covenant* between God and Israel, whereby Israel promised to God a sincere obedience to all his precepts, especially to the ten words; God on the other hand promised to Israel that such an observance would be acceptable to him, nor want its reward, both in this life, and in that which is to come, both as to body and soul. This reciprocal promise [pre]supposed a covenant of grace. For, without the assistance of the covenant of grace, man cannot sincerely promise that observance; and yet that an imperfect observance should be acceptable to God is wholly owing to the covenant of grace. It also [pre]supposed the covenant of works, the terror of which being increased by those tremendous signs that attended it, they ought to have been excited to embrace the covenant of God. This agreement therefore is a consequence both of the covenant of grace and of works; but was formally neither the one nor the other. . . .

The ten words or commandments therefore are not the form of a covenant properly so called, but the rule of duty: much less are they the form of the covenant of grace; because that covenant in its strict signification consists of mere promises and, as it related to elect persons, has the nature of a testament or last will rather than of a covenant strictly speaking and depends on no condition. . . .

John Calvin: Love of Neighbor and the Sermon on the Mount

Calvin conceives of love of neighbor as an expression of our love of God. In the first selection we see that the "neighbor" includes, in principle, all humanity; but under the exigencies of life in this world, the ethical command of neighbor-love does not exclude unique responsibilities within special relationships. The second selection is from Calvin's commentary on the Sermon on the Mount. It is noteworthy for the way in which it refuses to accept the rigorism and literalistic interpretation of the so-called left wing or radical reformation. For example, Anabaptists refused to swear official oaths out of strict adherence to Jesus' teaching, whereas the Reformed embraced the whole political realm. Similarly, for the Reformed, the admonition to "turn the other cheek" is not meant to eliminate all law and order. Calvin's interpretation here is in keeping with the vast majority of Reformed opinion, though the issue has attracted dissent and debate throughout the history of the Reformed tradition.

SOURCES

(A) *Institutes* II.8.54–55, pp. 417–19. **(B)** John Calvin, Commentary: Matthew 5:34, 37, 42 (and parallels) (1555); *CO* 45; ET: In *A Harmony of the Gospels: Matthew, Mark and Luke*, trans. A. W. Morrison, *Calvin's New Testament Commentaries* 1:90–100 (edited).

BIBLIOGRAPHY

Willem Balke, *Calvinism and the Anabaptist Radicals*, trans. William Heynen (Grand Rapids: Wm. B. Eerdmans, 1981). André Bielér, *The Social Humanism of Calvin*, trans. Paul T. Fuhrmann (Richmond: John Knox, 1964). W. Fred Graham, *The Constructive Revolutionary: John Calvin and His Socio-Economic Impact* (Richmond: John Knox, 1971). Georgia Harkness, *John Calvin: The Man and His Ethics* (New York: Henry Holt & Co., 1931). This work, and its perspective, are dated, but it contains useful information from the whole of Calvin's corpus. Richard Stauffer, *The Humanness of John Calvin*, trans. George Shriver (Nashville: Abingdon, 1971). Ernst Troeltsch, *The Social Teaching of the Christian Churches*.

A. LOVE OF NEIGHBOR

[O]ur life shall best conform to God's will and the prescription of the law when it is in every respect most fruitful for our brethren. In the entire law we do not read one syllable that lays a rule upon man as regards those things which he may or may not do, for the advantage of his own flesh. And obviously, since men were born in such a state that they are all too much inclined to self-love—and, however much they deviate from truth, they still keep self-love—there was no need of a law that would increase or rather enkindle this already excessive love. Hence it is very clear that we keep the commandments not by loving ourselves but by loving God and neighbor; that he lives the best and holiest life who lives and strives for himself as little as he can, and that no one lives in a worse or more evil manner than he who lives and strives for himself alone, and thinks about and seeks only his own advantage.

Indeed, to express how profoundly we must be inclined to love our neighbors [Lev. 19:18], the Lord measured it by the love of ourselves because he had at hand no more violent or stronger emotion than this. And we ought diligently to ponder the force of this expression. For he does not concede the first place to self-love as certain Sophists stupidly imagine, and assign the second place to love. Rather, he transfers to others the emotion of love that we naturally feel toward ourselves.

Now, since Christ has shown in the parable of the Samaritan that the term "neighbor" includes even the most remote person [Luke 10:36], we are not expected to limit the precept of love to those in close relationships. I do not deny that the more closely a man is linked to us, the more intimate obligation we have to assist him. It is the common habit of mankind that the more closely men are bound together by the ties of kinship, of acquaintanceship, or of neighborhood, the more responsibilities for one another they share. This does not offend God; for his providence, as it were, leads us to it. But I say: we ought to embrace the whole human race without exception in a single feeling of love; here there is no distinction between barbarian and Greek, worthy and unworthy, friend and enemy, since all should be contemplated in God, not in themselves. When we turn aside from such contemplation, it is no wonder we become entangled in many errors. Therefore, if we rightly direct our love, we must first turn our eyes not to man, the sight of whom would more often engender hate than love, but to God, who bids us extend to all men the love we bear to him, that this may be an unchanging principle: whatever the character of the man, we must yet love him because we love God.

B. SERMON ON THE MOUNT

Matt. 5:34. *Swear not at all.* The phrase *not at all* has deceived many, making them think that it was a general condemnation of every sort of swearing. Some men in former days were driven to this excessive rigour—not bad men, I may say—because of the unbridled freedom of swearing which they saw prevailing on all sides in their world. The Anabaptists, too, used this pretext for a great uproar, saying that Christ allowed no reason for taking oaths, in telling men to swear not at all. However, the exposition may be derived straight from the context itself. He goes directly on to say, "Neither by heaven, neither by the earth." Cannot we see that these particulars are added as explanation, to express precisely and categorically what the first part said? The Jews had roundabout or indirect, if that is the expression, forms of swearing. When they swore by heaven or earth or altar, they made virtually nothing of it, and as one fault gives rise to another, they dressed over their (less obvious) profanation of God's Name. Christ faces this mal-practice, and states that there is to be no swearing at all in this or that way, neither by heaven, nor by earth, etc. So we gather the phrase *not at all* does not apply to the substance but to the form: in other words, Neither directly, nor indirectly. Otherwise it would be superfluous to set down these instances. Hence the Anabaptists reveal both their passion for dispute, and their total lack of intelligence, when they stress one word with great earnestness and lose the whole tenor of the discourse, with their eyes shut. Suppose a man objects that no oath-taking is allowed by Christ. I answer—what the Law's interpreter says should be understood according to the Law's intention. Briefly, it comes back to this, that there are other ways than perjury for God's Name to be taken in vain. So we must abstain from all unnecessary freedom in swearing, for when a right reason compels it, the Law not only allows the oath but explicitly enjoins it. Therefore Christ's sole purpose was that all oaths should be illicit which by any abuse profane God's holy Name, when they should enhance His respect. . . .

Matt. 5:39. *Whosoever smiteth.* Julian and his like have absurdly slandered Christ's teaching, as though He made a complete reversal of law and order. As Augustine writes, with knowledge and discretion, in his fifth letter, Christ's purpose was purely to instruct the minds of the faithful in moderation and equity, in case after one or two knocks they should fail or weary. What Augustine says is true. The law is not confined to outward works, as long as you read it with intelligence. I grant that Christ holds back our hands from revenge, just as much as our minds, but where a man may, without taking revenge, protect himself and his own from injuries, Christ's words do not stop him from peaceably and non-violently deflecting the force as it runs onto him. Certainly Christ did not wish to urge His hearers to irritate the malice of those who were already over hot in their mood for trouble. Would it not be just such an irritation to turn the other cheek? Well, the fair and reasonable commentator will not strain at syllables, but concentrate on the intention that is in the speaker. It is quite unbecoming for Christ's disciples to trifle with turns of expression, when the Master's purpose is apparent. There is no doubt over Christ's aim, namely, that the end of one struggle would only be the beginning of another, and so in all the course of our lives the faithful must experience an unending succession of various hurts. Those who have been once wounded, He would have trained by that actual encounter to become tolerant, by their suffering to suffer more, with understanding. . . .

Matt. 5:42. *Give to him that asketh thee.* Though the effect of Christ's words, as Matthew records them, is to enjoin us to give to all without distinction, we gather a different sense from Luke, who takes the matter a little further. First it is certain that Christ's purpose was to make His disciples generous, not prodigal. There is stupid prodigality, which pours away the Lord's gifts recklessly, but we see how elsewhere the Spirit gives us a rule for the gifts we make. Take this point then, that Christ is first urging His disciples to be openhanded and benevolent. And the measure of it is that they are never to reckon they have done their duty when only a few have been helped, but they are to be eager to reach all with their alms, and not to grow weary as long as their means last out. In case anyone should find a loophole in Matthew's words, compare what we have in Luke. Christ says that we are not performing our service towards God, if in our sharing of goods or anything else we are looking to our mutual benefit and so He makes a distinction between charity and fleshly affection. Profane folk have love for themselves, not for nothing, but for the reward they hope to get. Thus it happens that a man turns back the love he shows for others upon himself—just as Plato wisely remarks. It is gratuitous well-doing that Christ demands from His people—zeal to aid the helpless, from whom they can expect nothing in return. Now we see what it means to keep our hand open to those who seek: it is to be stretched out generously to those who need our help, and who are unable to repay our beneficence. . . .

Matt. 5:48. *Ye therefore shall be perfect.* Perfection here, not in the sense of equality, but in relation to its likeness. However far we are from God, yet we are said to be perfect as he is, as long as we aim for the same goal, that He presents us with in Himself. If you prefer to put it differently, there is no comparison made here between God and ourselves, but it is called God's perfection when we show, first, sheer and free generosity, not spurred by any thought of gain, then, exceptional goodness, such as tackles the ill-will and ingratitude of men. It comes out better in Luke's words, *Be ye merciful, even as your Father* in heaven. Mercy is contrasted with the mercenary, that which is tied to personal advantage.

THE POLITICAL REALM AND ITS RELATION TO THE CHURCH

Government Ordained by God: Zwingli and Calvin

For the Reformed tradition, faith and politics have to be inextricably entwined; otherwise, both the unity of Christian experience and the unity of God's sovereign reign over all of life would be destroyed. The reign of God may not be limited to an internal transformation of the heart; it also has an external reach into every aspect of human culture. Thus, theologically speaking, no dimension of human activity can be relegated to a sphere beyond the reach of transforming grace. On the level of historical events themselves, the Protestant opposition to the papal church included by implication a challenge to the dominant political authorities, which defended Roman religion and received in return Rome's spiritual patronage. Therefore, the link between faith and political action was not merely theoretical but manifested itself practically throughout the course of the reform movement. For example, when Zwingli's parishioners gathered at the home of Christopher Froschauer on March 9, 1522, to proclaim their liberty by eating sausages and breaking the Lenten fast, this was a political as well as a religious act. Similarly, Calvin and many other Protestant leaders lived most of their lives as religious but also as political exiles.

Both Zwingli and Calvin, as inhabitants of free cities, believed that Christians should assume direct responsibility for extending the justice and righteousness of God into public life. This conviction distinguished them from the so-called radical reformers,[1] men such as Conrad Grebel (1498–1526), Menno Simons (1496–1561), Caspar Schwenkfeld (1490–1561), and Thomas Müntzer (1490–1525), who were equally earnest in wanting a transformation of life but who believed that the road to righteousness lay in a greater separation of the church from civil society. These more radical reformers sought a separated church of true believers and dissented from the magisterial reformers' failure to carry their reform far enough. In addition to the purging of papal practices, many of these more radical groups refused to take oaths in civil proceedings and refused public office and the payment of tithes; and many of them were pacifists, refusing military service. Moreover, they emphasized strict ecclesiastical discipline which they enforced through the exercise of the "ban." They opposed the practice of infant baptism, and quite often they connected their own suffering with a heightened expectation of the end times.

Neither Zwingli nor Calvin could embrace this sectarian alternative. Both pressed the reform, in principal part, through the structure of the city councils in Zurich and Geneva. The government was part of the created order, having been ordained by God and pronounced "good"; and so the institution of government must be embraced, even if its actual practices need to be redeemed. The task of government, as of all human institutions, was to be an instrument of God's reign; and so the preacher must hold nothing back in proclaiming God's Word in the public sphere. The following paragraphs give theological expression to these convictions.

SOURCES

(A) Huldrych Zwingli, *Von göttlicher und menschlicher Gerechtigkeit* (1523), in *Sämtliche Werke* 2:471–525; ET: *On Divine and Human Righteousness* (1523), in Zwingli, *In Search of True Religion*, 24–26. (B) John Calvin, "Civil Government," *Institutes* IV.20.1–16, 31, pp. 1485–1505, 1520–21 (edited).

---

1. The classic work is George H. Williams, *The Radical Reformation* (Philadelphia: Westminster, 1962).

BIBLIOGRAPHY

Willem Balke, *Calvinism and the Anabaptist Radicals*. Marc-Edourd Chenevière, *La Pensée Politique de Calvin* (Geneva: Labor; Paris: Je Sers, 1937). A. Farner, *Die Lehre von Kirche und Staat bei Zwingli* (Tübingen: J.C.B. Mohr, 1930). Ralph C. Hancock, *Calvin and the Foundations of Modern Politics* (Ithaca and London: Cornell University Press, 1989). Harro Höpfl, *The Christian Polity of John Calvin*, Cambridge Studies in the History and Theory of Politics (New York: Cambridge University Press, 1982). Bernd Möeller, *Imperial Cities and the Reformation*, ed. and trans. H.C.E. Midelfort and Mark U. Edwards (Philadelphia, 1972). Steven E. Ozment, *The Reformation in the Cities* (New Haven: Yale University Press, 1975). R. C. Walton, *Zwingli's Theocracy* (Toronto: University of Toronto Press, 1967).

A. HULDRYCH ZWINGLI

First of all, God commands, through the mouth of Paul, that everyone must be obedient unto the authorities; since all authority is from God. We discover here that even the evil, godless superiors are from God.

Yet there is nothing in their oath or obedience which entitles them to rule over the souls and consciences of people; for they are incapable of doing so. As little as they know what is in the heart of a person, so little are they capable of ruling the human heart, to make it good or evil, believing or unbelieving.

The human heart is known by no one except by the one God. Hence, no one but God is able to instruct it. For as long as God does not set a person free in his heart he is not free. As soon as he is liberated though, no one is able to enslave him. Though one might force him to believe differently, it cannot be done. Therefore the raging defenders of the Pope will have to become their tyrants—as were Nero and Domitian—before they shall be able to change their minds. Whenever they do so, however, one ought not obey them. For Christians have a rule that we ought to endure death rather than depart from or keep silent the truth we know, Luke 12:4. Therefore, no prince ought or is able to command anything that is against the word of God. Nor should one preach God's word in order to please people. For as soon as this happens, the messengers of God are to say, "One ought to obey God more than one obeys people," Acts 4:19 and 5:29. But the messengers who fail to speak thus—of whom we have some right now—who undertake to tie together Christ and Belial because they are afraid, are true distorters of the word of God which demands to be preached purely and cannot be mingled with the water of human pretense, Isaiah 1:22. As soon, then, as princes command anything that is against or denies divine truth, those who believe

God's word ought to endure death rather than depart from the truth. If they fail to do so, they are not followers of Christ. But this be far from you, superiors, that you should ever undertake to fight against God; it would be sheer presumption and should never succeed in the end, anyhow. For it should prove easier to a human being to bring down the heavens than to eradicate the comforting word of God. Heaven and earth shall pass away, but not God's word. Therefore, no magistrate ought to set itself up against this word or else it will destroy the magistrate. Thus we find here an area in which one is not bound to obey the authorities.

Secondly, it follows from Paul's words [Rom. 13:3] that superiors are not a deterrent to good works, but to evil ones. We note here, firstly, that evil hearts which are not manifest cannot be punished by superiors, for they cannot be recognized until they have been revealed through works. Therefore Paul does not say that they ought to deter or punish evil thoughts or hearts, but rather, evil deeds. And from that it may be concluded that human righteousness is a poor righteousness, though one is in need of it as much as one needs food. It comes into effect and punishes only after the evil has broken out which long before has been accomplished in the heart but is known to God only.

The fact that superiors are not a deterrent and threat to good works comes from their knowing which are good works and which are not. Where else but from the word of God are they to learn this? Therein they find the truth that does not deceive. Hence, no teaching serves a government and magistrate better than the teaching of Christ. It teaches what is good and what is evil. Not only does it teach external piety but it leads superiors and subjects alike to an internal piety and to greater perfection than is required by human righteousness, setting before both of them a common mind so that one does not hold for a good what the other does not consider thus. Now one may see in this that a great deal of controversy comes solely from the fact that not all of us believe the singular word of God and fail to learn from it alone what is evil and what is good.

B. JOHN CALVIN

Now, since we have established above that man is under a twofold government, and since we have elsewhere discussed at sufficient length the kind that resides in the soul or inner man and pertains to eternal life, this is the place to say something also about the other kind, which pertains only to the establishment of civil justice and outward morality.

For although this topic seems by nature alien to the spiritual doctrine of faith which I have undertaken to discuss, what follows will show that I am right in joining them, in fact, that necessity compels me to do so. This is especially true since, from one side, insane and barbarous men furiously strive to overturn this divinely established order; while, on the other side, the flatterers of princes, immoderately praising their power, do not hesitate to set them against the rule of God himself. Unless both these evils are checked, purity of faith will perish. Besides, it is of no slight importance to us to know how lovingly God has provided in this respect for mankind, that greater zeal for piety may flourish in us to attest our gratefulness. . . .

Yet this distinction does not lead us to consider the whole nature of government a thing polluted, which has nothing to do with Christian men. That is what, indeed, certain fanatics who delight in unbridled license shout and boast: after we have died through Christ to the elements of this world [Col. 2:20], are transported to God's Kingdom, and sit among heavenly beings, it is a thing unworthy of us and set far beneath our excellence to be occupied with those vile and worldly cares which have to do with business foreign to a Christian man. To what purpose, they ask, are there laws without trials and tribunals? But what has a Christian man to do with trials themselves? Indeed, if it is not lawful to kill, why do we have laws and trials? But as we have just now pointed out that this kind of government is distinct from that spiritual and inward Kingdom of Christ, so we must know that they are not at variance. For spiritual government, indeed, is already initiating in us upon earth certain beginnings of the Heavenly Kingdom, and in this mortal and fleeting life affords a certain forecast of an immortal and incorruptible blessedness. Yet civil government has as its appointed end, so long as we live among men, to cherish and protect the outward worship of God, to defend sound doctrine of piety and the position of the church, to adjust our life to the society of men, to form our social behavior to civil righteousness, to reconcile us with one another, and to promote general peace and tranquillity. All of this I admit to be superfluous, if God's Kingdom, such as it is now among us, wipes out the present life. But if it is God's will that we go as pilgrims upon the earth while we aspire to the true fatherland, and if the pilgrimage requires such helps, those who take these from man deprive him of his very humanity. Our adversaries claim that there ought to be such great perfection in the church of God that its government should suffice for law. But they stupidly imagine such a perfection as can never be found in a community of men.

Yet Government Subject to God:
Calvin, Knox, Vermigli, Mornay,
Grotius, Rutherford, Madison

Government ordained by God also meant government subject to God. An important thesis in Reformation studies maintains that the political theology of the Reformed tradition, forged as it was in the furnace of protracted persecution, helped sow the seeds of later Western democracy. While the Reformed do not have an exclusive claim to fostering nascent democratic sentiment,[2] their contributions were nonetheless historically significant.

In the sixteenth and seventeenth centuries, the cutting-edge issue was whether a tyrannical monarch who persecuted true religion, thus violating the command of God, could be resisted with impunity. Calvin was an aristocrat, and his answer to this question was that the people themselves could not resist or take up arms; they could do no more than patiently and prayerfully endure, even to the point of martyrdom, on the model of Romans 13. But if the situation became dire, the lesser magistrates did have the authority to rise up, on behalf of the people, to resist and bring down the tyrant.

Even though Calvin shared with most of his contemporaries an abhorrence of mob rule, nonetheless he had sounded an important principle: no one is above the law of God. This relativizing principle would be extended later in more democratic directions by other Reformed thinkers, especially those who lived, not in free cities like Geneva and Zurich, but as persecuted minorities within regional monarchies such as Scotland, England, and France. Thus the Scottish Reformer John Knox (1513–72), who had been among the Marian exiles, issued in his *First Blast* and *Second Blast* a more uncompromising denunciation of tyrannical monarchs.[3] Appealing to constitutional principles, Peter Martyr Vermigli (1500–1562) also put forward a widely disseminated political theory which upheld the right of magistrates to resist.[4]

The St. Bartholomew's Day Massacre in 1572, in which Catherine de' Medici ordered thousands of French Huguenots slain, sparked renewed attention to

2. E.g., some early Lutherans developed their own theories of resistance to government. See Quentin Skinner, *The Foundations of Modern Political Thought*, 2 vols. (New York: Cambridge University Press, 1978) 2:191–206.

3. John Knox, *The First Blast of the Trumpet Against the Monstrous Regiment of Women* (1558), rejected the monarchy of Mary of Guise, claiming that rule by a female violated God's law. The *Second Blast* (1558) was never finished, but its basic principles were listed by Knox in the passage quoted below.

4. Robert Kingdon offers the judgment that Vermigli mediated between Lutheran and Reformed theorists, and he notes that Vermigli's stance is less radical than many of the later Reformed. Part of the reason for Vermigli's less radical position, as Kingdon implies, may be that he wrote prior to the St. Bartholomew's Day massacre of 1572 (Robert M. Kingdon, ed., *The Political Thought of Peter Martyr Vermigli: Selected Texts and Commentary*, xvii–xxi).

the theology and politics of resistance. One of the most important treatises to arise out of these events was the *Vindiciae contra Tyrannos* (Defense of liberty against tyrants) which appeared in 1579 under the name Junius Brutus. It argues on covenantal grounds that monarchs who persecute religion are subject to the power of the people, who themselves are parties to the covenant. Some have attributed the work to Hubert Languet, but it was most likely written by Phillipe de Plessis-Mornay (Philippe de Mornay, sieur du Plessis-Marly) (1549–1623), perhaps in collaboration with others. Mornay was neither a pastor nor an academic but, rather, an educated soldier and statesman; he was Governor of Saumur from 1600 and a founder of the Saumur Academy in 1604.[5]

The final three selections illustrate seventeenth- and eighteenth-century Reformed political thought. Although we have already attended to some of the theological works of Hugo Grotius, he won lasting fame primarily as a jurist. For Grotius, justice and international law are grounded in an unchangeable law of nature and the existence of humanity as an intrinsically social being. His concern for justice and human rights anticipates similar concerns of later Reformed Christians. Samuel Rutherford (1600–1661) was a Scottish Presbyterian whose censure of absolute monarchy in *Lex Rex* (1644) is an important contribution to constitutional and natural law theory. Rutherford argued that monarchs are not above the law and must submit themselves to the power of the people and of Parliament as expressed in the constitutional framework. Unfortunately, Rutherford did not possess the tolerant spirit of Grotius and in 1646 argued against liberty of conscience because he thought it blasphemy to elevate conscience above the scriptural revelation of God.

The final contribution is from James Madison (1751–1836), the principal author of the United States Constitution. Madison had been a student of John Witherspoon, the Presbyterian minister and Princeton president from whom he learned covenant theology and the doctrine of human depravity. His defense of the separation of powers in *The Federalist*, number 10, derives in part from this theological background and is a classic text for students of American constitutional government.

SOURCES

(A) John Calvin, Commentary: Daniel 6:22. ET: In *Commentaries on the Book of the Prophet Daniel*, ed. and trans. Thomas Myers, 2 vols. (Edinburgh, 1853), 1:378–82; *Calvin's Commentaries*, vol. 12 (Reprint: Grand Rapids: Wm. B. Eerdmans, 1948). **(B)**

5. For an example of de Plessis-Mornay's theological interests, see his *De la verité de la religion chrestienne* (Antwerp, 1581); ET: *A Woorke Concerning the Trewnesse of the Christian Religion*, trans. Philip Sidney and Arthur Golding (London: Thomas Cadman, 1587); facsimile reproduction with introduction by F. J. Sypher (Delmar, N.Y.: Scholar's Facsimiles and Reprints, 1976).

John Knox, *The Second Blast* (1558), in *The Political Writings of John Knox*, ed. Marvin A. Brewlow (Washington: Folger Shakespeare Library, 1985), 159–60. **(C)** Peter Martyr Vermigli, "Commentary on Judges 1:36" (1564), in *Loci Communes* (London, 1576), vol. 4; ET: In *The Political Thought of Peter Martyr Vermigli: Selected Texts and Commentary*, ed. Robert M. Kingdon, Travaux D'humanisme et Renaissance 178 (Geneva: Librarie Droz, 1980), 87, 99–100 (orthography revised). **(D)** Phillipe de Plessis-Mornay, *Vindiciae Contra Tyrannos* (1579), in *Constitutionalism and Resistance in the Sixteenth Century*, trans. and ed. John H. Franklin (New York: Western Publishing, 1969), 180–85 (edited). **(E)** Hugo Grotius, *De Jure Bellie as Pacis* (Paris, 1625); ET: *The Rights of War and Peace* (1625), trans. A. C. Campbell, ed. David J. Hill (London: M. Walter Dunne, 1901; reprint: Westport, Conn.: Hyperion, 1979), 17–30, 280–84, 379–84 (edited). **(F)** Samuel Rutherford, *Lex Rex, or The Law and the Prince: A Dispute for the Just Prerogative of King and People* (1644) (Edinburgh: Robert Ogle and Oliver & Boyd, 1843), qs. 21, 26 (edited). **(G)** James Madison, *The Federalist*, no. 10 (1787), reprinted in *The Federalist Papers: Hamilton, Madison, Jay* (New York: New American Library, 1961), 79, 80–81, 82, 83 (edited).

BIBLIOGRAPHY

Primary Sources: Theodore Beza, *The Right of Magistrates* (1574). François Hotman, *Franco-Gallia* (1573). A partial translation of these two treatises may be found in John H. Franklin, *Constitutionalism and Resistance*. For a complete translation of Beza, see *Concerning the Rights of Rulers over Their Subjects and the Duty of Subjects Towards Their Rulers*, trans. Henri-Louis Gonin (Capetown, Pretoria: H.A.U.M., 1956).

Secondary Sources: Willem Balke, *Calvinism and the Anabaptist Radicals*, trans. William Heynen (Grand Rapids: Wm. B. Eerdmans, 1981). Harro Höpfl, *The Christian Polity of John Calvin*. Robert M. Kingdon, "Calvinism and Democracy: Some Political Implications of Debates on French Reformed Church Government, 1562–1572," *American Historical Review* 69 (1964): 393–401. Robert M. Kingdon and Robert D. Linder, eds., *Calvin and Calvinism: Sources of Democracy?* (Boston: Heath, 1970). David Little, *Religion, Order, and Law: A Study in Pre-Revolutionary England* (New York: Harper & Row, 1969). Nikolaus Paulus, *Protestantismus und Toleranz im 16. Jahrhundert* (Freiberg im Breisgau: Herder Verlag, 1911). W. Sanford Reid, "John Knox's Theology of Political Government," *Sixteenth Century Journal* 4 (1988): 529–40. Quentin Skinner, *The Foundations of Modern Political Thought*, 2 vols. (New York: Cambridge University Press, 1978), 2:191–206. James R. Smither, "The St. Bartholomew's Day Massacre and Images of Kingship in France: 1572–1574," *Sixteenth Century Journal* 12 (1991): 27–46. Mario Turchetti, "Religious Concord and Political Tolerance in Sixteenth- and Seventeenth-Century France," *Sixteenth Century Journal* 12 (1991): 15–25. Michael Walzer, *The Revolution of the Saints: A Study in the Origins of Radical Politics* (Cambridge: Harvard University Press, 1963).

For a contrary view on Calvinism and democracy, see George H. Sabine and Thomas L. Thorson, *A History of Political Theory*, 4th ed. (New York: Rinehart & Winston, 1973).

A. JOHN CALVIN

It is clear that the Prophet had violated the king's edict. Why, then, does he not ingenuously confess this? Nay, why does he contend that he has not transgressed against the king? Because he conducted himself with fidelity in all his duties, he could free himself from every calumny by which he knew himself oppressed, as if he had despised the king's sovereignty. But Daniel was not so bound to the king of the Persians when he claimed for himself as a god what ought not to be offered to him. We know how earthly empires are constituted by God, only on the condition that he deprives himself of nothing, but shines forth alone, and all magistrates must be set in regular order, and every authority in existence must be subject to his glory. Since, therefore, Daniel could not obey the king's edict without denying God, as we have previously seen, he did not transgress against the king by constantly persevering in that exercise of piety to which he had been accustomed, and by calling on his God three times a-day. To make this the more evident, we must remember that passage of Peter, "Fear God, honour the king." (1 Pet. ii. 17.) The two commands are connected together, and cannot be separated from one another. The fear of God ought to precede, that kings may obtain their authority. For if any one begins his reverence of an earthly prince by rejecting that of God, he will act preposterously, since this is a complete perversion of the order of nature. Then let God be feared in the first place, and earthly princes will obtain their authority, if only God shines forth, as I have already said. Daniel, therefore, here defends himself with justice, since *he had not committed any crime against the king;* for he was compelled to obey the command of God, and he neglected what the king had ordered in opposition to it. For earthly princes lay aside all their power when they rise up against God, and are unworthy of being reckoned in the number of mankind. We ought rather utterly to defy than to obey them whenever they are so restive and wish to spoil God of his rights, and, as it were, to seize upon his throne and draw him down from heaven.

B. JOHN KNOX

Because many are offended at *The First Blast of the Trumpet,* in which I affirm that to promote a woman to bear rule or empire above any realm, nation, or city is repugnant to nature, contumely to God, and a thing most contrarious to his revealed and approved ordinance, and because also that some hath promised—as I understand—a confutation of the same, I have delayed *The Second Blast* till such time as their reasons appear, by the which I either may be reformed in opinion or else shall have further occasion more simply and plainly to utter my judgment. Yet in the meantime, for the discharge of my conscience, and for avoiding suspicion which might be engendered by reason of my silence, I could not cease to notify these subsequent propositions which, by God's grace, I purpose to entreat in *The Second Blast* promised.

1. It is not birth only nor propinquity of blood that maketh a king lawfully to reign above a people, professing Christ Jesus and his eternal verity, but in his election must the ordinance which God hath established in the election of inferior judges be observed.

2. No manifest idolater nor notorious transgressor of God's holy precepts ought to be promoted to any public regiment, honor, or dignity in any realm, province, or city that hath subjected the self to Christ Jesus and his blessed Evangel.

3. Neither can oath nor promise bind any such people to obey and maintain tyrants against God and against his truth known.

4. But, if either rashly they have promoted any manifest wicked person, or yet ignorantly have chosen such a one as after declareth himself unworthy of regiment above the people of God—and such be all idolaters and cruel persecutors, most justly may the same men depose and punish him that unadvisedly before they did nominate, appoint, and elect.

"If the eye be single, the whole body shall be clear."

C. PETER MARTYR VERMIGLI

But thou wilt say: by what law do inferior Princes resist either the Emperor or Kings, or else public wealths, when as they [the Emperor and Kings] defend the sincere religion and true faith? I answer, by the law of the Emperor, or by the law of the King, or by the law of the public wealth. For they [the inferior Princes] are chosen of Emperors, Kings, and public wealths, as helpers to rule, whereby Justice may more and more flourish. And therefore were they ordained according to the office committed unto them, rightly, justly, and godly to govern the public wealth. Wherefore they do according to their duty, when in cause of religion they resist the higher power. Neither can that superior power justly complain, if in that case inferior power fall from it [i.e., resist]. . . .

[It may be asked,] Whether it be lawful for subjects to rise against their prince?

Let us divide subjects, so as some of them may be mere private men, and others in such sort inferior [magistrates/princes]. . . . Those which only are subject and counted altogether private, ought not to arise against their Princes and Lords. . . . But there be others in the Commonweale, which in place and dignity are inferior unto Princes, and yet in very deed do elect the superior power, and by certain laws do govern the Common-weale: as at this day we see done by the Electors of the [Holy Roman] Empire: And perhaps the same is done in other kingdoms. To these undoubtedly if the Prince perform not his covenants and promises, it is lawful to constrain and bring him into order, and by force to compel him to perform the conditions and covenants which he had promised, and that by war when it cannot otherwise be done. . . .

Some think that when superior powers go about to drive the inferior powers to wicked things, it were good and meet, that they which exer-cise the inferior office should resign and depart from their office. But I think not so, for this were to fall from his vocation, which ought not to be done, especially, when as we see that we must give over to the ungodly, which either resist or oppress the kingdom of God. I judge therefore that they ought to continue, until they be by force cast out by the superior powers, that they may in keeping their office gallantly defend the glory of God. But (alas) we see very many Dukes, Earls and Princes which if the King or Emperor would take away from them their dominions, they would not leave a stone unmoved, to defend and keep their own. There would they with all their force resist the higher powers for this cause and under this title, because they would unjustly deprive them of their things. But when the kingdom of God, godliness, and pure religion are assailed of them, and these inferior powers are required as Ministers to be at hand, and to help to overthrow them, they dare not speak or resist any thing at all. Wherefore we can think nothing else, but that they have little regard of the kingdom of Christ, and of true godliness.

D. PHILLIPE DE PLESSIS-MORNAY

The Covenant, or Compact,* Between the King and the People.

We have already said that the creation of a king involved a double compact. The first, between God, the king, and the people, has been discussed above. The second, between the king and the people, we shall now take up.

When Saul is made king, he accepts a *lex regia*[†] as the condition of his rule. David at Hebron, in the presence of God—with God, that is, as witness—enters into a covenant with all the elders of Israel, who repre-sented the people as a whole. Joash, too, covenanted with the people of the land in the House of the Lord, with the high priest Jehoiada presid-ing. We are told, indeed, that a "testimony" was imposed on him, and many interpreters take this to mean the Word of God which, in many passages, is called the "testimony." And Josiah also promises that he will observe the precepts, testimonies, and commandments included in the Book of the Covenant, and he is thus referring to the precepts of religion and justice.

In all the relevant passages, the compact is said to be made with the whole people, or the entire multitude, or all the elders, or all the men of Judah—so that we may understand, even if it were not expressly stated, that not only did the chiefs of the tribes attend, but also the lesser military chiefs and lower magistrates acting in the name of the towns, each of which covenanted of its own right with the king.

This compact created the king. For the people made the king, not the king the people. Therefore, there is no doubt that the people was the stipulator and the king the promiser. And the position of the stipulator is considered stronger under civil law.

By the first covenant, or compact, religious piety becomes an obligation; by the second, justice. In the first the king promises to obey God religiously, in the second, to rule the people justly; in the former, to maintain God's glory, in the latter, to preserve the people's welfare. The condition in the first is: "If you will observe My Law"; the condition in the second is: "If you will render each his own." If the king does not perform the conditions of the first, God is properly the avenger, while the whole people may lawfully punish non-performance of the second. . . .

But even if these ceremonies, these vows, these oaths did not take place, is it not clear, from the very nature of the case, that kings are created by the people on condition that they govern well, just as judges are established on condition that they do justice, and military commanders on condition that they lead their armies against foreign foes? And if kings become oppressors, if they commit injustices, if they become the enemy, they are no longer kings and should not be so regarded by the people. But, you may ask, what if a ruler forcibly compels a people to take an oath in his favor? What, I answer, if a robber, pirate, or tyrant— with whom, it is held, no legal bonds exist—should extort a promise at the point of a sword? Or are you unaware that a pledge elicited by force is void, and especially when the promise is against good custom and the laws of nature? And what is more at war with nature than for a people to promise a prince that it will put chains and fetters on itself, will put its throat beneath the knife, and will do violence to itself (for this is what that promise really means)? Thus, between king and people there exists a mutual obligation which, whether civil or only natural, explicit or tacit, cannot be superseded by any other compact, or violated in the name of any other right, or rescinded by any act of force. So great is its force that a king who breaks it willfully may properly be called a "tyrant," while a people that breaks it may be properly called "seditious."

Foedus sive pactum. Here and throughout *foedus* and *pactum* are used as equivalent. *Foedus* is the favored term where the agreement with God is mentioned. I have most often translated it as "covenant."
† Here used in a general sense as the "fundamental law of a kingdom."

E. HUGO GROTIUS

Now the Law of Nature is so unalterable, that it cannot be changed even by God himself. For although the power of God is infinite, yet there are some things, to which it does not extend. Because the things so expressed would have no true meaning, but imply a contradiction. Thus two and two must make four, nor is it possible to be otherwise; nor, again, can what is really evil not be evil. . . .

Whereas in reality there is no change in the unalterable law of nature, but only in the things appointed by it, and which are liable to variation. . . .

XII. The existence of the Law of Nature is proved by two kinds of argument, a priori, and a posteriori, the former a more abstruse, and the latter a more popular method of proof. We are said to reason a priori, when we show the agreement or disagreement of any thing with a reasonable and social nature; but a posteriori, when without absolute proof, but only upon probability, any thing is inferred to accord with the law of nature, because it is received as such among all, or at least the more civilized nations. . . .

XIII. It has been already remarked, that there is another kind of right, which is the voluntary right, deriving its origin from the will, and is either human or divine.

XIV. We will begin with the human as more generally known. Now this is either a civil right, or a right more or less extensive than the civil right. The civil right is that which is derived from the civil power. The civil power is the sovereign power of the state. A state is a perfect body of free men, united together in order to enjoy common rights and advantages. The less extensive right, and not derived from the civil power itself, although subject to it, is various, comprehending the authority of parents over children, masters over servants, and the like. But the law of nations is a more extensive right, deriving its authority from the consent of all, or at least of many nations. . . .

XV. The very meaning of the words divine voluntary right, shows that it springs from the divine will, by which it is distinguished from natural law, which, it has already been observed, is called divine also. This law admits of what Anaxarchus said, as Plutarch relates in the life of Alexander, though without sufficient accuracy, that God does not will a thing, because it is just, but that it is just, or binding, because God wills it. Now this law was given either to mankind in general, or to one particular people. We find three periods, at which it was given by God to the human race, the first of which was immediately after the creation of man, the second upon the restoration of mankind after the flood, and the third upon that more glorious restoration through Jesus Christ. These three laws undoubtedly bind all men, as soon as they come to a sufficient knowledge of them.

XVI. Of all nations there is but one, to which God particularly vouchsafed to give laws, and that was the people of Israel. . . .

[T]he old law, when compared with the Gospel, is said to have been neither perfect nor faultless, and Christ is said to be the end of the law, and the law our schoolmaster to bring us to Christ. Thus the old law respecting the Sabbath, and the law respecting tithes, show that Christians are bound to devote not less than a seventh portion of their time to divine worship, nor less than a tenth of their fruits to maintain those who are employed in holy things, or to other pious uses.

F. SAMUEL RUTHERFORD

QUESTION XXI.

WHAT POWER THE PEOPLE AND STATES OF PARLIAMENT HAVE OVER THE KING, AND IN THE STATE.

Arg. 3.—As God in a law of nature hath given to every man the keeping and self-preservation of himself and of his brother, Cain ought in his place to be the keeper of Abel his brother; so hath God committed the keeping of the commonwealth, by a positive law, not to the king alone, because that is impossible. (Num. xi.14, 17; 2 Chron. xix.1–6; 1 Chron. xxvii.)

Arg. 4.—If the king had such a power as king, and so from God, he should have power to break up the meeting of all courts of parliament, secret councils, and all inferior judicatures; and when the congregation of gods, as Psalm lxxxii., in the midst of which the Lord standeth, were about to pronounce just judgment for the oppressed and poor, they might be hindered by the king; and so they should be as just as the king maketh them, and might pervert judgment, and take away the righteousness of the righteous from him, (Isa. v.23,) because the king commandeth; and the cause of the poor should not come before the judge, when the king so commandeth. And shall it excuse the estates, to say, we could not judge the cause of the poor, nor crush the priests of Baal, and the idolatrous mass-prelates, because the king forbade us? So might the king break up the meeting of the lords of session, when they were to [discern] that Naboth's vineyard should be restored to him, and hinder the states to repress tyranny; and this were as much as if the states should say, We made this man our king, and with our good-will we agree he shall be a tyrant. For if God gave it to him as a king, we are to consent that he enjoy it. . . .

Arg. 9.—Those who make the king, and so have power to unmake him in the case of tyranny, must be above the king in power of government; but the elders and princes made both David and Saul kings.

Arg. 10.—There is not any who say that the princes and people, (1 Sam. xiv.) did not right in rescuing innocent Jonathan from death, against the king's will and his law.

QUESTION XXVI.
WHETHER THE KING BE ABOVE THE LAW OR NO.

Assert. 1.—The law hath a supremacy of constitution above the king:—

1. Because the king by nature is not king, as is proved; therefore, he must be king by a politic constitution and law; and so the law, in that consideration, is above the king, because it is from a civil law that there is a king rather than any other kind of governor. 2. It is by law, that amongst many hundred men, this man is king, not that man; and because, by the which a thing is constituted, by the same thing it is, or may be dissolved; therefore, 3. As a community, finding such and such qualifications as the law requireth to be in a king, in this man, not in that man,—therefore upon law-ground they make him a king, and, upon law-grounds and just demerit, they may unmake him again; for what men voluntary do upon condition, the condition being removed, they may undo again.

Assert. 2.—It is denied by none but the king is under the directive power of the law, though many liberate the king from the co-active power of a civil law. But I see not what direction a civil law can give to the king if he be above all obedience, or disobedience, to a law, seeing all law-direction is *in ordine ad obedientiam,* in order to obey, except thus far, that the light that is in the civil law is a moral or natural guide to conduct a king in his walking; but this is the morality of the law which enlighteneth and informeth, not any obligation that aweth the king; and so the king is under God's and nature's law.

G. JAMES MADISON

By a faction I understand a number of citizens, whether amounting to a majority or minority of the whole, who are united and actuated by some common impulse of passion, or of interest, adverse to the rights of other citizens, or to the permanent and aggregate interests of the community.

There are two methods of curing the mischiefs of faction: the one, by removing its causes; the other, by controlling its effects.

There are again two methods of removing the causes of faction: the one, by destroying the liberty which is essential to its existence; the other, by giving to every citizen the same opinions, the same passions, and the same interests.

It could never be more truly said than of the first remedy that it was worse than the disease. Liberty is to faction what air is to fire, an aliment without which it instantly expires. But it could not be a less folly to abolish liberty, which is essential to political life, because it nourishes faction than it would be to wish the annihilation of air, which is essential to animal life, because it imparts to fire its destructive agency.

The second expedient is as impracticable as the first would be unwise. As long as the reason of man continues fallible, and he is at liberty to exercise it, different opinions will be formed. As long as the connection subsists between his reason and his self-love, his opinions and his passions will have a reciprocal influence on each other; and the former will be objects to which the latter will attach themselves. The diversity in the faculties of men, from which the rights of property originate, is not less an insuperable obstacle to a uniformity of interests. The protection of these faculties is the first object of government. From the protection of different and unequal faculties of acquiring property, the possession of different degrees and kinds of property immediately results; and from the influence of these on the sentiments and views of the respective proprietors ensues a division of the society into different interests and parties.

The latent causes of faction are thus sown in the nature of man; and we see them everywhere brought into different degrees of activity, according to the different circumstances of civil society. A zeal for different opinions concerning religion, concerning government, and many other points, as well of speculation as of practice; an attachment to different leaders ambitiously contending for pre-eminence and power; or to persons of other descriptions whose fortunes have been interesting to the human passions, have, in turn, divided mankind into parties, inflamed them with mutual animosity, and rendered them much more disposed to vex and oppress each other than to co-operate for their common good. So strong is this propensity of mankind to fall into mutual animosities that where no substantial occasion presents itself the most frivolous and fanciful distinctions have been sufficient to kindle their unfriendly passions and excite their most violent conflicts. But the most common and durable source of factions has been the various and unequal distribution of property. Those who hold and those who are without property have ever formed distinct interests in society. Those who are creditors, and those who are debtors, fall under a like discrimination. A landed interest, a manufacturing interest, a mercantile interest, a moneyed interest, with many lesser interests, grow up of necessity in civilized nations, and divide them into different classes, actuated by different sentiments and views. The regulation of these various and interfering interests forms the principal task of modern legislation and involves the spirit of party and faction in the necessary and ordinary operations of government. . . .

It is in vain to say that enlightened statesmen will be able to adjust these clashing interests and render them all subservient to the public good. Enlightened statesmen will not always be at the helm. Nor, in many cases, can such an adjustment be made at all without taking into view indirect and remote considerations, which will rarely prevail over the immediate interest which one party may find in disregarding the rights of another or the good of the whole.

The inference to which we are brought is that the *causes* of faction cannot be removed and that relief is only to be sought in the means of controlling its *effects*.

If a faction consists of less than a majority, relief is supplied by the republican principle, which enables the majority to defeat its sinister views by regular vote. It may clog the administration, it may convulse the society, but it will be unable to execute and mask its violence under the forms of the Constitution. When a majority is included in a faction, the form of popular government, on the other hand, enables it to sacrifice to its ruling passion or interest both the public good and the rights of other citizens. To secure the public good and private rights against the danger of such a faction, and at the same time to preserve the spirit and the form of popular government, is then the great object to which our inquiries are directed. Let me add that it is the great desideration by which alone this form of government can be rescued from the opprobrium under which it has so long labored and be recommended to the esteem and adoption of mankind.

By what means is this object attainable? Evidently by one of two only. Either the existence of the same passion or interest in a majority at the same time must be prevented, or the majority, having such coexistent passion or interest, must be rendered, by their number and local situation, unable to concert and carry into effect schemes of oppression. If the impulse and the opportunity be suffered to coincide, we well know that neither moral nor religious motives can be relied on as an adequate control. They are not found to be such on the injustice and violence of individuals, and lose their efficacy in proportion to the number combined together, that is, in proportion as their efficacy becomes needful.

From this view of the subject it may be concluded that a pure democracy, by which I mean a society consisting of a small number of citizens, who assemble and administer the government in person, can admit of no cure for the mischiefs of faction. A common passion or interest will, in almost every case, be felt by a majority of the whole; a communication and concert results from the form of government itself; and there is nothing to check the inducements to sacrifice the weaker party or an obnoxious individual. Hence it is that such democracies have ever been spectacles of turbulence and contention; have ever been found incompatible with personal security or the rights of property; and have in general been as short in their lives as they have been violent in their deaths. Theoretic politicians, who have patronized this species of government, have erroneously supposed that by reducing mankind to a perfect equality in their political rights, they would at the same time be perfectly equalized and assimilated in their possessions, their opinions, and their passions.

A republic, by which I mean a government in which the scheme of representation takes place, opens a different prospect and promises the cure for which we are seeking. Let us examine the points in which it varies from pure democracy, and we shall comprehend both the nature of the cure and the efficacy which it must derive from the Union.

The two great points of difference between a democracy and a republic are: first, the delegation of the government, in the latter, to a small number of citizens elected by the rest; secondly, the greater number of citizens and greater sphere of country over which the latter may be extended.

The effect of the first difference is, on the one hand, to refine and enlarge the public views by passing them through the medium of a chosen body of citizens, whose wisdom may best discern the true interest of their country and whose patriotism and love of justice will be least likely to sacrifice it to temporary or partial considerations. . . .

The other point of difference is the greater number of citizens and extent of territory which may be brought within the compass of republican than of democratic government; and it is this circumstance principally which renders factious combinations less to be dreaded in the former than in the latter. . . .

Extend the sphere and you take in a greater variety of parties and interests; you make it less probable that a majority of the whole will have a common motive to invade the rights of other citizens; or if such a common motive exists, it will be more difficult for all who feel it to discover their own strength and to act in unison with each other. Besides other impediments, it may be remarked that, where there is a consciousness of unjust or dishonorable purposes, communication is always checked by distrust in proportion to the number whose concurrence is necessary.

Hence, it clearly appears that the same advantage which a republic has over a democracy in controlling the effects of faction is enjoyed by a large over a small republic—is enjoyed by the Union over the States composing it.

ECONOMY AND SOCIETY

Another important and widely debated thesis concerning Reformed theology, originally advanced by the sociologist Max Weber, is that there existed an "elective affinity" between Western capitalism and Calvinism, especially as the latter blended with various sectarian movements in the seventeenth century. The relevant factors that made for this affinity were doctrinal, motivational, and ethical in nature. The doctrine of election, said Weber, wherein one is chosen for salvation by the inscrutable will of God, created the motivation to test one's election in good works. The key to this motivation was the dutiful attention to one's "calling" as that calling took shape in the routine affairs of life in the world. In place of the "other-worldly" asceticism of medieval monasticism, the Reformed practiced an "inner-worldly" asceticism, open to ordinary believers. This in turn generated the peculiar Reformed ethos of thrift, hard work, and honesty that has been termed "the Protestant ethic."

Weber was not arguing that Calvinism created capitalism, any more than it created democracy. Rather the argument was that there existed a mutually interactive influence (not a causal relationship) between the religious ethos of Calvinism and the economic conditions which were ripe for capitalism's emergence. While Weber's thesis has been severely criticized and modified in recent years, Reformed Christianity has indeed displayed a vigorous social ethic which the following selections can only hope briefly to illustrate.

Zwingli provides an example of an early Reformed approach to usury.[6] For Zwingli, because human righteousness does not measure up to divine righteousness, God gave laws for the right ordering of life. We should relinquish all to care for the poor, but, under the rules of human righteousness, we may not be forced to. Taking advantage of the poor through usury is ungodly, but if the poor have entered into a usurious contract, they must honor it. Some argue that Reformed Christianity's opening the door to usury was helpful to the credit system needed for industrial capitalism. Still, Zwingli was very much concerned that the magistrate attempt to mitigate the harsh effects of usury on the poor. Moreover, Zwingli, Calvin, and the other reformers established systematic ways of caring for the poor within their cities.

Martin Bucer presents a view that simultaneously is open to free commerce but seeks to place limits upon business when its practices might be harmful to the common good.

The inclusion of Richard Baxter is particularly appropriate, since he is one of the figures whom Weber used to support his thesis. Baxter's writings entitled "Christian Economics" are voluminous and detailed. The piece below comes from his "Directions to the Rich."

Shifting themes from the economy to society, Jonathan Edwards, Jr., in a 1791 sermon delivered before the annual meeting of a Connecticut abolitionist society in New Haven, condemns the inhumanity of slavery, basing his argument on the golden rule. He criticizes the newly adopted United States Constitution for its inconsistency in proclaiming human freedom while allowing a whole racial group within the new nation to remain enslaved.

SOURCES

(A) Huldrych Zwingli, *Von göttlicher und menschlicher Gerechtigkeit* (1523); ET: *On Divine and Human Righteousness*, in Zwingli, *In Search of True Religion*, 15–16, 36. (B) Martin Bucer, "The Reform of Marketing," and "Poor Relief," *De Regno Christi* (1550), in *Melanchthon and Bucer*, 306–15, 342–45. (C) Richard Baxter, "Directions to the Rich," *Christian Directory* (1664–65), Part II, Christian Economics, chap. 28, in *The Practical Works of Richard Baxter*, 4 vols. (London, 1838), 1:517–19 (edited). (D) Jonathan Edwards, Jr., Sermon: "The Injustice and Impolicy of the Slave Trade, and of Slavery" (1791), in Jonathan Edwards, Jr., *Works* 2:75-82.

BIBLIOGRAPHY

André Bielér, *La pensée economique et social de Calvin* (Geneva: Librarie de L'Université, 1959.) Robert W. Green, *Protestantism, Capitalism, and Social Science: The Weber Thesis Controversy*, 2d ed. (Lexington, Mass.: D. C. Heath & Co., 1973). Robert M. Kingdon,

---

6. See also John Calvin, "On Usury," *CR* 51.247–48, in *Calvin's Ecclesiastical Advice*, trans. Mary Beaty and Benjamin W. Farley (Louisville, Ky.: Westminster/John Knox, 1991), 140–41.

"Social Welfare in Calvin's Geneva," *The American Historical Review* 76/1 (1971): 50–69. R. W. Henderson, "Sixteenth Century Community Benevolence: An Attempt to Resacralize the Secular," *Church History* 38/4 (1969): 421–28. Karl Koch, *Studium Pietatis: Martin Bucer als Ethiker*, Beiträge zur Geschichte und Lehre der Reformierten Kirche 14 (Neukirchen: Neukirchener Verlag, 1962). David Little, "Max Weber Revisited: The 'Protestant Ethic' and the Puritans," *Harvard Theological Review* 59 (1966): 415–28. John T. McNeill, *The History and Character of Calvinism* (New York: Oxford University Press, 1954). Jeannine E. Olson, *Calvin and Social Welfare: Deacons and the Bourse Français* (London and Toronto: Associated University Press, 1985). H. R. Robertson, *Aspects of the Rise of Economic Individualism: A Criticism of Max Weber and His School* (Cambridge: Cambridge University Press, 1933). R. H. Tawney, *Religion and the Rise of Capitalism* (New York: Harcourt Brace & World, 1926). Ernst Troeltsch, *The Social Teaching of the Christian Churches*. Max Weber, *From Max Weber: Essays in Sociology*, trans. H. H. Gerth and C. Wright Mills (New York: Oxford University Press, 1946). Idem, *The Protestant Ethic and the Spirit of Capitalism: The Relation Between Religion and the Economic and Social Life of Modern Culture*, trans. Talcott Parsons (New York: Charles Scribner's Sons, 1958). Idem, *The Sociology of Religion*, trans. Ephraim Fischoff (Boston: Beacon, 1963).

A. HULDRYCH ZWINGLI: ON USURY

When compared to the divine, human righteousness is not worthy to be called righteousness; nonetheless, God instituted it on account of our disobedience, and commanded us to follow it. . . .

God bids us give our possessions to the needy without compensation. If we should ever fail to do that, he bids us lend out money without profit, Ex. 22:25, Lev. 25:36. And if we should fail to do that, there is the teacher who teaches us how to give and take with gain.

And though the penalty for profit-taking is not clearly stated, it is, however, left to the judges who were established so that they might settle the resulting abuses and quarrels, Ex. 18:25–27. Now one who does not practice usury is considered good in human eyes because of it, for the authorities cannot get at him on account of usury. In God's sight, however, he is still not good unless he sells all he has and gives it to the poor, Lk. 12:33. If no one does that, then there is no one who is good according to divine righteousness. May we assume then that you know yourself a sinner?

On usury, I think as follows: in cases where a magistrate allows usury, the debtor is obligated to pay what is demanded of him. But no magistrate ought to be so unjust towards its subjects as to tolerate Jews or other usurers to compound interest on interest on a part or on the total sum. But in cases where the magistrate does tolerate usury and does not pronounce judgement on it, one is not obligated to pay. Indeed, the magistrate ought to punish both the ones who take and who receive it, whenever it is aware of what is going on, even though the one is obligated to return the capital—unless the magistrate goes by another rule. This prattle one may find among human law-givers (if I remember correctly) whom I have to use to get through the mire of usury; for to God, such a one is so offensive that he cannot tolerate him. Nonetheless, the magistrate has been instituted that it might deal as closely to divine righteousness as it is capable of in such matters. It is duty bound, therefore, to accept all such ungodly burdens, as far as this is possible without further damage. In short, no one should destroy human friendship for the sake of temporal goods. Rather, when one is concerned with something he does not want to forsake out of respect for the divine word, he should handle it through authority alone, and not tolerate that Christian teaching is charged with causing dissension. Further, the magistrate is to keep its eyes open so that all abuses which are so crassly against God might be removed; or else, long suffering to which nothing is conceded is twisted into nonsense in the end. How can an honorable magistrate tolerate the tomfoolery of the so-called spirituals? How can it watch its poor people being consumed by usurers and bailiffs? Therefore God kindles the light of his word once again so that his filth be washed out and cleaned for once.

B. MARTIN BUCER: THE REFORM
OF MARKETING

Marketing is a business which is honest and necessary for the commonwealth if it confines itself to the export and import of things that are advantageous to the commonwealth for living well and in a holy way, but not those which encourage and foster impious pomp and luxury. In order to benefit men's piety, this purpose ought never to be absent from the thoughts and deeds of Christians but should always be considered and weighed as scrupulously as possible.

Therefore, inasmuch as merchants pretty commonly reject this purpose, they burst forth with wickedness and greed, so that next to the false clergy there is no type of men more pestiferous to the commonwealth. For, in the first place, for the sweet odor of gain, of which they accumulate an intense amount with little work through their nefarious skills, and for the splendor of pomp and luxury, of which they recognize no measure or limit, they attract the more outstanding talents, which if they were dedicated to philosophy, could be of very great use both to the State and the Church.

Furthermore, they daily invent astonishing enticements for the purchase of their trifling wares, which are designed and prepared only for impious luxury and pomp, and they seduce nobles and other wealthy men of little thrift into buying them. And when they do not have enough money for these trifles which are esteemed as the ornaments of the nobility and its social status, there is at hand the money of the merchants, but at interest, and such a poisonous interest that within a very brief time whole families are destroyed and overthrown.

Since in so many ways this crooked kind of merchants and tradesmen is harmful and pernicious for the people of God, there must also be a chapter for the reform of merchandising in the law under which, for the suppression of godless idleness, a wholesome industry is to be restored.

And in this it must be ordered, first, that nobody should be allowed to enter merchandising whom officials have not judged suitable for this sort of thing, having found him to be pious, a lover of the commonwealth rather than of private interest, eager for sobriety and temperance, vigilant and industrious. Secondly, that these should not import or export merchandise other than what Your Majesty has decreed. And he shall decree that only those things are to be exported of which the people of the realm really have an abundance so that their export may be of no less benefit to the people of this realm, to whom these things are surplus, than to those who take them to foreign countries and make a profit on them. So also he should permit no merchandise to be imported except what he judges good for the pious, sober, and salutary use of the commonwealth. Finally, that a definite and fair price should be established for individual items of merchandise, which can easily be arranged and is very necessary (so fiery is human avarice) for conserving justice and decency among the citizens.

C. RICHARD BAXTER: DIRECTIONS TO THE RICH

Understand what it is to love and trust in worldly prosperity and wealth. Many here deceive themselves to their destruction. They persuade themselves, that they desire and use their riches but for necessity; but that they do not love them, nor trust in them, because they can say that heaven is better, and wealth will leave us to a grave! But do you not love that ease, that greatness, that domination, that fulness, that satisfaction of your appetite, eye, and fancy, which you cannot have without your wealth? It is fleshly lust, and will, and pleasure, which carnal worldlings love for itself; and then they love their wealth for these. And to trust in riches, is not to trust that they will never leave you; for every fool doth know the contrary. But it is to rest, and quiet, and comfort your minds in them, as that which most pleaseth you, and maketh you well, or to be as you would be.

Know therefore particularly what are the temptations of prosperity, that you may make a particular, prosperous resistance. And they are especially these:

1. Pride. The foolish heart of man is apt to swell upon the accession of so poor a matter as wealth; and men think they are got above their neighbours, and more honour and obeisance is their due, if they be but richer.

2. Fulness of bread. If they do not eat till they are sick, they think the constant and costly pleasing of their appetite in meats and drinks, is lawful.

3. Idleness. They think he is not bound to labour, that can live without it, and hath enough.

4. Time-wasting sports and recreations. They think their hours may be devoted to the flesh, when all their lives are devoted to it; they think their wealth alloweth them to play, and court, and compliment away that precious time, which no men have more need to redeem; they tell God that he hath given them more time than they have need of; and God will shortly cut it off, and tell them that they shall have no more.

5. Lust and wantonness, fulness and idleness, abolish both the cogitations and inclinations unto business; they that live in gluttony and drunkenness, are like to live in chambering and wantonness.

6. Curiosity, and wasting their lives in a multitude of little, ceremonious, unprofitable things, to the exclusion of the great businesses of life. Well may we say, that men's lusts are their jailors.

Let your fruitfulness to God, and the public good, be proportionable to your possessions. Do as much more good in the world than the poor, as you are better furnished with it than they. Let your servants have more time for the learning of God's word, and let your families be the more religiously instructed and governed. To whom God giveth much, from them he doth expect much.

Do not only take occasions of doing good, when they are thrust upon you; but study how to do all the good you can, as those "that are jealous of good works," Tit. ii. 14.

Do good both to men's souls and bodies; but always let bodily benefits be conferred in order to those of the soul, and in due subordination, and not for the body alone. . . .

Ask yourselves often, how you shall wish at death and judgment your estates had been laid out; and accordingly now use them. Why should not a man of reason do that which he knoweth beforehand he shall vehemently wish that he had done?

As your care must be in a special manner for your children and families; so take heed of the common error of worldlings, who think their children must have so much, as that God and their own souls have very little.

D. JONATHAN EDWARDS, JR.: CONDEMNATION OF SLAVERY

MATTHEW 7:12—*Therefore all things whatsoever ye would, that men should do to you, do ye even so to them; for this is the law and the prophets.*

This precept of our divine Lord hath always been admired as most excellent; and doubtless with the greatest reason. Yet it needs some explanation. It is not surely to be understood in the most unlimited sense, implying that because a prince expects and wishes for obedience from his subjects, he is obliged to obey them; that because parents wish their children to submit to their government, therefore they are to submit to the government of their children; or that because some men wish that others would concur and assist them to the gratification of their unlawful desires, therefore they also are to gratify the unlawful desires of others. But whatever we are conscious that we should, in an exchange of circumstances, wish, and are persuaded that we might reasonably wish, that others would do to us; that we are bound to do to them. This is the general rule given us in the text; and a very extensive rule it is, reaching to all our actions; and is particularly useful to direct our conduct toward inferiors, and those whom we have in our power. I have therefore thought it a proper foundation for the discourse, which by *the Society for the promotion of Freedom, and for the Relief of Persons unlawfully holden in Bondage,* I have the honor to be appointed to deliver, on the present occasion.

This divine maxim is most properly applicable to the slave trade, and to the slavery of the Africans. Let us then make the application.

Should we be willing, that the Africans or any other nation should purchase us, our wives and children, transport us into Africa and there sell us into perpetual and absolute slavery? Should we be willing, that they by large bribes and offers of a gainful traffic should entice our neighbors to kidnap and sell us to them, and that they should hold in perpetual and cruel bondage, not only ourselves, but our posterity through all generations? Yet why is it not as right for them to treat us in this manner, as it is for us to treat them in the same manner? Their color indeed is different from ours. But does this give us a right to enslave them? The nations from Germany to Guinea have complexions of every shade from the fairest white to a jetty black; and if a black complexion subject a nation or an individual to slavery, where shall slavery begin, or where shall it end?

It is unjust in the same sense, and for the same reason, that it is, to steal, to rob, or to murder. It is a principle, the truth of which hath in this country been generally, if not universally acknowledged, ever since the commencement of the late war, *that all men are born equally free.* If this be true, the Africans are by nature equally entitled to freedom as we are; and therefore we have no more right to enslave, or to afford aid to enslave them, than they have to do the same to us. They have the same right to their freedom, which they have to their property or to their lives. Therefore to enslave them is as really and in the same sense wrong, as to steal from them, or to rob or murder them.

CHRISTIANITY AND CULTURE

The conviction that God is Lord over all of life also prompted Reformed Christians to active involvement in every area of the wider culture. We cannot document this involvement in any detail in the present context and can only offer a few illustrations of this Reformed concern. First, John Calvin reflects upon the significance of science and the liberal arts generally and astronomy in particular. Second, Martin Bucer gives his theological reflections upon what makes for wholesomeness in various sorts of games. Third, we reproduce Robert Mather's recollections on the founding of Harvard, an institution which initially was intended to train Puritan clergy. And finally, there is a short portion of a much longer list of scientific phenomena which, in his youth, Jonathan Edwards, having been profoundly influenced by Sir Isaac Newton, once proposed to write a book to explain.

SOURCES

(A) *Institutes* II.2.14–15, pp. 273–75. (B) John Calvin, Commentary: Genesis 1:16; *CO* 23; ET: In *Commentaries on The First Book of Moses Called Genesis*, ed. and trans. John King, 2 vols. (Edinburgh, 1844); *Calvin's Commentaries* 1:86–87. (C) Martin Bucer, "Honest Games," *De Regno Christi* (1550), in *Melanchthon and Bucer*, 346–54. (D) Robert Mather, "New England's First Fruits," in *The American Puritans: Their Prose and Poetry*, ed. Perry Miller (Garden City, N.Y.: Doubleday, 1956), 323. (E) Jonathan Edwards, "Things to be Considered and Written Fully About," in Edwards, *Works* (Yale) 6:219–24.

BIBLIOGRAPHY

Quirinus Breen, *John Calvin: A Study in French Humanism* (Grand Rapids: Wm. B. Eerdmans, 1931). Herbert Butterfield, *The Origins of Modern Science, 1300–1800* (London: G. Bell & Sons, 1958). John Dillenberger, *Protestant Thought and Natural Science: A Historical Interpretation* (Garden City, N.Y.: Doubleday, 1960). Brian A. Gerrish, "The Reformation and the Rise of Modern Science: Luther, Calvin, and Copernicus," in idem, *The Old Protestantism and the New*, chap. 10, and sources cited therein. E. Harris Harbison, *The Christian Scholar in the Age of the Reformation* (New York: Charles Scribner's Sons, 1956). Karl Holl, *The Cultural Significance of the Reformation* (New York: Meridian Books, 1959). Richard Hooykaas, *Religion and the Rise of Modern Science* (Grand Rapids: Wm. B. Eerdmans, 1972).

A. JOHN CALVIN: SCIENCE AND
THE LIBERAL ARTS

Whenever we come upon these matters in secular writers, let that admirable light of truth shining in them teach us that the mind of man, though fallen and perverted from its wholeness, is nevertheless clothed and ornamented with God's excellent gifts. If we regard the Spirit of God as the sole fountain of truth, we shall neither reject the truth itself, nor despise it wherever it shall appear, unless we wish to dishonor the Spirit of God. For by holding the gifts of the Spirit in slight esteem, we contemn and reproach the Spirit himself. What then? Shall we deny that the truth shone upon the ancient jurists who established civic order and discipline with such great equity? Shall we say that the philosophers were blind in their fine observation and artful description of nature? Shall we say that those men were devoid of understanding who conceived the art of disputation and taught us to speak reasonably? Shall we say that they are insane who developed medicine, devoting their labor to our benefit? What shall we say of all the mathematical sciences? Shall we consider them the ravings of madmen? No, we cannot read the writings of the ancients on these subjects without great admiration. We marvel at them because we are compelled to recognize how preeminent they are. But shall we count anything praiseworthy or noble without recognizing at the same time that it comes from God?

It is no wonder, then, that the knowledge of all that is most excellent in human life is said to be communicated to us through the Spirit of God. Nor is there reason for anyone to ask, What have the impious, who are utterly estranged from God, to do with his Spirit? We ought to understand the statement that the Spirit of God dwells only in believers [Rom. 8:9] as referring to the Spirit of sanctification through whom we are consecrated as temples to God [1 Cor. 3:16]. Nonetheless he fills, moves, and quickens all things by the power of the same Spirit, and does so according to the character that he bestowed upon each kind by the law of creation. But if the Lord has willed that we be helped in physics, dialectic, mathematics, and other like disciplines, by the work and ministry of the ungodly, let us use this assistance. For if we neglect God's gift freely offered in these arts, we ought to suffer just punishment for our sloths. But lest anyone think a man truly blessed when he is credited with possessing great power to comprehend truth under the elements of this world [cf. Col. 2:8], we should at once add that all this capacity to understand, with the understanding that follows upon it, is an unstable and transitory thing in God's sight, when a solid foundation of truth does not underlie it.

B. JOHN CALVIN: ASTRONOMY

I have said, that Moses does not here subtilely descant, as a philosopher, on the secrets of nature, as may be seen in these words. First, he assigns a place in the expanse of heaven to the planets and stars; but astronomers make a distinction of spheres, and, at the same time, teach that the fixed stars have their proper place in the firmament. Moses makes two great luminaries; but astronomers prove, by conclusive reasons, that the star of Saturn, which, on account of its great distance, appears the least of all, is greater than the moon. Here lies the difference; Moses wrote in a popular style things which, without instruction, all ordinary persons, endued with common sense, are able to understand; but astronomers investigate with great labour whatever the sagacity of the human mind can comprehend. Nevertheless, this study is not to be reprobated, nor this science to be condemned, because some frantic persons are wont boldly to reject whatever is unknown to them. For astronomy is not only pleasant, but also very useful to be known: it cannot be denied that this art unfolds the admirable wisdom of God. Wherefore, as ingenious men are to be honoured who have expended useful labour on this subject, so they who have leisure and capacity ought not to neglect this kind of exercise. Nor did Moses truly wish to withdraw us from this pursuit in omitting such things as are peculiar to the art; but because he was ordained a teacher as well of the unlearned and rude as of the learned, he could not otherwise fulfil his office than by descending to this grosser method of instruction. Had he spoken of things generally unknown, the uneducated might have pleaded in excuse that such subjects were beyond their capacity. Lastly, since the Spirit of God here opens a common school for all, it is not surprising that he should chiefly choose those subjects which would be intelligible to all. If the astronomer inquires respecting the actual dimensions of the stars, he will find the moon to be less than Saturn; but this is something abstruse, for to the sight it appears differently. Moses, therefore, rather adapts his discourse to common usage. For since the Lord stretches forth, as it were, his hand to us in causing us to enjoy the brightness of the sun and moon, how great would be our ingratitude were we to close our eyes against our own experience? There is therefore no reason why janglers should deride the unskilfulness of Moses in making the moon the second luminary; for he does not call us up into heaven, he only proposes things which lie open before our eyes. Let the astronomers possess their more exalted knowledge; but, in the meantime, they who perceive by the moon the splendour of night, are convicted by its use of perverse ingratitude unless they acknowledge the beneficence of God.

C. MARTIN BUCER: HONEST GAMES

Further, since human nature has that weakness by which it cannot always concentrate on grave and serious matters but demands other rest besides sleep, there must also be provision made for certain relaxations from work and useful studies and a certain recreation of the strength both of the spirit and of the body in play and games, especially when grave and serious obligations have been satisfied, and by all means in proper moderation and prudence, so that the kind of games is prescribed and presented for adults and youth in which there need not be feared any relaxation of morals or delight in wicked idleness and from which there may also be gained a certain strengthening of health as well as some improvement in the cultivation of the mind. As a pagan philosopher wrote, "We have not been so fashioned by nature that we seem to have been made for sport and games but rather for hardship and for certain more serious and more important pursuits" (Cicero, *De officiis* I, 29).

These games must be derived from musical and gymnastic art. From music one will take poems and songs that present and proclaim nothing futile, nothing inappropriate to the Christian profession and nothing obscene and wicked, but rather the praises of God and the Savior derived from all his works and judgments as these are expressed in Holy Scripture; the praise of virtues and of men excelling in virtue; laws and precepts of a pious life, and well-known and helpful historical narratives.

To these may be added dances (but the dances of pious girls must be separate from the dances of young boys) which may be danced to pure and holy songs, with chaste and modest motion befitting those who profess piety.

Youth could also perform comedies and tragedies, and by such means a useful form of entertainment, honorable and contributing toward an increase of piety, may be staged for the people; but it will be necessary that devout and wise men experienced in the Kingdom of Christ compose these comedies and tragedies, in which there may be presented on the stage the plans, actions, and events of mankind, whether common and ordinary as it occurs in comedies or unique and eliciting admiration as it is characteristic of tragedies. All this will contribute toward a correction of morals and a pious orientation to life.

It must be observed, however, that when in both kinds of poetic material, comic and tragic, the activities and sins of men are described and actively presented to be seen with the eyes, it should be done in such a way that although the crimes of reprobate men are related, yet a certain terror of divine judgment and horror of sin should appear in these things, and a shameless daring and an exultant delight in crimes should not be expressed. It is better here to take something away from poetic fitness rather than from the concern for edifying the piety of the spectators, which demands that in every representation of sin there be felt the condemnation of one's conscience and the horrible fear of God's judgment.

But when pious and good actions are shown, they should express as clearly as possible a happy, secure, and confident sense of the divine mercy, but moderate and diffident as regards the self, and a joyful trust in God and his promises, with holy and spiritual pleasure in doing good.

D. ROBERT MATHER: HARVARD COLLEGE

After God had carried us safe to New England, and we had builded our houses, provided necessaries for our livelihood, reared convenient places for God's worship, and settled the civil government, One of the next things we longed for, and looked after was to advance learning and perpetuate it to posterity, dreading to leave an illiterate ministery [sic] to the churches when our present ministers shall lie in the dust. And as we were thinking and consulting how to effect this great work, it pleased God to stir up the heart of one Mr. Harvard (a godly gentleman and a lover of learning, there living amongst us). . . .

E. JONATHAN EDWARDS:
SCIENTIFIC INTERESTS

1. To observe that incurvation, refraction, and reflections from concave surfaces of drops of water, etc. is from gravity.

2. To observe that 'tis like that the attraction of particles of heat contributes as much towards the burning of bodies as the impulse.

3. To observe how water may quench fire by insinuating into the pores and hindering the free play of the particles, and, by reason of that softness and pliableness, deadening that motion like throwing a stone upon a featherbed.

4. To observe that if we do suppose an infinite number of surfaces in the universe, yet, according to the number of them, so must the smallness of them be.

5. To observe that the cause that an object appears not double, being seen with two eyes, [is that] all the parts upon the retina that exactly correspond end upon the same spot of the surface in the brain which receives the images.

6. To observe that one end of respiration is that the motion in [the] ribs may be communicated to the parts of the body.

7. To consider whether one use of air in preserving fire be not that the particles of it may be to counteract the fiery particles of the burning body; and whether that be not the reason that nothing shines, rotten wood, glowworms, nor coals, in the exhausted receiver; and that may be one use of air in respiration among the rest.

8. To shew that the probable reason why the light of *ignis fatuus*, rotten wood, glowworms, etc., are not accompanied with heat is because of the exquisite smallness of the rays; and to shew that if that were the reason the rays need not be the thousandth part so small as that of the sun.

9. To shew that the different refrangibility of rays must of necessity be either their different velocity or different magnitudes; because there can be no other reason of their different attractability, which indeed is refrangibility.

10. To shew the parvity of the rays of light, the elasticity of air, how wisely the eye is contrived so a man may see things colored.

11. To shew, from Isaac Newton's principles of light and color, why the sky is blue. . . .

8

ESCHATOLOGY

THE REIGN OF GOD AND
THE LAST THINGS

The Christian life orients itself by the prayer "Thy kingdom come." Through the centuries the Christian proclamation has included a vigorous hope that God's plan for believers will culminate in the return of Christ, the resurrection of the dead, the final judgment, and the coming of the fullness of God's reign in glory. The Heidelberg lectures of Zacharias Ursinus, based on the catechism, make up our first entry, and they are commendable in their concise and faithful summary of basic Reformed belief concerning eschatology.

When early Reformed theology took up the question of eschatology, or the last things, it did so largely as a complement to its gospel of salvation by grace through faith. A chief emphasis, therefore, was on glorification, the final link in the chain of salvation (*ordo salutis*), following election, calling, justification, and sanctification (pp. 107–15). In the readings below from William Ames and Herman Witsius, glorification is not treated primarily as the finale of history—though that it surely is—but as something which impinges upon the believer's present Christian experience.

One aspect of Christian eschatology is the belief in a thousand-year reign of Christ, derived from Revelation 20. This has been interpreted both literally by millennialists, and symbolically by amillennialists. The sixteenth-century magisterial reformers stood in an ambiguous relationship to the millennial expectations that were prominent in the late medieval period. On the one hand, these expectations played a pertinent part in laying the cultural and religious groundwork for the sixteenth-century reforms to take place. On the other hand, the magisterial Protestant reformers shied away from the theology and goals of the millennialists. Except for denunciations of the pope as the Antichrist, most magisterial reformers were amillennial, refraining from a literal interpretation of Revelation (Calvin refused to write a commentary on it) and avoiding fanaticism and speculation into the specifics of the last days. These millennial hopes were of course preserved by figures such as Thomas Müntzer and in the more radical groups such as the Anabaptists.

Nevertheless, Reformed theology from the sixteenth century on has experienced a profound tension: human effort by itself can neither effectuate salvation nor bring in the millennium; yet Reformed theology at its best, from Zwingli on, has strived to transform society according to the vision of the kingdom of God. Thus apocalyptic reflections continued to express themselves, here and there, in the sixteenth and early seventeenth centuries—John Foxe's *Book of Martyrs* is a prominent and influential example—and in the late seventeenth century millennial expectations reemerged among covenant theologians such as Cocceius and Witsius, from which apocalypticism flowed into Reformed pietism and into some branches of Puritanism. The depth of this late fascination was such that even the greatest scientist of the day, Isaac Newton (1642–1727), spent much time in apocalyptic inquiry.

We include here just one notable example of Reformed apocalyptic thought, drawn from the 1739 sermons of Jonathan Edwards, collected in *A History of the Work of Redemption*. Edwards was a post-millennialist, that is, one who believed a great outpouring of God's Spirit would usher in a thousand years of peace and righteousness, after which would occur Christ's second advent and the end of the world. In the sermons, Edwards chronicles the covenantal relationship between God and God's people which he believed would culminate in the millennium, an event which, for all its excellence, still would be only a foretaste of the ultimate glories of heaven. While Edwards hoped for this outpouring of the Spirit in his own time, and while he considered the eighteenth-century revivals a most "glorious work of God," it was never his considered judgment that the millennial age had already begun to dawn, and this was especially true once the revivals were on the wane.

BIBLIOGRAPHY

Jonathan Edwards, *Apocalyptic Writings*, in Edwards, *Works* (Yale), vol. 5. T. F. Torrance, *Kingdom and Church: A Study of the Theology of the Reformation* (Edinburgh: Oliver & Boyd, 1956). William J. Scheick, "The Grand Design: Jonathan Edwards' *History of the Work of Redemption*," *Eighteenth Century Studies* 8 (1975): 300–314.

Heidelberg and Zacharias Ursinus: The Final Judgment

SOURCES

(A) *Catechismus oder Christlicher Unterricht.* . . . (1563) = *Der Heidelberger Katechismus*, q. 52; ET: Heidelberg Catechism (1566), in Cochrane, *Confessions*, 313–14. **(B)** Zacharius Ursinus, *Explicationum catecheticarum* (1594), exposition of q. 52; ET: *Ursinus Commentary*, 260, 262–63, 264, 267–68.

A. HEIDELBERG CATECHISM

Q. 52: What comfort does the return of Christ "to judge the living and the dead" give you?

A. That in all affliction and persecution I may await with head held high the very Judge from heaven who has already submitted himself to the judgment of God for me and has removed all the curse from me; that he will cast all his enemies and mine into everlasting condemnation, but he shall take me, together with all his elect, to himself into heavenly joy and glory.

B. ZACHARIAS URSINUS: THE LAST THINGS

II. What the Final Judgment is.

In every judgment amongst men we have the accused, the accuser, the judge, the case, the trial, the law according to which a decision is given, the sentence of acquittal or condemnation, and the execution thereof according to the law. Hence a human judgment, in general, is the examination of a case by a regular judge according to just laws, and the passing and execution of the sentence either by acquitting or punishing the guilty.

From this it is easy to give a definition of the final judgment which God will execute through Christ. The judge, in this case, will have no need of accusers or witnesses, inasmuch as he himself will make the works of all manifest, being himself the searcher of hearts. There will then merely be the judge, the guilty, the law, the sentence and its execution. The final judgment is, therefore, that judgment which will take place at the end of the world, when Christ the judge will descend in a visible manner from heaven in a cloud in the glory and majesty of his Father and the holy angels, when all men who have lived from the beginning of the world will be raised, whilst those who will then be living shall be suddenly changed, and when all will stand before the judgment seat of Christ, who will pass sentence upon all, and who will then cast the wicked with the devils into everlasting punishment, but will receive the godly to himself, that they may, with him and the blessed angels, enjoy eternal felicity and glory in heaven. "He shall so come in like manner as ye have seen him go into heaven." (Acts 1:11.) Or, we may define the last judgment in a few words to be the disclosure of all hearts, and the revelation of all those things which have been done by men, and a separation between the righteous and the wicked, which God will execute through Christ, who will pronounce and execute sentence upon all according to the doctrine of the law and gospel, which will result in the perfect deliverance of the church, and the banishment of the wicked and devils into everlasting punishment.

III. Who will be the Judge?

The judge will be Christ, the same person who is the mediator. "The Father hath committed all judgment to the Son, and hath given him authority to execute judgment also, because he is the Son of man." (John 5:22, 27.) By this, however, we are not to understand that the Father and the Holy Ghost will have no part in this judgment, but it is committed to Christ because he will appear and pronounce the sentence in his human nature. But when he speaks, God will speak; when he judges, God will judge, and that not only because he is himself God, but also because the Father speaks and judges through him. "He was ordained of God to be the Judge of quick and dead." "He will judge the world in righteousness by that man whom he hath ordained." (Acts 10:42; 17:31.) This judgment, therefore, will belong to all the persons of the Trinity as it respects their consent and authority; but to Christ as it respects the visible scene, the announcement and execution of the sentence; for Christ will in a visible manner pass and execute sentence upon all. The church will also judge by giving its approbation to the decision of the judge. It is for this reason that Christ says that the apostles shall be seated upon twelve thrones, and that they shall judge the twelve tribes of Israel. Yea, we also shall approve and subscribe to the sentence which Christ will then pass.

VIII. Why will there be a judgment?

The chief cause of this judgment lies in the decree of God. God has decreed and declared that it shall be. Hence there is a necessity in view of this decree, that it should take place. It is also necessary that God may obtain the end for which he created man, and be eternally praised by his people—that he may declare his great goodness and mercy towards the faithful, who in this life suffer various trials and afflictions; and that he may manifest his justice and truth in the punishment of the wicked, who here flourish and prosper; for there is a necessity that it should at length be well with the righteous, and ill with the wicked both in body and soul. In a word, the end of the final judgment is, that God may cast away the wicked and deliver the church, that he may dwell in us and be all in all.

XII. Why this judgment is deferred.

The Lord defers his coming: 1. That he may exercise the godly in faith, hope, patience, and prayer. 2. That all the elect may be gathered into the church; for it is on their account, and not on account of the wicked, that the world is permitted to stand. The lower orders of creation were made for the children of God. The wicked use them as thieves and robbers. But when the whole number of God's people shall once have been gathered into the church, then will the end be. God, too, will have his people brought in by ordinary means; he will have them hear his word, and through this be converted and born again, the accomplishment of which will require time. 3. That he may afford all time for repentence, as in the days of Noah, and that this his delay may render the wicked and disobedient without excuse. "God endured with much long suffering the vessels of wrath fitted for destruction." "Not knowing that the goodness of God leadeth thee to repentence." (Rom. 9:22; 2:4.)

William Ames and Herman Witsius: Glorification

SOURCES

(A) William Ames, *Medulla SS. Theologiae*, Book 1, chap. 30, pars. 8–9, 15, 27, 29, 33–34, in Ames, *Marrow*, 171–74 (edited). **(B)** Herman Witsius, *De oeconomia foederium Dei cum hominibur libri quattuor* (1677), Book 3, Chapter 14; ET: "Of Glorification," *The Oeconomy of the Covenants Between God and Man* 2:331–41 (edited). **(C)** Jonathan Edwards, *A History of the Work of Redemption*, in Edwards, *Works* (Yale) 9:460–66 (edited).

A. WILLIAM AMES

[T]he first stage of beginning glorification is the apprehension and sense of the love of God shining forth in Christ, in the communion of believers with him. Rom. 5:5. . . .

[T]here comes about a certain friendship between God, Christ, and the faithful. John 15:15. . . . James 2:23. . . .

[T]he second stage is undoubting hope and expectation of the enjoyment of all those good things which God has prepared for his own. Rom. 5:2. . . .

[F]or this reason we are free to come to God with trust, Eph. 2:18 and 3:12; Heb. 10:22 . . . [and with] the certainty of perseverance and salvation, Rom. 8:38. . . .

[T]his truth is perceived and made certain in us in these ways. First,

by a certain spiritual sense in which the grace of God now present
becomes known and evident to the believer. Second, by the gift of dis-
cernment through which believers distinguish true grace from its
shadow. Third, by the whisper and witness of conscience in which grace
and salvation are made fast for believers, just as sin and death are for
unbelievers. Fourth, the Spirit of God so confirms to believers these
ways of perceiving that they have the same certainty as faith itself. Rom.
8:16 . . . Cor. 2:12 . . . 2 Cor. 13:5 . . . 1 John 4:16. . . .

[T]he third stage is the possession of spiritual gifts of grace in overflowing abundance, Col. 2:2, 7, 10. . . .

[T]he fourth stage is the experience of God's benevolence or good will,
Ps. 31:19 . . . Ps. 65:4. . . . These all show that the faithful are rooted and
grounded in the love of God, Eph. 3:17.

[P]erfect glorification is in the taking away of every imperfection
from soul and body and the bestowal of total perfection.

[T]his is granted to the soul immediately after the separation from
the body, 2 Cor. 5:2; Phil. 1:23; Heb. 12:23. . . . It is not ordinarily to
be granted to the soul and body together until that last day when all
the faithful shall in one moment be perfected in Christ, Eph. 4:13; Phil.
3:20, 21.

B. HERMAN WITSIUS

As all God's works tend to his glory, so also to the *glorification* of his
chosen people. This doubtless is the glory of God, to manifest himself in
his elect, to be what he is to himself, the fountain of consummate
happiness. . . . 2 Thess. 1:10 . . . Rom. 5:2. . . . Our glorification is called
the glory of God, not only because it comes from, and is freely bestowed
on us by God; but also because the magnificence of the divine majesty
displays itself nowhere more illustriously than in the glorious happiness
which he makes to shine in his beloved people. . . .

Glorification is *the gracious act of God, whereby he actually translates
his chosen and redeemed people from an unhappy and base to a happy and
glorious state.* And it may be considered, either as *begun in this life*, or as
consummated in the next. "The first fruits of the Spirit" [Rom. 8:23], who
is the "Spirit of glory," [1 Pet. 4:14] are even in this life granted to the
children of God; not only that by these they might comfort themselves in
adversity; but also that, from these, they might in some measure infer,
what and how great that future happiness is, which is reserved for them
in heaven; and that, having had a foretaste of that great reward they
expect, they may be the more cheerful in the course of faith and holiness. Now these first-fruits consist of the following things:

First, in that most excellent *holiness*, which is freely bestowed on the elect. . . . [Rom. 3:23; Jer. 3:24; Exod. 15:11; 1 Cor. 11:7; Ps. 19:8, 10]. . . .

Secondly, in that *vision of God*, with which he honors the saints even in this life. . . . [T]he complete happiness of the life to come consists in the perfect vision of God. That vision, therefore, which is the privilege of believers here, is certainly the beginning of that other. Now God presents himself here to be seen, (1) *By faith*, which indeed is mere darkness when compared with the light of glory, and in that respect is distinguished from *sight* . . . [2 Cor. 5:7; Heb. 11:1; 2 Cor. 4:4; Heb. 11:37; 2 Cor. 3:18; Eph. 2:8; John 5:24]. . . . (2) God is also seen by an *experimental sense* of his goodness, which intimately insinuates itself into the soul, in the holy use of the creatures . . . so that . . . [he] has the experience of it both by sight, sense, and taste, while God himself, by means of his creatures, wonderfully delights the soul . . . Ps. 34:8. . . . (3) He is seen still more *immediately* when he reveals himself to the soul, while deeply engaged in holy meditation, prayer, and other exercises of devotion, as the fountain of life and the source of light; so as wonderfully to affect it with the immediate darting of his rays into it . . . Ps. 27:4; 63:2. . . . (4) Something peculiar is at times imparted to sick and dying Christians, in whose *imagination* God sometimes draws so distinctly the brightest images of heavenly things, that they seem to see them before their eyes. . . . The nearer the soul to heaven, it is also enlightened with the brighter rays of supercelestial light, flowing from him, who, being light itself, dwells in light inaccessible. . . .

Thirdly, *in the gracious possessions and enjoyment of God;* when God himself, according to the promise of his covenant, holds communion with them, and gives them not only to see him, but also to possess and enjoy him . . . and in this consists salvation . . . [Ps. 145:15; 16:5–6; 73:23; 65:4]. . . .

Fourthly, such magnificent beginnings of glory beget *all riches of the full assurance of understanding* [Col. 2:2] and the firmest certainty of consummate happiness to be enjoyed in its appointed time . . . [2 Tim. 1:12; Rom. 8:38–39]. . . . And indeed I know not whether anything more delightful and pleasant can be desired in this life, than with full assurance of our faith, which entirely calms the conscience, and delights it with the ineffable sweetness of consolations.

Fifthly, These so many and so great benefits joined together beget *a joy unspeakable and full of glory*, whereby Peter testifies, "though now not seeing yet believing they rejoice" [1 Pet. 1:8]. For that God with whom they have fellowship as their God is their exceeding joy . . . [Ps. 43:4]. . . . Nothing exceeds this joy in efficacy; for it penetrates into the inmost soul, and is alone sufficient to sweeten the most grievous of all afflictions, let them be ever so bitter, and easily dispel the greatest anguish of soul: so that the faithful martyrs of Christ, who had tasted the sweetness of it, have gone, with joy and songs of praise, to the most cruel torments, as to the most sumptuous feasts. Nothing is more pure. . . .

C. THE MILLENNIUM: JONATHAN EDWARDS

[I] proceed now to show how this glorious work [the millennium] shall be accomplished:

1. God's Spirit shall be gloriously poured out for the wonderful revival and propagation of religion. This great work shall be accomplished, not by the authority of princes, nor by the wisdom of learned men, but by God's Holy Spirit, Zech. 4:6–7. . . .

This pouring out of the Spirit of God, when it is begun, shall soon bring great multitudes to forsake that vice and profaneness that now so abundantly prevails, and shall cause that vital religion that is now so despised and laughed at in the world to revive. . . .

2. This pouring out of the spirit of God shall not effect the overthrow of Satan's visible kingdom till there has first been a violent and mighty opposition made. In this the Scripture is plain, that when Christ is thus gloriously coming forth, and the destruction of Anti-Christ is ready at hand, and Satan's kingdom begins to totter and to appear to be eminently threatened, the powers of the kingdom of darkness will rise up and mightily exert themselves to prevent their kingdom's being overthrown. . . . We know not particularly in what manner this opposition shall be made. 'Tis represented as a battle, 'tis the "battle of the great day of God Almighty." . . .

3. Christ and his church shall in this battle obtain a complete and entire victory over their enemies; they shall be totally routed and overthrown in this their last effort. . . .

4. Consequent on this victory, Satan's visible kingdom on earth shall be destroyed. . . .

DEATH AND ETERNAL LIFE

For the classical Christian witness, death is not the end; Christians look forward in hope to eternal life. Our opening passage, once again, comes from Zacharias Ursinus's Heidelberg lectures which state the Reformed theology very well and which make it clear that the resurrection and eternal life are not the culmination of a self-centered and utilitarian religion but, as in all areas of Reformed theology, are secondary to the goal of giving glory and praise to the living God. The second reading is one of the most remarkable to be found in Zwingli's corpus. Here he gives his description of the joyful fellowship in heaven which will include all the elect from the beginning of time, among them pious pagans, some of whom Zwingli even has the boldness to name! This passage is intelligible only against the background of Zwingli's understanding of the unity of God and of God's ways with humanity. Basing his thoughts on Mal. 1:11, Zwingli believes that God has been working graciously among all people since the beginning; and any of them who are saved are saved only through the work of Christ.[1] This passage arises in the context of a rejection, typical of Reformed eschatology, of the Anabaptist doctrine of the sleep of the soul during the intermediate state between death and the final resurrection. According to Reformed doctrine, believers upon death go immediately to be with God.

We know of no more fitting way for this volume to conclude than with Jonathan Edwards's sermon "Heaven is a World of Love," a portrayal, similar to that of Augustine, of eternal life as a condition of harmonious and balanced sharing of all things in the love of God. Some saints, who have run a good race and lived life in close communion with God, receive a greater portion of grace in heaven; but this is not begrudged by those in a lower station, for all the abundance of grace creates an abundance of satisfaction. Those in closer communion completely condescend to those in humbler states; none is diminished for each one is ennobled by receiving as much love as he or she desires.[2] In eternal happiness they dwell giving praise and glory to God.

BIBLIOGRAPHY

John Calvin, *Psychopannychia* (Aureliae, 1534; 2d rev. ed., Basel, 1536; 3d ed., Strasbourg, 1542); *CO* 5:165–232; ET: *Tracts and Treatises* 3:441–490.

Huldrych Zwingli: The Intermediate State and the Eternal Fellowship of the Saints

SOURCE

Huldrych Zwingli, *Fidei expositio* (1536), in *SS*; ET: "Eternal Life," *Exposition of the Christian Faith*, in *Zwingli and Bullinger*, 273–76.

---

1. W. P. Stephens, *The Theology of Huldrych Zwingli* (Oxford: Clarendon, 1986), 122–27.
2. Cf. Augustine: "No one will wish to be what it has not been granted him to be; and yet he will be bound in the closest bond of peaceful harmony with one to whom it has been granted; just as in the body the finger does not wish to be the eye, since both members are included in the harmonious organization of the whole body. And so although one will have a gift inferior to another, he will have also the compensatory gift of contentment with what he has" (*City of God*, Book 22, trans. Henry Bettenson [New York: Penguin, 1972], p. 1088).

Finally, we believe that after this existence, which is captivity and death rather than life, there is for saints and believers an everlasting life of joy and felicity, but for the wicked and unbelieving, of misery and wretchedness. In this regard we do not accept the view of the Anabaptists that the soul as well as the body sleeps until the resurrection. We maintain that the souls of angels and men can never sleep or rest. For their teaching is contrary to all reason. The soul is so vital a substance that not only does it have life in itself, but it gives life to the dwelling-place in which it resides. . . .

"He that believeth shall not come into condemnation, but is passed from death unto life." If this is the case, then he who believes in this present life experiences already how good the Lord is and enjoys a foretaste of the life of heaven. But if the soul which now lives in God were to fall asleep the moment it left the body, the life of a Christian would be better in the world than when he has left the world. . . .

We believe, then, that as soon as they depart the body the faithful fly away to God, joining themselves to God and enjoying eternal felicity. Therefore, most religious king, if you discharge the office entrusted to you, as David, Hezekiah and Josiah did, you may look forward first to seeing God himself in his very essence and majesty and with all his attributes and powers. And this you will enjoy, not sparingly, but in full measure, not with the satiety which always accompanies abundance, but with that agreeable fulfilment which no surfeit can destroy, like rivers which flowing unceasingly to the sea and returning through the heart of the earth never become displeasing to men but constantly bring them profit and gladness, watering and fertilizing and bringing forth the seeds of new life. The good which we shall enjoy is eternal: and the eternal can never be exhausted. For that reason surfeit is impossible, for it is always new and yet constantly the same.

After that you may expect to see the communion and fellowship of all the saints and sages and believers and the steadfast and the brave and the good who have ever lived since the world began. You will see the two Adams, the redeemed and the Redeemer, Abel, Enoch, Noah, Abraham, Isaac, Jacob, Judah, Moses, Joshua, Gideon, Samuel, Phinehas, Elijah, Elisha, Isaiah and the Virgin Mother of God of whom he prophesied, David, Hezekiah, Josiah, the Baptist, Peter, Paul; Hercules too and Theseus, Socrates, Aristides, Antigonus, Numa, Camillus, the Catos and Scipios; Louis the Pious and your predecessors the Louis, Philips, Pepins and all your ancestors who have departed this life in faith. In short there has not lived a single good man, there has not been a single pious heart or believing soul from the beginning of the world to the end, which you will not see there in the presence of God. Can we conceive of any spectacle more joyful or agreeable or indeed sublime? Is it not right to direct all our soul's energies to the attainment of such a life? And let the dreaming Anabaptists deservedly sleep in the nether regions that sleep from which they will never awake. The source of their error is their ignorance of the fact that in Hebrew the word to sleep is used as the equivalent of "to die," as is often the case with Paul too when he has occasion to use the word.

Heidelberg and Zacharias Ursinus: Resurrection and Eternal Life

SOURCES

(A) *Catechismus oder Christlicher Unterricht* . . . . (1563) = *Der Heidelberger Katechismus*, qs. 57 and 58; ET: Heidelberg Catechism, in Cochrane, *Confessions*, 315. **(B)** Zacharius Ursinus, *Explicationum catecheticarum* (1594); ET: Ursinus, *Commentary*, 310, 312–13, 316, 317, 318, 319, 323. **(C)** Jonathan Edwards, Sermon: "Heaven is a World of Love," *Charity and Its Fruits* 15 (1738), in Edwards, *Works* (Yale) 8:366–86 (edited).

A. HEIDELBERG CATECHISM

Q. 57: What comfort does "the resurrection of the body" give you?

A: That after this life my soul shall be immediately taken up to Christ, its Head, and that this flesh of mine, raised by the power of Christ, shall be reunited with my soul, and be conformed to the glorious body of Christ.

Q. 58: What comfort does the article concerning "the life everlasting" give you?

A: That, since I now feel in my heart the beginning of eternal joy, I shall possess, after this life, perfect blessedness, which no eye has seen, nor ear heard, nor the heart of man conceived, and thereby praise God forever.

B. ZACHARIAS URSINUS

The doctrine of immortality of the soul is established by such declarations of the word of God as these: "For when he dieth, he shall carry nothing away; his glory shall not descend after him. Though, while he lived, he blessed his soul." "As thou livest, and as thy soul liveth, I will not do this thing." "Fear not them which kill the body, but are not able to kill the soul." "As touching the dead, that they rise, have ye not read in the book of Moses, how in the bush God spake unto him, saying, I am the God of Abraham, and the God of Isaac, and the God of Jacob? He is not the God of the dead, but the God of the living." (Ps. 49:17, 18. 2 Sam. 11:11. Matt. 10:28. Mark 12:26, 27.) Christ when hanging upon the cross said to the thief, "To-day shalt thou be with me in Paradise." (Luke 23:43.) But he could not be there in his body, because that was dead, and buried. Therefore his soul was brought with Christ into Paradise, and hence the soul must live after death. Paul said; "I have a desire to depart and be with Christ." (Phil. 1:23.) He spoke this in reference to the rest, and joy which he would have with Christ after death. But what can be the joy or blessedness of those, who are in a state of unconsciousness? Hence those who imagine that the soul sleeps after death, and so deny its immortality, are refuted by this passage of Scripture. "Father into thy hands, I commend my spirit." "Lord Jesus, receive my spirit." "I am the Resurrection and the Life; he that believeth in me though he were dead, yet shall he live." "We are willing rather to be absent from the body, and to be present with the Lord." (Luke 23:46. Acts 7:59. John 11:25. 2 Cor. 5:8.) The soul therefore, does not sleep after death, but enjoys immortal life, and heavenly glory with the Lord.

The resurrection, then, will consist, first, in the restoration of the same body, or the bringing together the mass or matter which now constitutes our bodies, but which, after death, is scattered, and dissolved in the different elements. Secondly, it will consist in the re-union of the body with the same soul which it had at first, by which it will also be quickened, and be made immortal. The resurrection will, in the last place, consist in the glorification of the elect, and the eternal banishment of the wicked from the presence of God.

There are three great errors in relation to the doctrine of the resurrection: 1. There are some who deny it altogether, and affirm that the soul dies with the body. This was the view which the Sadducees entertained, as is evident from what is said of them in Acts 23:8. "For the Sadducees say that there is no resurrection, neither angel, nor Spirit." 2. There are others who have admitted the immortality of the soul, but understand by the resurrection nothing more than regeneration. They deny that the bodies of the saints will rise, although their souls enjoy eternal felicity after death. The authors of this heresy seems to have been Hymeneus and Philetus, of whom Paul speaks: (2 Tim. 2:17, 18) "Who concerning the truth have erred, saying, That the resurrection is past already; and overthrow the faith of some." 3. Others again, as the Anabaptists, deny that the very same bodies which we now have will rise again, and contend that God will create new bodies at the second coming of Christ. In opposition to all these errors, it becomes us to believe what the Scriptures affirm in relation to this subject, that the dead will most certainly rise again.

How will the Resurrection be effected?

The resurrection will be accomplished openly, and gloriously, and not secretly, nor hastily. It will be far different from that which occurred in relation to certain persons, when Christ rose from the dead. It will take place in the sight of angels, men and devils, and will be a scene of inexpressible joy to the righteous, but of unutterable anguish, and horror to the wicked. Christ shall descend from heaven, accompanied by the angels, with a shout, with the voice of the Arch-angel, and with the trumpet of God, at whose sound all the dead shall awake and come forth from their graves, and stand before the judgement seat of Jesus Christ. Those who will remain alive until the coming of Christ shall be suddenly changed from a state of mortality to immortality, which change will be to them in the place of death, and the resurrection. (Thes. 4:14, 18. 1 Cor. 15:50, 55.)

When will the Resurrection take place?

The resurrection will take place at the end of the world, in the last day, according as it is said, "I will raise him up at the last day." "I know that he shall rise again in the resurrection at the last day." (John 6:44; 11:24.) But when the last day will arise no one knows, but God alone.

For what purpose, and to what state will the dead be raised?

The ultimate end of the resurrection of the dead is the glory of God; for he will then manifest and exercise his mercy in its highest form in the glorification of the faithful, whilst his justice will be displayed in the damnation of the reprobate; and thus he will declare the certainty of his promises and threatenings in relation to both. *The next end,* and the one that is subordinate to the former, is the salvation and glory of the elect; and on the other hand the punishment and rejection of the reprobate: for the former shall be raised to eternal life, whilst the latter shall come forth to everlasting punishment.

What is everlasting life?

This question seems at first inexplicable, especially in view of what the Apostle says concerning it: "Eye hath not seen, nor ear heard, neither have entered into the heart of man, the things which God hath prepared for them that love him." (1 Cor. 2:9.) We may, however, form some faint idea of what eternal life is, from the analogy of life, of which philosophers are wont to dispute much, and of which the Scriptures also speak. The term life is variously defined by philosophers. It may in general be defined as the very being of that which lives, when used in reference to God, angels, and living beings and plants. Spirits also live; but have not their existence from any quickening soul, but from their essence or nature. In creatures, however, possessed of a soul, life is properly the being of that which lives, which is the same thing as to be endowed with a soul, or to have in oneself a living soul. For the soul is that by which such a being lives; or it is the essential form of life, by which those live who are endowed therewith. It is taken for the first and second actions; that is, for the very being, action or living, and for the acting of a living thing. We may now define life more fully thus: natural life is the existence or dwelling of the soul in a body which is animated, and the acting of a living being. Or, it is the perfection (ἐντελέχεια) of the soul accomplishing those works which are proper to that which has life. Or, finally, it is the adaptedness of a living being to effect such things as are proper to itself; and is also the things themselves by virtue of the union which exists between the body and the soul.

That is called *everlasting*, 1. Which is without beginning or end, as God is. 2. That which is without a beginning, but which has an end, as the decrees of God. 3. That which has a beginning, but will have no end, as the angels, &c. It is in this third sense that our heavenly life is called everlasting, by which we mean, that whilst it has a beginning, it will have no end. The everlasting life of man, then, is the eternal being of man, regenerated and glorified, which will consist in having the image of God perfectly restored in him, as it was when he was first created, having perfect wisdom, righteousness, and happiness, or being endowed with the true knowledge and love of God, in connection with eternal joy. And here for the sake of plainness we shall include among these *acts* the *powers* themselves of knowing and loving God; for to *be able* rightly to know and love God, belongs equally as much to spiritual life as to know and love him, inasmuch as the natural man receiveth not the things of the Spirit of God. (1 Cor. 2:14.)

When is Eternal Life given?

The beginning of everlasting life is given already in this world; but the consummation of it, is reserved for the life to come, which none receive, but those in whom it is here begun. Hence it is said, "In this we groan, earnestly desiring to be clothed upon, with our house which is from heaven; if so be that being clothed, we shall not be found naked." "Whosoever hath, to him shall be given, and he shall have more abundance; but whosoever hath not from him shall be taken away, even that he hath." (2 Cor. 5:23. Matt. 13:12.)

There are two degrees in the consummation of eternal life. The one is when the souls of the righteous, being freed from the body, are immediately carried into heaven; for in death they obtain a deliverance from all the evils of this life. The other is that greater, and more glorious degree to which we shall attain in the resurrection of our bodies, when we shall ascend into heaven perfectly redeemed and glorified, and see God as he is, face to face. "He that heareth my word, and believeth in him that sent me, hath everlasting life, and shall not come into condemnation, but is passed from death unto life." "Now are we the sons of God, and it doth not yet appear what we shall be; but we know that when he shall appear, we shall be like him, for we shall see him as he is." (John 5:24. 1 John 3:3.)

C. JONATHAN EDWARDS

First, . . . Most of the love which there is in this world is of an unhallowed nature. But in heaven, the love which has place there is not carnal, but spiritual; not proceeding from corrupt principles, not from selfish motives, and to mean and vile purposes; but there love is a pure flame. The saints there love God for his own sake, and each other for God's sake, for the sake of that relation which they bear to God, and that image of God which is upon them.

Second. With respect to the degree of their love, it is perfect. The love which is in the heart of God is perfect, with an absolute, infinite and divine perfection. . . .

Those who have a lower station in glory than others suffer no diminution of their own happiness by seeing others above them in glory. On the contrary they rejoice in it. All that whole society rejoice in each other's happiness; for the love of benevolence is perfect in them. Everyone has not only a sincere but a perfect good will to every other. Sincere and strong love is greatly gratified and delighted in the prosperity of the beloved. And if the love be perfect, the greater the prosperity of the beloved is, the more is the lover pleased and delighted. For the prosperity of the beloved is, as it were, the food of love; and therefore the greater that prosperity is, the more richly is love feasted. The love of benevolence is delighted in beholding the prosperity of another, as the love of complacence is delighted in viewing the beauty of another. So that the superior prosperity of those who are higher in glory is so far from being any damp to the happiness of saints of lower degree that it is an addition to it, or a part of it. There is undoubtedly an inconceivably pure, sweet and fervent love between the saints in glory; and their love is in proportion to the perfection and amiableness of the objects beloved. . . . And therefore it must necessarily cause delight in them when they see others' happiness and glory to be in proportion to their amiableness, and so in proportion to their love of them. Those who are highest in glory are those who are highest in holiness, and therefore are those who are most beloved by all the saints. For they love those most who are most holy, and so they will all rejoice in it that they are most happy. And it will be a damp to none of the saints to see them who have higher degrees of holiness and likeness to God to be more loved than themselves; for all shall have as much love as they desire, and as great manifestations of love as they can bear; all shall be fully satisfied.

And when there is perfect satisfaction, there is no room for envy. And they will have no temptation to envy those who are above them in glory from their superiors being lifted up with pride. We are apt to conceive that those who are more holy, and more happy than others in heaven, will be elated and lifted up in their spirit above others. Whereas their being above them in holiness implies their being superior to them in humility; for their superior humility is part of their superior holiness. Though all are perfectly free from pride, yet as some will have greater degrees of divine knowledge than others, will have larger capacities to see more of the divine perfections, so they will see more of their own comparative littleness and nothingness, and therefore will be lowest abased in humility. And besides, the inferior in glory will have no temptation to envy those who are higher. For those who are highest will not only be more beloved by the lower saints for their higher holiness, but they will also have more of a spirit of love to others. They will love those who are below them more than other saints of less capacity. They who are in highest degrees of glory will be of largest capacity, and so of greatest knowledge, and will see most of God's loveliness, and consequently will have love to God and love to saints most abounding in their hearts. So that those who are lower in glory will not envy those who are above them. They will be most beloved of those who are highest in glory, and the superior in glory will be so far from slighting those who are inferior, that they will have more abundant love to them, greater degrees of love in proportion to their superior knowledge and happiness; the higher in glory, the more like Christ in this respect. . . .

First. Love there always meets with answerable returns of love. Love is always mutual, and the returns are always in due proportion. Love always seeks this. In proportion as any person is beloved, in that proportion his love is desired and prized. And in heaven this inclination or desire of love will never fail of being satisfied. No one person there will ever be grieved that he is slighted by those whom he loves, or that he has not answerable returns. . . .

Second. The joy of heavenly love shall never be damped or interrupted by jealousy. . . .

Third. They shall have nothing within themselves to clog them in the exercises and expressions of love. In this world they find much to hinder them. They have a great deal of dullness and heaviness. . . .

Fourth. In heaven love will be expressed with perfect decency and wisdom. . . .

Fifth. There shall be nothing external to keep them at a distance or hinder the most perfect enjoyment of each other's love. There shall be no separation wall to keep them asunder. They shall not be hindered from the full and constant enjoyment of each other's love by distance of habitation, for they shall be together as one family in their heavenly Father's house. . . .

Sixth. They shall all be united together in a very near relation. Love seeks a near relation to the object beloved. And in heaven all shall be nearly related. They shall be nearly allied to God, the supreme object of their love; for they shall all be his children. And all shall be nearly related to Christ; for he shall be the Head of the whole society, and husband of the whole church of saints. All together shall constitute his spouse, and they shall be related one to another as brethren. It will all be one society, yea, one family. Eph. 2:19, "Ye are fellow citizens with the saints, and of the household of God."

Seventh. All shall have *propriety* in one another. Love seeks to have the beloved its own, and divine love rejoices in saying, "My beloved is mine, and I am his," as Cant. 2:16. And in heaven all shall not only be related one to another, but they shall be each other's. The saints shall be God's. He brings them hence to him in glory, as that part of the creation which he has chosen for his peculiar treasure. And on the other hand God shall be theirs. . . .

Eighth. They shall enjoy each other's love in perfect and undisturbed prosperity. . . .

Ninth. All things in that world shall conspire to promote their love, and give advantage for mutual enjoyment. . . .

Tenth. And lastly. They shall know that they shall forever be continued in the perfect enjoyment of each other's love. They shall know that God and Christ will be forever, and that their love will be continued and be fully manifested forever, and that all their beloved fellow saints shall live forever in glory with the same love in their hearts. And they shall know that they themselves shall ever live to love God, and love the saints, and enjoy their love. They shall be in no fear or any end of this happiness, nor shall they be in any fear or danger of any abatement of it through a weariness of the exercises and expressions of love, or cloyed with the enjoyment of it, or the beloved objects becoming old or decayed, or stale or tasteless. All things shall flourish there in an eternal youth. . . .

Thus having taken notice of many of the blessed circumstances with which love in heaven is expressed and enjoyed, I proceed now.

VI. And lastly, to speak of the blessed fruits of this love, exercised and enjoyed in these circumstances. And I shall mention only two at this time.

First. The most excellent and perfect behavior of the inhabitants of heaven towards God and one another. Divine love is the sum of all good principles, and therefore is the fountain whence proceed all amiable actions. . . .

Second. The other fruit of this love in heaven exercised in such circumstances is perfect tranquility and joy. Holy, humble and divine love is a principle of wonderful power to give ineffable quietness and tranquility to the soul. It banishes all disturbance, it sweetly composes and brings rest, it makes all things appear calm and sweet. . . .

All shall stand about the God of glory, the fountain of love, as it were opening their bosoms to be filled with those effusions of love which are poured forth from thence, as the flowers on the earth in a pleasant spring day open their bosoms to the sun to be filled with his warmth and light, and to flourish in beauty and fragrancy by his rays. Every saint is as a flower in the garden of God, and holy love is the fragrancy and sweet odor which they all send forth, and with which they fill that paradise. Every saint there is as a note in a concert of music which sweetly harmonizes with every other note, and all together employed wholly in praising God and the Lamb; and so all helping one another to their utmost to express their love of the whole society to the glorious Father and Head of it, and [to pour back] love into the fountain of love, whence they are supplied and filled with love and with glory. And thus they will live and thus they will reign in love, and in that godlike joy which is the blessed fruit of it, such as eye hath not seen, nor ear heard, nor have ever entered into the heart of any in this world to conceive [cf. 1 Cor. 2:9]. And thus they will live and reign forever and ever.

INDEX

Ames, William, xvi, 6–9, 124–26, 174–75, 229, 255–57, 325, 327–29, 333–34, 377–78, 381–82
Amyraut, Moïse (Moses Amyrauldus), xvi, 39–40, 87, 99–104, 224–25
Anselm of Canterbury, 40, 213 n.5
Arminius, Jacob, xvi, 13, 94–99, 114, 153–56, 162, 188, 189–90, 222–24, 229, 262–65, 288–91, 301–4
Arndt, Johann, 13
Athanasius, xxi
Augsburg Confession (1530), 299 n.3
Augustine of Hippo, xxi, xxxi, 17, 49 n.1., 86, 146, 158, 161, 187 n.5, 385 n.2

Baillie, Donald, xxx
Baillie, John, xxx
Barth, Karl, xxvi, xxx, 73 n.9
Baxter, Richard, xvi, 224–25, 227, 260, 272, 279, 281–84, 325, 330–31, 365–66, 368–70
Bayle, Pierre, xvi, 42–44
Belgic Confession, 95, 108 n.21, 306–7
Bellamy, Joseph, xxvii
Beza, Theodore, xvi, 77–78, 108, 111–12, 206–10
Braun, Johannes, 107–9
Bruner, Emil, xxx
Bucer (Bützer), Martin, xix, 247, 279–80, 325, 327–28, 371–72, 374–75
Bullinger, Heinrich, xvi, xix, xxi, xxv, xxvi, 10, 22–25, 49, 62–65, 87–90, 116–18, 146–49, 247–49, 284–85, 294–97, 299–301
Bunyan, John, 269–72

Calvin, John, xvi, xix, xxi, xxii, xxiii, xxiv, xxv, xxvi, 2–4, 10, 19–22, 33–34, 51–52, 57–59, 67–69, 75–77, 90–94, 107, 118–19, 131–34, 136–38, 141–42, 144–46, 158–61, 164–65, 170–72, 192–93, 193–94, 196–99, 206, 212–13, 214–16, 221–22, 239–41, 249–52, 262, 267, 268–69, 293–94, 299–300, 308–11, 310–11, 316–18, 325–27, 339–40, 342–46, 346–48, 349–50, 371–74
Cameron, John, 224 n.7
Capito, Wolfgang, 247
Cappel, Louis, 29
Caroli, Pierre, 67
Chandieu (Sadeel or Sandeel), Antoine de la Roche, xvi, 25–27
Chisholm, Roderick M., 45
Chrysostom, xxi
Cocceius, Johannes, xvi, 9–13, 62–63, 65–66, 126–31, 174, 176–79, 228, 229
Colloquy of Poissy, 321
Consensus Tigurinus, 319–21
Copernicus, Nicholas, xxviii
Cotton, John, xvi, 306–7
Council of Trent (1545–63), 19
Cowper, William, 172–73

Darwin, Charles, xxviii
de Labadie, Jean, xvi, 13, 14, 265–66